Library of
Davidson College

THREATS, WEAPONS, AND FOREIGN POLICY

Editorial Board

LJUBIVOJE ACIMOVIC
 Institute of International
 Politics and Economics
 Belgrade, Yugoslavia
MICHAEL BRECHER
 The Hebrew University
 Jerusalem, Israel
 and McGill University
 Montreal, Canada
ERNST-OTTO CZEMPIEL
 Goethe-Universitat
 Frankfurt, GFR
WOLFRAM F. HANRIEDER
 University of California
 Santa Barbara, California USA
MICHAEL HAAS
 University of Hawaii
 Honolulu, Hawaii USA
CHARLES F. HERMANN
 The Mershon Center
 and Ohio State University
 Columbus, Ohio USA
JOHAN J. HOLST
 Norwegian Institute of
 International Affairs
 Oslo, Norway
MOHAMED KHAIRY ISSA
 The American University in Cairo
 and The University of Cairo
 Cairo, Egypt
EDWARD L. MORSE
 Woodrow Wilson School of
 Public and International Affairs
 Princeton University
 Princeton, New Jersey USA

KINHIDE MUSHAKOJI
 Sophia University
 Tokyo, Japan
RICHARD ROSECRANCE
 Cornell University
 Ithaca, New York USA
DIETER SENGHAAS
 Hessian Foundation for
 Peace and Conflict Research
 Frankfurt, GFR
ESTRELLA D. SOLIDUM
 University of the Philippines
 Quezon City, Philippines
DENIS STAIRS
 Dalhousie University
 Halifax, Nova Scotia, Canada
JANICE STEIN
 McGill University
 Montreal, Canada
YASH TANDON
 Institute for Development Studies
 Nairobi, Kenya
W. SCOTT THOMPSON
 Fletcher School of Law and Diplomacy
 Tufts University
 Medford, Massachusetts USA
LADISLAV VENYS
 Charles University
 Prague, Czechoslovakia
WILLIAM J.L. WALLACE
 University of Manchester
 Manchester, United Kingdom

Volume 5. Sage International Yearbook of Foreign Policy Studies

THREATS, WEAPONS, AND FOREIGN POLICY

edited by

Pat McGowan
Department of Political Science
Arizona State University

Charles W. Kegley, Jr.
Department of Government and International Studies
University of South Carolina

SAGE Publications   Beverly Hills   London

Copyright © 1980 by Sage Publications, Inc.

All rights reserved. No part of this book may be reproduced or utilized in any form or by any means, electronic or mechanical, including photocopying, recording, or by any information storage and retrieval system, without permission in writing from the publisher.

327.07
T531

For information address:

SAGE Publications, Inc.
275 South Beverly Drive
Beverly Hills, California 90212

SAGE Publications Ltd
28 Banner Street
London EC1 Y 8 QE, England

Printed in the United States of America

Library of Congress Cataloging in Publication Data

Main entry under title:

Threats, weapons, and foreign policy.

   (Sage international yearbook of foreign policy studies ; v. 5)
     Bibliography: p.
     1. International relations. 2. Military policy.
3. Armaments. I. McGowan, Patrick J. II. Kegley, Charles W. III. Series
JX1291.S25 vol. 5 [JX1391]   327'.07'2s . 79-26659
ISBN 0-8039-1154-8   [327.1'17]
ISBN 0-8039-1155-6 pbk.

FIRST PRINTING

8ﾉ-7429

*DEDICATED TO THE MEMORY
OF
JOHN V. GILLESPIE
1943-1979*

CONTENTS

Preface   9

Introduction
        PAT McGOWAN and CHARLES W. KEGLEY, Jr.   11

PART I: THREATS AND FOREIGN POLICY

1. Threat and Foreign Policy: The Overt Behavior of States in Conflict
   GERALD W. HOPPLE, PAUL J. ROSSA, and JONATHAN WILKENFELD   19
2. Images and Threats: Soviet Perceptions of International Crises, 1946-1975
   ROBERT B. MAHONEY, Jr. and RICHARD P. CLAYBERG   55
3. Threat, Public Opinion, and Military Spending in the United States, 1930-1990
   FARID ABOLFATHI   83

PART II: WEAPONS AND FOREIGN POLICY

4. Determinants of French Arms Sales: Security Implications
   EDWARD A. KOLODZIEJ   137
5. Legislative Control of Weapons System Acquisition: A Comparative Analysis of the United Kingdom and the United States
   NORMAN A. GRAHAM and DAVID J. LOUSCHER   177
6. Military Production in Third World Countries: A Political Study
   ILAN PELEG   209
7. A Comparative Analysis of Nuclear Armament
   CHARLES W. KEGLEY, Jr., GREGORY A. RAYMOND, and RICHARD A. SKINNER   231

PART III: MODELING ARMS RACES

8. Accounting for Superpower Arms Spending
   MICHAEL DAVID WALLACE 259
9. Sensitivity Analysis of an Armaments Race Model
   JOHN V. GILLESPIE, DINA A. ZINNES, PHILIP A. SCHRODT,
   and G. S. TAHIM 275

PART IV: BIBLIOGRAPHY

10. Bibliography of Recent Comparative Foreign
    Policy Studies, 1975-1979
    CONSTANCE J. LYNCH 313

About the Authors 321

PREFACE

As we completed the last stages in the preparation of this volume, we learned of the utterly premature death of our friend and colleague, John V. Gillespie of Indiana University. With the approval of his wife, Judith, we proudly dedicate this volume to John's living memory.

Throughout his all too brief academic career, John Gillespie demonstrated in his teaching and research the greatest possible dedication to rigorous thought, analysis, and communication. More importantly, perhaps, he was among the most warm and agreeable of men imaginable.

It is certain that his impact on the study of foreign policy and international politics will continue to grow. Not only did he author and edit four books and twenty-three important articles in just nine years, but he chaired the committees of eleven Ph.D. candidates at Indiana and served on twenty-nine other committees. John's publications, many of them in collaboration with Dina A. Zinnes and Indiana graduate students, are so advanced and complex that it will only be during the 1980s, as the profession matures, that their full impact will be felt. Moreover, as John's students mature—and this includes all who worked in any way with him—the standards he set by example, the questions he asked, and the enthusiasm that so characterized him will spread and deepen in the profession.

Among John's central concerns were arms race phenomena and the interface between threats, weapons, and foreign policy behavior. This is reflected in his contribution with Zinnes, Schrodt, and Takim to this volume. It is with the most profound sadness that we publish here one of his last major contributions. It is, also, with equally deep feelings of gratification that we shall remember John Gillespie as our friend, co-worker, and exemplar.

> Pat McGowan
> Tempe, Arizona
>
> Charles W. Kegley, Jr.
> Columbia, South Carolina
>
> October 1, 1979

INTRODUCTION

PAT McGOWAN
Arizona State University

CHARLES W. KEGLEY, Jr.
University of South Carolina

Division of labor leads to increased economic productivity and other material advantages, but it has resulted in serious problems for students of foreign policy behavior. This can be seen in the separation between "theorists" and "empirical researchers," the one producing largely nonoperational theoretical sketches and the other engaging in post hoc rationalizations of empirical findings. Rare, indeed, are the Michael Brechers or James Rosenaus who have theorized creatively and accomplished extensive systematic research as well.

Another equally deplorable form taken by the intellectual division of labor in our discipline is the growing separation between scientific foreign policy studies on the one hand and national security/defense studies on the other hand. Everyone would agree in principle that the external relations of states comprise the full range of activities from the most routine consular tasks of low-level bureaucrats to the very high politics of national security decisions by prime ministers, party chairmen, and presidents. Defense policy and foreign policy are two sides of the same coin—each aiming to adapt national societies to their ever-changing environments. Yet, they are seldom integrated either theoretically or empirically. It is difficult to identify prominent specialists in comparative foreign policy analysis who have focused on security and defense issues. Similarly rare is the defense analyst who is conversant with the theoretical approaches and methodology of the scientific foreign policy literature.

Why this is so is difficult to understand and in our view impossible to justify. Clearly, defense analysts must make a considerable investment in mastering the scientific and technological aspects of their subject, but if anything one would expect that such exposure would make them open to social science as well. Defense analysts, more so than academic foreign policy specialists, tend to have a strong applied orientation and a willingness to make their skills available to their national governments. But this is a difference in degree and not in kind, for many foreign policy and area experts participate in this form of service as well. Comparative foreign policy specialists often overemphasize their theory-building efforts, yet it can be argued that only in theories of deterrence and arms races does international relations possess powerful and parsimonious explanatory models.

Instead of worrying overly about the apparent lack of communication between defense and foreign policy experts, this fifth volume of our *Yearbook* is devoted to fostering exchange between these two subjects and communities of scholars. By focusing on *Threats, Weapons, and Foreign Policy Behavior,* our intention was to bring together in one volume studies by foreign policy and defense experts on the interface between national security and foreign policy behavior that were unique because of their application of newer social science methodologies to the perennial questions of defense and security. Unfortunately, as in all ambitious enterprises, we have only partially achieved our goals.

Among nine substantive chapters and eighteen authors, we have not elicited contributions from specialists primarily identified with defense and strategic studies. Most of our authors are academic specialists in quantitative international politics and comparative foreign policy analysis. However, applied research on defense and foreign policy matters is increasingly being done at research corporations in the greater Washington, DC area and elsewhere throughout the United States. Six of our authors—Tahim, Abolfathi, Clayberg, Mahoney, Rossa, and Hopple—are affiliated with three such enterprises—IPPRC, CACI, and the General Electric Space Center—and others of our authors frequently consult with government and research corporations reflecting strong applied experience and concerns which should make this volume of great interest to our absent defense specialists as well as to the general reader.

We are quite pleased that our original primary concern, to apply newer concepts and methodologies to the study of national security and defense issues, has been abundantly achieved. While diverse and hardly exhaustive of the possible topics that could have been studied in this volume, our chapters can be grouped under three broad headings of threats, weapons, and arms races. Let us review each category and contribution in turn.

Based on the creative theoretical work of Thomas Schelling, Kenneth Boulding, and particularly Charles McClelland, the concepts of threat, threat systems, and threat agendas, burdens, fields, and regions may provide the needed conceptual linkage between foreign and defense policy studies. Threats are anticipations of approaching harm that trigger feelings of stress that lead to responses generally known as coping or adaptive behavior. In their rich opening chapter Hopple, Rossa, and Wilkenfeld develop these and related concepts and relate them "the overt behavior of states in conflict." In their view threats are antecedent to international crises which are, in turn, a central focus of national security studies. Environmental change that carries threat messages resulting in societal stress may result in adaptive responses designed to lessen threat. This is entirely consistent with certain macrotheoretical approaches to comparative foreign policy studies (Rosenau, 1970; Hansen, 1974; McGowan and Gottwald, 1975).

It is a truism that one man's threat is another man's opportunity. How does the Soviet Union view international threat phenomena and how may Western scholars validly record Soviet perceptions of threats and crises? These fascinating questions represent the central thrust of Mahoney and Clayberg's chapter on "Images and Threats." Not surprisingly, the Soviet literature demonstrates a more historical and structural view of threats to Soviet security and interests than do comparable American writings. Comparison of the Soviet crisis data to comparable data sets produced by Brookings and CACI permits the authors to highlight the similar and different correlates of superpower threat concerns over the past thirty years, an entirely original contribution to the literature.

Military spending—the generally accepted measure of arms race phenomena—is of more continuous concern to elites and mass publics than any other defense phenomenon. Since Lewis F. Richardson's pioneering studies of arms races (1960), most analysts have emphasized the stimulus-response mechanisms of one nation arming in response to another's initiatives. It is entirely possible, however, that in democratic societies the people's willingness to pay via taxes, as this is affected by their perceptions of threat, is the determining variable. How else can one explain the failure of certain experts and their allies in Congress to achieve significant increases in the U.S. defense budget at this time of massive Soviet expenditures? The international system is relatively tranquil at present, and not feeling directly threatened, U.S. public opinion does not support increased military spending whatever may be the nature of warnings issued by the Committee on the Present Danger and similar groups. These hypotheses are the central concern of Chapter 3 by Farid Abolfathi.

Part II of our volume presents four chapters that examine the impact of weapons and weapons systems procurement on foreign policy and the policy making process.

Edward Kolodziej breaks entirely new ground in his study of "French Arms Sales." Basing his analysis on a newly created, more accurate data base, Kolodziej is able to show that French sales are greater than previously thought. Via an analysis of French balance of payments and the interpretation of the French armaments industry and government, he is able to show the structural necessity for France to export weapons so that it can maintain a modern, independent military-industrial complex. A system has evolved over time in directions quite different from what was intended in the early days of the Fifth Republic.

Among Western democracies it is axiomatic that civilians control the military. A central mechanism in this structure of responsibility is legislative oversight of military expenditure and weapons system acquisition. While there is an extensive case study literature on the American Congress's role in this area, there are hardly any comparisons of legislative control in different national settings. Norman Graham and David Louscher accomplish this in their innovative comparison of behavior in hearings by members of the British Parliament's External Affairs Subcommittee of the Select Committee on Expenditure and the United States House of Representatives's Armed Services Committee. Their research leads to the troubling conclusion that in both countries elected representatives of the people are largely acquiescent and loath to challenge the initiatives of the military and civilian military experts when it comes to acquiring new weapons systems as long as these systems fall within general budget guidelines.

The other side of arms sales to Third World countries—a topic often studied—is the local production of conventional weapons in Third World countries themselves. About this important phenomenon and its implications for international security, we know very little, which makes Ilan Peleg's contribution to this volume so useful. Led by Argentina, Brazil, India, Israel, and South Africa, some twenty-seven Third World countries self-produce at least some of their weapons. Peleg theorizes that the necessary condition for military production by such states is an adequate level of scientific technology and economic development. If this condition is met, then what triggers production is the political will to produce weapons derived from feelings of threat and insecurity. Statistical analysis generally supports this theory.

No volume devoted to *Threats, Weapons, and Foreign Policy Behavior* would be complete without giving attention to nuclear weapons and their proliferation. Nothing is more likely to complicate the formulation of foreign policy throughout the rest of this century than nuclear proliferation. Gregory Raymond, Richard Skinner, and Charles Kegley approach the study of proliferation in a novel fashion in their chapter on "Nuclear Armament." They reject the traditional perspective on this issue which has emphasized indigenous phenomena such as scientific expertise, technological skill, and economic wealth as prerequisites for acquiring nuclear weapons. More likely to affect the spread of nuclear arms they feel is the international environment involving nuclear technology commerce, increased energy needs, and general technological diffusion. To evaluate this hypothesis they statistically compare forty-six countries grouped into four categories of "nuclear states," "latent nuclear aspirants," "nuclear aspirants," and "nonnuclear states." It would appear from their analysis that the growing international availability of nuclear technology is the key factor affecting proliferation today.

The last Part of this volume contains two rigorous studies of arms races from quite different perspectives. Writing in the tradition of Richardson, Michael Wallace empirically analyzes military spending by the United States and the Soviet Union over the period 1950-1976. While both superpowers positively react to each other's arms spending and the pressure of serious disputes between them, they differ in one key respect—the Soviet Union responds to Chinese military spending but the United States is not affected by this variable. The implications of this finding for the future foreign and defense policies of the superpowers are profound.

Chapter 9 by the late John Gillespie and his coworkers Dina Zinnes, Philip Schrodt, and G. Takim presents a pioneering "Sensitivity Analysis of an Armaments Race Model." Building upon Richardson's (1960) simple differential equation model of arms races, they use sophisticated mathematics to develop a model of an optimal defense policy for any nation involved in an arms race that incorporates national goals and objectives. Because of its mathematical formulation, once the basic model parameters have been estimated from data, sensitivity coefficients may be derived and the behavior of the parameters over time in response to changes in the coefficients may be investigated. This is done for the United States, USSR, NATO, Warsaw Pact, Israel, and its opposing Arab states. In our view the major contribution of this chapter is its policy relevance, for sensitivity analysis permits one to ask vital "what if" questions.

Finally, as in the previous four volumes of the *Yearbook* we include a bibliography of recent foreign policy studies covering the period 1975-1979, with special emphasis on the most recent two-year period.

Taken as a whole, our authors have clearly advanced our understanding of the interface between foreign and defense policy. Their chapters contribute in another important fashion as well, increased attention to model specification and the dynamic analysis of time series data. One of us recently argued (McGowan, 1976) that greater attention to theory and the abandonment of cross-sectional correlation analysis were necessary if comparative studies of foreign policy were to advance in quality and impact. The chapters in this volume demonstrate what, in our view, should be done and how to do it. We hope our readers will agree.

REFERENCES

HANSEN, P. (1974) "Adaptive behavior of small states: the case of Denmark and the European Community," pp. 143-174 in P. J. McGowan (ed.) Sage International Yearbook of Foreign Policy Studies 2. Beverly Hills: Sage Publications.

McGOWAN, P. J. (1976) "The future of comparative studies: an evangelical plea," pp. 217-325 in J. N. Rosenau (ed.) In Search of Global Patterns. New York: Free Press.

――― and GOTTWALD, K. P. (1975) "Small state foreign policies." International Studies Quarterly 19 (December): 469-500.

RICHARDSON, L. S. (1960) Arms and Insecurity. Chicago: Quadrangle.

ROSENAU, J. N. (1970) The Adaptation of National Societies. New York: McCaleb-Seiler.

PART I

THREATS AND FOREIGN POLICY

Chapter 1

THREAT AND FOREIGN POLICY: THE OVERT BEHAVIOR OF STATES IN CONFLICT

GERALD W. HOPPLE
PAUL J. ROSSA

International Public Policy Research Corporation
McLean, Virginia

JONATHAN WILKENFELD

University of Maryland,
College Park

THREAT ANALYSIS: AN OVERVIEW

Concepts such as *crisis,* conflict, war, and alliance have traditionally been the building blocks of both substantive and analytical theory construction in international political and comparative foreign policy analysis.[1] *Threat* has generally been treated as a vital but presumably implicitly "understood" facet of reality. Aside from the work of Charles McClelland, few researchers have attempted to analyze the idea of threat as either a theoretical concept or an empirical phenomenon.[2] McClelland has argued

EDITORS' NOTE: This chapter was first submitted for review May 1, 1979. The version published here was received July 13, 1979. The authors report that the data presented herein are available from the Inter-University Consortium for Political and Social Research in Ann Arbor, Michigan.

AUTHORS' NOTE: This is a revised version of a paper which was presented at the 1979 Meeting of the International Political Science Association in Moscow. The

that crisis analysts may achieve more progress if they "retreat" one step from the level of crises per se to the more temporally and causally primordial stage of threat recognition and analysis.[3]

In traditional international relations, crisis has a distinct meaning. The concept refers to a discrete episode and focused attention on a particular state between war and peace.[4] While the historical context may shift, the common attributes remain. Thus, McClelland (1977: 16-18) isolates three crisis series:

(1) the pre-World War I era (1904-1914);
(2) the pre-World War II period (1935-1939);
(3) the Cold War pattern (1948-1964).

More recently, however, a crisis is seen as "simply an emergency situation that is responded to according to a perception of danger and an urge to act against the danger" (McClelland, 1977: 25).

Perceived dangers and emergency situations include traditional military-national security crises, energy and environmental crises, economic crises, and a bewildering profusion of other "crises." McClelland (1977: 22) notes that of ten "high tension" international episodes in the decade from 1966 to 1975, only three conformed to the Cold War crisis series patterns; all three occurred in the Middle East arena.

McClelland (1977: 25) views threat recognition and threat response as "better objects for theory development that crisis itself." While the concept of *threat* is not systematically articulated as a component of any "theory" of international relations, the idea does play a pivotal role in deterrence theory in the field of national security studies (McClelland, 1974: 1).[5] In both national and international political analysis, threats—which involve the anticipation of approaching "harm" from the individual perspective and impending *"ruin"* from the systematic vantage point—are

---

chapter itself should be viewed as one aspect of a larger research project which has spanned several years. The research was supported by the Cybernetics Technology Office of the U.S. Department of Defense Advanced Research Projects Agency (DARPA) and was monitored by ONR under Contract No. N00014-76-C-0153. More recently, support for the first two authors was provided by DARPA and monitored by ONR under Contract No. N00014-79-C-0101. The views and conclusions contained in this chapter are those of the authors and should not be interpreted as necessarily representing the official policies, either expressed or implied, or DARPA or the U.S. Government. We are grateful for the assistance of Lee Decker and Amy Favin of IPPRC. We would like to express our appreciation to the following individuals for their helpful comments and suggestions: Michael A. Daniels of IPPRC; Charles W. Kegley, Jr. of the University of South Carolina; Patrick J. McGowan of Arizona State University; and Milton Rokeach of Washington State University. None of the individuals, however, should be held responsible for the specific contents of the chapter.

almost universal stimulants of action. *Threat "regions"* on the cognitive map and specific active *threat "fields"* in threat regions can be pinpointed.

SCIENTIFIC FOREIGN POLICY ANALYSIS AND "THREAT SCIENCE": ILLUMINATING THE NEXUS

Our prior work in the scientific study of foreign policy has involved the construction of a comprehensive analytical framework, the operationalization of concepts, and the testing of a series of preliminary models. The focus here is much more restricted in scope; we shall report some empirical findings on the determinants of external behavior and attempt to relate these to the McClelland threat framework. Initially, however, we shall offer a brief overview of the research directions which have led up to this point.

Background

Our overall research design has featured an explicitly cross-national orientation, involving a set of fifty-six states selected on the basis of volume of activity in the international system during the 1966 to 1970 time frame. Only thirty-nine of these countries will be dealt with in this chapter.[6] The country "sample" includes actors from every region of the world and represents every type of state (with the exception of very small entities).

In the course of conducting our research, we specified a large number of discrete indicators, indices, and variable clusters in an effort to "map" conceptually and empirically the primary internal and external determinants of foreign behavior. This effort was anchored in the process of constructing and refining a general framework for analyzing the sources and processes of foreign or external behavioral outputs (Andriole et al., 1975; Wilkenfeld et al., 1978a).

The culmination of this conceptual work—as well as the extensive data collection which it entailed—was the systematic assessment of the relative contribution of the various determinants to the ultimate behavior of states. We have examined this issue in a variety of analytical contexts. The general research design is portrayed in Figure 1.

A series of conceptual and empirical analyses has provided the foundation for pursuing more sophisticated causal modeling approaches in the future.[7] Initial conceptual and empirical research sought to establish the validity of three assumptions:

(1) The behavioral domain of state action in the sphere of foreign policy can be dimensionalized into distinct types (constructive

FIGURE 1.1 Cross-National Foreign Policy Analysis: General Research Design

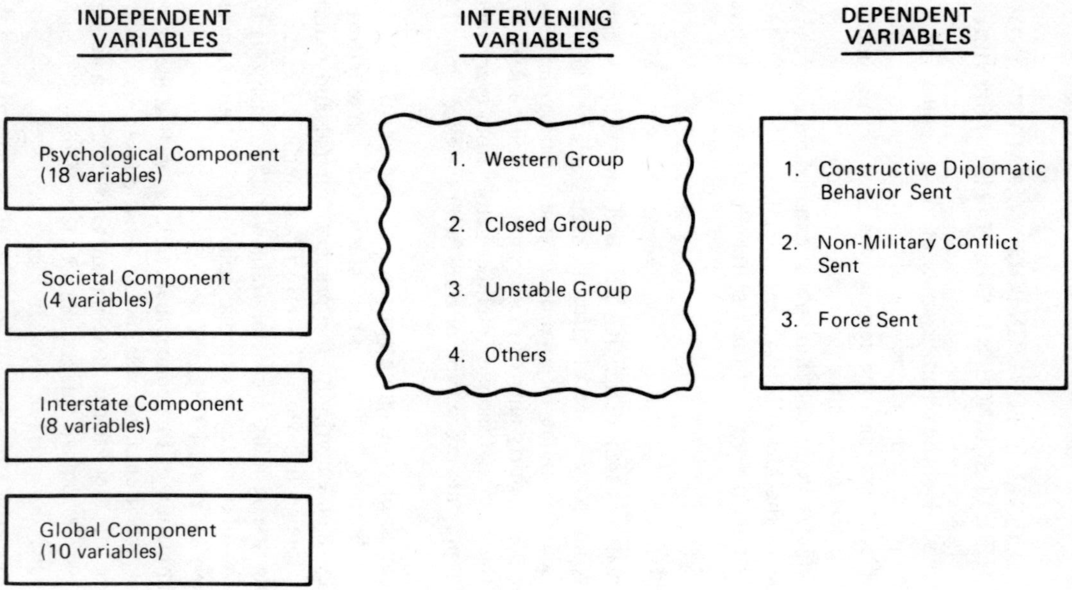

INDEPENDENT VARIABLES

- Psychological Component (18 variables)
- Societal Component (4 variables)
- Interstate Component (8 variables)
- Global Component (10 variables)

INTERVENING VARIABLES

1. Western Group
2. Closed Group
3. Unstable Group
4. Others

DEPENDENT VARIABLES

1. Constructive Diplomatic Behavior Sent
2. Non-Military Conflict Sent
3. Force Sent

diplomatic behavior, nonmilitary conflict behavior, and force behavior).
(2) The determinants or "sources" of state behavior can be clustered into at least four realms (psychological, internal or societal/political, interstate, and global).
(3) Countries can be distinguished on the basis of four sets of structural attributes (economic structure, governmental structure, capabilities, and political stability).

The analytical phase of inquiry has revolved around the issue of relative potency assessment. This question has been explored via two primary analytical strategies. One, based on the Partial Least Squares (PLS) methodology, allowed us to construct "latent" (not directly observable) variables (from manifest or measured indicators) in the realms of foreign behavior (the dependent cluster), determinants of such behavior (the independent clusters), and the state classification scheme (the intervening clusters).[8] The use of moderators to represent static structural (contextual) factors (with and without the action-reaction element of the interstate cluster) permitted us to derive country-specific parameters.[9]

The other analytical strategy—the Coleman research strategy—was initially employed in the now famous *Equality of Educational Opportunity* (Coleman et al., 1966). Figure 1.2(a) depicts the Coleman research design. Coleman sought to explain educational achievement in terms of family background and school quality and to assess the relative potency of these two blocks of variables. As Figure 1.2(b) illustrates, we substitute foreign behavior for the dependent variable; variable blocks P, S, I, and G represent the four independent variable realms.

The Coleman strategy was designed to accommodate a larger number of predictive variables and ascertain their relative efficacy in accounting for a criterion (foreign behavior). An earlier publication contains some preliminary results derived from applying this perspective (Hopple et al., 1977). We now extend that earlier effort by incorporating a variety of additional potential determinants and by analyzing a modified set of foreign behavior categories. The specific indicators and more general conceptual and empirical clusters are listed in summary form in Table 1.1.[10]

We introduce the control for type of state (i.e., the structural dimensions) into the analysis by performing separate regressions on the total group of states, followed by analyses within each of the subgroups. Since only thirty-nine of our original fifty-six states are represented in the psychological data base, we have modified the state clusters somewhat. Table 1.2 lists the groupings and the states in each. While the Western, Closed, and Unstable groups remain unchanged (cf., Wilkenfeld et al., 1978b), we have collapsed the Large Developing and Poor groups (along

FIGURE 1.2 Coleman Analysis

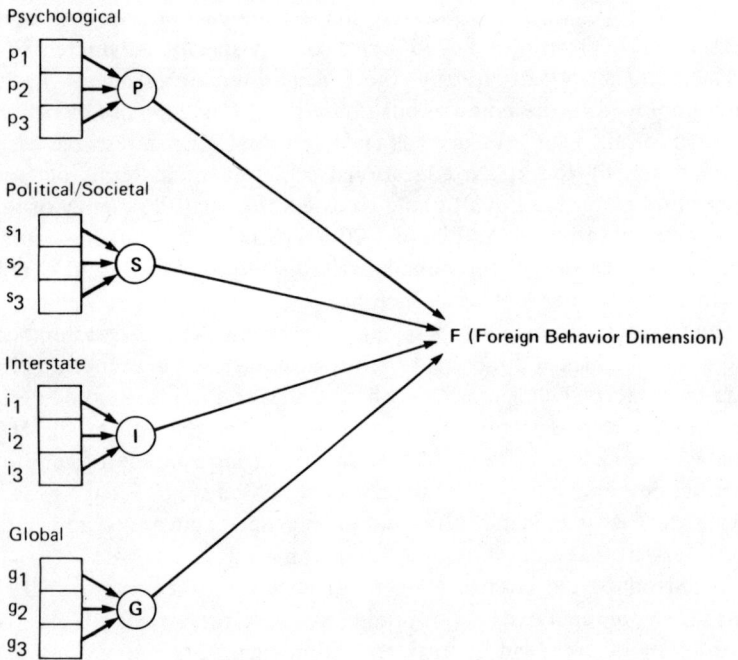

TABLE 1.1 List of Variables and Conceptual Clusters*

SOURCE VARIABLES

A. <u>Psychological Component</u> (Decision-Maker Values)
   1. A comfortable life
   2. A world of peace
   3. Equality
   4. Freedom
   5. Happiness
   6. Governmental security
   7. Honor
   8. Justice
   9. National security
   10. Public security
   11. Respect
   12. Social recognition
   13. Wisdom
   14. Progress
   15. Unity
   16. Ideology
   17. Cooperation
   18. Support of government

B. <u>Political/Societal Component</u>
   1. Merchandise balance of payments (economic performance)
   2. Population growth rate
   3. Governmental instability
      • Purges
      • Revolutions
      • Number of coups
      • Number of changes in the executive
      • Number of changes in the cabinet
      • Number of changes in the constitution
   4. Societal unrest
      • General strikes
      • Riots
      • Anti-government demonstrations

C. <u>Interstate Component</u>[a]
   1. Interstate energy relationships
      • Energy interdependency
      • Energy market strength
      • Energy dependency
   2. General trade relationships
      • Neo-colonial dependency
      • Economic involvement (total trade)
   3. Food dependency and advantage
      • Food dependency
   4. General interstate economic relationships
      • Import concentration
      • Export concentration

D. <u>Global Component</u>
   1. International governmental organization (IGO) membership
      • Total IGO memberships per year
      • Total new IGO memberships per year
   2. Conflict within bordering states[b]
      • Total number of force events sent and received by nations land-bordering State X
      • Total number of force events sent and received by nations sea-bordering State X
      • Total number of force events sent and received by nations with colonies land-bordering State X
      • Total number of force events sent and received by nations with colonies sea-bordering State X
      • Total number of conflictual events (excluding force) sent and received by nations land-bordering State X
      • Total number of conflictual events sent and received by nations sea-bordering State X
      • Total number of conflictual events sent and received by nations with colonies land-bordering State X

TABLE 1.1 List of Variables and Conceptual Clusters* (Cont)

- Total number of conflictual events sent and received by nations with colonies sea-bordering State X

INTERVENING STATE CLASSIFICATION SCHEME DIMENSIONS AND VARIABLES[c]

A. Economic Dimension
   1. Gross National Product per capita
   2. Percent of Gross Domestic Product originating in agriculture
   3. Percent of Gross Domestic Product originating in industry
   4. Energy consumption per capita
   5. Percent of economically active male population in agricultural occupations
   6. Percent of economically active male population in professional-technical occupations

B. Capability Dimension
   Size:
   7. Total area
   8. Total population
   9. Gross National Product
   Military:
   10. Military manpower
   11. Defense expenditures
   12. Defense expenditures per capita
   Resource Base:
   13. Percent of energy consumed domestically produced

C. Political Dimension
   Development:
   14. Number of political parties
   15. Horizontal power distribution
   16. Local government autonomy
   Structure:
   17. Selection of effective executive
   18. Legislative effectiveness
   19. Legislative selection
   Stability (1946–1965)
   20. Average number of coups per year
   21. Average number of constitutional changes per year
   22. Average number of major cabinet changes per year
   23. Average number of changes in effective executive per year

DEPENDENT (FOREIGN BEHAVIOR SENT) VARIABLES[d]

1. Constructive diplomatic behavior sent
   - yield
   - comment
   - consult
   - approve
   - promise
   - grant
   - reward
   - agree
   - request
   - propose
   - reject
   - deny
   - warn
   - negative sanctions
2. Non-military conflict behavior sent
   - accuse
   - protest
   - demand
   - threaten

TABLE 1.1 List of Variables and Conceptual Clusters* (Cont)

- demonstrate
- expel
- seize

3. Force acts sent
   - force

*See Hopple (1978a) for a discussion of data sources and other pertinent details.

[a] See Appendix B for formulae.

[b] This is based on the WEIS classification of conflictual and force events. The borders data consist of aggregated neighboring conflict scores for each state and total number of borders of each type (nation land, nation sea, colony land, colony sea).

[c] For factor analytic and other results, see Wilkenfeld et al. (1978b).

[d] These variables are from the World Event Interaction Survey (WEIS) data base (see Burgess and Lawton, 1972). Factor analyses of the behavior sent and received domains of WEIS are discussed in Rossa et al. (1979).

TABLE 1.2 Groupings of States[a]

WEST	THIRD WORLD
West Germany Israel Japan France United States	**Large Developing** India Pakistan Turkey Indonesia China South Korea
CLOSED Poland Rumania Czechoslovakia Bulgaria USSR Hungary East Germany Yugoslavia	**Poor** Cyprus Lebanon Cambodia Jordan Laos Yemen
UNSTABLE Syria Iraq Algeria Egypt Iran Cuba South Vietnam	**Unclassifiable** Thailand Ghana Kenya Greece Nigeria Saudi Arabia

a. This List is based on Q-factor analysis groupings for the larger 56-state List; see Wilkenfeld et al. (1978b) for details.

with countries which had previously been unclassifiable) into an "Others" category; this cluster comprises what is primarily a Third World grouping.[11] Since each state-year between 1966 and 1970 constitutes a separate case for analysis, our total N is 131, broken down by cluster as follows:

(1) Western (N=24);
(2) Closed (N=35);
(3) Unstable (N=27);
(4) Third World (N=45).

The Threat Linkage

In discussing the linkage between threat science and the work which is chronicled in this chapter, it is helpful to introduce McClelland's (1977: 34-35) schematization of current prospects for crisis research in a 2 X 3 matrix that identifies *Charting* and *Modeling* as row labels and *Conditions, Situations,* and *Events* as column labels:

	Conditions	Situations	Events
Charting			
Modeling			

The empirical results which are presented later in this chapter exemplify what could be referred to as "static threat analysis." In terms of McClelland's tripartite scheme of conditions, situations, and events, our indicators, indices, and clusters fall into the situations and (primarily) conditions cells of the matrix. In contrast, the *D-files* data base typifies situations analysis, while the computer-based *Early Warning and Monitoring System* at the International Public Policy Research Corporation provides an illustration of an events analysis approach to international affairs tracking and crisis anticipation.[12]

In terms of the charting/modeling dichotomy, most of the work reported in this chapter pertains to the charting process. Some of our other research—especially the PLS-based analyses—shades over into the domain of "soft" modeling. From an applied or policy-relevant threat assessment vantage point, we are offering tools and products which are potentially relevant to basic or background intelligence and foreign affairs analysts. From a basic or scientific frame of reference, the research summarized here constitutes (systematic) description much more than explanation or theorizing.

The relative potency approach enables us to begin to confront the fundamental proposition in threat theory (McClelland, 1975a: 17) that events and event sequences are linked to the recognition of threats and the latter are in turn associated with crisis phenomena. According to McClelland, the identification of the limiting/facilitating conditions for the two linkage processes emerges as the central theory problem of threat analysis. Diagrammatically, the focus can be depicted in the following fashion:

```
                    Events and Event Sequences ➤ Routine Behavior
                   ↗
       Conditions
                   ↘
                    Events and Event Sequences ➤ Threats ➤ Conflict/crisis
```

By profiling *"threat burdens"* which emanate from various levels of analysis, we can discuss in a very preliminary fashion the relative potency of the determinants of external behavior in relation to the subject of threat burdens across national systems and within distinct types of systems.[13] For example, if external factors invariably override potential internal determinants, then a theory of foreign policy threat should highlight interstate and perhaps global context determinants. If, alternatively, domestic forces play a role in the process, then linkage politics interpretations and spillover syndromes become pertinent.

An extreme interactional (action-reaction) model—a caricature of the spiral model—undoubtedly drives some threat systems. Similarly, there is also evidence for the existence of a nexus between internal and external threats.[14] However, mechanistic stimulus-response and automatic spillover models rarely hold. Reality is much more complex.[15]

What we view as static threat analysis can facilitate the process of identifying the parameters of the configurations which characterize the dynamics of internal and external sources of threats to a nation-state. A country or state type in which internal factors shape external behavior (and/or interact with interstate or systemic sources of foreign behavior) clearly faces a different *threat agenda* (and must cope with a qualitatively distinct threat burden) in comparison with a state or grouping in which external stimuli tend to be more potent.[16] This general argument will be fleshed out in some detail in our discussion of the findings; at this point, it is vital to emphasize that different *types of states* confront varying *stress* levels (internally, externally, or in terms of the intermix) and can be expected to exhibit divergent *coping styles* and patterns.

The Objective and Subjective Aspects of Threat Science

In addition to the general internal/external threat nexus question, the recurring perceptual/psychological and interactional/systemic "debate" is also relevant to efforts to chart and account for the determinants of threat.[17] At the extremes of the continuum, either perceptions or environmental (external) influences may function in a deterministic fashion. A paranoid leader (Hitler, perhaps Stalin, or Johnson, etc.) has a belief system (and an underlying psychodynamic pattern) which can convert even "innocent" stimuli into "dangerous" threats; elite perceptions (or misperceptions) dominate the process in this relatively rare situation. Alternatively, overwhelming environmental threats (objectively defined) may eventually penetrate even the most impermeable or resistant barrier; Britain in the 1930s is an extreme example.[18] Generally, however, foreign policy decision-makers must navigate in a situation where there are many potential sources of threat activation. Perceptual and environmental factors both play a role in the processes of threat assessment, anticipation, and reaction.

Objective sources of potential threats to a decision system range from the actions of other states (threats, accusations, and other verbal and physical forms of conflict) to interstate economic relationships (food dependency, energy dependency, etc.) to internal economic patterns (such as a decline in economic performance). Across temporal and spatial parameters, we can conceive of delineating profiles and trends which assess threat burden configurations across the dimensions of:

(1) State or state types (e.g., differences by level of economic development or political stability);
(2) time (e.g., pre- and post-crisis periods, the impact of systemic changes such as the transition from loose bipolarity to multipolarity, etc.); and
(3) space and time (e.g., the developed world before and after the Arab oil embargo, the client states of the United States or the Soviet Union before and after a superpower crisis with a recalcitrant, weak ally, etc.).

Two actors may confront identical threat agendas (in terms of the nature, internal-external distribution, and range of issues) and threat burdens (in terms of the quantity or "load" on the decision-making system) and may nevertheless differ considerably with respect to external patterns of behavior. The relevant distinguishing characteristic here is the elite's system of perceptions and beliefs.

The obstacles to acquiring valid, reliable elite belief systems data are formidable—especially on a cross-national basis.[19] For obvious reasons, the individual or psychological variable domain is the most elusive and the least amenable to systematic empirical analysis of all the potential sources of external behavior. Prior research has identified three distinct levels of analysis or variable domains in the interface area between political psychology and foreign policy analysis: psycho-dynamic factors; personality traits; and belief systems.[20] Our focus is exclusively on the third.

Our psychological data set relies on the use of content analysis as a research technique and concentrates on the *value* subsystem of a decision-maker's belief system as the substantive focus of inquiry.[21] These data, which refer to the foreign policy elite of the state (i.e., the head of state and the foreign minister), are based on speeches and interviews during the 1966-1970 period. The specific variables are listed in Table 1.1.

The eighteen values are derived from Rokeach's (1973) list of universal values and from exploratory research; the last five foreign policy-specific values in Table 1.1 were added as a result of our exploratory content analysis pretests. The source for speech material was the *Daily Report* of the U.S. Foreign Broadcast Information Service (FBIS).[22]

The *Daily Report* consists of material which is obtained through U.S. monitoring of foreign broadcasts. Included is a variety of speeches and interviews of heads of state and foreign ministers.

The actual coding process was very straightforward. The speech was the primary unit of analysis; within a speech, the sentence was the operational coding unit. A given sentence could contain no values, one value, two values, and so on. For each speech, a frequency count was made for each of the eighteen values (based on the explicit appearance of the given value or of a keyword/synonym).

Values and Threats

Other discussions of the value data base have highlighted such issues as reliability, validity, and the role of foreign policy decision-makers' values and value rankings in the context of a more general cognitive or belief systems framework.[23] Our concern in this chapter is with a much more general set of issues: Do the articulated values of foreign policy-making elites affect external behavior of various forms? How important are these phenomena vis-à-vis other factors? In a much more fundamental sense, can elite values be viewed as preferred terminal goals or end-states of existence which also reflect those threats which are salient to decision-makers?

This more basic question is the most interesting and—from a threat science vantage point—the most relevant of these issues. McClelland (1974) points out that threat situations have a linkage with "objective realities" but that, simultaneously, the individual (or elite unit) "reads" arriving signs and signals in terms of dominant personal values and interests.

Extensive evidence suggests that value hierarchies differ across the subgroups of a population in a systematic, predictable fashion. The empirical data reinforce the fundamental theoretical proposition that values and value systems function as standards for action and as general plans for conflict resolution and decision-making (Rokeach, 1973: 13-14). For example, strikingly disparate relative rankings of core political values (freedom and equality) characterize the value profiles of diverse conservative, liberal, and left and right authoritarian leaders (Rokeach, 1973: 171-178). Within a variety of mass and elite samples, quite a few value-ranking differences have been isolated; these relate to attitudinal and behavioral variations in an impressive number of instances.[24] Searing's (1978) study of value rankins in the British House of Commons provides more recent supportive evidence. Relative ranks for the core political values of freedom and social equality show the expected differences; while 85% of the conservative MPs rank freedom over social equality, 79% of the Labour members rank the latter above the former.[25]

An individual who ranks a given value higher is more likely to be sensitized to perceive threats in that area. For example, Rokeach (1973) demonstrates that blacks in the United States tend to rank equality differently than whites. Of all thirty-six terminal and instrumental values in the Rokeach value inventory, *equality* shows the largest interracial differences; its overall rank order is second for blacks and eleventh for whites (Rokeach, 1973: 69).[26] *Threats* related to equality would presumably be more salient to blacks that to whites. The point is not that equality (conceived as an abstract value or as a guide to opinion and behavior) is *irrelevant* to the typical white; the threat sensitivity threshold is simply much higher. Similarly, certain values (cleanliness, a comfortable life, etc.) are ranked higher in the working as opposed to the middle class, not because they are intrinsically more important to those in lower social strata but simply because such individuals lack these particular values (Rokeach, 1973: 62; see also Kohn, 1969). Analogously, states which lack security (objectively and/or perceptually) would presumably rank certain types of values higher than countries which "possess" larger quantities of this precious and scarce commodity.

This argument is strengthened when we note that values can be regarded as fundamental orientations or as structuring mechanisms:

> The value screen of culture appraises and selectively perceives stimuli which act on it. Stimuli which are congenial are accepted and allowed to act on the social process. Those which are not tend to be screened out. Other stimuli are accepted, but they are shaped by the values of the culture before they act on the social process [Devine, 1972: 10].

Elite values comprise the core of the individual's belief system, which is an organized entity by definition. As Meddin (1975) notes, all research on subjective (belief systems) phenomena accepts the principle of hierarchy—

the idea that there is a continuum from discrete to general. One plausible scheme extends from fundamental value-orientations to very specific opinions:

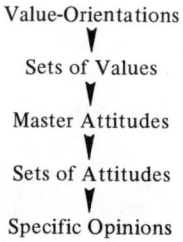

By profiling elite value systems, we are presumably tapping phenomena which shape the awareness of threat (in a static sense) and structure or screen the perception of threat (in a dynamic context).

From the perspective of international conflict and crisis analysis, foreign policy *elite value profiles* may be homogeneous. This expectation conforms to the research findings of Rokeach, who has attempted to map the value systems of such *institutions* as science and religion.[27] The theoretical literature on national security, deterrence, and strategy also suggests that a dominant profile would exist across states; in a world in which security is inevitably a scarce commodity, all decision-makers confront the same agenda and must formulate policies and engage in actions which are directed toward the goals of maximizing security and minimizing insecurity.[28] Foreign policy elites in different states, then, may tend to emphasize (and rank) values in a similar fashion.

In contrast, some of the available evidence indicates that the state value patterns differ.[29] This would be consistent with the earlier argument that salient threats vary on the basis of the particular decision-maker's or elite's value screen. In addition, state and state type variations might produce divergent value profiles; such diversity across our sample of national decision systems would be analogous to the distinct tendency of subgroups within the U.S. population to exhibit differing value patterns.

ANALYSIS

The unexplored but very fundamental threat-value linkage and the related question about interstate homogeneity versus diversity are complex theoretical concerns which will not be confronted here. The focus of this analysis is the more general issue of the impact of elite values on foreign behavior in comparison with other types of source factors.

Relative Potency Assessment

The foreign policy analyst's concern with estimating the relative potency of general source clusters, which may be traced to the work of Rosenau (1966), has spawned a series of empirical studies.[30] Frequently, the question revolves around the assessment of the relative importance of internal versus external sources of behavior—or between comparative and international politics approaches to the study of the sources of external behavior or the processes of foreign policy decision-making.

We have already reviewed the series of relative potency tests in our research program. The specific analysis discussed below entailed five distinct steps:

(1) Regress the three dependent variables (constructive diplomatic behavior, nonmilitary conflict, and force), one at a time, on the eighteen value variables, generating betas and predicted values of the dependent variables. Perform the regressions on the total group (thirty-nine states) and on the four subgroups (Western, Closed, Unstable, and Third World).
(2) Repeat the procedure, substituting the four societal/political variables for the eighteen value variables.
(3) Repeat the procedure, substituting the eight interstate variables for the eighteen value variables.
(4) Repeat the procedure, substituting the ten global variables for the eighteen value variables.
(5) Regress the three dependent variables, one at a time, on the four sets of predicted values derived from the first four steps. Perform the regressions on the total group of thirty-nine and on each of the four subgroups (Western, Closed, Unstable, and Third World).

In the first four steps, the three dependent variables are each regressed upon the indicators from one of the four independent variable clusters. The beta-weights index the effects of discrete variables within the cluster. For example, the impact of freedom, national security, or any of the eighteen values could be assessed *in relation to the effects of other decision-maker values*. The same holds for the societal/political variables of step 2, the interstate variables of step 3, and the global variables of step 4.

In contrast to these isolated variable cluster analyses, step 5 is a direct *relative potency* test. A single indicator is developed for each of the four components; this summary measure reflects the combined effects of all variables within each cluster in terms of explaining foreign behavior. The input values for the independent variables are the predicted values for the three forms of foreign behavior that were produced in the first four stages. Relative potency is directly estimated by regressing the dependent variable upon the set of predictions, thus generating comparative betas which can be viewed as *relative potency scores*.

FINDINGS

Severe limitations of length preclude a detailed discussion of all aspects of the analysis. The focus here will be the relative potency results since these are the most relevant from the threat science perspective. The findings for the preliminary component-by-component regressions (i.e., steps 1-4) are presented elsewhere.[31]

The relative potency results are presented in summary form in Table 1.3. The states in the various subgroups are listed in Table 1.2. Overall, the lowest percentage of variance explained figure is twenty-six (the force dimension for the Unstable states); the highest is eighty-six (constructive diplomatic behavior for the same cluster of states). All of the R^2's are statistically significant.

These results should be considered in the context of an earlier relative potency test (Hopple et al., 1977). In that analysis, only two components were included: the societal and a modified insterstate cluster. The latter incorporated WEIS behavior received variables as well as the interstate economic indicators which comprise the interstate cluster of Table 1.3. In addition, fifty-six states were examined, whereas this test involves a

TABLE 1.3 Relative Potency of Predictors of Foreign Policy Behavior (nation-years aggregated, 1966-1970)[a]

	Psychological	Societal	Interstate	Global	R^2
Total Group					
Constructive Diplomatic	.18*	.28*	.15*	.42*	.56*
Non-Military Conflict	.21*	.04	.15*	.49*	.46*
Force	.29*	.15*	.14*	.29*	.34*
Western Group					
Constructive Diplomatic	−.03	.58*	.01	.30	.61*
Non-Military Conflict	.07	−.05	.10	.72*	.61*
Force	.24	.29	.09	.31	.43*
Closed Group					
Constructive Diplomatic	.28*	.48*	.13	.20	.74*
Non-Military Conflict	.25*	.47*	.29	.15	.68*
Force	.55*	.16	.17	.07	.45*
Unstable Group					
Constructive Diplomatic	−.05	.09	−.01	.90*	.86*
Non-Military Conflict	.09	−.10	.30*	.50*	.56*
Force	.41*	.29	.04	.18	.26*
Others[b]					
Constructive Diplomatic	.82*	−.09	.01	.21*	.59*
Non-Military Conflict	.62*	.11	.04	.23	.80*
Force	.21*	−.07	.05	.67*	.59*

a. Numbers in first four columns are beta weights.
b. This group consists of all large developing, poor, and unclassifiable states.
*Beta or R^2 significant at the .05 level.

thirty-nine-member subset of the fifty-six (see Appendix A). This simpler relative potency test yielded a single dominant conclusion: the interstate domain accounted for an overwhelming portion of the variance in a direct "contest" with the societal realm.

This pattern clearly does not characterize the analysis reported in Table 1.3. The fact that the value or psychological data are significantly related to foreign behavior outputs in ten of fifteen cases (the total group, all three forms of behavior; the Closed states, all three forms of behavior; the Unstable states, force behavior; and the Third World group, all three forms of behavior) provides striking support for the need to operationalize all of the major source variable domains in foreign policy analysis. In comparison, the interstate economic beta weights are statistically significant in only four of fifteen instances.

The extensive literature which deals with the potential impact of psychological factors on foreign policy phenomena has generally focused on the questions of *when* psychological forces exert an impact and *which particular variables* are relevant. Regarding the former issue, it is obvious that certain situations and variable configurations maximize the impact of psychological factors.[32] Various propositions *specify* the expected relationship between decision-maker characteristics (personality traits, values, beliefs, age, education, etc.) and external behavior.

An array of factors inhibits the influence of the inidividual actor (or foreign policy elite). Among these are numerous bureaucratic and role constraints. The need to respond to inputs from other countries constitutes a restraint of undeniable impact, as the earlier discussion of objective/subjective and perceptual/interactional levels of analysis demonstrated. International systemic parameters also limit the role of the individual foreign policy-maker.

One factor which has been singled out as an especially potent determinant of individual influence is *position in the hierarchy* (Kelman and Bloom, 1973: 269). Another set of modifying forces emanates from the *nature of the situation,* such as routine versus unprecedented or crisis decision contexts (Paige, 1968). A third noteworthy determinant is *the type of state* (Quandt, 1970: 198; Zimmerman, 1979).

Presumably, elites in closed regimes would shape foreign behavior to a greater extent than is the case for their peers in more accountable or democratic polities. The latter face an array of expectations, demands, and "pressures" from an institutionalized and autonomous bureaucracy, a competitive party system, attentive and mass public opinion, and other centers of influence which transmit inputs in a pluralistic system.

Generally, decision-makers' characteristics can also be expected to display more efficacy as predictor variables in developing systems. Power in such states is often concentrated in a charismatic leader or a ruling clique; roles are less clearly delineated and are comparatively uninstitutionalized.

Theoretically, then, there are three sets of conditions which maximize the impact of individual-level factors:

(1) level in the hierarchy (the higher the position, the greater the impact);
(2) type of situation (the less routine or more crisis-like the context, the greater the impact); and
(3) type of state (the more closed or developing the state, the greater the impact).

Empirically, the findings conform impressively to the predictions. Level in the hierarchy is a constant, since all of the decision-makers are representatives of the highest stratum (head of state and foreign minister). The psychological beta weights are generally lowest for the Western (democratic or politically open) states, especially for the more routine constructive diplomatic and nonmilitary conflict forms of behavior; the force beta is a much higher (but nonsignificant) .24.

The closed and the two developing clusters display the significant findings in the value realm. For the Closed countries, a grouping which consists primarily of the Soviet Union and Eastern European states (see Table 1.2),[33] the beta is highest for force, the least routine form of behavior.

The force behavior of the unstable countries is clearly determined primarily by the values of decision-makers; across the Unstable entries, the relative potency scores (betas) are: .41 (values); .29 (societal); .04 (interstate); and .18 (global). However, the psychological scores for the other two behavior dimensions are very low; the global domain is the key predictor of constructive diplomatic behavior and interstate and global forces interactively determine nonmilitary conflict outputs.

As Table 1.2 demonstrates, the states in the Third World category are basically members of the developing bloc or Third (and Fourth) Worlds. Included are such "large developing" polities as China and India and such generally "poor" (and small and weak) states as Cambodia, Jordan, and Laos. Articulated elite values are the basic determinants of both constructive diplomatic and nonmilitary conflict behaviors. Along with the global source domain, values play a role in the force behavior sent process as well.

Given our previous inability to account for force acts sent—aside from the pervasiveness of the action-reaction dynamic—these results are certainly nontrivial. In fact, the consistency and strength of the pattern within the Closed and the two developing groupings are striking: the psychological component predicts to force behavior in all three tests and is virtually the sole determinant in two of the three.

The findings are also relevant to the more general internal-external relative potency question. Whereas some of the earlier empirical work in comparative foreign policy identified the external realm as the more potent, these results suggest that both sets of source factors should be analyzed. In addition to the psychological domain, the societal cluster exerts an impact (on constructive diplomatic behavior within the Western and Closed groups and on nonmilitary conflict behavior within the Closed states).

One of the two external realms, the global is the more important; it displays a very significant effect on nonmilitary conflict within two clusters (Western and Unstable), shares influence in two other cases (with the interstate cluster for nonmilitary conflict within the Unstable group and with the psychological cluster for constructive diplomatic behavior within the Third World group), and is the most potent source of behavior sent within the Third World category.

IMPLICATIONS

While the results presented above provide a static "snapshot" of the threat environment rather than a dynamic process-oriented analysis, the former is a not insignificant product in and of itself. Further, it provides the basis for developing more dynamic models and for moving from conditions to situations and events analysis.

From the vantage point of ascertaining the sources of threats, it is clear that the Closed states react to psychological as well as societal inputs; note the robust societal betas of .48 (constructive diplomatic) and .47 (nonmilitary conflict) in Table 1.3. Societal forces also impinge upon the process of sending external constructive diplomatic outputs within the Western states (beta weight = .58).

Objective diffusion or interstate spillover interpretations are supported by the instances in which the global source domain is significant: the Western group (nonmilitary conflict); the Unstable group (constructive diplomatic and nonmilitary conflict); and the Third World group (constructive diplomatic and force). Interstate determinants are influential with respect to the nonmilitary conflict behavior of Unstable states and, to a lesser extent, the same type of behavior of Closed states (a respectable but nonsignificant beta of .29).

Foreign policy can be conceptualized in cybernetic terms as a process of steering and coordination. Foreign behavior data bases such as WEIS capture the public manifestations of these steering and coordination efforts. While events (as opposed to transactions) are by definition "nonroutine" interactions, many are nevertheless substantively "routine." Perhaps the bulk of the constructive diplomatic events can be so characterized. Many comments, consultations, agreements, and even denials and warnings would presumably exemplify this pattern.

Threat awareness and management processes become activated and are expressed via such "constructive diplomatic" categories as negative sanctions and especially by accusations, demands, and other words and deed in the nonmilitary conflict realm. Demonstrations, expulsions, and seizures are at the extreme threat end of the nonmilitary conflict "spectrum." When force occurs, threat (and conflict and crisis) management has "failed." Interestingly, the three forms of external behavior identified initially in our factor analytic work make sense from a "threat theory" perspective.

Threat science will be a science of complexity. A cybernetic threat steering model must incorporate internal and external sources and deal with "hard" (objective, interstate/systemic) and "soft" (subjective, perceptual/psychological) phenomena. This chapter hopefully makes a modest contribution toward the goal of illuminating the neglected subject of threat:

> To make a science of threats ... is to threaten the threat system itself, for a system so inefficient in producing welfare as the threat system is can only survive as long as it is supported on folk ignorance. It is little wonder, therefore, that the science of threat systems has been so slow to develop [Boulding, 1963: 434].

NOTES

1. The term *crisis* is defined in the Glossary of Concepts at the end of the chapter; the Glossary contains concepts which are central to our discussion and often tend to be defined ambiguously or implicitly. The first time that a particular term from the Glossary appears in the text, it will be underlined.

2. Noteworthy exceptions include Boulding (1963), Rosenau (1970), and Singer (1963). Brecher (1977, 1978) and C. F. Hermann (1969, 1972) both treat threat as one of three elements of crisis perception. Brecher's definition consists of threat, time, and war likelihood dimensions; threat perception incorporates activity, potency, and affect (central, peripheral). Thus, the most active and/or strong and/or central the values which are threatened, the higher the perceived probability of military hostilities and the more limited the perceived time for response. Brecher has explored additional interactional relationships involving the three elements of crisis perception; the dominant conclusion is that the three crisis elements form mutually interacting relationships.

3. This perspective is developed in detail in McClelland (1974, 1975a, 1975b, 1975c, 1976, 1977); see also McClelland et al. (1976). The empirical dimension of

the research will not be discussed here; on "dangers" or D-files data, see McClelland (1978a, 1978b), McClelland et al. (1976), McClelland and Simon (1979), and Simon (1979).

4. See also Snyder and Diesing (1977: 3-4). The conceptual literature on international crises, which is voluminous and heterogeneous, is reviewed in Hopple (1978a); see also C. F. Hermann (1969), 1972).

5. The threat concept is also featured in the various arms race and action-reaction models; see, e.g., Richardson (1960) and North et al. (1968). On threat and deterrence, see also Boulding (1963).

6. The original set of fifty-six states has since been expanded to seventy-seven; the data currently span the period 1966-1975. Hopple (1978a) discusses the total sample of seventy-seven; the countries are listed in Appendix A, with the core group of thirty-nine denoted by asterisks.

7. Potential causal models are sketched out in Rosa (1979b). Details on the conceptualization, operationalization, empirical mapping, (factor analysis, index and scale construction, etc.) and phases of inquiry are provided in Hopple (1978a) and Wilkenfeld et al. (1978a, 1978b).

8. PLS is described in detail in Hopple (1978a, 1978b), Rossa (1979a), and Wold (1978, 1979). For applications to foreign behavior, see Rossa et al. (1979) and Wilkenfeld et al. (1979b). The state classification scheme refers to the structural attribute dimensions (economic structure, etc.) which were identified via R-factor analysis of the state attributes data set as well as the five country groupings revealed by Q-factor analysis; both are described in detail in Wilkenfeld et al. (1978b).

9. The action-reaction element of the interstate component refers to World Event Interaction Survey or WEIS behavior received data (treated as independent variables within the interstate domain); action-reaction factors were included in the research design of Rossa et al. (1979) but excluded from the otherwise comparable model tested by Wilkenfeld et al. (1979b).

10. These indicators and clusters are discussed in detail in Rossa (1976) and Wilkenfeld et al. (1978a).

11. The states included in this group are Greece, Cyprus, Ghana, Nigeria, Kenya, Turkey, Lebanon, Jordan, Saudi Arabia, Yemen, China, South Korea, India, Pakistan, Thailand, Cambodia, Laos, and Indonesia. See Appendix A for the list of states.

12. See, respectively, McClelland (1977, 1978a, 1978b) and IPPRC (1978); see also the Glossary of Concepts at the end of this chapter.

13. Moderator analysis is more useful than the approach employed here for the purpose of generating state-specific portraits, but it introduces added complexity to the model. State groupings represent a compromise between purely nomothetic modeling and system-specific studies.

14. The research reported in the voluminous domestic conflict/foreign conflict literature is mixed and far from supportive; for a recent example, see Kegley et al. (1978). More relevant evidence can be gleaned from initial results generated with McClelland's D-files methodology (see McClelland et al., 1976: 32-38), where a robust inverse relationship characterizes the nexus between the number of domestic and international *threats* for a four-month span (January to April of 1976) over weekly and three-day intervals. The internal-external crisis model is reviewed in Hopple (1978a: 222-233).

15. The array of internal and external factors is cataloged in the comparative foreign policy literature; for a recent overview which emphasizes the role of external variables (in the context of also considering the internal policy processes which

convert global inputs into "adaptive" outputs), see Kegley and McGowan (1979: 18-27). See also East et al. (1978).

16. Since our focus is external behavior, we have not attempted to track or profile all of the factors which would be relevant to assessing a country's purely internal threat agenda. For analyzing the entire range of internal and external threats and illuminating the various conceivable linkages (internal⟶external; internal⟶external, internal⟶external, etc.), it would be necessary to adopt some form of systematic internal situation profiling. While we are at a relatively advanced state for monitoring interstate affairs, our methodologies for tracking intrastate affairs are primitive.

17. See especially Hopple and Rossa (1979), Kinder and Weiss (1978), and Tanter (1978). Perceptual and belief systems phenomena are treated in a number of recent studies of international crisis and conflict; see especially Bobrow et al. (1979) and Snyder and Diesing (1977). The more general theme of environmental influences and decision-maker perceptions is discussed in Gold (1978).

18. Even more aberrant are the occasional instances when a genuine threat does not even pass from a latent "threat region" to the active "threat field" of a cognitive map (in McClelland's terminology) until an actual attack occurs (e.g., Barbarossa from the perspective of Stalin). Even instances of "surprise" (e.g., Pearl Harbor, the outbreak of the October War in 1973, etc.) generally occur in contexts characterized by heightened tension and hostility.

19. Several projects which feature such data are described in Falkowski (1979a, 1979b); see also Hopple (1980) and M. G. Hermann (1977, 1978).

20. See Hopple (1978b, 1980) and Hopple and Favin (1978).

21. The psychological realm of our research is described in more detail in Hopple (1978b).

22. For the United States itself, the source was the *Department of State Bulletin*. For generating yearly samples, all states for which there were three or more speeches were included. Thirty-nine states satisfied this criterion at least once during the five-year period from 1966 to 1970. The annual state samples vary from 31 (1966, 1967) to 20 (1969). A core group of fourteen states appears in all five yearly samples, including, among others, the United States, USSR, China, most Eastern European states, and several Middle Eastern states.

23. See especially Hopple (1979a, 1980).

24. See Rokeach (1973) and Table 8-2 of Wilkenfeld et al. (1978a: 217-218); also relevant are two recent works by Rokeach (1979b, 1979c).

25. See Searing (1978: 77); expected differences also emerge for factional groups within parties.

26. See also Rokeach and Parker (1970) and Rokeach (1979c).

27. See, respectively, Rokeach (1975) and Rokeach (1968a, 1968b); see also Rokeach (1979a).

28. From a game theoretic or macro perspective, crisis, conflict, and war *can* occur because of the ultimate and pervasive structural factor (the anarchy of the international supergame and the consequent security dilemma); all nations pursue a basic security strategy via a number of core "tactics" (acquisition of armaments, formation of alliances, direct actions gainst adversaries, etc.). See Snyder and Diesing (1977) for details.

29. See Wilkenfeld et al. (1978a: 223-226). This question, it should be emphasized, has been explored in a very preliminary fashion; we plan to offer a more definitive assessment on the basis of subsequent inquiry.

30. Examples include Hopple et al. (1977), Rosenau and Hoggard (1974), and Rosenau and Ramsey (1975).

31. See Hopple (1979a) and Wilkenfeld et al. (1979a).

32. See Holsti (1976) and M. G. Hermann (1976), 1978).

33. The two exceptions (Portugal and Spain) were politically closed during the research design time frame (1966-1970). Neither country, it should be noted, is among the thirty-nine in the value data subsample discussed in this chapter. Neither China nor Cuba loaded on the Closed factor; China was initially a Large Developing (the Third World category in this study) and Cuba is one of the Unstable states.

GLOSSARY OF CONCEPTS

CONDITION: From McClelland's (1977) perspective, this is the third and most remote level of analysis for disaster warning and crisis anticipation. Unlike situations (q.v.), conditions do not include the data of interactive behavior. A climate change that reduced food production and spawned shortages and internal stress is cited by McClelland (1977: 33) as an example of "conditions" analysis.

CRISIS: Definitions of international crisis have proliferated. The conceptual labyrinth of the concept of crisis is reflected by the array of existing conceptual definitions and empirical measures. Conceptual discussions often bifurcate crisis research into two distinct realms: the situational/decision-making/intraunit perspective and the systemic/interactional/interunit vantage point. The former is treated in Brecher (1977, 1978) and C. F. Hermann (1969, 1972); the latter is illuminated in McClelland (1961, 1972). See also the discussion and citations in Hopple (1978a) and Thompson (1979). Crisis and threat (q.v.) as concepts are compared in McClelland (1975a).

To a considerable extent, the researcher's choice of a definition is shaped by the purposes of analysis and the focus of concern. From the perspective of the United States, for example, definitions would vary from the State Department to the defense milieu to the (political) intelligence community. One common U.S. military-oriented definition is:

> A "crisis" is a period of increased military management activity at the national level that is carried on in a sustained manner under conditions of rapid action and response from unexpected events or incidents that have occurred internationally, internally in a foreign country, or within the responding country (such as the domestic United States) and that have inflicted or threatened to inflict violence or significant damage to actual or perceived national interests, personnel, or facilities [Hazelwood et al., 1977: 79].

DANGER: Danger as a concept is inextricably linked with threat (q.v.), stress (q.v.), tension, crisis (q.v.), and similar phenomena. Dangers encompass situations which contain present or forthcoming threats to safety, security, survival, welfare, or well-being and thus constitute the essence of threat recognition (McClelland, 1978b: 13). Approaching hazards and dangers include coups, earthquakes, riots, revolts, border classes, guerilla attacks, atmospheric catastrophes, ecological upsets and tragedies, and a potentially infinite number of additional items (McClelland, 1978b: 6-7). Note that McClelland defines a danger as *any* source of a current or potential sign or indicator of warning; the range of items is much broader than the traditional economic, political, and military classification scheme. Note also that dangers may be purely internal, may involve two or more countries, and may even apply to the entire international system; the traditional distinction between internal and external political analysis (i.e., comparative and international politics as separate fields) is abandoned. On the conceptualization of intrastate crises in general, see Hopple (1978a).

DANGERS FILES (D-FILES): Charles McClelland's Current World Stress Studies (CWSS) Project at the University of Southern California is designed to develop and apply a methodology to monitor and forecast stress and tension. Prestige newspapers (the New York *Times* and, until the *Times* of London shutdown ends, the Los Angeles *Times*) serve as sources for D-files data, which operationalize the concept of threat recognition. The coding procedure involves daily data collection from the newspapers in order to extract "D"-related (i.e., accounts of dangers, disasters, disturbances, etc.). As McClelland and Simon (1979) point out, each data item consists of a line of codes followed by a descriptive account of the threat situation. Included in the code line are the date of the item, sequence number, source, judge, country (maximum of three), level (domestic, international, global), category (apprehension, agitation, life support breakdown, accident/natural disaster, assault, warfare), and judge's assessments (degree of severity, anticipated development or tilt, speed, and spread). In addition to McClelland and Simon (1979), see McClelland (1978a, 1978b), McClelland et al. (1976), and Simon (1979).

EARLY WARNING AND MONITORING SYSTEM (EWAMS): Described in IPPRC (1978), the Early Warning and Monitoring System (EWAMS) is a computer-based, user-oriented, early warning system that reflects as realistically as possible— and detects as early as possible—changes in the interactions of nation-states and other actors in the international arena. Combining techniques from quantitative political science and international relations, computer science, decision theory, and forecasting methodology, the EWAMS is currently based on World Event Interaction Survey (WEIS) event (q.v.) data from the New York *Times* (1966 to the present) and the *Times* of London/Manchester *Guardian* (1978 to the present). Designed eventually for transfer to U.S. government analysts with concerns in foreign affairs and intelligence, the EWAMS will ultimately incorporate a number of data bases and forecasting methodologies.

ELITE VALUE PROFILES: The foreign policy elite (i.e., head of state and foreign minister) for each country in the world features a value system with values (q.v.) or ultimate, preferred end-states of existence ranked in a hierarchy. Values comprise the core of an individual's (or institution's) belief system and function as guides to action and decision-making. Evidence concerning the value profiles of various political elites is presented in Hopple (1979a, 1980), Rokeach (1973), and Searing (1978).

EVENT (EVENT/INTERACTION): The events data movement in international politics and comparative foreign policy transforms the multifaceted, elusive construct of "foreign policy" into the more measurable concept of "foreign behavior" or "foreign outputs." An event is a discrete, observable physical or verbal action. All events data sets feature time or date of occurrence, actor/s, event types, and one or more targets as central variables; there are, however, significant differences across data sets in terms of spatial and temporal parameters, types of actors and targets, categorization versus scaling, and other dimensions. Events data are used for short-term forecasting in the event analysis mode (see McClelland, 1977: 34-35). Events data and D-files (q.v.) are contrasted in McClelland (1978a, 1978b).

RUIN: A ruin outcome is a potential end-state of the threat process. Ruin for a social system is not necessarily isomorphic to extinction as a potential end-state for a biological system. McClelland provides a systems framework for analyzing threat (q.v.) in terms of functions, essential variables, and critical ranges. A threat situation in a social system can be defined as "a particular sequence of change-steps, these being successive system states still emerging in the social system with the potential end state being a condition of ruin" (McClelland, 1974: 17).

SITUATION: Situations, unlike conditions, include the data of interactive behavior; according to McClelland (1977: 33), they are " 'states of affairs' with some fairly stable patterning and some endurance across time but without permanence." McClelland (1977) offers several examples of situations analysis (e.g., schemes for tracking nation-to-nation commitments). Situations analysis should be compared to conditions (q.v.) analysis and events (q.v.) analysis.

STRESS: This term has been defined in various ways; the version here is based on Wiegele (1978a). Stress connotes the idea that the individual is "beset by powerful pressures which greatly tax the adaptive resources of the biological or psychological system" (Lazarus, 1966: 10). Stress is a stimulus condition which produces systemic disequilibrium. A stressful event is one which causes a high degree of emotional tension and also inhibits normal response modes. See also Wiegele (1978b) and the sources cited there.

THREAT: For the individual, a threat is the "anticipation of approaching harm that triggers a characteristic response called 'stress' " (McClelland, 1975a: 19). Stress (q.v.) in turn produces behavioral reactions and effects referred to in the aggregate as "coping." McClelland (1974: 5) distinguishes between issued threats (issued from one actor and directed toward another) and situational threats ("state of affairs" threats). Situational threat has "two faces": the objective/state of affairs aspect and the subjective/image dimension. McClelland (1974: 9) labels the entire perceptual or psychological process "threat prevision," which he defines as "patternings of perceptions that are oriented to foreseen future states of affairs that are, at once, undesirable, avoidable, and to be warned against." McClelland (1974: 19) emphasizes that the objective (threat process identification) and subjective (threat prevision) aspects are in a transactional relationship (i.e., the prevision is conditioned by empirical influences while the empirical element of a threat situation is modified by the imagery of the prevision). Both McClelland's 1974 report "Threat Situations: A Search for a Controlled Definition" and the 1975a citation ("Crisis and Threat in the International Setting: Some Relational Concepts") provide discussions of threat as a concept and flesh out the hypothesized event (q.v.) threat-crisis (q.v.) linkage process. Also relevant are McClelland (1975b, 1975c, 1976, 1977) and McClelland et al. (1976). Boulding's (1963) abstract discussion of threat systems, exchange systems, and integrative systems is very helpful; he notes that deterrence systems—which are based on threats—tend to exhibit long-run instability because either capability or credibility (or both) decline over time. Boulding also offers some interesting analogies between the competition of states via threats and the competition of firms in an economy via exchange; the game theoretic and bargaining studies of Thomas Schelling and others provide pertinent analytic perspectives for efforts to develop and apply threat as a central concept in the study of international politics and foreign policy.

THREAT AGENDA: Each society has an agenda of active issues; the list is usually relatively short and even in open societies the items are often chosen by a relatively small segment of the attentive public. The media and government are primary actors in the process of fashioning an agenda and are characterized by a complex web of reciprocal influences. The threat agenda is that part of the general agenda which features issues with a potential or actual capacity for harm and ruin (q.v.). As much as is possible, the government reduces the vast incoming stream of matters to the level of the routine and assigns them to the bureaucracy or administrative apparatus; reports of warning and threat, for example, are initially routed to the middle and lower levels of the bureaucracy. There is a bimodal pattern of organizational behavior: the routine "default option" (which usually prevails) and the emergency approach. If a series of reported events fits in with a latent threat region (q.v.), it may spur a transition to an active threat field (q.v.); the issue then appears on the threat agenda. McClelland (1975a) provides a detailed discussion of agendas. The contents of general agendas and threat agendas vary across national systems and across time within a system. Pertinent dimensions of variation include substantive issues, the internal versus external mix, and the range of issues.

THREAT BURDEN: A threat burden is the threat "load" on a decision system. Burdens are reflected by the media of public communication, as McClelland (1975a) notes. However, this assumes an objective view of threat burdens; threat burdens may also be viewed as perceptual phenomena. In either case, the burden fluctuates in terms of the proportion of internal, external, and the intermix of threats and, like the threat agenda (q.v.) per se, may vary across systems (e.g., the threat load on Italy versus Switzerland) and within a system across time (e.g., Lebanon in the late 1950s versus the same country in the late 1970s). McClelland's (1978a, 1978b) D-files data (q.v.) should provide an empirical foundation for profiling and assessing threat burdens by issue area on cross-national and temporal bases.

THREAT FIELD: There are specific active threat "fields" in the threat region (q.v.) of an individual's (or institution's) cognitive map. Events can set off a movement from the region to the field and back to the region; in the 1950s, the "Communist threat" was a salient element of the threat field of the United States and many other Western countries. Active threat fields display a tendency to persist when activated and are often generalized. The former tendency explains the frequent "staying power" of irrelevant threats and the latter accounts in part for the common pattern in which decision-makers use analogies to generate sweeping (and often inappropriate or misleading) lessons of history (e.g., extrapolations from the Munich threat field of 1938 to the Korean attack in 1950 or the Cuban missile crisis in 1962). This definition is based on McClelland (1975a).

THREAT REGION: McClelland (1975a: 19) defines a cognitive map as the "stored and partly ordered assembly of one's awareness and understanding of many ranges of topics, conditions, and circumstances." A cognitive map contains a "region" which is especially sensitive to cognitively established events which indicate that danger (q.v.) is present or imminent. The threat region, which is not always active, performs an early warning function. Inactive threat regions may be appropriate responses to reality or may represent potentially disastrous instances of misperception. Threat regions may have specific active threat fields (q.v.). McClelland (1975a), who provides the basis for this capsule description of the threat region concept, emphasizes that threat regions and fields are not isomorphic at the individual and collective levels of analysis. At the societal level, for example, the threat region of the cognitive map is probably not identical across a large number of individuals. At the level of the collectivity, the media of mass communication provide threat signs and pinpoint the salient cues which illuminate threat regions and fields.

VALUE: According to Rokeach (1973: 5), a value

> is an enduring belief that a specific mode of conduct or end-state of existence is personally or socially preferable to an opposite or converse mode of conduct or end-state of existence. A *value system* is an enduring organization of beliefs concerning preferable modes of conduct or end-states of existence along a continuum of relative importance.

The Rokeach belief systems framework incorporates a range of levels of objects: responses, opinions, beliefs, attitudes, and values. The foreign policy-relevant belief systems landscape is surveyed and the various terms defined in Hopple (1978b, 1980) and Hopple and Favin (1978: 16-30). Value theory per se is discussed in Rokeach (1979a, 1979b, 1979c).

Values embody ideas of the desirable and serve as internalized criteria and standards of evaluation; values are few in number, are basic and general in nature, and are causually primordial in the individual's belief system. Operationally, Rokeach (1973) identifies eighteen terminal and eighteen instrumental values. Respondents typically rank values in order of their importance. Values and value rankings can be obtained from *individuals* (through questionnaires and surveys) and from *institutions* (through content analysis and other methods); see Rokeach (1979a) for details.

APPENDIX A: LIST OF STATES[a]

State	No. Code	Letter Code	State	No. Code	Letter Code
Western Hemisphere:					
1. United States*	002	USA	40. Ethiopia	530	ETH
2. Canada	020	CAN	41. Zambia	551	ZAM
3. Cuba*	040	CUB	42. Rhodesia	552	RHO
4. Mexico	070	MEX	43. Mozambique	555	FRE
5. Panama	095	PAN	44. South Africa	560	SAF
6. Venezuela	101	VEN	45. Angola	561	ANG
7. Brazil	140	BRA			
8. Chile*	155	CHL	**Middle East:**		
9. Argentina	160	ARG			
			46. Morocco	600	MOR
Europe:			47. Algeria*	615	ALG
			48. Libya	620	LBY
10. United Kingdom	200	UNK	49. Sudan	625	SUD
11. Netherlands	210	NTH	50. Iran*	630	IRN
12. Belgium	211	BEL	51. Turkey*	640	TUR
13. France*	220	FRN	52. Iraq*	645	IRQ
14. Spain	230	SPN	53. United Arab Rep.*	651	UAR
15. Portugal	235	POR	54. Syria*	652	SYR
16. West Germany*	255	GMW	55. Lebanon*	660	LEB
17. East Germany*	265	GME	56. Jordan*	663	JOR
18. Poland*	290	POL	57. Israel*	666	ISR
19. Austria	305	AUS	58. Saudia Arabia*	670	SAU
20. Hungary*	310	HUN	59. Yemen*	678	YEM
21. Czechoslovakia*	315	CZE	60. Kuwait	690	KUW
22. Italy	325	ITA			
23. Albania	339	ALB	**Asia:**		
24. Yugoslavia*	345	YUG			
25. Greece*	350	GRC	61. China*	710	CHN
26. Cyprus*	352	CYP	62. Taiwan	713	CHT
27. Bulgaria*	355	BUL	63. North Korea	731	KON
28. Rumania*	360	RUM	64. South Korea*	732	KOS
29. USSR*	365	USR	65. Japan*	740	JAP
30. Sweden	380	SWD	66. India*	750	IND
31. Denmark	390	DEN	67. Bangladesh	765	BGD
32. Iceland	395	ICE	68. Pakistan*	770	PAK
			69. Thailand*	800	TAI
Africa:			70. Cambodia*	811	CAM
			71. Laos*	812	LAO
			72. N. Vietnam	816	VTN
33. Ghana*	452	GHA	73. S. Vietnam*	817	VTS
34. Nigeria*	475	NIG	74. Malaysia	820	MAL
35. Zaire	490	COP	75. Philippines	840	PHI
36. Uganda	500	UGA	76. Indonesia*	850	INS
37. Kenya*	501	KEN			
38. Tanzania	510	TAZ	**Oceania:**		
39. Somalia	520	SOM			
			77. Australia	900	AUL

a. Standard World Event Interaction Survey (WEIS) number and letter codes
*Value subsample of states (one or more years, 1966-1970)

APPENDIX B: INTERSTATE ECONOMIC INDEX FORMULAE

Interstate Energy Relationships (Indices)

1. Energy Interdependency =
$$\frac{\text{energy imports} + \text{energy exports}}{\text{energy consumption}}$$

2. Energy Market Strength =
$$\frac{\text{energy exports}}{\text{energy production} + \text{imports}}$$

3. Energy Dependency =
$$\frac{\text{energy imports}}{\text{energy consumption} + \text{exports/production}}$$

General Trade Relationships (Indices)

4. Neo-Colonial Dependency =
$$\frac{(\text{industrial imports} + \text{unrefined exports}) - (\text{unrefined imports} + \text{industrial exports})}{\text{total imports} + \text{total exports}}$$

5. Economic Involvement = total exports + total imports

Food Dependency and Advantage (Index)

6. Food Dependency =
$$\frac{\text{food imports} - \text{food exports}}{\text{food imports} + \text{food exports}}$$

General Interstate Economic Relations (Indices)

7. Import Concentration = $\sqrt{\dfrac{(S_i)^2 - 1/10}{1 - 1/10}}$

8. Export Concentration = $\sqrt{\dfrac{(T_i)^2 - 1/10}{1 - 1/10}}$

REFERENCES

ANDRIOLE, S. J., J. WILKENFELD, and G. W. HOPPLE (1975) "A framework for the comparative analysis of foreign policy behavior." International Studies Quarterly 19 (June): 160-198.
BOBROW, D. B., S. CHAN, and J. A. KRINGEN (1979) Understanding Foreign Policy Decisions: The Chinese Case. New York: Free Press.
BOULDING, K. E. (1963) "Toward a pure theory of threat systems." American Economic Review 53 (May): 424-434.
BRECHER, M. (1978) "A theoretical approach to international crisis behavior." Jerusalem Journal of International Relations 3 (Winter-Spring): 5-24.
——— (1977) "Toward a theory of international crisis behavior: a preliminary report." International Studies Quarterly 21 (March): 39-74.
BURGESS, P. M. and R. W. LAWTON (1972) Indicators of International Behavior: An Assessment of Events Data Research. Beverly Hills: Sage Publications.
COLEMAN, J. S. et al. (1966) Equality of Educational Opportunity. Washington, DC: Department of Health, Education, and Welfare.
DEVINE, D. J. (1972) The Political Culture of the United States: The Influence of Member Values on Regime Maintainance. Boston: Little, Brown.
EAST, M. A., S. A. SALMORE, and C. F. HERMANN [eds.] (1978) Why Nations Act: Theoretical Perspectives for Comparative Foreign Policy Studies. Beverly Hills: Sage Publications.
FALKOWSKI, L. [ed.] (1979a) "Proceedings of the IPPRC Symposium on Biopolitics and Political Psychology." McLean, VA: International Public Policy Research Corporation, Publication No. 79-8.
——— (1979b) Psychological Models in International Politics. Boulder, CO: Westview.
GOLD, H. (1978) "Foreign policy decision-making and the environment: the claims of Snyder, Brecher, and the Sprouts." International Studies Quarterly 22 (December): 569-586.
HAZELWOOD, L., J. J. HAYES, and J. R. BROWNELL, Jr. (1977) "Planning for problems in crisis management: an analysis of post-1945 behavior in the U.S. Department of Defense." International Studies Quarterly 21 (March): 75-106.
HERMANN, C. F. [ed.] (1972) International Crises: Insights from Behavioral Research. New York: Free Press.
——— (1969) "International crisis as a situational variable," pp. 409-421 in J. N. Rosenau (ed.) International Politics and Foreign Policy: A Reader in Research and Theory. New York: Free Press.
HERMANN, M. G. (1978) "Effects of personal characteristics of political leaders on foreign policy," pp. 49-68 in M. A. East et al. (eds.) Why Nations Act: Theoretical Perspectives for Comparative Foreign Policy Studies. Beverly Hills: Sage Publications.
——— [ed.] (1977) A Psychological Examination of Political Leaders. New York: Free Press.
——— (1976) "When leader personality will affect foreign policy: some propositions," pp. 326-333 in J. N. Rosenau (ed.) In Search of Global Patterns. New York: Free Press.
HOLSTI, O. R. (1976) "Foreign policy formation viewed cognitively," pp. 18-54 in R. Axelrod (ed.) Structure of Decision. Princeton, NJ: Princeton Univ. Press.
HOPPLE, G. W. (1980) The Psychological and Psychophysiological Foundations of Elite Foreign Policy Behavior. Boulder, CO: Westview.

—— (1979a) "Elite values and foreign policy analysis: preliminary findings," in L. S. Falkowski (ed.) Psychological Models in International Politics. Boulder, CO: Westview.

—— (1979b) "Soft modeling in the social sciences: applications of partial least squares in political science." Presented at the Conference on Soft Modeling in the Social Sciences, University of Geneva, October.

—— (1978a) "Final report of the Cross-National Crisis Indicators Project." College Park, MD: University of Maryland, December.

—— (1978b) "Mapping the terrain of command psychophysiology: a preliminary design for an emerging applied science." McLean, VA: International Public Policy Research Corporation, Cybernetics Sciences Evaluation Project, Technical Assessment Report 78-2-1, August.

—— and A. J. FAVIN (1978) "The domain of command psychophysiology: a scientific/technical literature review." McLean, VA: International Public Policy Research Corporation, Cybernetics Sciences Evaluation Project, December.

HOPPLE, G. W. and P. J. ROSSA (1979) "Recent developments and future directions in international crisis research." Presented at the Annual Meeting of the International Studies Association, Toronto, Canada, March.

HOPPLE, G. W., J. WILKENFELD, P. J. ROSSA, and R. N. McCAULEY (1977) "Societal and interstate determinants of foreign conflict." Jerusalem Journal of International Relations 2 (Summer): 30-66.

International Public Policy Research Corporation (IPPRC) (1978) "The Early Warning and Monitoring System," pp. 146-166 in J. A. Daly (ed.) Proceedings of the DARPA/CTO Crisis Management Seminar. Arlington, VA: Defense Advanced Research Projects Agency, October.

KEGLEY, C. W., Jr. and P. J. McGOWAN (1979) "Introduction," pp. 13-33 in C. W. Kegley, Jr. and P. J. McGowan (eds.) Challenges to America: United States Foreign Policy in the 1980s. Sage International Yearbook of Foreign Policy Studies 4. Beverly Hills: Sage Publications.

KEGLEY, C. W., Jr., N. R. RICHARSON, and G. RICHTER (1978) "Conflict at home and abroad: an empirical extension." Journal of Politics 40 (August): 742-751.

KELMAN, H. C. and A. H. BLOOM (1973) "Assumptive frameworks in international politics," pp. 261-295 in J. N. Knutson (ed.) Handbook of Political Psychology. San Francisco: Jossey-Bass.

KINDER, D. R. and J. A. WEISS (1978) "In lieu of rationality: psychological perspectives on foreign policy decision making." Journal of Conflict Resolution 22 (December): 707-735.

KOHN, M. L. (1969) Class and Conformity: A Study in Values. Homewood, IL: Dorsey.

LAZARUS, R. (1966) Psychological Stress and the Coping Process. New York: McGraw-Hill.

McCLELLAND, C. A. (1978a) "Current world stress studies: the basics." Los Angeles: University of Southern California, October.

—— (1978b) "D-files for monitoring and forecasting threats and problems abroad." Presented at the Annual Meeting of the International Studies Association, Washington, DC, February.

—— (1977) "The anticipation of international crises: prospects for theory and research." International Studies Quarterly 21 (March): 15-38.

—— (1976) "Warning in the international event flow: EFI and ROZ as threat indicators." Los Angeles: University of Southern California, Threat Recognition and Analysis Project Technical Report, July.

——— (1975a) "Crisis and threat in the international setting: some relational concepts." Los Angeles: International Relations Research Institute, University of Southern California, Threat Recognition and Analysis Project Technical Report 28, June.

——— (1975b) "Defense against threat." Los Angeles: International Relations Research Institute, University of Southern California, Threat Recognition and Analysis Project Technical Report 29, September.

——— (1975c) "Toward dynamic threat control: statement around a research design," pp. 119-127 in C. F. Hermann (ed.) "Research tasks for international crisis avoidance and management." Columbus, OH: Mershon Center, Ohio State University, Final Report, October.

——— (1974) "Threat situations: a search for a controlled definition." Los Angeles: International Relations Research Institute, University of Southern California, Threat Recognition and Analysis Project, January (mimeo).

——— (1972) "The beginning, duration, and abatement of international crises: comparisons in two conflict arenas," pp. 83-108 in C. F. Hermann (ed.) International Crises: Insights from Behavioral Research. New York: Free Press.

——— (1961) "The acute international crisis." World Politics 14 (January): 182-204.

——— and J. D. SIMON (1979) "Dangers files data: January-February 1979." Los Angeles: University of Southern California, Current World Stress Studies Project, May.

———, P. J. Mc GOWAN, and W. R. MARTIN (1976) "Threat, Conflict, and Commitment." Los Angeles: University of Southern California, Threat Recognition and Analysis Project Final Technical Report, September.

MEDDIN, J. (1975) "Attitudes, values and related concepts: a system of classification." Social Science Quarterly 55 (March): 889-918.

NORTH, R. C., O. R. HOLSTI, and R. A. BRODY (1968) "Perception and action in the 1914 crisis," pp. 160-186 in J. D. Singer (ed.) Quantitative International Politics. New York: Free Press.

PAIGE, G. D. (1968) The Korean Decision. New York: Free Press.

QUANDT, W. B. (1970) The Comparative Study of Political Elites. Sage Professional Papers in Comparative Politics 01-004. Beverly Hills: Sage Publications.

RICHARDSON, L. F. (1960) Arms and Insecurity. Pittsburgh: Boxwood.

ROKEACH, M. (1979a) "From individual to institutional values," in M. Rokeach (ed.) Understanding Human Values: Individual and Social. New York: Free Press.

——— [ed.] (1979b) Understanding Human Values: Individual and Social. New York: Free Press.

——— (1979c) "Value theory and communication research: review and commentary," in D. Nimmo (ed.) Communication Yearbook 3. New York: Transaction Books.

——— (1975) "Value images of science and the values of science." Pullman, WA: Washington State University, mimeo.

——— (1973) The Nature of Human Values. New York: Free Press.

——— (1968a) Beliefs, Attitudes, and Values: A Theory of Organization and Change. San Francisco: Jossey-Bass.

——— (1968b) "A theory of organization and change within value-attitude systems." Journal of Social Issues 24 (January): 13-33.

——— and S. PARKER (1970) "Values as social indicators of poverty and race relations in America." The Annals 388: 97-111.

ROSENAU, J. N. (1970) "Foreign policy as adaptive behavior." Comparative Politics 2 (April): 365-389.

––– (1966) "Pre-theories and theories of foreign policy," pp. 27-92 in R. B. Farrell (ed.) Approaches to Comparative and International Politics. Evanston, IL: Northwestern Univ. Press.

––– and G. HOGGARD (1974) "Foreign policy behavior in dyadic relationships: testing a pre-theoretical extension," in J. N. Rosenau (ed.) Comparing Foreign Policies: Theories, Findings, Methods. Beverly Hills: Sage Publications.

ROSENAU, J. N. and G. RAMSEY (1975) "External vs. internal sources of foreign policy behavior," pp. 245-262 in P. J. McGowan (ed.) Sage International Yearbook of Foreign Policy Studies 3. Beverly Hills: Sage Publications.

ROSSA, P. J. (1979a) "Explaining international political behavior and conflict through partial least squares modeling." Presented at the Conference on Systems under Indirect Observation (Causality/Structure/Prediction), Geneva, Switzerland, October.

––– (1979b) "Latent variable causal models of international conflict." McLean, VA: International Public Policy Research Corporation, Publication No. 79-3.

––– (1976) "A Q-factor analysis of the state attribute domain." College Park, MD: University of Maryland, Interstate Behavior Analysis Project Research Report 24, December.

–––, G. W. HOPPLE, and J. WILKENFELD (1979) "Crisis indicators and models." International Interactions, forthcoming.

SEARING, D. D. (1978) "Measuring politicians' values: administration and assessment of a ranking technique in the British House of Commons." American Political Science Review 72 (March): 65-79.

SIMON, J. D. (1979) "Crisis forecasting: D-Files report for February 1-15, 1979." Los Angeles: University of Southern California, Current World Stress Studies Project, February (mimeo).

SINGER, J. D. (1963) "Inter-nation influence: a formal model." American Political Science Review 57 (June): 420-430.

SNYDER, G. H. and P. DIESING (1977) Conflict Among Nations: Bargaining, Decision Making, and System Structure in International Crises. Princeton, NJ: Princeton Univ. Press.

TANTER, R. (1978) "International crisis behavior: an appraisal of the literature." Jerusalem Journal of International Relations 3 (Winter-Spring): 340-374.

THOMPSON, W. R. (1979) "Definitional and dating problems in the analysis of international crises." McLean, VA: International Public Policy Research Corporation, Publication No. 79-1.

WIEGELE, T. C. (1978a) "The psychophysiology of elite stress in five international crises: a preliminary test of a voice measurement technique." International Studies Quarterly 22 (December): 467-511.

––– (1978b) "Remote psychophysiological assessment of elites during international crises," pp. 61-72 in J. A. Daly (ed.) Proceedings of the DARPA/CTO Crisis Management Seminar. Arlington, VA: Defense Advanced Research Projects Agency, October.

WILKENFELD, J., G. W. HOPPLE, and P. J. ROSSA (1979a) "Determinants of conflict and cooperation in interstate relations." Presented at the Annual Meeting of the International Political Science Association, Moscow, August

––– (1979b) "Indicators of conflict and cooperation in the interstate system, 1966-1970," in J. D. Singer and M. D. Wallace (eds.) To Augur Well: Early

Warning Indicators in Interstate Conflict. Beverly Hills: Sage Publications.
——— and S. J. ANDRIOLE (1978a) "Final report of the interstate behavior analysis project." College Park, MD: University of Maryland, December.
WILKENFELD, J., G. W. HOPPLE, S. J. ANDRIOLE, and R. N. McCAULEY (1978b) "Profiling states for foreign policy analysis." Comparative Political Studies (April): 4-35.
WOLD, H. (1979) "Model construction and evaluation when theoretical knowledge is scarce: an example of the use of partial least squares," in J. Kmenta and J. Ramsey (eds.) Evaluation of Econometric Models, forthcoming.
——— (1978) "Ways and means of multidisciplinary studies," pp. 1071-1095 in the Transactions of the Sixth International Conference on the Unity of the Sciences, San Francisco. New York: International Cultural Foundation.
ZIMMERMAN, W. (1979) "Elite perspectives and the explanation of Soviet foreign policy." Journal of International Affairs 24: 84-98.

Chapter 2

IMAGES AND THREATS: SOVIET PERCEPTIONS OF INTERNATIONAL CRISES, 1946-1975

ROBERT B. MAHONEY, Jr.
RICHARD P. CLAYBERG

CACI, Inc.-Federal

Since the close of World War II, the leadership of the Soviet Union has perceived an international environment filled with both threats and opportunities. During this period, Soviet leaders have been particularly concerned with international crises. This chapter analyzes the Soviet Union's postwar experience with foreign political-military crises. It deals with those events in which the Soviets engaged in what has become known in the West as military "crisis management" as well as with the broader range of cases that were of concern to the Soviets but in which they did not conduct a Western-style crisis management operation. The three sections

EDITORS' NOTE: This chapter was first submitted for review May 2, 1979. The version published here was received July 9, 1979. The authors report that the data presented in this study will be made available to the Inter-University Consortium for Political and Social Research at Ann Arbor, Michigan.

AUTHORS' NOTE: The research presented in this chapter is based on a project sponsored by the Cybernetics Technology Office of the Defense Advanced Research Projects Agency (DARPA/CTO). More detailed presentations of the analysis can be found in that project's final technical report (CACI, 1978) and in Mahoney and Clayberg (1979). The arguments and conclusions presented in this chapter are solely those of the authors and should not be attributed to DARPA or any other component of the U.S. Government.

of this chapter present the research strategy used to identify Soviet crisis concerns, some of the aggregate patterns taken by these incidents, and some of the ways in which they have fit into the broader context of international relations during the postwar period.

RESEARCH STRATEGY

Introduction

Unconscious enthnocentrism is one of the most significant problems faced by comparative foreign policy researchers. Because of their familiarity and demonstrated utility for the analysis of Western foreign policy, it is all too easy to assume that standard Western sources also accurately capture the concerns of non-Western actors. While comforting, this assumption is contradicted by the findings of a number of studies (for example, Bobrow et al., 1979) that show that foreign media often trace out significantly different patterns than are found in their Western counterparts. The net result, in all too many cases, is that we end up seeing others as the Western media see them, rather than as they see themselves.

To avoid this problem, Soviet sources have been used to identify the crisis of concern to the Soviet leadership, in order to get at the perceptions that are likely to prompt and correlate with Soviet actions. This solution, however, raises another class of problems since it is desirable for a number of reasons to produce a data base of Soviet crisis concerns that is compatible to the extent practical (that is, without losing the crucial Soviet vantage point provided by the sources used) with existing U.S. crisis data files (for example, CACI, 1976). This would allow for comparisons of the crisis management experiences of the two superpowers. These two considerations pose significant analytical problems, since Soviet and Western approaches to crises and crisis management differ substantially. Their reconciliation (which makes up the core of the research strategy) involves the use of Soviet sources to identify "events," with these events being defined in terms similar to those used in Western crisis studies.

The remainder of this section outlines the problem in greater detail by comparing Western and Soviet approaches to crisis analysis and crisis management, and then goes on to detail the research strategy adopted to respond to key differences between the two vantage points.

Comparison of Soviet and Western Approaches

Soviet approaches to the analysis of crises and crisis management differ from Western practices in a number of key respects.[1] An immediate problem is that Soviet authors do not distinguish between "political" and "military" factors in the way commonly found in the West. Soviet analysts, for example, adamantly maintain that the balance of power (correlation of forces) cannot be evaluated solely on the basis of "military" factors. Instead, they contend, economic, political, and psychological considerations must also be taken into account as equally integral factors (Tomashevsky, 1974: 73). This Soviet analytical orientation has direct bearing on the analysis of the Soviet crisis management experience. In a sense that is not true in the West, it is fair to say that the Soviets have not had (in their eyes) any "military" crises since World War II. Instead, they have been involved in what they would term (Tomashevsky, 1974) "military-political" and "military-strategic" events. Military-political events are the elements involved in Soviet perceptions of crises.

A second distinction of relevance is based on the use of Marxist and Marxist-Leninist concepts in Soviet analyses. It is a major mistake to assume that these concepts are mere window dressing. Instead, it appears that Soviet analysts, using their "dialectical" approach, are more oriented toward contextual/systemic factors (the relations that sets of events have with one another) and toward longer-term trends and processes than is the case in many Western crisis studies. Emphasis on clusters of factors and longer-term perspectives often leads to the classification of events in terms of stages that are longer in duration and broader in scope than comparable "crisis events" in Western data files; for example, Yukhananov's (1972) analysis of the stages in the Southeast Asian conflicts since World War II.[2]

A third point of relevance has to do with the position from which the Soviet Union approached crisis management in the postwar period. While militarily victorious, the Soviets were devastated during the war. Their economic base was substantially damaged, casualties were severe, and their forces were not structured for distant crisis operations. Moreover, a combination of Soviet miscalculations and Western policies largely isolated the Soviets from contacts with what would become the Third World nations. This situation had two impacts. The first was that the Soviets had proportionately less in the way of resources to devote to "crisis-managing" forces (for example, general purpose naval forces). Perhaps more significantly, their relative isolation presented them with a different set of crisis management problems than were faced by Western states. While Western nations faced the problem of marshalling forces to support allied nations or factions, particularly in the Third World, the Soviets faced the problem of developing contacts to gain allies among the newly independent states. These differences in position, in all likelihood, affected the types of crisis management practiced by the two superpowers.

A fourth point of concern has to do with the style of crisis management practiced by the Soviet Union. Since World War II the Soviets have placed less emphasis on the development of crisis management-oriented projection forces, particularly naval forces, than has the United States. While the absence of these forces during the early postwar period could be attributed to the impact of the war, the persistence of these gaps in Soviet crisis management capabilities is the product of implicit and explicit resource allocation decisions by the Soviet leadership. A similar matter of leadership choice is reflected in the ways the Soviet armed forces have been employed in areas that do not border on the homeland. The Soviet Union has been much less prone than Western states such as the United States to employ its forces actively in political-military roles (military aid excepted) in the Third World, the locale for many postwar crises (Blechman and Kaplan, 1978). This policy style has even extended to relatively innocuous forms of activity such as naval port visits, which did not begin in the postwar era until 1953 and did not become relatively frequent until the mid-1960s, two decades after the war (MccGwire, 1975).

Whatever the reasons for this distinctively Soviet style (the factors proposed range from Soviet beliefs that the mix of policy instruments employed should have a higher proportion of nonmilitary factors to a concern for the potential consequences of escalation if Soviet forces are engaged in more active roles), its import for the analysis of the Soviet crisis management experience is clear.

When dealing with U.S. crisis behavior, overt military operations can be used to index American concerns. When analyzing the Soviet crisis management experience, on the other hand, this approach will not suffice, since out of choice or necessity the Soviets do not always make an overt military response to all crises of concern to them.

The final points of concern have to do with some important similarities between Soviet and Western approaches to the analysis of crises, as revealed in the Soviet crisis management literature, a relatively recent body of research. Soviet analyses in this literature contain some striking points in common with Western ones in their treatment of signaling and communication in crises and in their evaluation of attempts to formally model international conflicts.

One of the key concepts in the Western crisis literature has been the importance of signaling (particularly signaling involving the "language of deeds" or movements of armed forces) in crisis interactions (George and Smoke, 1974). This emphasis on intracrisis communication has direct counterparts in the Soviet literature (for example, Gantmann, 1972; Gromyko, 1972). This recognition of the importance of signaling is significant because it suggests (without necessarily proving) that the Soviets may also recognize broader forms of crisis signaling that are required to allow antagonists to make predictions about one another's behavior. It is possible that the Soviets use their open literature to index their principal concerns (that subset of crises of particular concern to them) to both foreign and domestic audiences. This would seem to be particularly likely where the Soviets have made the special effort of translating such writings into one or more common international languages.

A related development of interest, found in both the Soviet crisis management literature and, more generally, throughout Soviet social science, is a sympathetic attitude toward attempts to formally model political phenomena through techniques such as factor analysis and regression (for example, Melikhov, 1977; Fedorov, 1975; Osipov and Andreyenkov, 1974). The Western efforts reviewed by these authors are criticized for their "bourgeois" theoretical bases and their failures to consider the systemic aspects of behavior, particularly the complex interdependencies that exist among political, military, and sociological variables. Nevertheless, there is a genuine sympathy toward the use of such formal analytical procedures. The significance of this analytical trend for our work is direct. It suggests that the present attempt to develop a systematic account of Soviet crisis concerns is consistent with Soviet analytical emphases and hence that the style of our analysis does not do violence to Soviet analytical perceptions.

Methodology

The research strategy was developed with two ends in mind: capturing *Soviet* perceptions (and, to the extent feasible, incorporating Soviet analytical perspectives) while at the same time developing the data in a form compatible with Western crisis data bases to allow for later comparisons.[3] The research strategy developed is to use *Soviet sources* to identify *Western-style* crises. This strategy employs elements for both Soviet and Western approaches to crisis analysis and management. Major elements taken from Western approaches include:

(1) The treatment of crisis events as discrete episodes (in contrast to the Soviet tendency to focus on longer-run processes which, in some cases, span decades).
(2) A focus on negative events (viewing crises as turning points, Soviet authors would also cite some positive events, such as the accords which settled the status of Berlin; moreover, few (if any) things are completely negative or positive from a dialectical perspective).
(3) The definition of crises in terms of their actual or potential negative impact on political-military values or interests (one of the three defining elements of crisis specified by Hermann [1972]).
(4) The employment of an organizational process—citation of an incident in a Soviet source—to identify cases. Each of the three major recent U.S. crisis studies (Blechman and Kaplan, 1978; Mahoney, 1977a; CACI, 1976) used organizational processes to identify

cases. Since Soviet sources are both approved and published by party and government bodies, publication constitutes a form of organizational process in a way that is not true for the Western open source literature.

Major elements taken from the Soviet perspective include:

(1) A focus on political-military rather than simply military events.
(2) The use of a case identification criterion (appearance in a Soviet source) that takes into account differences between Soviet and U.S. crisis management styles and positions by not focusing exclusively on the overt operations of military forces.
(3) The recognition accorded in Soviet literature to the need for crisis communications by examining explicit open source Soviet communications regarding crises.

Like all compromises, this research strategy is by no means perfect. While structured in Western-style crisis events, the Soviet data base deals with Soviet crisis concerns rather than with crisis operations. However, given the character of the problem, it appears to be the best technical solution available.

Based on the preceding analysis, crises of concern to the Soviet Union are defined as:

(1) events involving foreign nations (domestic and international),
(2) involving conflict (violent or nonviolent), significant trends, and "structural" changes which might negatively affect Soviet political-military interests,
(3) which are cited in certain classes of Soviet sources (described below).

Like many operational definitions, this one serves to bracket, rather than to precisely delimit, the objects of concern. It needs to be read in the context of the preceding discussion of Soviet-Western differences and in terms of the sources employed (described below). The first term in the definition fixes the geographic scope of the concerns; crises internal to the USSR are excluded due to the lack of reliable, systematic data sources. The second term lists three generic types of events of concern. The first are conflict events, where concern is with the character of the events themselves rather than Soviet conflict, per se. The second set consists of trends and turning points to which the Soviets call attention in their writings (for example, West German rearmament). The third category encompasses what the Soviets see as significant "structural" threats, for example, the formation of NATO and other "anti-Soviet" alliances.

The final term in the definition pertains to the sources used to identify Soviet crisis concerns. Six sets of materials were employed: Soviet statements in the United Nations, the Soviet crisis management literature,

Soviet "State of the World" messages, Soviet texts dealing with international events, Krushchev's memoirs, and Soviet chronologies.

Soviet statements in the United Nations (a forum to which it attaches great importance [Zhurkin and Primakov, 1972]) were identified by a detailed analysis of all *UN Yearbooks* published since 1946. The Soviet crisis management literature was examined by reviewing the three major works published by the Soviets: Zhurkin and Primakov, 1972; Zhurkin, 1975; and Kulish, 1972. Soviet "State of the World" assessments are published at the apex of the formal Soviet policy process: the Congresses of the Communist Party of the Soviet Union. Each postwar Congress has included an assessment of the Soviet Union's international position; all such assessments were incorporated into the data base.

The Soviet Union publishes a large number of books, many dealing with international affairs. In some, but by no means all cases, the Soviets translate these works into English and arrange for their distribution in the West. Using the catalogs of the two major outlets for Soviet books in the United States and ordering all titles that appeared to deal with international events resulted in forty-five volumes being included in the data base.

Khrushchev's memoirs (1970, 1974) are another form of Soviet communication to the West. While clearly not official publications and not translated by the Soviets for foreign distribution, the sheer volume of material provided by Western publishers, the prominence of the author, and some of the "editorial" changes in the transcripts prior to their arrival in the West suggests that there may have been informal acquiesence in their publication on the part of at least a portion of the Soviet leadership. As a result, they were included in the survey.

Finally, the survey of sources included chronologies published in English by the Soviets (in addition to chronologies found in the works cited previously): *Milestones of Soviet Foreign Policy, 1917-1967* and the "Chronicle of Soviet Major Foreign Policy Acts" series in the journal *International Affairs* (Moscow) for the period 1946-1975.

Using these sources, 386 crises of concern to the Soviet Union over the period 1946-1975 were identified. Using both Soviet and Western sources, we also coded the characteristics of these events, ranging from initiation and termination dates for the incidents through their strategic implications.[4]

THE PATTERN OF SOVIET CRISIS CONCERNS

The Character of the Events

While considerations of space preclude the presentation of all 386 crises of concern to the Soviets during the postwar period, some insights into their character can be obtained by examining the incidents which occured in one recent year: 1973 (Table 2.1). The six incidents presented in the table aptly characterize the wide range of events included on the total list. The final phase of U.S. involvement in the Indochina War (the first incident) was a case in which the Soviets were involved in the conflict, but only in an indirect way (provision of military and economic aid and advisory assistance to the Democratic Republic of Vietnam, and so forth).

The second entry, dealing with events in Uruguay, illustrates a quite different type of concern which runs through Soviet commentaries on international affairs. While the Soviets did not engage in gunboat diplomacy in response to the incident (nor for that matter to the Chilean and Argentine incidents also listed in the table), it is clear from Soviet writings that incidents such as this in which parties or movements favored by the Soviets are repressed are of considerable concern to them. One indication of this concern is the special section in the Documents and Resolutions of the twenty-fifth Congress of the CPSU (1975), which has a special section devoted to the fate of such movements in Latin America.

The 1973 coup d'état in Afghanistan was of concern to the Soviets for a number of reasons, for example, its proximity to the Soviet homeland. The final entry in the table presents a major crisis in which the Soviet Union was a major participant, the 1973 October War.

As can be seen even from this review of only six cases, the 386 crises of concern to the Soviet Union differ from one another in many ways. Each, however, shares one critical factor in common with the others: of all the

TABLE 2.1 Example of Crises of Concern to the Soviet Union, 1973

Date	Events
730127–750430	U.S. involvement in the Indochina war comes to an end. New phase in struggle of Vietnam, Cambodia, and Laos initiated as United States continues to provide aid to nonprogressive forces.
730627–731201	Uruguay: President Bordaberry dismisses congress, ending constitutional government; initiates period of intense repression against progressive forces within Uruguay; all Marxist parties banned on December 1.
730707	Afghanistan: Military coup overthrows monarchy.
730911	Military coup overthrows Allende in Chile.
730925–	President Peron begins campaign of repression against progressive forces in Argentina.
731003–731114	October Middle East war.

myriad postwar events that might have been singled out by the Soviets in their commentaries, these are the incidents cited in Soviet sources.

Crisis Trends

The relative frequency of incidents is only one limited aspect of Soviet crisis concerns. As shown, the events have varied along many dimensions. Nevertheless, an examination of the frequency of these events can present some insights into the amount of threat perceived by the Soviets (Figure 2.1).

There was a moderately high number of events of concern in the immediate postwar period (1946-1948), followed by a drop in the relative frequency of crisis events during the remainder of the Stalin era (1949-1953). The next significant modalities in the chart are the relatively high number of events in the periods following the twenty-second (1962-1964) and the twenty-third (1966-1970) Congresses of the Communist Party of the Soviet Union, including the peak year of the entire thirty-year span (1967). Interestingly, 1967 is also the year in which the political-military activism of the Soviet Navy began to increase, as demonstrated by its activities during the June Middle East War.

The final point of interest is the drop in the frequency of incidents in the period between the twenty-fourth and twenty-fifth Party Congresses

FIGURE 2.1 Yearly Frequency of Crises of Concern to the Soviet Union

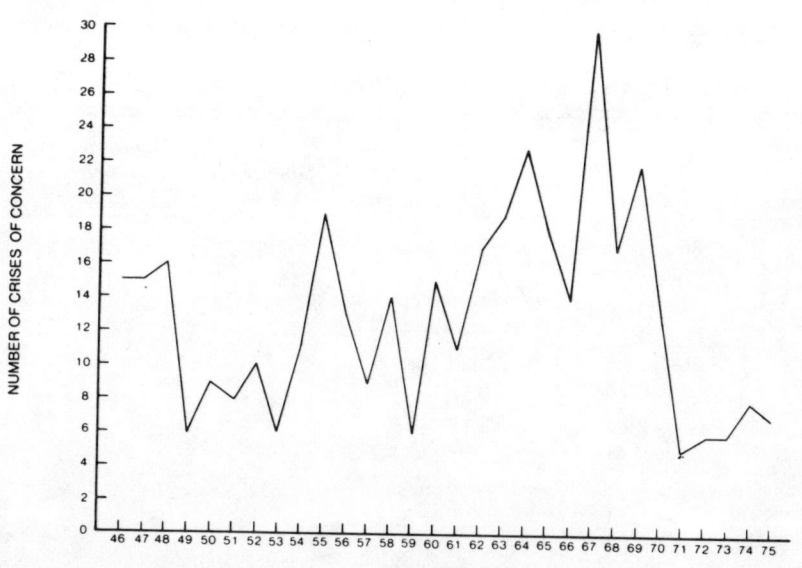

(1971-1975). This sharp decline appears to be more than simply an artifact of the source materials. The materials reviewed give good coverage at least through 1973-1974 (the October War and Cyprus crises). In 1971 there is a concomitant qualitative shift in the Soviet *International Affairs* chronology that covers the entire thirty-year span, with a marked decrease after 1970 in the number of events reported that might negatively affect Soviet political-military interests. Moreover, in 1971-1972 there was a leveling off, followed by a downturn, in world wide Soviet naval operations (Westwood, 1978).

It is also conceivable that the post-1971 shift might reflect greater confidence on the part of the Soviet leadership. Many of the types of events that caused concern in earlier years are no longer common problems, for example, colonialism issues and the status of Berlin. Perhaps more significantly, in the 1970s the United States began to accord greater recognition (through the SALT negotiations and other means) to the superpower status of the Soviet Union (for a Soviet perspective, see Zhurkin, 1975). This might have led to lessened relative concern on the part of Soviet leaders.

Trends in Crisis Characteristics

On the basis of the time series patterns presented in Figure 2.1, the 386 crises can be divided into four phases, using Party Congresses as the division points (Table 2.2). During the first phase, the average number of crises of concern was close to the thirty-year average of 12.8 events/year. The second and third phases reflect the higher average annual levels

TABLE 2.2 Phases in Soviet Crisis Concerns

Phase	Dates	Party Congress Period	Number of Crises	Average Number of Crises/Year
1	January 1964–October 1961	From the end of World War II to the 21st Congress[a]	180	11.1
2	October 1961–March 1966	22nd Congress	81	18.4
3	March 1966–March 1971	23rd Congress	95	22.1
4	March 1971–December 1975	24th Congress	30	6.3

a. This set includes one case that began in 1945 and continued into 1946.

following the twenty-second and twenty-third Congresses. The final phase depicts the lower levels of concerned evidenced since the twenty-fourth Congress.

Using the phases presented in Table 2.2, Table 2.3 presents the geographic distribution of the events of concern to the Soviet Union. Two notable points are the breadth of crisis concerns, even in the earliest period, and the decline during the last period (1971-1975) in the relative frequency of events involving the Soviet homeland and Eastern Europe, probably due in large part to the settlement of the Berlin question.

Some of the general characteristics of the 386 events are presented in Table 2.4. Notable patterns and trends include:

(1) a higher percentage of interstate incidents over time;
(2) a consistently low level of strategic confrontation over all periods, with a marked variation on potential confrontations over the spans;
(3) a steady overall level of threat to Communist Parties (CP's), movements, and regimes, accompanied by a decline in perceived threats to their survival;
(4) some increase in the relative frequency of violent events since the pre-1962 period; and
(5) a not unexpected increase in Soviet in-theater military crisis management capabilities during the incidents.

SOVIET CRISIS CONCERNS IN CONTEXT

Introduction

Most analyses of crises focus on single incidents or involve a comparison of a handful of major cases. While such studies can be extremely useful, this type of analytical emphasis automatically excludes some major aspects of crisis behavior, such as emerging patterns and trends and the interconnections that crisis operations and concerns have with other facets of East-West competition. These can only be analyzed by reviewing a large number of cases in conjunction with these other factors. Analyses of U.S. crisis behavior have shown that these operations exhibit clear patterns in the period since World War II and have varied in accordance with changes in other central aspects of interbloc relations such as Soviet-U.S. strategic parity (Mahoney, 1977b).

This section deals with the context within which Soviet crisis concerns have occurred since 1946. The first portion reviews previous research dealing with the context in which U.S. crisis operations have occurred since World War II. It then uses these findings to suggest factors (for example, superpower strategic parity) that might have influenced and/or been influenced by Soviet crisis concerns and sets the stage for comparisons of the Soviet and U.S. crisis management experiences. The second

TABLE 2.3 Geographic Focus of Soviet Crisis Concerns by Period[a] (percentages)

	1(1945–1961)	2(1961–1966)	3(1966–1971)	4(1971–1975)	5(1946–1975)
Region					
North America	1.7	0.0	1.1	3.3	1.3
Central, South America	17.8	17.3	13.7	13.3	16.3
Western Europe, Mediterranean, Atlantic	12.8	8.6	14.7	13.3	12.5
Eastern Europe, Soviet Union	12.8	11.1	10.5	6.7	11.4
Middle East, Northern Africa	24.4	14.8	21.1	20.0	21.3
Southern Asia, Indian Ocean, Sub-Saharan Africa	8.3	23.5	11.6	16.7	13.1
Pacific, Eastern Asia	21.1	24.7	26.3	26.7	23.6
Other, Multiple Regions	1.1	0.0	1.1	0.0	0.8
Geopolitical Area					
Soviet homeland	2.8	13.6	7.4	3.3	6.2
Germany/Berlin (East or West)	7.8	2.5	6.3	0.0	5.7
Primary buffer zone (Warsaw Pact states)	6.7	0.0	1.1	3.3	3.6
People's Republic of China	7.2	12.3	15.8	10.0	10.6
Border states	2.2	0.0	4.2	13.3	3.1
Middle East	21.1	16.0	23.2	26.7	21.0
Other	52.2	55.6	42.1	43.3	48.4

a. Because of rounding, percentages do not total to exactly 100.

TABLE 2.4 Crisis Characteristics by Period (percentages)

	1(1945-1961)	2(1961-1966)	3(1966-1971)	4(1971-1975)	5(1946-1975)
Scope					
Domestic[a]	38.9	35.8	22.1	20.0	32.6
International	61.1	64.2	77.9	80.0	67.4
Strategic confrontation					
None	78.9	91.4	80.0	93.3	82.9
Potential	20.0	6.2	18.9	3.3	15.5
Actual	1.1	2.5	1.1	3.3	1.6
Threat to CP, CP/movement, or CP regime					
No threat	56.7	59.3	51.6	56.7	56.0
Well-being activities threatened	27.2	28.4	41.1	36.7	31.6
Survival threatened	16.1	12.3	7.4	6.7	12.4
Level of violence					
Nonviolent events	41.1	38.3	26.3	33.3	36.3
Violent events	58.9	61.7	73.7	66.7	63.7
Soviet in-theater, military crisis management capabilities					
Uncodable	1.1	0.0	0.0	3.3	0.8
Substantial	22.2	19.8	27.4	33.3	23.8
Moderate	0.6	1.2	24.2	30.0	8.8
Minor/negligible	76.1	79.0	48.4	33.3	66.6

a. Within a nation other than the Soviet Union.

portion uses these and other factors to analyze how Soviet crisis concerns have fit into larger frameworks or structures of relations during the postwar period (for example, the structures of East-West relations and Soviet-Chinese competition).

Review of Research on U.S. Crises in Context

Mahoney (1978) examined 215 separate U.S. political-military crisis operations conducted over the period 1946-1975. These data were taken from a major DARPA-sponsored study (Blechman and Kaplan, 1978) conducted at the Brookings Institution. The 215 operations were instances in which the U.S. Armed Forces:

(1) engaged in some physical action(s);
(2) At the direction of the U.S. National Command Authorities;
(3) in order to influence events abroad, either by taking direct action (short of war) or by establishing a presence targeted at specific nations and events.

The Korean and Vietnamese wars were excluded from the data base.

These 215 operations differ from one another along many dimensions. At the same time, however, each shares the common characteristic of being a case in which the U.S. Armed Forces were used for political-military ends. As a result, the relative frequency of crisis operations over time provided a *partial* perspective on the incidence of U.S. political-military operations and of the propensity of U.S. leaders to use the armed forces as policy instruments.

It is not a simple matter to relate these operations to the context of the postwar international environment. Not enough theoretical work has been carried out in the fields of defense analysis and international relations to allow for the development of strong model specifications of the type required for many types of formal causal inference. Instead of searching for the "causes" or causal consequences of U.S. crisis operations (which is beyond the state of the art), the most that can be done in this area is to identify significant common modalities—trends and patterns in crisis operations and other factors of significance (such as Soviet-U.S. strategic parity).

A literature review (Mahoney, 1977b) suggests that four factors are of particular relevance for an understanding of the context within which U.S. crisis operations have taken place:

(1) the state of the strategic balance between the superpowers;
(2) Soviet-U.S. interactions;
(3) the amount of conflict occurring throughout the world; and
(4) U.S. involvement in limited wars since 1946.

The frequency of U.S. crisis operations is taken from Blechman and Kaplan's (1978) study.

The Soviet-U.S. strategic balance is indexed by a four-value-ordinal variable based on an interpretation of Goldmann's (1974) analysis of the postwar strategic competition. In this scheme a low number indexes a low level of "objective" tension in the balance. In Goldmann's assessment the most balanced (and least tense) period has been the phase of mutual second strike capabilities (parity) since the mid-1960s. The next most stable/least tension phase was 1948-1956, when only the United States possessed the capacity to attack the other superpower's homeland with a major strategic strike. This is followed by the period in which neither superpower had significant nuclear forces. Finally, the period with the most "objective" tension was 1957-1965, when both superpowers had counterhomeland nuclear capabilities, but where the United States had a significant lead over the Soviet Union. Parity (achieved sometime during the mid-1960s) ended this imbalance.

The behavioral dimension of Soviet-U.S. relations can be indexed by an event data measure of Soviet conflict behaviors directed toward the United States over the period 1948-1973. This measure is taken from the Azar-Sloan (1975) event data file and deals primarily with verbal behaviors.

Most U.S. political-military operations involve actual (or perceived potential) conflict in the Third World. This facet of the international environment will be measured by a frequency index based on a data file developed by Edward E. Azar (1973). The file contains major domestic and international conflicts: coups and other irregular regime transfers, border incidents and wars, and major domestic disturbances.

U.S. involvement in limited wars will be reflected by a dichotomous variable. For the Korean War, this variable takes on positive values for the years 1950-1953. For the Vietnam/Indochina War, the positive values begin in 1965 with the introduction of large numbers of U.S. military personnel into Vietnam. The end of the limited war commitment in the Southeast Asia theater is set in 1970. While one can argue for other termination dates (for example, 1972 and 1975), a 1970 endpoint is consistent with the Blechman-Kaplan data base. From early 1965 through the end of 1970 there are no U.S. political-military operations in the file that involve the core states of Southeast Asia. In 1971 such operations begin to appear. While U.S. involvement in the theater certainly continued after 1970, it is consistent with the data base being employed to index a shift in the character of this involvement in 1970. The correlations between the frequency of U.S. crisis operations and the other four factors are given in Table 2.5.

TABLE 2.5 Correlation: Frequency
of U.S. Crisis Operations[a]

Variable	Correlation
Strategic balance	.74
Soviet conflict behaviors toward the United States	.38
Frequency of conflict throughout the world	.49
U.S. involvement in limited wars	−.34

a. All corrections are significant at the .05 level. These and subsequent statistics were computed using the pair-wise deletion option of the Statistical Package for the Social Sciences.

U.S. crisis operations fall into a pattern that is shared, to varying degrees, by the other elements. Moreover, these are reasonable relationships. The signs of the correlations in Table 2.5 are intuitively interpretable. U.S. crisis operations were more likely when:

(1) the strategic balance was in phases that were more conducive to tension;
(2) the level of conflict in Soviet behaviors increased;
(3) the amount of conflict throughout the world increased; and
(4) the United States was not involved in a limited war.

The final step in relating the operations to their structural context involves determining the fit between the operations and the other four factors, taken as a set, using ordinary least squares (OLS) regression. Because of the weak specifications involved in this analysis, attention will be confined to the R^2 value and the fit between actual and estimated values, as presented in Figure R.2 and below.

$R = .84$ $R^2 = .70$ $F = 12.6$

Standard deviation of residuals = 2.7

Durbin-Watson statistic = 1.94.

Two points stand out in this analysis. First, it is apparent that there is a good fit between the pattern taken by U.S. crisis operations since 1946 and the set of contextual factors. The operations share better than two-thirds of their variance in common with the other elements; the standard deviation of the residuals is not a bad estimate; and the estimated curve reproduces, in essence, the most prominent features of the crisis opera-

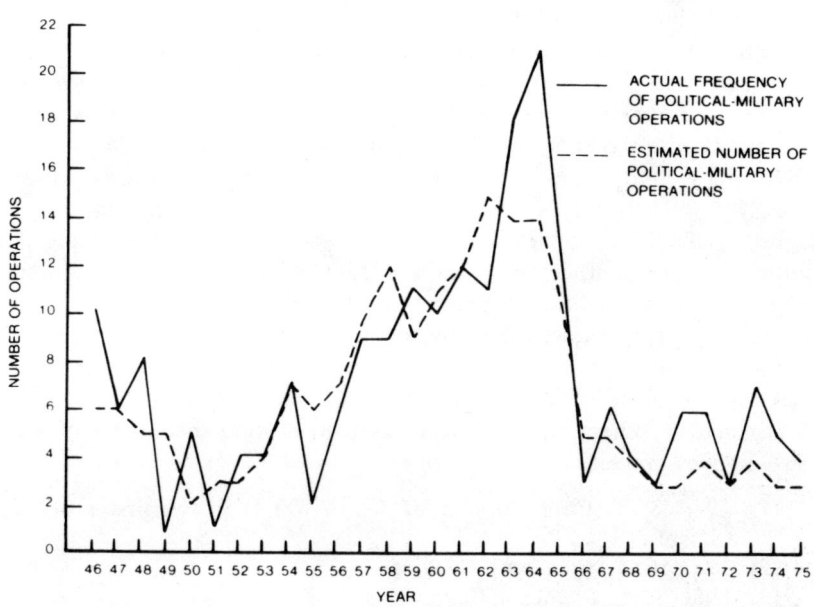

FIGURE 2.2   Actual and Estimated Number of Operations

tions frequency curve, notably the "peaking" in the late 1950s and early 1960s followed by a sharp decline in 1966. Postwar U.S. crisis operations take on patterns that are quite similar to those taken by other significant facets of East-West relations and international affairs.

Second, this analysis shows four classes of factors that might also be relevant for explaining Soviet crisis concerns:

(1) the state of the strategic balance,
(2) Soviet-U.S. interactions,
(3) the level of conflict throughout the world, and
(4) U.S. involvement in limited wars.

Factors Bearing on Soviet Crisis Concerns

The review of U.S. crisis analyses and the Soviet studies literature suggests a number of factors that might have influenced, and been influenced by, Soviet crisis concerns. As was true in the review of the U.S. crises in the previous section, any analysis of the similarities of patterns taken by these factors and the set of crises of concern to the Soviet Union is subject to two caveats. The first is that the relative frequency of these events over time is only one limited aspect of Soviet crisis concerns. The second is that because of the limited amount of research performed to date in this area no attempts to uncover "causal" patterns can be supported. The most that can be done is to search for similarities in patterns as indications of the broader contexts into which the events of concern to the Soviets might have fallen in the postwar period.[5]

The analyses in this section will follow the format used in the previous section: an initial presentation of potentially relevant factors, followed by a correlation analysis to observe bivariate pattern similarities, and a final multivariate comparison of patterns. Two general classes of factors will be related to the pattern of Soviet crisis concerns. The first set pertains to the Soviet Union itself and includes indicators of the formal Soviet policy process; Soviet conflict behaviors toward the United States, West Germany, and China; and Soviet perceptions of the strategic balance.

Earlier analysis showed that the frequency of crisis concerns varied in accordance with the cycles traced by the Congresses of the Communist Party of the Soviet Union. Dichotomous indicators indexing the periods demarcated by these Congresses are used to capture this aspect of the Soviet policy process:

(1) 1946-1952 (from the end of World War II to the first postwar Congress),
(2) 1953-1955, Nineteenth Congress,
(3) 1956-1958, Twentieth Congress,
(4) 1959-1961, Twenty-first Congress,
(5) 1962-1965, Twenty-second Congress,
(6) 1966-1970, Twenty-third Congress, and
(7) 1971-1975, Twenty-fourth Congress.

Three major Soviet crisis antagonists are the United States, the Federal Republic of Germany, and the People's Republic of China. Soviet conflict toward these nations (primarily verbal behavior) is indexed using the Azar-Sloan (1975) event data scale.

In an unpublished analysis, Kjell Goldmann of the University of Stockholm has analyzed major power relations from 1950 through 1975.[6] Using official government statements, Goldmann has computed mean tension levels for the major power dyads, for example, mean tension in U.S. statements regarding the Soviet Union. To index these perceptual/psychological dimensions of Soviet behavior, Goldmann's scores for Soviet tension perceptions regarding the United States will be employed.

The final Soviet factor to be considered will be changes in national leadership, with dichotomous indicators representing the Stalin, Khrushchev, and Brezhnev-Kosygin eras.

The second class of factors consists of items that are not Soviet actions, perceptions, or aspects of the Soviet policy process. Items to be considered are the frequency of conflict throughout the world; the frequency of U.S.

crisis management operations; conflict behavior directed by the United States, Federal Germany, and China toward the Soviet Union; articulated U.S. perceptions relating to U.S.-Soviet relations; Western perceptions of the strategic balance; and U.S. involvement in limited wars (Korea and Vietnam).

The frequency of domestic and interstate conflicts is indexed using measures developed by Azar (1973). The frequency of U.S. crisis operations is measured using two major projects conducted by the Brookings Institution (Blechman and Kaplan, 1978; CACI, 1976). The Azar-Sloan event data file is used to assess conflict behaviors directed toward the Soviet Union. The Goldmann perceptual data base discussed previously is used to measure U.S. perceptions of tension in relations with the Soviet Union. A dichotomous indicator is used to index U.S. involvement in limited wars. Western perceptions of the strategic balance are indexed by the four value ordinal variable based on an interpretation of Goldmann's (1974) analysis of the postwar strategic competition presented previously in the discussion of U.S. crises.

Analysis

Table 2.6 presents the correlations that the Soviet and non-Soviet factors have with the yearly frequency of crises of concern to the Soviet

TABLE 2.6 Correlation of Factors with Soviet Crisis Concerns

	Correlation With Frequency of Soviet Crisis Concerns, 1946–1975[a]
Soviet factors	
CPSU Congress Periods:	
Prior to 19th	−.22
19th	−.04
20th	−.04
21st	−.12
22nd	.39
23rd	.47
24th	−.48
Soviet conflict behavior toward:	
United States	.50
West Germany	.22
People's Republic of China	.37

TABLE 2.6 Correlation of Factors with Soviet Crisis Concerns (Cont)

	Correlation With Frequency of Soviet Crisis Concerns, 1946–1975[a]
Goldmann, Soviet expressions of tension toward the United States	−.42
Leaders:	
Stalin	−.22
Khrushchev	.18
Brezhnev-Kosygin	.02
Non-Soviet factors	
Frequency of conflicts throught the world	.54
U.S. crisis operations:	
CACI	.25
Brookings	.35
Conflict behaviors of major nations toward the Soviet Union:	
United States	−.38[b]
West Germany	.04
People's Republic of China	.41
Goldmann, U.S. expressions of tensions toward the Soviet Union	.13
Strategic balance (Western views)	.15
U.S. involvement in limited wars	.19

a. Underlined correlations are ⩾.30 and are statistically significant at the 0.05 level.
b. The sign of this correlation is anomalous, associating higher levels of U.S. conflict toward the Soviet Union with lower levels of crisis concern on the part of the Soviet Union. While this could be interpreted as a plausible relationship (with received hostility from the United States causing the Soviet Union to focus its concerns on a narrower range of topics), there is a strong possibility that the relationship is artifactual. A comparison of the time series for Soviet conflict toward the United States and U.S. conflict toward the Soviet Union suggests that the former presents a perspective that is more in harmony with traditional interpretations of postwar superpower relations. For example, the Soviet-to-U.S. series has a peak in conflict in 1962, the year of the Cuban missile crisis, which the U.S.-to-Soviet series lacks. Because of the anomalous sign, this variable will be excluded from subsequent analyses. Apart from this case, all signs of the significant correlations are intuitively interpretable, for example, those of the Goldmann tensions variable, which is scored with low values refelecting high levels of tension.

Union. It is evident that a large number of factors (predominantly Soviet) have appreciable correlations with the pattern taken by Soviet concerns over the thirty-year period. Rather than being idiosyncratic events, Soviet concerns varied in ways that were related to the patterns taken by other factors.

Using a .30 threshold, six of the nine correlates of the crisis concerns are Soviet factors. The first three pertain to the Soviet policy process and are indicators for the periods following the twenty-second, twenty-third, and twenty-fourth Congresses of the CPSU. The next two variables are Soviet conflict behaviors toward the United States and China (interestingly, neither Soviet conflict toward Federal Republic of Germany nor German conflict toward the USSR shows an association above the .30 threshold). The remaining factor deals with articulated Soviet perceptions of tension concerning Soviet-U.S. relations.

Of the non-Soviet factors, only three have substantively meaningful relationships above the .30 threshold: Azar's index of the frequency of domestic and interstate conflict throughout the world, the Brookings Institution index of the frequency of U.S. crisis operations, and Chinese conflict toward the Soviet Union.[7]

The results of regressing the frequency of Soviet crisis concerns against the nine factors with significant bivariate relationships are as shown:

$R = .85$ $R^2 = .73$ $F = 4.29$

Standard deviation of residuals = 4.2

Durbin-Watson statistic = 2.37.

The results show that there is a good fit between the aggregate pattern traced by these nine factors and the crises, with the incidents sharing almost three-quarters of their variance in common with the set of predictors. The Durbin-Watson statistic indicates a modest degree of negative autocorrelation.

The fit between the pattern of the crises and the set of predictors is confirmed in Figure 2.3. The estimated and actual frequencies are very close in the early Cold War years (1946-1954). The estimates then miss a peak in Soviet concerns in the mid-1950s and return on track in the late 1950s and early 1960s. The estimated curve catches the general rise in the frequency of events of concern to the Soviets during the periods following the twenty-second and twenty-third Congresses (1962-1970), but falls short of capturing the peaks, especially in 1967, the year with the highest number of events of concern. The fit between the actual and estimated curves then becomes quite close for the most recent years (1971-1975).

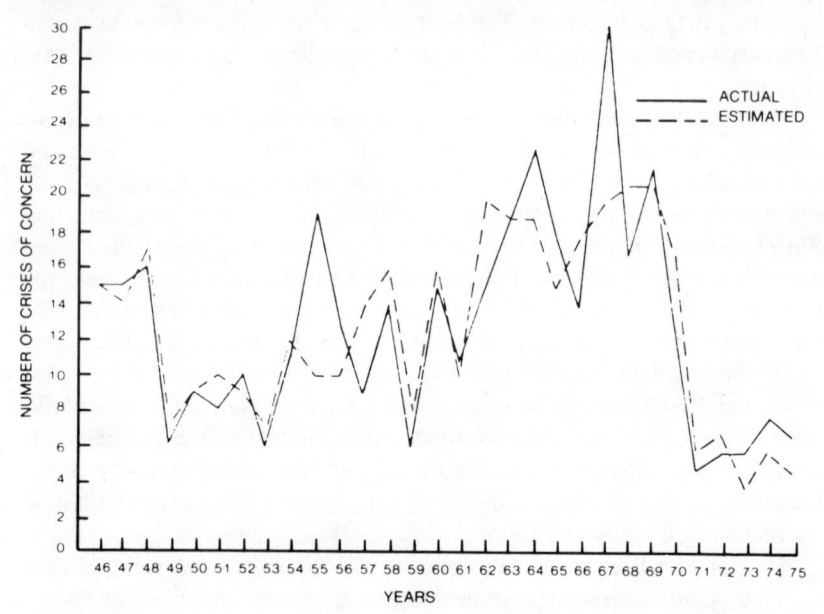

FIGURE 2.3   Actual and Estimated Crisis Frequencies

CONCLUSIONS

Listening to others and hearing what they have to say, rather than what we expect to hear, is never easy. It becomes even more difficult when the speaker and listener are separated by cultural and political differences. Soviet foreign policy concerns are part and parcel of a policy-process that often appears enigmatic to Western observers (and it may at times even be so to the Soviets themselves). We have attempted to learn from the Soviets by listening to what they are attempting to tell the West through the medium of open source publications.

Three points stand out in the analysis. The first is that the Soviets have gone to very considerable lengths to communicate their crisis concerns to the West by discussing just under 400 postwar incidents. Second, when arrayed over time, the pattern of these incidents matches portions of the patterns taken by a number of other factors of interest to students of comparative foreign policy, such as the rhythm of the formal Soviet policy process.[8] Finally, the results of the comparisons of patterns suggest a number of factors (for example, the frequency of U.S. crisis operations and Chinese actions) that may have played a major role in shaping the

Soviet perceptions and concerns. The patterns uncovered show that Soviet crisis concerns, in the aggregate, are far from being idiosyncratic phenomena; instead they appear to be part of a larger, interpretable context of postwar international relations.

These points have implications for both practitioners and analysts of comparative foreign policy. From the standpoint of policy, one of the most important findings is that Soviet perceptions (and, by implication, policy actions) "dance" to a somewhat different "beat" than is the case for Western nations. Some suprises are in store for planners who don't stop to listen to this music.

Of equal interest to policy-makers is the likelihood that Soviet concerns, as reported in open source Soviet media, may foreshadow future areas and focuses of activity. To a large extent early postwar Soviet policy was constrained by the devastating effects of World War II. Now that these constraints are gone, greater activism is a distinct possibility. This is *not* to say that the Soviets are likely to respond in every case with a Western-style crisis operation. It is to say that the Soviets are global actors, as defined by the scope of their own expressed interests, and that they are likely to seek their quite diverse ends with their own distinctive mixes of policy instruments.

Finally, the results of the aggregate analyses suggest a number of factors which are likely to be related to Soviet perceptions, ranging from the rhythm of the formal Soviet policy process through the level of U.S. crisis management activity and Chinese behaviors toward the Soviet Union. These aggregate relationships, while necessarily only suggestive at this point, serve as useful counterpoints to the common emphasis upon personalities and bureaucratic factors in the analysis of Soviet policy.[9]

For the student of comparative foreign policy there are two significant findings. Substantively, the analysis identifies some correlates of the events that were of concern to the Soviet leadership during the postwar period. Some of the dynamics of the process of superpower "crisis management" are thereby revealed.

On a more general, methodological level, the results indicate that a more "structural" approach to analysis provides a valid and useful vantage point for the comprehension of foreign policy.[10] When viewed over substantial periods of time, both U.S. crisis operations and Soviet crisis concerns take on patterns which have appreciable, coherent correlations with other aspects of the environments within which both superpowers have conducted their crisis policies since World War II. Much more analysis of this type is required to move beyond a focus on seemingly unique crises to obtain an understanding of the roles played by crises and superpower crisis management within the fabric of international relations.

NOTES

1. Obviously, all Western approaches to the analysis and practice of crisis management are not alike. Some Western Marxian analyses share many of the emphases found in Soviet approaches, for example, the stress on structural factors. The distinctions being made in this section are, however, valid for the "mainstream" body of Western approaches to crises being considered.

2. Reinforcing this point is the common criticism in the Soviet scholarly literature that Western analyses employing quantitative techniques tend to focus on too narrow a range of concerns and thereby miss the systemic context which influences behaviors; for example, Melikhov's recent (1977) review of U.S. quantitative international relations studies employing factor analysis.

3. Considerations of space severely constrain the amount of discussion that can be given to the methodology employed. For a much more complete presentation, see Mahoney and Clayberg (1979) or CACI (1978).

4. Publishing inevitably involves delays between the completion of a manuscript and the publication of a book or article. This created a problem for the project in the later years of the survey since some of the relevant Soviet sources had not yet been printed. In response to this problem, Western sources were also used, in an adjunct role, to identify crisis events for the years 1974 and 1975. Use of Western materials to code the attributes of the crisis events did not create major methodological difficulties, since the important point was to use Soviet sources to identify the events themselves.

5. This lack of strong theoretical priors is taken into account in the regression analyses performed in this section. The relationships between the factors and Soviet crisis concerns are likely, in many cases, to be ones in which influence moves in both directions. However, in the absence of strong a priori specifications of such equations, the use of more powerful forms of regression that can capture such interactive effects is impractical because the coefficients of such equations cannot be interpreted with reference to priors. Similarly, there is no good solution to the problem of multicollinearity except the use of priors, which are not available. As a consequence, the regression analysis will focus on the pattern-matching components of ordinary least square regression (the simplest, most robust, and best understood model of regression)—R^2 and residuals. This methodological response to the problem of incomplete specifications is detailed at greater length in Mahoney (1977b).

6. These data, provided by Professor Goldmann in a seminar presentation conducted at CACI on April 5, 1978, deal with the entire range of Soviet-U.S. relations. A similar data set dealing only with European affairs is presented in detail in Goldmann (1974).

7. The difference in correlation between the Brookings and CACI crisis lists is apparently due to different patterns of coverage in the first postwar decade. The correlation between the two is .56 for 1955-1975 but only .32 for the entire thirty-year span. Appendix B in CACI (1978) compares these data bases in greater detail.

8. The comparison of patterns can be viewed as falling half-way between hypothesis testing and a weak form of construct validation. We would be unlikely to place much import on the frequency of the concerns if they had no appreciable correlations with other factors of interest. At the same time, however, the specific correlations were far from predetermined.

9. To a large extent the salience of explanations based on the characteristics and preferences of individual leaders, bureaucratic politics, and organizational processes

appears to depend on the level of aggregation at which an analysis is pitched. On an hourly or day to day basis, individual, small group, and bureaucratic processes have their greatest salience as explanatory factors. As the temporal scope of the analysis increases, interaction processes achieve more analytical prominence. Over more substantial intervals of time (decades or longer), structural explanations achieve more analytical salience. The salience of individual- and bureaucracy-level explanations within the policy community is in large part due to the pressures of the in-box, which gives policy (and analysis) a very short-term focus. One of the reasons why practitioners sometimes have difficulties coming to terms with the work of comparative foreign policy researchers is that the latter often pitch their theoretical efforts at higher levels of aggregation, e.g., Rosenau's (1966) pretheory, two of whose key elements are the structure-defining attributes of size and development. Braudel's analysis of Mediterranean politics in the age of Philip II (1973) presents an excellent illustration of ways in which individual and bureaucratic factors can be integrated within a broader structural context.

10. An important assumption in this argument is that the larger trans- and inter-national systems within which superpower crisis management operations were conducted consist of two types of structural elements. Following Braudel (1972), we can distinguish between "structures" and "conjunctures," with the former denoting long-term, and the latter, short-term, realities. A key implicit assumption in the argument is that certain types of conjunctures, such as daily event interactions between the United States and Soviet Union, can, when viewed in the aggregate over a substantial period of time, be viewed as a form of "emergent" structural element within, for example, a system of East-West competition and collaboration. While there is much variance from event to event, the general tone of relations changes more slowly, and thereby shades into the structural category. Lazarsfeld and Menzel (1961) make a related distinction between the "global" and "analytical" attributes of organizational systems, with the former being characteristics which inhere in the system itself while the latter are aggregates of lower-level elements' attributes.

REFERENCES

AZAR, E. E. and T. SLOAN (1975) Dimensions of Interaction: A Source Book for the Study of the Behaviors of 31 Nations From 1948 Through 1973. Pittsburgh: International Studies Association.

––– (1973) Probe for Peace. Minneapolis: Burgess.

BLECHMAN, B. M. and S. S. KAPLAN (1978) Force Without War. Washington, DC: Brookings Institution.

BOBROW, D. B., S. CHAN, and J. KRINGEN (1979) Understanding Foreign Policy Decisions: The Chinese Case. New York: Free Press.

BRAUDEL, F. (1973) The Mediterranean and the Mediterranean World in the Age of Philip II, Volume II. New York: Harper & Row.

––– (1972) The Mediterranean and the Mediterranean World in the Age of Philip II, Volume I. New York: Harper & Row.

CACI (1978) Analysis of the Soviet Crisis Management Experience: Technical Report. Arlington, VA: CACI, Inc.-Federal.

––– (1976) Planning for Problems in Crisis Management. Arlington, VA: CACI, Inc.-Federal.

"Chronicle of Soviet major foreign policy acts," International Affairs Moscow (title varies; covers period 1946-1975).

Documents and Resolutions, Congresses of the Communist Party of the Soviet Union (various dates, nineteenth through twenty-fifth Congresses, 1952-1976). Moscow.

FEDOROV, Y. (1975) "Methods and deadlocks in U.S. simulation modeling." Mirovaya Ekomika I Mezhdunarodnyye Otnesheniya (June). (JPRS Translations on USSR Political and Sociological Affairs, 12 August, No. 663.)

GANTMANN, V. I., (1972) "The Types, content, structure, and phases of development of international conflicts," in V. V. Zhurkin and YE. M. Primakov, International Conflicts. Moscow: Izdatel'stvo Nauka.

GEORGE, A. L. and R. SMOKE (1974) Deterrence in American Foreign Policy: Theory and Practice. New York: Columbia Univ. Press.

GOLDMANN, K. (1974) Tension and Detente in Bipolar Europe. Stockholm: Scandinavian University Books.

GROMYKO, A. A. (1972) "The Caribbean Crisis," in V. V. Zhurkin and YE. M. Primakov, International Conflicts. Moscow: Izdatel'stvo Nauka.

HERMANN, C. F. (1972) "Some issues in the study of international crisis," in C. F. Hermann (ed.) International Crises. New York: Free Press.

KHRUSHCHEV, N. S. (1974) Khrushchev Remembers: The Last Testament, trans. and ed. Strobe Talbot. Boston: Little, Brown.

----- (1970) Khrushchev Remembers, trans. and ed. Strobe Talbot. Boston: Little, Brown.

KULISH, V. M. (1972) Military Force and International Relations. Moscow: International Relations Publishing House (JPRS, 58947, 8 May 1973).

LAZARSFELD, P. F. and H. MENZEL (1961) "On the relation between individual and collective properties," in Amitai Etzioni (ed.) Complex Organizations. New York: Holt, Rinehart & Winston.

MAHONEY, R. B., Jr. (1978) "The employment of U.S. naval forces in crisis management, 1966-1975." Presented at the Annual Meeting of the International Studies Association, Washington, D.C.

----- (1977a) U.S. Navy Responses to International Incidents and Crises, 1955-1975, Survey of Navy Crisis Operations. Arlington, VA: Center for Naval Analyses.

----- (1977b) "American political-military operations and the structure of the international system, 1946-1976." Revised version of a paper presented at the meeting of the Section on Military Studies of the International Studies Association, Ohio State University, October 1976.

----- and R. CLAYBERG (1979) "The Soviet Union and international crises: 1946-1975." Presented at the Annual Meeting of the International Studies Association, Toronto.

MccGWIRE, M. (1975) "Foreign-port visits by Soviet naval units," pp. 387-418 in M. MccGwire et al., Soviet Naval Policy. New York: Praeger.

MELIKHOV, S. V. (1977) "Factor analysis in study of world affairs." U.S.A.: Economics, Politics, Ideology (April). (JPRS Translation, 6 May.)

Milestones of Soviet Foreign Policy, 1917-1967 (1967) Moscow: Progress Publishers.

OSIPOV, G. V. and V. G. ANDREYENKOV (1974) "Empirical substantiation of hypotheses in sociological research." Sociological Studies. (JPRS Translations on USSR Political and Sociological Affairs, September 9, No. 674.)

ROSENAU, J. N. (1966) "Pre-theories and theories of foreign policy," in R. B. Farrell (ed.) Approaches to Comparative and International Politics. Evanston, IL: Northwestern Univ. Press.

TOMASHEVSKY, D. (1974) Lenin's Ideas and Modern International Relations. Moscow: Progress Publishers.

WESTWOOD, J. T. (1978) "Soviet naval strategy, 1968-1978: a reexamination." U.S. Naval Institute Proceedings (May).
YUKHANANOV, YU. A. (1972) "The United States aggression in Indochina," in V. V. Zhurkin and YE. M. Primakov, International Conflicts. Moscow: Izdatel'stvo Nauka.
ZHURKIN, V. V. (1975) The USA and International Political Crises. Moscow: Izdatel'stvo Nauka. (JPRS Translations on USSR Political and Sociological Affairs, No. 658, July 29.)
––– and YE. M. PRIMAKOV (1972) International Conflicts. Moscow: Izdatel'stvo Nauka. (JPRS Translation 58443, March 12, 1973.)

Chapter 3

THREAT, PUBLIC OPINION, AND MILITARY SPENDING IN THE UNITED STATES, 1930-1990

FARID ABOLFATHI
CACI, Inc.-Federal

Defense spending represents consumption of real goods and services in return for provision of a public good—national security from external threats. Since neither national security nor external threats can be defined clearly, it is hardly surprising that the size of resource allocations for defense are often a subject of public controversy (Kanter, 1979; Aspin, 1979).

Since defense is among the "purest" public goods provided by the federal government, it would be natural to expect a large volume of literature in economics and political science on the impact of public opinion on allocation of defense spending. Unfortunately, however, there are only a few such studies. Economists generally exclude defense spending from their studies of public goods (Kennedy, 1975: 17) and political scientists have generally ignored the role of public opinion in their studies of defense spending.[1]

The voluminous literature on military spending includes both some of the most elegant formal theoretical works (e.g., Richardson, 1960) and huge amounts of informal anecdotal analyses (e.g., Kistiakowsky, 1979). Cross-sectional analyses of military spending identify three types of independent explanatory variables for military spending:

EDITORS' NOTE: This chapter was first submitted for review June 6, 1979. The version published here was received August 12, 1979. The author reports that the data analyzed here are available from him at CACI-Inc.-Federal, 1815 N. Fort Myer Drive, Arlington, VA 22209

(1) economic wealth,
(2) interstate conflict or threat, and
(3) domestic conflict or threat (Abolfathi, 1977).

Time series analyses generally support economic wealth as a major long-term constraining factor for defense spending of most countries (Coward, 1964), but fail to support consistently the other independent variables. Most time series studies focus on two types of processes that determine armament spending:

(1) action-reaction or arms race processes typified by Richardson equations (Richardson, 1960; Hollist, 1977), and
(2) bureaucratic processes of budgetary spending such as the incremental demand model (Ostrom, 1977; Rattinger, 1975).

These studies generally exclude public opinion from the determinants of arms spending or deal with it implicitly.

The only significant work on the relationship between public opinion and defense spending is Russett's (1972a, 1974, 1975). However, his work mainly focuses on public opinion with respect to defense spending without any systematic assessments of its multivariate relationships. Moreover, by focusing his analyses only on major *shifts* in public opinion data, he failed to adequately analyze the long-term relationship between public opinion and defense spending. His major conclusions in this regard, based on cursory data analyses, were that there are "no simple explanations of public attitudes toward defense spending," and, more specifically, there is "no relationship" between changes in defense spending and public opinion (Russett, 1972a: 312-313).[2]

The role of public opinion, at least in democratic countries, deserves far more attention than students of defense spending have devoted to it. A fresh look at the impact of public opinion on U.S. defense spending is particularly relevant to U.S. military policy for the 1980s, when the defense budget is expected to face severe competition from nondefense budgetary demands (Kanter, 1979). Already some special interest groups have discovered the importance of public opinion in an era of economic scarcity (Committee on the Present Danger, 1979).

This chapter analyzes the impact of public opinion on defense spending since the 1930s. The objectives of the study are:

(1) to identify the major trends in external threat, public perceptions of threat, public support for defense spending, and aggregate defense expenditures in the United States since the 1930s;
(2) to specify a model of linkages among threat, public opinion, and defense spending and estimate the model parameters; and

(3) to utilize the model to forecast future trends in defense spending under various external threat scenarios.

Among the relationships analyzed in this study, three linkages are germane. At the simplest level, these relationships can be viewed as:

External Threats ➤ Public Perception of Threats ➤ Public Support for Defense ➤ Changes in Defense Spending

Or more formally stated:

(1) Changes in U.S. defense spending are a function of public support for defense spending;
(2) public support for defense spending is a function of public perception of external threats to U.S. interests; and
(3) public perception of external threat is a function of actual levels of external threats.

By focusing on explanatory variables such as public opinion and external threats to national security, these relationships form the basic structure for a model of U.S. defense spending that is intuitively reasonable. Yet, as far as could be determined, except for Russett's limited analyses (see note 2), no previous study has systematically analyzed these linkages and no model incorporating them has been estimated by either political scientists or economists. However, it could be argued that these basic relationships are implicit in the analytical frameworks of many students of defense spending. For instance, Richardson (1960: 16) had a term in his famous arms race equations that represented "grievances" and can be interpreted as the national "mood" or public opinion of a country. Unfortunately, Richardson's followers generally have ignored this parameter because of lack of data or conveniently assumed it to be constant (Hollist, 1977; Rattinger, 1975).

Since no previous study has collected and validated the data required for this study, the bulk of the chapter is devoted to the development of appropriate indicators and descriptions of the trends and major discontinuities, if any, in the data. For each of the four major concepts—actual external threat, perception of threat, support for defense, and increase in defense—the historical developments in relevant variables and their trends and major discontinuities are described. Because of the centrality of the defense-related variables, such as real defense spending and defense share in the federal budget, they constitute the bulk of the descriptive sections of this chapter.

In addition to analyzing trends in single variables, the study demonstrates that it is feasible to specify and estimate a relatively simple model of the relationship between public opinion and defense spending in the United States and utilize it to produce reasonable forecasts. The most likely model-generated forecast for increases in U.S. defense spending during the 1980s appears to be an annual real growth rate of 3.2%. This would imply an increase in the Department of Defense (DoD) budget from 129 billion dollars in 1980 to 177 billion in 1990 (at 1980 prices).[3]

Excluding the introduction and conclusions, the chapter is organized into five sections. The first three sections describe the development of actual external threats to the United States, public opinion, and defense spending since the 1930s. The data used throughout the study are presented in these sections. The fourth section analyzes the data and presents the variable structure and an estimated three-equation model of external threat, public opinion, and defense spending. Finally, the fifth section applies the model to forecasting diverse scenarios for U.S. defense spending, focusing on what would appear to be the most likely scenario for the 1980s.

EXTERNAL THREATS TO THE UNITED STATES

Every year the U.S. Congress reviews in detail the annual appropriation requests of the Department of Defense for the next fiscal year and demands justifications for both the overall size and, sometimes, each item within the budget. The major public justifications for U.S. defense spending are based on the threat analyses contained in the annual posture statements of the Secretary of Defense and his Chiefs of armed forces.[4] These analyses generally concern two major types of threats:

(1) Strategic threats to the continental United States from the Soviet Union and its allies; and
(2) Nonstrategic military threats to U.S. overseas interests, such as U.S.-flag shipping, U.S. nationals abroad, U.S. foreign investments, and trade with other countries.[5]

The term "strategic threats," when narrowly defined, is often used to describe the potential threats of Soviet intercontinental nuclear weapons that are capable of reaching the United States. In this study the term strategic threat is used to indicate situations in which the U.S. mainland is in imminent danger of conquest or widespread destruction by either nuclear or conventional forces. This definition is still considerably narrower than when the terms "strategy" is used to refer to "the art of distributing and applying military means to fulfil the end of policy" (Liddel Hart, 1968: 334).

Strategic Threats to the United States

During the one hundred years that followed the Civil War no foreign power ever seriously challenged the security of the U.S. mainland. During the zenith of Axis power in World War II not a single German or Japanese bomber attacked the continental United States. Hitler's dream of building a huge bomber for the sole purpose of taking the European airwar across the Atlantic went up in smoke with the German setback in the Battle of Britain and the more serious failure of the Luftwaffe against Soviet air power.

America's military security was greatly enhanced during the early postwar period by the nation's possession of nuclear weapons and its overwhelmingly powerful naval and air forces. The Communist threat as envisaged by alarmists in the 1940s ignored the fact that the U.S. military could potentially take a war to the Soviet heartland while the Soviet Union had no such capability against the United States.[6] Although the Soviet Union had developed a strategic air capability by the late 1950s, that force would have had great difficulty penetrating the North American air defenses in large numbers (Menaul and Gunston, 1977; Donnelly and Guston, 1978). Indeed, for all practical purposes, the actual military balance greatly favored the United States until the mid-1960s.[7]

The first time since the Civil War that the U.S. mainland became vulnerable to the threat of large scale destruction from a potential adversary was probably between the 1962 Cuban missile crisis and the 1967 Arab-Israeli war (Kegley and Wittkopf, 1979: 59). During this period the U.S.-Soviet military strategic balance went through a transition from a state of approximate U.S. first strike capability (with no major Soviet second strike response capability) to one of Soviet second strike capability. Many analysts believe this transition occurred between 1962 and 1963, but given the poor quality of Soviet strategic weapons during the first half of the 1960s, it probably happened a few years later. Since then, both sides have had enough nuclear forces to survive a first strike from the other and launch a retaliatory strike hopefully with enough destructive power to make the other side perceive nuclear war as unacceptable. Since the stability of such "mutually assured destruction" (MAD) requires only the survival of a relatively small number of missles out of the total missle forces of each side, theoretically the strategic security of the United States should remain unthreatened for many years to come.[8]

In summary, two points related to strategic threats to the United States need to be emphasized:

(1) The continental United States has not faced a serious threat of invasion or widespread destruction by means of external conventional military forces since at least the Civil War.

(2) The Soviet nuclear threat to the United States was matched by a far greater U.S. nuclear deterrent until the late 1960s. Since then, there has been rough equivalence with neither side capable of a surprise attack that could destroy the other side's nuclear deterrent capability (Brown, 1979).

Thus, since there has been little variation over time in the *strategic* security of the U.S. mainland, it does not merit inclusion in the study as a major determining factor in U.S. defense spending. That is not to say that strategic forces are not an important element of U.S. defense spending. On the contrary, U.S. strategic forces have been a significant component of U.S. defense spending since World War II (e.g., 8% in the 1980 budget). The argument simply is that the continental United States has generally faced little *imminent* (versus *potential*) strategic threat during the past several decades. Hence, because of insufficient variance, it is not possible to analyze the role of this variable as an element of the external threat that may have determed past military spending. Since the Soviet nuclear forces could pose an imminent strategic threat were not for the U.S. nuclear deterrent, there is an obvious linkage between Soviet *potential* nuclear threat and U.S. strategic defense spending. However, to study this linkage would greatly increase the complexity of the basic structure of the model of defense spending presented above. In particular, because of the high capital intensity of strategic forces and their relatively low operating costs, modeling their linkage to potential Soviet strategic threat would require incorporating into the model such complex concepts as the utility of military capital stocks and separating both investment and operating costs of strategic forces from the total defense budget. Such a modeling effort would be beyond the scope of the present study. Therefore, for the present strategic threats to the United States are excluded from consideration.

Nonstrategic Threats

Although the U.S. mainland is likely to remain safe from destruction and conquest, its worldwide interests enjoy no such security. The overseas economic, diplomatic, and military interests of the United States, which had grown considerably during prewar years, proliferated at an extremely rapid rate during and after World War II. These interests have been a major cause of U.S. involvement in wars and other overseas military conflicts.

For instance, overseas spheres of influence were a major reason for Japan's 1941 Pearl Harbor attack[9] and similar disputes contributed greatly to the U.S.-Soviet disagreements at the Yalta and Potsdam conferences that initiated the Cold War (Mee, 1975; Clemens, 1970). U.S. worldwide interests at times created conflicts even with its Western allies. For instance, U.S. demands for decolonization of Asia and Africa were a major source of friction with Britain and France during and for some years after World War II (Louis, 1978).

In addition, the worldwide interests of the United States were major reasons for U.S. involvement in such post-World War II conflicts as Korea, Vietnam, Laos, Cambodia, and the Middle East. Although more recent trends indicate that the United States may have shifted its role from containment of communism toward involvements resulting from general goals of global peace and regional stability, it appears that there has been no shift away from globalism and the anticipated "new isolationism" (Tucker, 1972) does not appear to have arrived yet (Abolfathi et al., 1979). Furthermore, existing international U.S. military commitments appear to be a continuing source of entanglement in overseas conflicts (McClelland et al., 1976; Paul 1973).

By reasons of geography alone, the overseas interests of the United States have always been more vulnerable to military threats from potential adversaries than the U.S. mainland. The security of these interests has dictated the large size of U.S. general purpose forces since the end of World War II (Koehler and Pirie, 1977). However, the exact nature of the threats to the U.S. overseas interests is the subject of intense controversy. Some writers have argued that the threat is local nationalism while others argue that it is international communism. There are many other variations to these themes,[10] but it would be beyond the scope of this study to try to review them. Moreover, an understanding of the sources of the threats to U.S. overseas interests is not essential to this study as long as it is possible to identify the major trends in the level of threats.

In light of the preceding discussions, it appears reasonable to argue that, with the possible exception of World War II, the major threats to the United States since the 1930s have been mainly those that involved overseas interests and required conventional and limited military responses.[11] Even the few major postwar U.S. military challenges that required rapid increases in defense spending and substantial mobilization of manpower, such as Korea and Vietnam, generally involved defense of territory or other interests far removed from the continental United States. The other decidedly less demanding challenges to the United States have come during periods of high international tension and most are identified by such major military crises as Berlin, 1948; Cuba, 1962; and the Middle East, 1973 (CACI, 1976; Blechman and Kaplan, 1978; Abolfathi et al., 1979).

On the basis of the above arguments, it is reasonable to assume that there have been two types of conventional and/or theater-oriented threats (see note 5) involving U.S. overseas interests:

(1) threats to U.S. overseas interests, from both local and international actors, during "peacetime" crises and periods of high international tension; and
(2) threats of potential military setbacks after the transition from crisis to war. At the very least, such setbacks are likely to involve U.S. prestige as a major power or U.S. economic and military stakes abroad. If, however, the conflict escalates to a world wide nuclear war the very survival of the United States would be endangered.

On the basis of the above assumptions, the nonstrategic threats to the United States can be viewed as being a function of the level of international tensions involving U.S. overseas interests and the degree of U.S. involvement in overseas conflicts. Therefore, it is feasible to measure threats to U.S. interests by the level of *international tensions* involving U.S. overseas interests and the degree of *U.S. war involvement*. In a preliminary effort these two variables were coded as dummy variables with only two values—zero and one.[12] For the present study it was decided to introduce greater variation in the two variables by extending their range.

The definitions used for coding these dummy variables are admittedly crude and depend greatly on the coder's judgment and historical knowledge:

(1) *U.S. war involvement* is a variable indicating the geographic scope and intensity of U.S. involvement in overseas wars. Its values are:[13]
    ○ no war involvement = 0;
    ○ limited war involvement = 1;
    ○ worldwide war not threatening the U.S. mainland = 2; and
    ○ worldwide war threatening the U.S. mainland = 3.
(2) *International tension levels* is a variable indicating the geographic scope and intensity of international conflicts (both "hot" and "cold") involving U.S. overseas interests during periods in which the United States is not involved in total wars.[14] Its values are:
    ○ no significant international conflicts affecting U.S. interests = 0;
    ○ low levels of tension = 0.5[15]
    ○ moderate levels of tension = 1;
    ○ high levels of tension = 2; and
    ○ extremely high tension levels = 3

The procedure used to code the variables involved two steps. First, the high and low points on the scale for the whole period were identified and coded. Then, the intermediate cases were coded. The codes for U.S. war involvement are likely to have greatly higher intercoder reliability than international tension because coder information about events as important as wars are likely to be similar and relatively little individual judgment is required for coding. The codes for international tension levels involving U.S. interests are likely to be less reliable and could vary greatly among coders with different levels of knowledge of U.S. history since the 1930s.[16]

Both variables were coded judgmentally by the author based on a detailed historical review of 1930-1979 carried out in a previous study (Abolfathi, 1978). In Table 3.1 the codes for the two variables are

TABLE 3.1 War and International Tension Dummy Variables, 1930-1979 (range = 0.0 to 3.0)

	War Involvement of the United States[a]	International Tension Levels[b]	Major Crises of Concern to the United States[c]
1930	0	0	International trade war
1931	0	0	Japan invades Manchuria
1932	0	0	Philippine independence crisis
1933	0	0	Default of U.S. war debts by Europe
1934	0	0.5	Hitlers' Blood Purge
1935	0	0.5	Militarization of Germany
1936	0	0.5	Spanish Civil War
1937	0	0.5	Japan Invades China
1938	0	1	Austria and Czech crises
1939	0	1	Poland and Finland crises
1940	0	2	Indochina crisis
1941	1	2	U.S. enters WWII
1942	2	0	Battle for North Africa
1943	2	0	German counteroffensives in Italy
1944	2	0	Battle of the Bulge
1945	1	0	Soviet demands at Potsdam
1946	0	0.5	Iran crisis
1947	0	1	Greek Civil War
1948	0	3	Berlin blockage/Czech coup
1949	0	2	China becomes Communist
1950	0.5	2	Korean War
1951	1	3	Iran oil crisis
1952	1	3	Burma-Nationalist China crisis
1953	0.5	3	Turmoil in East Germany and Poland
1954	0	2	Indochina conflict

TABLE 3.1 War and International Tension Dummy
Variables, 1930–1979 (range = 0.0 to 3.0) (Cont)

	War Involvement of the United States[a]	International Tension Levels[b]	Major Crises of Concern to the United States[c]
1955	0	1	Egypt-Israeli border clash
1956	0	1	Hungarian turmoil/Suez crisis
1957	0	2	Syrian crisis
1958	0	2	Taiwan Straits crisis
1959	0	2	Algerian war
1960	0	3	Congo crisis/Laos crisis
1961	0	3	Berlin Wall
1962	0	3	Cuban missile crisis
1963	0	2	Algeria-Morocco conflict
1964	0	1	Cuban exports of revolution
1965	0.5	2	Vietnam War
1966	1	3	Cultural Revolution in China
1967	1	2	Middle East War
1968	1	2	Czechoslovakia crisis
1969	0.5	1	Nigerian Civil War
1970	0.5	1	Jordanian Civil War
1971	0.5	1	Indo-Pakistani War
1972	0.5	0.5	Major North Vietnamese offensive
1973	0	1	Middle East War
1974	0	1	Portuguese coup/Cyprus crisis
1975	0	1	Fall of South Vietnam
1976	0	1	Angolan crisis
1977	0	1	Somalia-Ethiopia War
1978	0	1	Iran crisis
1979	0	1	Vietnam-China War

a. Judgmental codes; with 0 representing no war involvement, 0.5 representing limited, low-level war involvement, 1 representing high-level limited war involvement, 2 representing involvement in a world war, and 3 representing worldwide nuclear war.
b. Judgmental codes ranging from 0 (no significant world tension) to 3 (high tension).
c. Partial list of major international crisis that have concerned the United States since 1930.

presented along with selected major international crises of the period. The crises are mainly from the CACI (1976) and Brookings (Blechman and Kaplan, 1978) crisis data sets. Because of space limitations only a selected list of major crises is presented here to illustrate some of major events of concern to the United States. Since crises involving the United States appear to be good reflectors of international tension levels, the crisis data sets proved highly useful in coding the tension levels that affect U.S.

overseas interests. As can be noted in Table 3.1, the level of international tensions peaked during such major Cold War crises as the 1948 Berlin blockade and the 1951-1953 Korean conflict. Tension levels for the period of pre-World War II crises were generally coded lower than the Cold War period because the former did not affect U.S. overseas interests to the same degree as postwar crises.

The periods of highest sustained tension generally coincide with crises series that McClelland (1977) has labeled the "Cold War pattern" (1948-1964) and the pre-World War II high tension roughly fits his 1935-1939 crisis series. The postwar high tension period also coincides with some of the high tension years that can be identified from data collected by Gamson and Modigliani (1971), Goldman (1972), and Azar and Sloan (1975). However, the pattern inconsistencies among these data sets are so great that they are not likely to be a good test of validity for the present tension variable (Abolfathi, 1978: 10). Given the high inconsistencies among such "reliable" indicators, the validity of the international tension variable can only be judged on the basis of our knowledge and interpretation of U.S. history since the 1930s which introduces an element of arbitrariness into the evaluation (see note 16). However, because this variable is treated as an exogenous factor in the model of U.S. defense spending, any alternative views of international tensions can be incorporated into the model. The use of simple dummy variables greatly eases the tasks of recoding the tension variable and reestimating the equations. If, for instance, a survey of historians or the literature leads us to two different sets of tension variables, both can be used as alternative assumptions in reestimating the model of U.S. defense spending. Although the implications of accepting the wrong assumption is serious, its consequences are no more disturbing than model specification errors. In this study only one set of tension data are used for estimation, but the full data sets are made available in Tables 3.1 to 3.6 for anyone who wishes to test a different tension data series.

The U.S. war involvement variable has three peaks, during 1942-1944, 1951-1952, and 1966-1968, which indicate the height of U.S. involvements in one unlimited war (World War II) and two limited wars (Korea and Vietnam, respectively). The three peak years of the unlimited war were given codes of 2.0 and the 5 peak years of limited wars were coded 1. As is common with dummy variables (e.g., Singh et al., 1977: 144), the first years of each war period were divided by 2 in order to correct for the absence of intense fighting during the whole of those years (see note 13). Similarly, the codes for the years of deescalation were divided by 2 in order to correct for the reduced intensity of fighting.

A valid criticism of these decisions would be that by reducing all variance to a few codes they do not adequately account for the extended escalations and deescalations during wars. However, improvements incorporating such variances in the measurement procedures and would prove too costly for the marginal improvements in the variance of the variables. Using a crude dummy variable may not satisfy the exacting standards of some scholars, but it has proved to be an adequate measurement device for many of the weakly developed concepts in economics (e.g., Singh et al., 1977: 113-114).

It should be noted that the U.S. war involvement data only range up to a value of 2 whereas the maximum possible code is 3. The maximum historical code indicates the period of unlimited war against the Axis which can be roughly delineated from the U.S.-British invasion of North Africa in 1942 to the last full year of war in 1944. The reason for not assigning the maximum possible code to World War II is that this conflict never seriously threatened the continental United States (Russett, 1972b). However, the possibility of such a war cannot be ruled out for the future. Therefore, the higher code is a device that can be used in simulating the impact of a future world war on defense spending. Inferences from any such simulation, however, will have severe limitations. Since, as was detailed earlier, the U.S. mainland has not faced an imminent external threat for many years, there is no empirical evidence to show what the behavioral response of the relevant variables would be to such an external threat. Therefore, simulating the impact of a world-wide war threatening the continental United States is not unlike taking a submarine to a depth below its safety margin—it is hard to predict at what point things will begin to go wrong.

PUBLIC OPINION ON THREATS AND DEFENSE

Public Perception of International Threats

One of the three basic relationships in the model of defense spending introduced at the beginning of this chapter is the linkage between actual external threat and public perception of threat. The concept of threat perception at the individual and systemic level has only recently received attention from scholars. Most of the effort has been led by McClelland et al. (1976) and has been directed toward threat recognition and anticipation techniques. The efforts so far have not progressed much beyond early conceptualization and limited data analysis and are not directly useful for the present study.[17]

The best available source of information for assessing U.S. public perceptions of international threat over a long time period is a series of

Gallup opinion surveys of national samples involving questions about the important problems facing the United States. The exact format of the questions has changed slightly over the years but its general form has remained basically the same:

> What do you think is the most important problem facing the country today?[18]

While this question does not directly ask what are the major threats facing this country, it is not unrealistic to expect that whenever external threats are perceived to be of great importance they would be mentioned in the responses. One major shortcoming of the data is that they can only measure the importance of international problems *relative* to other problems. Because of improvements in polling techniques, the reliability of the measure is likely to range from fair in the early years to excellent in recent years.

Table 3.2 presents the relevant survey results. The first column on the left presents the average annual percentage of respondents identifying

TABLE 3.2 U.S. Public Perception of Most Important Problem, 1935–1978

Year	Percentage of Population Identifying International Problems as Most Important[a]	The Most Frequently Identified Important Problems During the Course of a Year[b]	Most Important International Problem(s) Identified During the Course of a Year[c]
1935	11	employment	neutrality
1936	26	employment	neutrality
1937	23	employment	neutrality
1938	33[d]	keeping out of war	keeping out of war
1939	42	keeping out of war	keeping out of war
1940	48	national defense	national defense
1941	75	national defense/war	national defense/war
1942	95[d]	war effort	war effort
1943	95[d]	war effort	war effort
1944	80[d]	war effort	war effort
1945	9	employment	making peace
1946	26	inflation	maintaining peace
1947	39	labor strikes/inflation	international relations
1948	53	inflation/peace	peace/foreign policy
1949	33	peace/labor strikes	peace/foreign conflict
1950	42	war efforts	war effort
1951	58	war	war
1952	65[d]	war	war
1953	62	war	war
1954	37	war	war

TABLE 3.2 U.S. Public Perception of Most Important Problem, 1935–1978 (Cont)

Year	Percentage of Population Identifying International Problems as Most Important[a]	The Most Frequently Identified Important Problems During the Course of a Year[b]	Most Important International Problem(s) Identified During the Course of a Year[c]
1955	47	foreign policy	foreign policy
1956	48	threat of war	threat of war
1957	41	foreign policy/civil rights	foreign policy/peace
1958	40	peace/economy	peace
1959	46[d]	peace	peace
1960	46	foreign policy	foreign policy
1961	46[d]	inflation	Russia
1962	63	peace/war	peace/war
1963	44	Cuba/racial problems	Cuba/foreign policy
1964	43	racial problems/Cold War/foreign policy	foriegn policy/Cold War
1965	55	Vietnam	Vietnam
1966	58	Vietnam	Vietnam
1967	50	Vietnam	Vietnam
1968	48	Vietnam	Vietnam
1969	40	Vietnam	Vietnam
1970	36	Vietnam	Indochina/Vietnam
1971	34	Vietnam/economy	Indochina/Vietnam
1972	37	Vietnam	Vietnam
1973	17	inflation	international problems[e]
1974	4	energy crisis/inflation	international problems[e]
1975	4	inflation	international problems[e]
1976	5	inflation	international problems[e]
1977	7	inflation	international problems[e]
1978	8	inflation	international problems[e]

a. Average percentage of all surveys conducted during each year.
b. Only the most frequently cited most important problem of each survey is listed. If more than one survey was carried out then it is possible to have more than one during the year.
c. Most frequently cited international problem.
d. Estimated on the basis of newspaper accounts, historical analyses, and related opinion polls for the relevant period.
e. In recent years, because the level of concern for international problems has been so low, the poll results were not published by issue. Instead, they were aggregated under the general label of "international problems."
Sources: Gallup (1972), *Gallup Opinion Index* (various issues), and Almond (1960).

international problems as "the most important." The most striking aspect of the data is the high preoccupation of the U.S. public with international problems over most of the period. Economic problems, however, which dominated up to the closing years of the Great Depression, have once again become dominant during the 1970s. The long-term changes in the data do not indicate any volatility in the U.S. foreign policy mood (Almond, 1960) which is consistant with Caspary's (1970) finding.

Another significant point is that the public disenchantment with foreign affairs that followed the Vietnam War reached a turning point in 1974-1975, when only an average of 4% of the public was greatly concerned about foreign issues. Since then there has been a slight upward trend in concern with international problems. This has been partially the result of extensive press coverage of Soviet involvement in crises such as Angola (1976), Ethiopia (1978), and Zaire (1978) and allegations of Soviet involvement in the recent coups d'etat in South Yemen and Afghanistan (Rielly, 1979). If Soviet involvement in international crises (or claims of such involvement by the press) increases during the 1980s, then public concern for international crises is likely to rise.[19] However, any such increase will be constrained by the level of public concern for economic problems such as inflation, unemployment, balance of payment problems and Government budget deficits (*Gallup Opinion Index,* March 1979: 4).

Public Support for Increased Defense Spending

Public support for defense spending has been a controversial subject for many years. National opinion polls on this issue sometimes tend to be misleading because their question formats may be biased. For instance, a recent poll sponsored by the Committee on the Present Danger (1979) has been used to show that public views on defense issues are greatly different from those that had been inferred from most other polls. Nevertheless, public opinion surveys are the only reasonably valid indicator of public support for defense spending available. Furthermore, their reliability can be significantly improved by substantial pruning of some of the biased polls in order to increase the similarity among the remaining survey results.

Table 3.3 presents the average of annual results for forty-three opinion surveys on defense spending since 1935. These surveys were selected from a larger list of national opinion polls on defense-related issues. In order to minimize question (stimuli) variability and hence the range of errors in the answers (responses), many of the surveys were excluded from the data set.[20] Among the remaining survey results the most common question asked was:

Do you feel we are spending too little, too much, or about the right amount on defense?

A major problem was that there were no data for many years between 1935 and 1978. Among the three columns in Table 3.3, the most complete

TABLE 3.3 U.S. Public Opinion on Defense Spending,
1935–1978 (percentages)[a]

Year	Percentage Supporting Increased Defense Spending	Percentage Supporting Decreased Defense Spending	Percentage in Favor of Maintaining Defense Spending at the Same Level
1935	48	11	41
1936	59[b]	...	...
1937	69	...	...
1938	74	...	...
1939	83	...	...
1940	82	...	...
1941	64	...	...
1942	70[c]	...	...
1943	43	...	...
1944	40[c]	...	...
1945	30[c]	...	...
1946	61	20	...
1947	60	34	...
1948	61	29	10
1949	56	29	15
1950	57	16	36
1951	73[d]	18	...
1952	29	26	25
1953	22	20	45
1954	16[b]	...	...
1955	9	19	72
1956	16[b]	...	...
1957	22	9	60
1958	63	...	...
1959	42[b]	...	...
1960	21	18	45
1961	31[d]	...	...
1962	38[e]	...	...
1963	38[e]	...	...
1964	38[e]	...	...
1965	38[e]	...	...
1966	38[e]	...	...
1967	38[e]	...	...
1968	38[e]	...	...
1969	8	52	31
1970	10	49	34
1971	10	47	33
1972	9	48	40
1973	10	44	35

TABLE 3.3 U.S. Public Opinion on Defense Spending,
1935–1978 (percentages)[a] (Cont)

Year	Percentage Supporting Increased Defense Spending	Percentage Supporting Decreased Defense Spending	Percentage in Favor of Maintaining Defense Spending at the Same Level
1974	12	50	32
1975	22	36	32
1976	25[b]	20	...
1977	27	23	40
1978	30[d]	15	47

a. Average percentage of all surveys conducted during each calendar year.
b. Estimated by averaging the results of surveys for adjacent years.
c. Estimated on the basis of newspaper accounts and inferences from polls indirectly related to defense spending issues.
d. Based on a survey during the last month of the preceding year.
e. Estimated by averaging the surveys for 1955–61.
... Not available.
Sources: compiled and estimated from Gallup (1972), Huntington (1961), Russett (1972a), Louis Harris and Associates, (1971, 1975, 1976), and *Gallup Opinion Index* (various issues).

data set over the whole period was in the left hand column, which indicates the percentage of respondents who supported *increased* defense spending. This variable had 35% missing cases (years). Most of its missing cases were estimated using a conservative approach of averaging values for the years adjacent to the missing cases.[21] The data for 1942, 1944, and 1945 were estimated on the basis of newspaper accounts and inferences indirectly related to defense spending issues. For instance, the 1945 estimate of 30% supporting increased defense spending is based on three considerations:

(1) Although the available data for 1946-48 show very high support for increased defense spending (60 to 61%), the 1945 major defense cuts by Truman (1965) did not create strong opposition.
(2) During the last three years of World War II the polls generally showed that there was public satisfaction with the current level of defense effort and a lack of enthusiasm for increasing the level of effort which by all objective measures was quite high (see the next section for further detail).
(3) By early 1945 the public was confident of defeating Germany and Japan and both had been accomplished by the middle of the year.

Therefore, support for *increased* defense spending could not have been very high at any time during 1945. Average support for the year as a whole could have been low to very low (i.e., 10 to 30%). By assuming a 30%

estimate for the level of public support for defense spending increases any potential error is likely to be on the conservative side.[22]

The data show a generally high level of public support for defense spending through 1960. Thereafter, the available data indicate a much lower level of support.[23] Clearly the Vietnam disillusionment could have been partly responsible for this transformation, but the lower level of Cold War tensions may also have been a factor (Watts and Free, 1976). During the last few years there has been a resurgence of public support for defense spending. This is often attributed to the new "Soviet threat" (Rielly, 1979). However, other contributing factors could include:

(1) recognition of increasing U.S. economic dependence on overseas markets, which often are in unstable regions;
(2) fading from memory of the Vietnamese experience and the associated antimilitarism of the period; and
(3) improvement in the economic situation of the vast majority of Americans during the 1976-1978 economic recovery from the major recession of 1974-1975.

This study focuses mainly on public opinion with respect to external threat and defense spending. Since the public opinion variables (such as those relating to the economy) are also reasonable contributing factors to defense spending (Ladd et al., 1979), the analysis will be somewhat incomplete and the model will be subject to some degree of specification error.

THE DEFENSE SECTOR

In this study defense-related variables are used in three different roles:

(1) as an indicator of the economic value of defense spending, commitment, effort, and so on;
(2) as an indicator of sufficiency or adequacy of the national defense capability; and
(3) as an indicator of the adequacy of federal concern for the national defense capability.

Greater detail on the role of these variables in the model of U.S. defense spending as specified in this study is presented in the next section. In this section, the development of defense-related variables since the 1930s is described.

Department of Defense Outlays

The most commonly used indicators of U.S. defense spending are outlays of the Department of Defense (DoD) and total federal outlays for national defense, which in any case differ only slightly. Another common measure is DoD outlays as a percentage of total federal outlays. Table 3.4 presents all three measures and the value of total federal outlays since 1930. Since all currency values are shown at current prices, they do not represent *real* outlays.

DoD outlays were less than two billion dollars annually until FY 1941, when they increased to 6.25 billion dollars. In the next fiscal year, with the United States fully engaged in the Pacific war, DoD outlays reached 22.9 billion dollars. The outlays were further increased to 63.4 billion dollars in FY 1943 in order to meet the additional requirements of U.S. operations in North Africa and Southern Europe and prepare for the invasion of Western Europe. Thus, during the first three years of the war, DoD outlays were increased by an average of 228% each year. The last two years of the war saw more modest increases to a peak outlay of 80.5 billion dollars in FY 1945.

TABLE 3.4 Department of Defense and Total Federal Budget of the United States, 1930–1983 (billion U.S. dollars at current prices)

Fiscal Year	Outlays of the Department of Defense (DoD)	Total Federal Outlays for National Defense	Total Federal Outlays of the United States	DoD Outlays as Percentage of Total Federal Outlays (percentage)
1930	0.839	...	3.320	25.3
1931	0.840	...	3.577	23.5
1932	0.834	...	4.659	17.9
1933	0.784	...	4.599	17.1
1934	0.706	...	6.644	10.6
1935	0.924	...	6.497	14.2
1936	1.148	...	8.422	13.6
1937	1.185	...	7.733	15.3
1938	1.240	...	6.674	18.3
1939	1.368	...	8.841	15.5
1940	1.799	1.504	9.055	19.9
1941	6.252	6.062	13.255	47.2
1942	22.905	23.970	34.037	67.3
1943	63.414	63.212	79.368	79.9
1944	75.976	76.874	94.986	80.0
1945	80.537	81.585	98.303	81.9
1946	43.151	44.731	60.326	71.5
1947	14.769	13.059	38.293	37.9
1948	11.983	13.015	32.955	36.4
1949	13.988	13.097	39.474	35.4

TABLE 3.4 Department of Defense and Total Federal Budget of the United States, 1930–1983 (billion U.S. dollars at current prices) (Cont)

Fiscal Year	Outlays of the Department of Defense (DoD)	Total Federal Outlays for National Defense	Total Federal Outlays of the United States	DoD Outlays as Percentage of Total Federal Outlays (percentage)
1950	13.440	13.119	39.544	34.0
1951	20.857	22.544	43.970	47.4
1952	40.536	44.015	65.303	62.1
1953	44.014	50.413	74.120	59.4
1954	40.626	46.645	70.890	57.3
1955	35.630	40.245	68.509	52.0
1956	35.693	40.305	70.460	50.7
1957	38.719	42.760	76.741	50.5
1958	39.817	44.371	82.575	48.3
1959	44.603	46.617	92.105	48.4
1960	43.696	45.908	92.223	47.7
1961	45.688	47.381	97.795	46.7
1962	49.283	51.097	106.813	46.1
1963	49.243	52.257	111.311	44.2
1964	50.703	53.591	118.583	42.8
1965	47.179	49.578	118.430	39.8
1966	55.445	56.785	134.652	41.2
1967	68.763	70.081	158.254	43.5
1968	78.673	80.517	178.833	44.0
1969	79.145	81.232	184.556	42.9
1970	78.360	80.295	196.588	39.9
1971	75.500	77.800	211.400	35.7
1972	76.200	78.400	231.900	32.9
1973	74.300	76.100	246.500	30.1
1974	77.600	79.600	268.400	28.9
1975	85.000	87.600	324.600	26.2
1976	88.000	92.800	366.500	24.0
1977	95.700	97.500	401.900	23.2
1978[a]	105.300	107.700	460.400	22.9
1979[a]	115.300	117.800	500.200	23.1
1980[b]	125.800	...	535.300	23.5
1981[b]	136.500	...	...	24.0
1982[b]	147.900	...	...	...
1983[b]	159.500	...	...	...

a. Preliminary estimate.
b. Projections of U.S. Department of Defense.
Sources: Compiled and estimated from U.S. Department of Commerce (1975, 1978) and U.S. Department of Defense (1978, 1979).
... Not available.

The peacetime decline of DoD outlays was not as spectacular as the wartime rise, but was impressive. By FY 1947, outlays were down to 14.8 billion dollars and were cut by a further 2.8 billion in FY 1948. However, by 1948 the Cold War was already fully underway even though its scope and intensity were still unknown quantities.

During the first few years of the Cold War, annual DoD outlays remained below 14 billion dollars. After the U.S. involvement in the Korean War, however, the Cold War entered a more intense phase and rearmament became rapid. By FY 1952 DoD spending had topped 40 billion dollars and total federal defense spending was over 44 billion dollars. The peak DoD outlay for this first phase of the Cold War rearmament was 44 billion dollars in FY 1953. Total federal defense spending in the same year was over 50 billion dollars.

The fiscally conservative Republican administration cut DoD spending to less than 37 billion dollars by the mid-1950s but received a chorus of abuse from the opposition Democrats and a host of military and civilian defense experts. To the extent that one could identify a military-industrial complex in the United States, the mid-1950s can be considered the period when it reached maturity. President Truman had successfully dealt with it in 1945 by overriding the objections and protests to major cuts in defense spending (Truman, 1965). The efforts of President Eisenhower met a far stronger interest group. The result was that after Korea, total federal defense spending never again fell below the 40 billion dollar level. In fact, by FY 1959, DoD outlays at current prices had surpassed the peak spending level of the Korean War.[24]

During the 1960s DoD outlays continued to rise rapidly in order to meet the requirements of new nuclear strategic weapons systems and finance the war in Vietnam. Unlike earlier periods, however, nondefense federal outlays either kept up with or surpassed defense outlays. This explosion of federal spending was checked for a short period in the early 1970s when U.S. forces rapidly withdrew from Vietnam. However, while DoD outlays were somewhat curtailed, other federal outlays continued their rapid rise. Consequently, the ratio of DoD to total federal outlays declined from 48% in 1960 to 23% in 1978.

The decline in the DoD share of federal spending by itself does not indicate declining commitment to national security. This secular, long-term decline mainly reflects rapidly rising civilian federal expenditures. The rise in civilian needs has been largely the result of:

(1) the U.S. population's age structure becoming older and requiring more government assistance;
(2) urbanization of the U.S. population and the growth of large,

complex cities, which in many cases have inadequate financial bases;
(3) the maturity of many industrial sectors of the U.S. economy and the relative decline of certain industries, which has resulted in regional dislocations that require public support;
(4) the increasing demand for government contributions to research and development activities, which increasingly have become dependent on government subsidy;
(5) the growth of demand for public regulation of commerce and industrial activities in order to protect citizens against unscrupulous practices and safeguard public resources and the environment against abuses;
(6) the increase in demand for public services such as transportation, recreational areas, education, and (increasingly) health; and
(7) greater expectations from governments as a result of sociological changes such as urbanization, industrialization and an older population structure.[25]

Thus, the decline in the DoD share in total federal spending is largely a result of the rapid expansion of the government's role in society. This role expansion reflects greater societal maturity and complexity and resultant changes in social values. Thus, because of secular trends, the ratio of DoD to total federal spending would have eventually declined because nondefense needs were growing far more rapidly than defense needs. In order to test whether the decline in the DoD share can be associated to an absolute (rather than relative) decrease in resource commitment to defense, other variables need to be analyzed.

Total National Defense Consumption

Two ways to show the real size of income/product consumption by the defense sector are to compare it to the total income/product of the nation or deflate it to a constant price currency. Table 3.5 presents the defense variable in relation to gross national product (GNP) and in constant 1957 prices. In addition, defense consumption and GNP at current prices and the GNP deflator are presented.

Defense as a Percentage of GNP. Defense consumption's share of total income/product absorption (GNP) in the United States is presented by the middle column in Table 3.5. This variable is based on current price values of defense consumption and GNP. Assuming no significant price differences between the two variables, their ratio represents a reasonable indicator of the nation's real defense burden or commitment in relation to total available resources.

TABLE 3.5 Defense Consumption in Relation to GNP in the United States, 1930–1985 (billion U.S. dollars)

Calendar Year	Consumption for Defense, at Current Prices	Gross National Product at Current Prices	Consumption for Defense as a Percent of GNP (percentage)	Index of GNP Implicit Price Deflator (1957 = 100)	Government Consumption for Defense at Constant 1957 Prices
1930	0.8	90.4	0.88	49.3	1.6
1931	0.8	75.8	1.06	44.8	1.8
1932	0.8	58.0	1.34	40.2	2.0
1933	0.8	55.6	1.44	39.3	2.0
1934	0.7	65.1	1.08	42.2	1.7
1935	0.9	72.2	1.25	42.6	2.1
1936	1.1	82.5	1.33	42.7	2.6
1937	1.1	90.4	1.22	44.5	2.5
1938	1.2	84.7	1.42	43.9	2.7
1939	1.2	90.8	1.32	43.6	2.8
1940	2.2	100.0	2.20	44.7	4.9
1941	13.7	124.9	10.97	48.4	28.3
1942	49.4	158.3	31.21	53.5	92.3
1943	79.7	192.0	41.51	55.9	142.6
1944	87.4	210.5	41.52	57.1	153.1
1945	73.5	212.3	34.62	58.4	125.9
1946	14.8	209.6	7.06	67.5	21.9
1947	9.0	232.8	3.87	76.4	11.8
1948	10.7	259.1	4.13	81.6	13.1
1949	13.2	258.0	5.12	80.8	16.3

TABLE 3.5 Defense Consumption in Relation to GNP in the United States, 1930–1985 (billion U.S. dollars) (Cont)

Calendar Year	Consumption for Defense, at Current Prices	Gross National Product at Current Prices	Consumption for Defense as a Percent of GNP (percentage)	Index of GNP Implicit Price Deflator (1957 = 100)	Government Consumption for Defense at Constant 1957 Prices
1950	14.0	286.2	4.89	82.4	17.0
1951	35.5	330.2	10.15	88.1	38.0
1952	45.8	347.2	13.19	89.2	51.4
1953	48.6	366.1	13.28	90.5	53.7
1954	41.1	366.3	11.22	91.8	44.8
1955	38.4	399.3	9.62	93.8	40.9
1956	40.2	420.7	9.56	96.8	41.5
1957	44.0	442.8	9.94	100.0	44.0
1958	45.6	448.9	10.16	101.7	44.8
1959	45.6	486.5	9.37	104.0	43.9
1960	44.5	506.0	8.79	105.7	42.1
1961	47.0	523.3	8.98	106.7	44.1
1962	51.1	563.8	9.06	108.6	47.1
1963	50.3	594.7	8.46	110.2	45.6
1964	49.0	635.7	7.71	112.0	43.8
1965	49.4	688.1	7.18	114.4	43.2
1966	60.3	753.0	8.01	118.2	51.0
1967	71.5	796.3	8.98	121.7	58.8
1968	76.9	868.5	8.85	127.1	60.5
1969	76.3	935.5	8.16	133.5	57.2

TABLE 3.5 Defense Consumption in Relation to GNP in the United States, 1930–1985 (billion U.S. dollars) (Cont)

Calendar Year	Consumption for Defense, at Current Prices	Gross National Product at Current Prices	Consumption for Defense as a Percent of GNP (percentage)	Index of GNP Implicit Price Deflator (1957 = 100)	Government Consumption for Defense at Constant 1957 Prices
1970	73.5	982.4	7.48	140.7	52.2
1971	70.2	1,063.4	6.60	147.9	47.5
1972	73.5	1,171.1	6.28	153.9	47.8
1973	73.5	1,306.6	5.63	162.9	45.1
1974	77.0	1,412.9	5.45	172.0	44.8
1975	83.9	1,528.8	5.49	188.5	44.5
1976	86.8	1,700.1	5.11	198.5	43.7
1977[a]	94.3	1,887.2	5.00	209.8	43.0
1978[a]	102.5	2,106.6	4.87	225.3	45.5
1979[b]	114.2	2,331.8	4.90	244.5	46.7
1980[b]	...	...	...	...	47.7
1981[c]	...	...	...	...	49.1
1982[c]	...	...	...	...	50.6
1983[c]	...	...	...	...	52.1
1984[c]	...	...	...	...	53.7
1985[c]	...	...	...	...	55.1

a. Preliminary estimates
b. Rough estimates
c. Projection based on 3% annual growth under NATO program.
... Not available
Sources: Compiled and estimated from U.S. Department of Commerce (1975, 1978) and U.S. Department of Defense (1978, 1979).

The U.S. defense burden or commitment was only about 1% of GNP during the 1930s, but it rose rapidly to a remarkable peak of 41.5% during the height of World War II. In the postwar period, it rapidly declined to 3.9% in 1947, only to rise again during the Korean War to a peak of 13.3% in 1953. The period since World War II, however, has been a period of nearly continuous growth for the U.S. economy averaging 3.6% per annum between 1947 and 1979. This rapid economic growth provided a continuously increasing resource base for potential defense and nondefense uses. Since the Korean War peak defense allocation of 13.3%, however, the defense share has generally declined. The decline became particularly rapid after the initiation of the U.S. withdrawal from Vietnam, and in 1978 reached its lowest level since 1948.

With the anticipated slowdown in the U.S. economy during the early 1980s (C.B.O., 1979) and the Carter administration's commitment to U.S. allies to raise defense spending by 3% per annum (Brown, 1979), the defense share is likely to gradually rise for the next few years. Any such rise will not be very large and is likely to be offset if the economy resumes its rapid growth. Most observers expect defense's share of the U.S. GNP to experience very gradual decline in the long run.[26] As long as world tensions remain at present low levels, the rate of decline is not expected to accelerate significantly. It is worth noting that ironically the rapid post-Vietnam decline was largely a result of the U.S. economic boom during the second half of the 1960s. Had there been no need for major increases in defense spending during Vietnam, then the decline in defense's share of GNP would have been far more gradual and orderly between 1960 and 1975.

The impact of changing GNP growth rates on defense's share of GNP makes the latter a poor indicator for measuring trends in real defense consumption. Such disturbances may have been responsible for Russett's (1972a) failure to find statistical support for a relationship between public opinion and defense spending.

Defense at Constant Prices. The best single indicator of defense consumption, commitment, or value would be a variable that measures the absorption of resources by the defense sector at *constant* prices. Unfortunately, the U.S. Commerce Department, which is responsible for estimating U.S. national accounts statistics, publishes "Government consumption for defense" figures only at current prices. Consequently, the DoD has been publishing its own constant price figures for defense outlays using price deflators that are either arbitrarily selected or have known biases (such as exaggerating the long-term decline in a defense outlays).

The constant price figures for defense consumption in Table 3.5, are based on GNP implicit price deflators with 1956 as the base year. The deflator is a combination of two series from the Department of Commerce with two different base years.[27] Before proceeding with a discussion of the results, it is worth reviewing the appropriateness of using a GNP deflator on defense consumption, which in recent years has been only 5% of total absorption (or GNP).

The alternatives available to using a GNP deflator are few. They include:

(1) using another national account deflator published by the Department of Commerce, such as those for "total Federal government purchases of goods and services," "personal consumption expenditures," or others;
(2) using one of the numerous price indexes compiled by the Department of Labor; or
(3) using one of the several reliable existing price indexes estimated privately for various industries by independent analysts that are generally based on Labor Department data.

Using any one of these alternative indexes can lead to significantly different results. For instance, using a national account deflator for "total federal government consumption" will result in a smaller defense value in 1979 than using, say, that for "personal consumption expenditures." It may be argued that the federal government consumption deflator is the most appropriate one available, since it includes defense spending. However, this deflator is notoriously unreliable because it deals with government services whose *real* value is never calculated directly but estimated by inference from purchase costs taking into account parallel price increases in the private sector.

Many services provided by government are those that are by nature difficult for the private sector to provide. For instance, they may be a service that the private sector could no longer provide because of small demand, large overhead costs, or inherent inefficiencies. Thus, the federal government's spending includes financing of many inefficient services and industries. The costs of some of these often escalate rapidly after the government takes over in order to make up for the years of neglect of capital stocks during the years of private sector ownership (e.g., the U.S. passenger rail system). The U.S. defense sector has very little in common with any of these problem industries (Gansler, 1979). Defense has always been a government function in the United States. Furthermore, defense spending largely involves the development and maintenance of military equipment.[28] These tasks are much easier to administer efficiently than, say, Health, Education and Welfare (HEW) programs that provide far more heterogenous services and have far less control over customer selection and payment transfers. The 30-billion dollar Medicare program by itself is probably far less manageable than the whole 126-billion dollar defense program. There is little reason, therefore, to assume that the defense program suffers from the same runaway costs as less manageable federal programs or problem industries (such as the railroads) that are subsidized by the government (Gansler, 1979).

Thus, the total federal consumption deflator is probably inferior to the GNP deflator for application to defense consumption. If one has to make a selection among various deflators, the total GNP deflator is the most appropriate because by taking into account all goods and services produced in the economy, it would be the most conservative choice. The other deflators should be used only if one has reasons to prefer them. Since no such reasons could be found, in this study only the total GNP deflator was employed. (The result of deflating defense consumption by the GNP deflator is presented in Table 3.5)

As would be expected from previous discussions of the trends in military spending, defense consumption at constant 1957 prices, which was small during the 1930s, rose rapidly during World War II. The postwar decline was brief and was followed by the Korean escalation period. By 1953, the value of defense (at 1957 prices) had peaked at just under 54 billion dollars. The Eisenhower cuts brought it down to 41 billion by 1955. Thereafter, defense consumption fluctuated at well above the 41 billion level. If one ignores the Vietnam escalation, the defense consumption shows a roughly level long-term trend since 1957.

In other words, defense spending at constant 1957 prices has remained at about 43-45 billion dollars since 1957. The data certainly show no secular long-term decline, as has long been claimed by the advocates of higher defense spending. In fact, the Carter administration's pledge to U.S. allies to increase defense spending by 3% per annum (Brown, 1979), if sustained, will increase U.S. spending to over 55 billion dollars (at 1957 prices), which is well above the post-Korean average.

In sum, U.S. real defense consumption has generally remained constant over the last twenty-five years and, according to current plans, is likely to rise gradually over the next few years. The first part of this conclusion can be supported by evidence that the defense sector of the United States has been constantly improving its managerial efficiency (Steadman, 1978; Scott, 1979), particularly since the major innovations of the Kennedy administration (Agapos, 1975). Moreover, although the unit costs of weapon systems have been rising rapidly, weapons capabilities have probably increased far more rapidly. Finally, although the personnel costs of the U.S. armed forces have increased due to inflation and the transition to all-volunteer force, the deflated personnel costs have remained nearly unchanged.[29] There has, however, been a very rapid increase in retirement

TABLE 3.6 Number of Active
Military Personnel in the U.S. Armed
Forces, 1930–1980 (millions)

Years	Military Personnel on Active Duty[a]
1930	0.256
1931	0.253
1932	0.245
1933	0.244
1934	0.247
1935	0.252
1936	0.291
1937	0.312
1938	0.323
1939	0.335
1940	0.458
1941	1.801
1942	3.859
1943	9.045
1944	11,452
1945	12.123
1946	3.030
1947	1.583
1948	1.446
1949	1.615
1950	1.460
1951	3.249
1952	3.636
1953	3.555
1954	3.302
1955	2.935
1956	2.806
1957	2.796
1958	2.601
1959	2.504
1960	2.476
1961	2.494
1962	2.808
1963	2.700
1964	2.687
1965	2.655
1966	3.094
1967	3.377
1968	3.547
1969	3.460

TABLE 3.6 Number of Active
Military Personnel in the U.S. Armed
Forces, 1930–1980 (millions) (Cont)

Years	Military Personnel on Active Duty[a]
1970	3.066
1971	2.714
1972	2.322
1973	2.252
1974	2.161
1975	2.127
1976	2.081
1977	2.074
1978	2.061
1979	2.050
1980	2.050

a. Excludes civilian employees of the Department of Defense.
Sources: Compiled and estimated from U.S. Department of Commerce (1975) and U.S. Department of Defense (1978, 1979).

pay partly because of the post-Vietnam reduction in active military personnel.

U.S. Military Manpower

As shown in Table 3.6, the major changes over time in the number of active military personnel in the U.S. armed forces roughly parallel the real defense consumption. Military personnel increased rapidly to an all-time peak of over 12 million in 1945 and then declined to a postwar nadir of 1.45 million in 1948. The Korean War peak of over 3.6 million was reached in 1952. After the Korean demobilization, active personnel ranged between 2.5 and 2.8 million until the Vietnam escalation. The Vietnam peak was reached in 1968 at 3.55 million. The disengagement from Vietnam after 1968 was accompanied by a gradual demobilization and reduction of armed forces. The reduction of military manpower continued well after disengagement was complete as part of the transition to a small, efficient all-volunteer force. In 1978 there were about 2.1 million active personnel in the U.S. armed forces—a level expected to continue during the 1980s. Among the indicators of defense spending, this variable is probably the most appropriate measure for the U.S. public's view of level of defense effort. Whenever the size of armed forces has increased through rapid mobilization, public support for increased defense spending has noticeably declined. Therefore, even though military manpower by itself may mean little in terms of actual military capability, for the U.S. public this variable is a good measure of the adequacy of U.S. defense capability.[30]

DATA ANALYSES

The model of U.S. defense spending analyzed in this study consists of three equations or sets of relationships that sequentially determine the

(1) level of public concern for international problems,
(2) level of public support for defense spending, and
(3) rate of increase in real defense spending.

This section first describes the indicators used to operationalize the model variables. Then the model structure is outlined. Finally, the estimated equations are presented.

The Variables

In this study six major types of variables are used to model U.S. defense spending:

(1) real change in U.S. defense spending,
(2) public support for increased defense spending,
(3) public perception of external threats,
(4) actual external threats,
(5) (public's view of the adequacy of) U.S. defense capability, and
(6) (public's view of the adequacy of) U.S. Government concern and commitment to national defense.[31]

The first four variables, which were described in the preceding sections, constitute the basic structure of the model. Their three primary linkages were described as a simple sequence:

Actual Threat → Perception of Threat → Public Support for Defense Spending → Change in Defense Spending

The last two variables are additions to the basic model structure. Their purpose is to introduce damping influence in the model so that, once there is an increase in external threats, there will be mechanisms for eventually halting the growth in defense expenditures. The precise manner in which these dampening influences take effect will become more clear in the discussions of the model that will follow brief descriptions of the indicators used to measure each of the six variable types.

Real Change in Defense Spending. This variable is measured in terms of annual percentage compound growth rates of defense consumption in 1957 prices. The original variable at current prices was deflated using the U.S. GNP deflator. All data are derived from U.S. national accounts estimated by the Commerce Department. It should be noted that this variable includes all resource consumption for national defense by the federal government but it does not generally differ greatly from the DoD annual outlays. Reliable data for this variable were available for 1929 to 1977.

Public Support for Increased Defense Outlays. Public support for greater defense expenditures is indicated by the annual average percentage of respondents in national opinion surveys supporting increases in such spending. The data for this variable were available for most years during the 1935-1977 period. The missing years were estimated conservatively by the author using newspaper accounts, opinion poll data for the available years adjacent to the missing years, and other poll data on issues indirectly related to support for defense spending.

Public Perception of Threat. The level of public concern for external threats to U.S. national interests is indicated by the annual average percentage of respondents in national opinion surveys singling out international and foreign policy issues as the most important problems facing the United States. The data for this variable were available for most years from 1935 to 1978. The data for the seven missing years were estimated conservatively using newspaper accounts, opinion polls on related issues, and historical analyses of U.S. public perceptions for the relevant years (e.g., Levering, 1978).

Actual External Threats. The *actual* (versus publicly perceived) level of external threats to U.S. national interests are represented by the two dummy variables representing U.S. war involvement and international tensions affecting U.S. interests. Both variables have a range of zero to three and were coded for the full 1930-1979 period. Since both variables were judgmentally coded, their reliabilities are the most questionable among the seven variables used in the analysis.

(Perception of Adequacy of) Defense Capability. In this study it is assumed that public perception of threat is a function of perception of the *adequacy*[32] of the country's defense capability as well as the levels of external threats. Since adequate data on public perceptions of the U.S. defense capability over time could not be found, measures of actual defense capability had to be utilized. Candidates for such a variable are

many. They include most measures of quantity and quality of armed forces and weapon systems. Rather than try many different indicators, it was decided to utilize the number of active military personnel in U.S. armed forces. Although this indicator by itself is a poor measure of total capability, it is one of the most easily identifiable military variables for the U.S. public. Hopefully, better variables will be found for future studies. For instance, one could develop indicators of U.S. military capability that use major adversaries' capabilities as benchmarks (e.g., U.S.-Soviet military balance). The data set used for this variable covered all years between 1929 and 1978.

(Perception of Adequacy of) Government Concern for Defense. Public support for military spending is assumed to be a function of the *adequacy*[33] of existing government defense efforts as well as public perceptions of external threats. As in the case of the preceding variable, because of the absence of public opinion data, this variable is indicated by an actual measure of government concern or commitment to defense. The most obvious such indicator is the percent of the government budget devoted to defense. In this study the specific variable used is the percentage of the federal budget allocated to the Department of Defense between 1929 and 1978. The original data were the federal government expenditure statistics by fiscal year.

The Model

The model of U.S. public opinion and defense spending estimated in this study consists of a recursive system with three endogenous and four exogenous variables. The direction and sign of the relationships among the variables are outlined in Figure 3.1. The model's three recursive equations describe three sets of relationships:

(1) Public concern for international problems is related positively to U.S. war involvement and international tensions affecting U.S. interests and is inversely related to the number of active military personnel (which for the U.S. public is a measure of adequacy of defense capability).
(2) Public support for increased defense spending is related positively to public concern for international problems and negatively to the defense share of the federal budget (which for the U.S. public is a measure of the adequacy of government concern for national defense).
(3) The rate of increase in real defense spending is related positively to public support for increased defense, U.S. war involvement, and international tensions affecting U.S. interests.

The model's intuitive reasonableness can be demonstrated easily by means of an example. If there is an increase in external threats to the

FIGURE 3.1 Diagram of a Model of Public Opinion and Defense for the United States

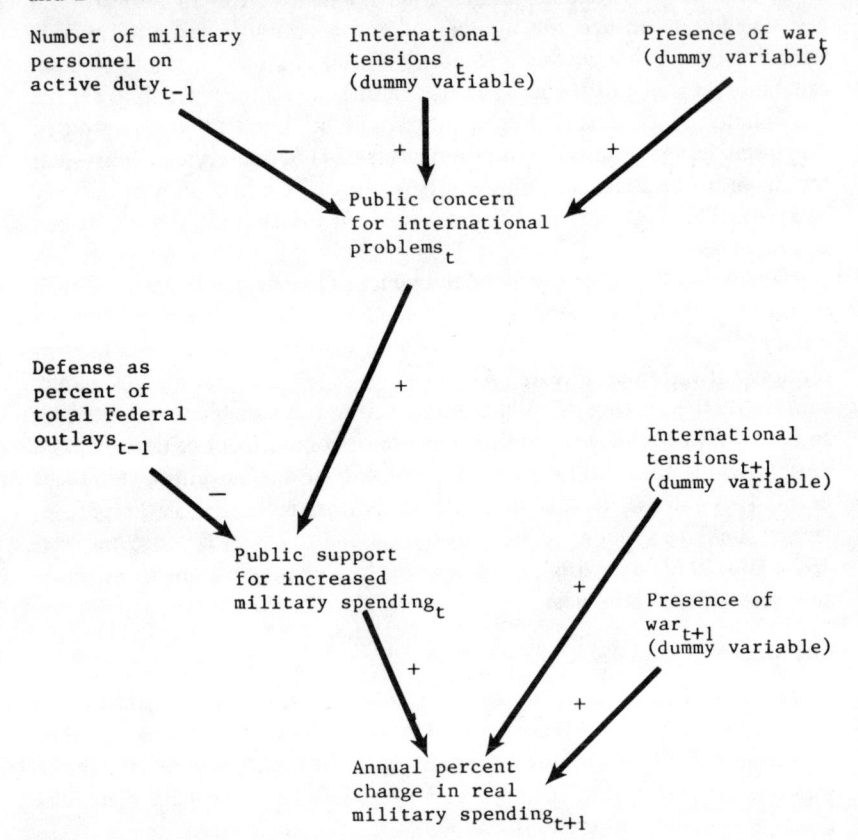

```
Number of military        International          Presence of war_t
personnel on              tensions_t              (dummy variable)
active duty_{t-1}         (dummy variable)

              —              +              +
                    Public concern
                    for international
                    problems_t

Defense as
percent of
total Federal                                      International
outlays_{t-1}              +                       tensions_{t+1}
                                                   (dummy variable)

              —
                    Public support
                    for increased                  Presence of
                    military spending_t            war_{t+1}
                                              +    (dummy variable)

                          +
                    Annual percent         +
                    change in real
                    military spending_{t+1}
```

Note: t-1 represents a one-year backward lag and t+1 a one-year forward lag.

United States either through international tension affecting U.S. overseas interests or U.S. involvement in wars, the model assumes that there will be an increase in defense spending through two linkages. First, there will be a direct linkage through the bureaucrats in charge of defense who immediately try to raise actual defense spending by either seeking new supplemental authorizations or by spending previously authorized appropriations at a faster rate. These methods were clearly used to increase the defense budget during the Vietnam War (Taylor, 1974). The second linkage is indirect and involves the two intermediate public opinion variables. Here external threats lead to increased public concern for international problems, which leads to greater public support for military spending, which leads to increased defense spending after a lag of one year. This indirect linkage is dampened by two lagged exogenous variables: the number of military personnel on active duty and the defense share of total federal outlays. The reasoning behind these two dampening influence are as follows:

(1) For any given level of external threat, public concern for international problems is likely to decline as public perception of the adequacy of national defense capability (indicated by the number of active military personnel) increases.
(2) For any given level of public concern for international problems, public support for defense spending is likely to decrease as the public perception of the adequacy of federal government concern for defense (indicated by the defense share in the federal budget) increases.[34]

Obviously, the relationships in the present model are not complete. There are other relevant variables that one could add such as elite attitudes toward defense, the economic burden of defense, bureaucratic "inertia" in government spending, U.S.-Soviet competitive arms accumulation, and congressional support for defense (for alternative models, see Ostrom, 1978; Strauss, 1972). In defense of the model, it can be argued that it is reasonable (i.e., has face validity), and it is simple enough to allow empirical analyses using statistical techniques.

Estimated Equations

The three linear recursive equations constituting the model of U.S. public opinion and defense spending were estimated using an ordinary least squares (OLS) technique.[35] The data used to estimate the equations covered most years between 1930 and 1978, but the last two years of data were excluded because they included preliminary estimates. The estimated parameters for the three equations and their statistics are presented in Table 3.7, but the discussion here will only involve the most important statistics.

Compared to most economic regression equations, the three equations have very small multiple correlation coefficients (R^2s). However, most of the variables in the model are not economic. Moreover, two of the most important variables are based on public opinion surveys that generally show statistically weak relationships with other variables. Another general weakness of the estimated equations is the presence of autocorrelation evidenced by the very low values of the Durbin-Watsin (D.W.) statistics. The autocorrelation problem appears serious despite the fact that the final dependent variable (change in defense spending) and defense GNP are substantially detrended variables. Since further detrending of the variables would violate basic model structure or would require better data quality, it

TABLE 3.7 Estimated Equations for the
Three Major Dependent Variables, 1935–1976

PRB	=	23.72 + 28.47 WAR − 1.26 MIL_{t-1} + 7.72 TEN (4.30) (7.39) (1.36) (3.29) $\bar{R}^2$ = 0.58; F = 20.06; D.W. = 0.89; n = 42
SUP	=	45.20 − 0.50 DOG_{t-1} + 0.37 PRB (4.88) (2.70) (2.38) $\bar{R}^2$ = 0.20; F = 4.99; D.W. = 0.53; n = 42
DDI	=	−65.39 + 1.34 SUP_{t-1} + 48.83 WAR + 9.64 TEN (2.24) (2.47) (2.34) (0.79) $\bar{R}^2$ = 0.26; F = 5.68; D.W. = 1.31; n = 42

Note: The t-statistics are presented in brackets. The variables and the statistics are represented as follows:

PRB	=	Public concern for international problems (percentage)
WAR	=	A dummy variable for years the United States has been at war (values range from zero to three)
TEN	=	A dummy variable for years in which international tensions affecting U.S. interests have been high (values range from zero to three)
MIL	=	Number of military personnel on active duty (millions)
SUP	=	Public support for increased military spending (percentage)
DOG	=	Defense as a percentage of total U.S. federal spending (percentage)
DDI	=	Annual percentage change in real military spending (percentage)
n	=	Number of years of data (in all cases: 1935–1976)
D.W.	=	Durbin-Watson statistics for the equation
F	=	F-statistic for the regression equation
$\bar{R}^2$	=	Multiple correlation coefficient for the regression equation (adjusted for degrees of freedom)

was judged inadvisable.[36] Moreover, the remaining autocorrelations are more likely to be due to omitted independent variables and misspecification of the equation form (both of which are common in social science models) than a result of true autocorrelation (Koutsoyiannis, 1973: 198). This suspicion is supported by the low R^2s, which indicate substantial unexplained variance for the dependent variables. Moreover, the presence of autocorrelation in OLS estimation does not lead to biased estimated parameters or forecasts (Johnston 1972: 246). It leads to inefficient estimates and high forecasting uncertainty. These problems are serious only if one is interested in selecting among two or more competing models based on their t- and F-statistics. Since in the present study only a single model is presented, these problems are not serious.[37]

Because of the presence of autocorrelation, the t-statistics may be inflated and cannot be used as a measure of statistical significance of individual parameters. However, as a general rule, higher t-statistics indicate greater reliability of the parameters. In the three equations, all parameters except two have t-statistics that are greater than 2 (which is only an arbitrary standard). More importantly, all estimated parameters have theoretically correct signs. The estimated equations support the overall model of U.S. defense spending presented in this study. In particular the equation for change in defense spending (DDI) indicates that there is a signficant positive relationship between defense spending and public support for defense, a relationship that had not been supported by Russett's analysis (1972a). Since this estimated model is the first to successfully link public opinion with defense spending, it represents a significant breakthrough in linking defense spending to variables other than the economic resource base (Coward, 1964) and external threat (Rattinger, 1975).

SCENARIOS AND FORECASTS

In order to observe the dynamics and test the robustness of the model of U.S. public opinion and defense spending, six scenarios were constructed and the performance of the model under each case was observed and evaluated. Finally, the likely levels of defense spending as predicted by the model were identified.

The six scenarios included:

(1) a standard scenario or the most likely situation,
(2) a very low international tension scenario,
(3) a no tension scenario,
(4) a scenario of sudden increase in world tensions,
(5) a limited war scenario, and
(6) a worldwide nuclear war scenario.

Each scenario consists of a set of general assumptions about the domestic and international political system and more specific assumptions for the four exogenous variables in the forecasting model. The standard scenario's assumptions consist of the most likely developments during the 1980s, based on recent trends. Therefore, it can be considered as a baseline for all the other scenarios.

Standard Scenario: The Most Likely Situation

Given the developments of the 1970s, the most likely scenario for the 1980s appears to be one in which:

(1) the United States remains at peace (war dummy = 0);
(2) world tension levels remain low compared to the Cold War era (world tension dummy = 1.0);

(3) the United States maintains its current all-volunteer armed forces at roughly the present level (armed forces = 2.05 million);
(4) as a result of public revolt against government spending, the ratio of defense to nondefense spending remains constant; and
(5) no world-shaking political or economic disasters occur (such as the breakup of NATO or a major world economic depression).[38]

Applying the above assumptions to the estimated three-equation model gives the following results:

- percentage of the U.S. public concerned with international problems = 29,
- percentage of the U.S. public supporting increased defense spending = 44, and
- percentage annual change in real defense spending = +3.2.

Compared to the Cold War years, the predicted level of public concern for international problems is low whereas support for defense spending is relatively high. Also, the rate of growth of defense spending is rather high for a low tension scenario. However, recent data indicate that despite detente, public concern for international problems and support for defense spending are rising very rapidly and the United States has plans for increasing its real defense spending by at least 3% per annum (Rielly, 1979; Brown, 1979).

Very Low Tension Scenario

If the United States and the Soviet Union are successful in resolving most major conflictual issues between them (such as disagreement over human rights in the Soviet Union, Soviet support for national liberation and Communist movements abroad, and strategic arms control), then the current level of international tension could be greatly reduced. Under such circumstances, it is reasonable to assume that the world tensions dummy (TEN) will be equal to 0.5 compared to 1.0 coded for the last few years. Assuming that values of all other exogenous variables remain the same, the results will be:

- percentage of the U.S. public concerned with international problems = 25,
- percentage of the U.S. public supporting increased defense spending = 43, and
- percentage annual change in real defense spending = -3.5.

The high levels of public concern for international problems and support for defense under the assumption of very low tension are puzzling. There are two likely reasons for this. First, the model could be biased because most of its data base includes years of either high international tension or war. Since the historical "experience" of low tension in the data base is very limited, the model could be subject to error when forecasting low tension scenarios. Another likely source of error is the lack of variables representing the importance of domestic problems, such as inflation and unemployment, which can dominate public attention at the expense of international problems.

No Tension Scenario

An unlikely but interesting scenario would be one in which all U.S.-Soviet animosity disappeared and other world tensions were reduced to the comparatively low levels of the 1925-1934 period. Under such conditions the world tensions dummy (TEN) will be equal to zero and the forecast variables will be as follows:

- percentage of the U.S. public concerned with international problems = 21,
- percentage of the U.S. public supporting increased defense spending = 41, and
- percentage annual change in real defense spending = -10.3.

The possible sources of bias described for the preceding scenario are likely to be more serious for the no tension scenario.

Scenario: Sudden Increase in World Tensions

If world tensions suddenly were increased considerably (for instance, as a result of the introduction of Soviet combat troops in Southern Africa), then it would be reasonable to assign a 2.0 code to the tension dummy (TEN). The result of this exogenous change on the dependent variables of the model will be as follows:

- percentage of the U.S. public concerned with international problems = 37,
- percentage of the U.S. public supporting increased defense spending = 47, and
- percentage annual change in real defense spending = +16.7.

If defense spending increased by nearly 17% during the first year then the level of military manpower (MIL) is bound to increase and dampen defense spending. The increasing share of defense in the federal budget (DOG) will also have a dampening influence. In order to show the impact of these dampening influences on the second year of the forecast, it was assumed that by the end of the first year military manpower increased to 3 million and the defense share of the federal budget increased to 40%. The results were:

- percentage of the U.S. public concerned with international problems = 35,
- percentage of U.S. public supporting defense spending = 38, and
- percentage annual change in real defense spending = +5.3.

Thus, after the large increase in defense spending in the first year, the model predicts a reduction in public support for defense during the second year which leads to a *slower increase* in defense spending (5.3%). This type of negative feedback is characteristic of most stable processes in both the natural and social sciences. Unfortunately, in the social sciences such models are generally too complex to be estimated empirically. The simulated feedback in this scenario was made possible only by intervention in the operation of the model, which has no explicit feedback loops.

Limited War Scenario

This scenario assumes that the U.S. suddenly becomes involved in a highly escalatory conflict situation and becomes engaged in a limited war with a major adversary such as the Soviet Union. Therefore, the value of war dummy (WAR) becomes one and world tension (TEN) takes a value of three. The results for the first year of conflict were as follows:

- percentage of the U.S. public concerned with international problems = 73,
- percentage of the U.S. Public supporting increased defense spending = 60, and
- percentage annual change in real defense spending = +93.3.

The predicted values of the two public opinion variables in this scenario are comparable to the worst years of the Cold War which match the assumptions of the scenario (a situation similar to the first year of the Korean conflict). The sudden 93% increase in defense spending is reasonable as the increases will be from a period of relatively low tension levels (which is similar to the Korean experience, as well).

World War III Scenario

If the United States becomes engaged in a worldwide war involving the use of nuclear weapons, the value of the war dummy takes on a value of three (compared to 2.0 for WWII), international tensions will become irrelevant (TEN = 0), and the impact on the three dependent variables will be as follows:

- percentage of the U.S. public concerned with international problems = 107,[39]
- percentage of the U.S. public supporting increased defense spending = 73, and
- percentage annual change in real defense spending = +179.

Since this scenario is an obvious extreme situation and is beyond the data experience of the model, its results are subject to forecasting errors similar to those described for the low tension scenario. Therefore, one should not be surprised to see that the predicted percentage of the public concerned with international problems is greater than 100% which clearly is not possible (see note 39).

Forecasts for the 1980s

Among the above scenarios the most likely is the standard scenario under which U.S. defense spending is projected to rise at a rate of 3.2% per year. The next most likely scenarios are the cases of "very low tensions" and "sudden increase in tensions," which forecast defense spending changes ranging from -3.5 to +16.7% for the first year, respectively. Thus, if there are substantial changes in international tensions affecting U.S. overseas interests, the range of forecast uncertainty would be very high.

Currently, most observers of U.S. defense appropriations project a 2-4% annual growth for real defense spending during the 1980s based on the assumption that the U.S.-Soviet agreement on the Strategic Arms Limitation Talks (SALT II) will be successfully completed before the 1980 U.S. elections.[40] When this assumption is relaxed, most (but not all) experts project a higher level of defense spending increase ranging from 3 to 7% per annum between 1980 and 1985.[41] Therefore, the 3.2% annual increase forecast by the three-equation model of this study falls within the first set of projections that are based on the approval of SALT II. If one accepts the 3.2% annual increase as reasonable, then U.S. defense spending will increase from 129 billion dollars in 1980 to 151 billion in 1985 and 177 billion in 1990 (at 1980 prices).

SUMMARY AND CONCLUSIONS

This study is the first to systematically analyze the long-term trends and relationships among external threat, public opinion, and defense spending. The descriptive sections of the study emphasize that, aside from Soviet nuclear capability, which has been at least balanced by the U.S. nuclear deterrent, the United States has been secure from imminent threats of conquest or widespread destruction for many decades. Yet, despite this long history of security, for most of the postwar period the

American public has been highly concerned with foreign problems. The instances of highest concern have generally been during U.S. involvements in overseas wars and international crises involving U.S. overseas interests. Public concern with international problems began a slow decline in the late 1960s, reached its nadir in the mid-1970s, and began to increase in 1976. The latest data show a rapid increase during the first quarter of 1979. In general, the long-term stability of the data supports Caspary's (1970) finding that the U.S. foreign policy "mood" is not volatile.

U.S. public support for defense spending tends to be more volatile than public concern for international problems. However, this variable reflects many exogenous factors. Public concern for the defense of the nation is likely to reflect existing defense capability, Government military spending, and levels of external threat. Therefore, the level of support for defense spending is likely to be as volatile as the exogenous variables and also vary with the degree of government responsiveness to defense needs.

Real U.S. defense spending, measured by a national defense consumption series at constant 1957 prices, indicates that military expenditures went through volatile changes during the 1930s and 1940s but remained relatively stable after 1957. This finding runs counter to the popular myth that defense spending has been declining. However, defense as a ratio of total federal spending and GNP did decline rapidly during the post-Vietnam period. A similar decline can be observed in the number of active military personnel in U.S. armed forces which can be partly attributed to the reorganization of the military to an all-volunteer basis.

The examination of all the above trends reveals that, after the Vietnam deescalation, with the reduction of international tension levels affecting U.S. overseas interests during the 1970s, public concern for international problems declined. Low public support for defense spending during the 1970s reflects that decline, but in recent years there has been a resurgence of public support for defense spending that has outpaced the growth of the public concern for international problems. This lag may be due to the severity of economic problems facing Americans. Inflation and energy problems have been dominating the public's concerns, but this does not mean that international problems are considered unimportant. Therefore, in light of the continuing severity of economic problems, the recent *growth* in national concern indicated by the public opinion polls may be far more significant than their low *levels* imply.

The planned growth in real defense spending of the United States for the 1980s probably reflects the growing public support for defense as well as the perception of a need for greater defense spending on the part of U.S. decision-makers. If so, this statement runs counter to findings of previous research, which found no direct relationship between defense spending and public opinion (Russett, 1972a; Huntington, 1961).

In order to provide a more systematic analysis of the relationships among variables, a relatively simple model of U.S. defense spending was specified. The model consisted of three equations linking changes in defense spending to public opinion, international tensions, and U.S. war involvement. In addition, indicators of defense capability (measured by military manpower) and government concern for defense (measured by percent share of defense in federal outlays) were linked exogenously to the model. The three equations were estimated using annual data for 1935-1976. The statistical results are not strong in all cases but are consistent with all the hypothesized linkages. That is, all the estimated coefficients have the correct signs and six out of eight have t-statistics greater than two. Specifically, the estimated model provides further support for linkage among the four central concepts of this study: actual external threats, public perception of threats, public support for defense spending, and actual change in defense spending.

Finally, the model's forecasting performance was tested using a number of scenarios. It was found that, although the model apparently has certain biases and probably cannot forecast scenarios representing extreme cases of tension and war, its forecasting capability for more normal scenarios is promising. In fact, its most likely forecast for the 1980s appears highly plausible. This baseline forecast was based on a scenario of continued low international tensions and no U.S. war involvement. The resulting forecast indicates that real U.S. defense spending will grow at about 3.2% per year. At this rate, the DoD budget will grow from 129 million dollars in 1980 to 177 billion in 1990 (at 1980 prices).

NOTES

1. Among empirical studies of military spending, only Russett (1972a, 1974), Huntington (1961), and Ostrom (1978) have analyzed public opinion as an explanatory variable. Huntington's work, however, was related only to a very brief period in U.S. history and Ostrom's limited analysis involved using a binary dummy variable in place of actual public opinion data.

2. Russett (1972a) used only bivariate analysis and post-World War II defense spending data. Another problem with his analysis was that he used a *relative* measure of defense spending rather than an absolute measure. Finally, he did not use any coherent framework or structural model to analyze his data.

3. This chapter is part of a much larger continuing study on defense spending started by the author in 1972. For previous publications see Abolfathi and Park (1975) and Abolfathi (1979).

4. The annual report of the Secretary of Defense (Brown, 1979) is the most comprehensive of the annual posture statements. The reports by the various Chiefs of armed forces tend to be more specialized and generally avoid discussing general threats to the United States.

5. Military threats to the United States are often distinguished by only the terms "strategic" and "theater." The latter refers to theaters of military operations, such as the Central European theater or the Southeast Asian theater, whereas the former is used to identify intercontinental nuclear threats. However, there are many areas in which the two concepts overlap (Deitchman, 1969: 32). For the evolution of U.S. strategic policy with respect to the western hemisphere see, Child (1979). For a much broader concept of strategic threat in the context of the present international system, see Freedman (1979).

6. The alarmists claims have been analyzed by many historians and political scientists. For a recent critical review of the claims see Kistiakowsky (1979).

7. Soviet historians, such as Sivachev and Yakovlev (1979), while sometimes admitting Soviet military inferiority during the early postwar years, downplay its significance by pointing out the complexity of the U.S.-Soviet balance of power. However, Western analysts generally agree that the strategic balance favored the United States at least through the early 1960s (Kistiakowsky, 1979; Collins and Cordesman, 1978).

8. In recent years some of the assumptions behind the MAD system have been rejected by critics of U.S.-Soviet detente. These critics believe that even marginal "strategic superiority" by the Soviet Union could enable it to blackmail the West. Moreover, they contend that Soviet strategists have never accepted the MAD system and actively plan to win a nuclear war (rummel, 1976; Pipes, 1978; Keegan, 1977). However, for deterrent purposes, U.S. strategic forces do not appear to be inferior to those of the Soviet Union, and so far no convincing evidence exists to support the contention that the Soviet Union believes a nuclear world war would have a less destructive impact on the Socialist countries than on the West. In fact, given the geographic concentration of the urban, developed, and industrial regions of USSR it appears likely that the Soviet Union will suffer more severely in a nuclear war (Lewis, 1979).

9. The United States and Japan had conflicts of interests over many issues including immigration of Japanese nationals to the United States, trade restrictions in China and Southeast Asia, maritime ambitions in the Pacific, and Japanese aggressions on the Asian mainland (DE Conde, 1971; Feis, 1950).

10. See, for instance, Walton (1973), Horowitz (1967), Payne (1970), and Keegan (1977).

11. With minor qualifications, the same could be said of World War II. It is the author's opinion that the Axis threat to the United States has been greatly exaggerated (Abolfathi, 1978). As Russett (1972b) has argued, there was "no clear and present danger" to the security of the U.S. mainland. Moreover, it is now widely accepted by many historians that neither Japan nor Germany saw war with the United States as a winning proposition. Logistical problems alone made war with the United States impossible to win. Therefore, the major reasons for U.S. involvement were overseas interests rather than security of the U.S. mainland.

12. A major advantage of using dummy variables in model building is that their coding requires relatively little investment of resources of a project. In principle, there can be no difference between *dummy* and *ordinal* variables. However, dummy variables gave greater flexibility for use in statistical analysis. For instance, a dummy

variable with three values (such as zero, one, and two) can be replaced by two dummy intercept variables each with values of zero and one. In this study, I have used the term "dummy" instead of "ordinal" variable in order to emphasize the tentativeness of the measurement procedure and their weak theoretical groundings. For the use of dummy variables in a variety of roles, see Singh et al. (1977: 113-114).

13. In cases where a war was experienced for roughly half a year or less, the appropriate code was reduced by dividing it by two. For example, if a limited war was experienced for only part of 1953, then the code for limited war (= one) was divided by 2 to obtain 0.5. This decision was made after an examination of the mobilization rates experienced during the first years of U.S. war involvements, which showed that a six month period is a reasonable minimum required time for a major response to a new war. Similarly, the codes for those periods of deescalation when a war was continuing at a greatly reduced scope and intensity (e.g., Vietnam, 1969-1972) were divided by two.

14. It is assumed that once a *total* war (such as World War II) begins, it absorbs most energy and attention of the nations involved and peacetime tensions become irrelevant or take a back seat to the business of winning the war. For instance, if an unlimited war breaks out between the United States and the Soviet Union, the threat to survival is likely to completely overshadow international tensions.

15. Initially the dummy variable did not include any fractions. However, in reviewing the coding it was found that there was a need for further variance at the low end of the range.

16. Although a number of more "reliable" data sets were examined, none proved adequate for a variety of reasons, most particularly the lack of face validity. Moreover, the data sets examined appeared to be inconsistent among themselves. In the author's evaluation, for forecasting purposes, it is preferable to code some variables as crude dummy variables with low intercoder reliability than to rely on supposedly reliable data which are often coded by college students with very limited interest and knowledge of the subject. For a comparison of several of these data sets, see Abolfathi (1978).

17. The conceptual developments have been highly abstract in order to accommodate cross-national analysis such as Hopple et al. (in this volume). In the author's evaluation, the concepts are not appropriate for analyzing military threats to a single country over a long time period. At any rate, the data collected so far by McClelland and his colleagues cover only a short time period. Furthermore, the data do not deal directly with public perception of threat.

18. In each survey, respondents were asked to make selections among a series of general problems, such as the economy, inflation, crime, race problems, international problems, foreign affairs, and the energy crisis. The list sometimes also included more specific problems, such as the Vietnam war, campus unrests, and corruption in government (Gallup, 1972).

19. In fact, a 1979 survey, which was released after data analyses of this study were completed, indicated that in early 1979 18% of the U.S. public were concerned with international problems. This dramatic increase could be either the result of the foreign policy setbacks that the U.S. allegedly suffered in early 1979 in Iran, South Yemen, and Afghanistan or the result of long-term trends, such as those identified by Klingberg (1979).

20. For the larger data set, see Abolfathi (1978).

21. The alternatives for dealing with missing data are generally of two types. One set of alternatives involves reducing the data matrix through either pairwise or listwise deletions. The second set of alternatives involves estimating the missing cases

by taking averages (e.g., of adjacent data elements), using related information (e.g., similar variables), or using judgmental coding. In this study, the second alternative was employed. More specific information on the procedures used to estimate missing cases is provided in Table 3.3.

22. The estimate is conservative because during 1945 U.S. defense spending was drastically reduced for the next fiscal year. This means that the lower the estimate of public support for increased defense spending in 1945 the higher its correlation with changes in defense spending.

23. The last survey available prior to the Vietnam War indicates that in December 1960 about 31% of the respondents supported *increased* defense spending. Thereafter, no surveys are available until 1969, when only 8% of respondents are recorded as supporting increased defense spending.

24. See Truman (1965), Kinnard (1977), Aliano (1975), Kistiakowsky (1979), and Huntington (1961).

25. The trends in U.S. public expenditure pattern are generally similar to those of other advanced industrial, open economies. For instance, see Stahl (1978).

26. If one uses the postwar experience of other advanced industrial, open economies as a standard, a reasonable long-term floor level for defense/GNP would be 2-3%. Very few major powers have lower rates. For various projections of U.S. defense spending, see Brown (1979), Kanter (1979), Assistant Secretary of Defense (Comptroller) (1979), Aspin (1979), and Pechman (1979).

27. The data sources are listed in the footnotes of Table 3.5.

28. For instance, during the 1978 fiscal year over 65% of the DoD budget was for procurement, operation, maintenance, and R&D. Transfer payments were less than 2% of the total budget.

29. Military personnel costs at current prices increased from 13 billion dollars in 1964 to 29 billion in 1979. This represents an increase of 123%, which is not significantly greater than the increase in the GNP deflator over the same period, which was 118%. For a major study of resource management in DoD, see Rice (1979).

30. It is possible that an increase in military manpower causes antimilitarism because of the disruptive effects of the draft on society and in turn leads to reduced public support for defense spending. However, the proportion of the public that generally supports increased military spending tends to consist largely of hard-core prodefense and highly patriotic groups who are in favor of the draft. For a detailed examination of public opinion on defense issues, see Bobrow and Wilcox (1966).

31. The bracketed terms in variables 5 and 6 are for drawing attention to the fact that these variables ideally should measure public attitude. But because adequate public opinion polls on these variable were not available, it was decided to use the variables that are outside the brackets.

32. The term "perception of adequacy of military capability" is used in the sense that, for any level of threat, there is a certain level of perceived need for military capability, which increases with the level of threat.

33. The term "perception of adequacy of government concern for defense" is used in the sense that, for any level of public perception of external threat, there is a level of perceived need for government defense effort, which increases with the level of perceived threat.

34. The term "adequacy" usually implies cost-benefit evaluation. As used in this study, it involves simpler concepts. For instance, public perception of adequacy of defense capability assumes that as defense capability increases, public concern for

external threats diminishes. Therefore, for high external threats, high defense capability is likely to be perceived as adequate and vice versa.

35. The three equations constitute a recursive model which can be optimally estimated using OLS (Johnston, 1972: 376).

36. For instance, the public opinion data are not of sufficiently high quality to allow any detrending. Also, detrending a variable such as change in defense spending violates the model's basic structure by introducing a concept of change, which may be useful in Newtonian physics but not in the present model of U.S. defense spending.

37. In general, any detrending or other means of reducing *true* autocorrelation problems requires that we first rule out *quasi*-autocorrelation (Koutsoyiannis, 1973: 211). In practice, this is only possible with highly developed models and reliable data (at least by the standards of economists). In international relations these requirements can seldom be satisfied.

38. For various assessments of likely trends during the 1980s, see Brown (1979), C.B.O. (1976), and Kegley and McGowan (1979).

39. Obviously, in reality this variable cannot exceed 100% and in practice should generally be less than 100%.

40. For various projections of U.S. defense spending, see Brown (1979), Kanter (1979), Aspin (1979), Pechman (1979), Sorrels (1976), Assistant Secretary of Defense (Comptroller) 1979), and C.B.O. (1979).

41. The July 1979 congressional public hearings on the SALT ratification have shown that there are substantial differences among the various estimates of future defense spending under no-SALT scenarios.

REFERENCES

ABOLFATHI, F. (1979) "Defense expenditures in the Persian Gulf," in W. L. Hollist (ed.) Exploring Competitive Arms Processes. New York: Marcel Dekker.
––– (1978) "External threat, public opinion, and military spending: the case of the United States since the 1930s." Prepared for delivery at the 19th Annual Meeting of the International Studies Association, Washington, DC, February 22-25.
––– (1977) Determinants of Military Spending. Ann Arbor, MI: University Microfilms.
––– J. HAYES, and R. HAYES (1979) "Trends in United States response to international crises: policy implications for the 1980s," in C. W. Kegley and P. J. McGowan (eds.) Challenges to America: United States Foreign Policy in the 1980s. Beverly Hills: Sage Publications.
ABOLFATHI, F. and T. W. PARK (1975) "Military spending in the third world," in C. Liske, W. Loehr, and J. McCamant (eds.) Comparative Foreign Policy: Issues, Theories, and Methods. Beverly Hills: Sage Publications.
AGAPOS, A. M. (1975) Government-Industry and Defense: Economics and Administration. University: Univ. of Alabama Press.
ALIANO, R. A. (1975) American Defense Policy from Eisenhower to Kennedy. Athens: Ohio Univ. Press.
ALMOND, G. A. (1960) The American People and Foreign Policy. New York: Praeger.
ASPIN, L. (1979) "The three percent solution: NATO and the U.S. defense budget." Challenge 22, 2: 22-29.

Assistant Secretary of Defense (Comptroller) (1979) National Defense Budget Estimates for FY 1980. Washington, DC: U.S. Department of Defense.

AZAR, E. E. and T. J. SLOAN (1975) "Dimensions of interaction." International studies occasional paper 8. Pittsburgh: University of Pittsburgh.

BLECHMAN, B. M. and S. S. KAPLAN (1978) Force Without War. Washington, DC: Brookings Institution.

BOBROW, D. B. and A. R. WILCOX (1966) "Dimensions of defense opinion: the American public." Peace Research Society (International) papers 6: 101-142.

BROWN, H. (1979) Department of Defense Annual Report, Fiscal Year 1980. Washington, DC: U.S. Government Printing Office.

CACI (1976) Planning for Problems in Crisis Management. Arlington, VA: CACI, Inc.-Federal.

CASPARY, W. R. (1970) "The mood theory: a study of public opinion and foreign policy." American Political Science Review 64, 2: 536-547.

C.B.O. (1979) Five Year Budget Projections and Alternative Budgetary Strategies for Fiscal Years 1980-1984. Washington, DC: Congressional Budget Office.

––– (1976) International Political Assumptions in Defense Posture Statements. Washington, DC: Congressional Budget Office.

CHILD, J. (1979) "From 'color' to 'rainbow': U.S. strategic planning for Latin America 1919-1948." Journal of Interamerican Studies 21, 2: 233-259.

CLEMENS, D. S. (1970) Yalta. New York: Oxford Univ. Press.

COLLINS, J. M. and A. H. CORDESMAN (1978) Imbalance of Power: Shifting U.S.-Soviet Military Strengths. San Rafael, CA: Presido Press.

COMMITTEE on the Present Danger (1979) Public Attitudes on Salt II. Washington, DC: Committee on the Present Danger.

COWARD, H. R. (1964) Military Technology in Developing Countries. Cambridge, MA: Center for International Studies, Massachusetts Institute of Technology.

DE CONDE, A. (1971) A History of American Foreign Policy. New York: Charles Scribner's.

DEITCHMAN, S. J. (1969) Limited War and American Defense Policy. Cambridge, MA: M.I.T.

DONNELLY, C. and B. GUNSTON (1978) Soviet Ground and Rocket Forces. New York: Paradise Press.

FEIS, H. (1950) The Road to Pearl Harbor. Princeton, NJ: Princeton Univ. Press.

FREEDMAN, L. (1979) "Has strategy reached a dead-end?" Futures 11, 2: 122-131.

GALLUP, G. H. (1972) The Gallup Poll: Public Opinion 1935-1971. New York: Random House.

GAMSON, W. A. and A. MODIGLIANI (1971) Untangling the Cold War: A Strategy for Testing Rival Theories. Boston: Little, Brown.

GANSLER, J. S. (1979) "The nation effectively achieves its objectives." Defense Management Journal 15, 2.

GOLDMAN, K. (1972) "Bipolarization and tension in the international system." Cooperation and Conflict 7: 37-63.

HOLLIST, W. L. (1977) "An analysis of arms processes in the United States and the Soviet Union." International Studies Quarterly 21, 3: 503-528.

HOROWITZ, D. (1967) From Yalta to Vietnam: American Foreign Policy in the Cold War. London: Penguin.

HUNTINGTON, S. P. (1961) The Common Defense: Strategic Programs in National Politics. New York: Columbia Univ. Press.

JOHNSTON, J. (1972) Econometric Methods. New York: McGraw-Hill.

KANTER, H. (1979) "The current budget debate: implications for defense." Strategic Review 7, 2: 40-49.
KEEGAN, G. J. (1977) "New assessment put on Soviet threat." Aviation Week and Space Technology (March 28): 38-48.
KEGLEY, C. W. and P. J. McGOWAN [eds.] (1979) Challenges to America: United States Foreign Policy in the 1980s. Beverly Hills: Sage Publications.
KEGLEY, C. W., and E. R. WITTKOPF (1979) American Foreign Policy: Pattern and Process. New York: St. Martin's.
KENNEDY, G. (1975) The Economics of Defense. Totowa, NJ: Rowman Littlefield.
KINNARD, D. (1977) President Eisenhower and Strategy Management. Lexington, KY: Univ. Press of Kentucky.
KISTIAKOWSKY, G. B. (1979) "False alarm: the story behind Salt II." New York Review of Books 26, 4: 33-38.
KLINGBERG, F. L. (1979) "Cyclical trends in American foreign policy: moods and their policy implications," in C. W. Kegley and P. J. McGowan (eds.) Challenges to America: United States Foreign Policy in the 1980s. Beverly Hills: Sage Publications.
KOEHLER, J. E. and R. B. PIRIE (1977) Planning U.S. General Purpose Forces: Overview. Washington, DC: Congressional Budget Office.
KOUTSOYIANNIS, A. (1973) Theory of Econometrics. London: Macmillan.
LADD, E. C., M. POTTER, L. BASILICK, S. DANIELS, and D. SUSZKIW (1979) "The polls: taxing and spending." Public Opinion Quarterly 43, 1: 126-135.
LEVERING, R. B. (1978) The Public and American Foreign Policy, 1918-1978. New York: William Morrow.
LEWIS, K. N. (1979) "The prompt and delayed effects of nuclear war." Scientific American 241, 1: 35-47.
LIDDELL HART, B. H. (1968) Strategy: The Indirect approach. London: Faber & Faber.
Louis Harris and Associates, Inc. (1976) The Harris Survey Yearbook of Public Opinion 1972: A Compendium of Current American Attitudes. New York: Louis Harris & Associates.
----- (1975) The Harris Survey Yearbook of Public Opinion 1971: A Compendium of Current American Attitudes. New York: Louis Harris & Associates.
----- (1971) The Harris Survey Yearbook of Public Opinion 1970: A Compendium of Current American Attitudes. New York: Louis Harris & Associates.
LOUIS, W. R. (1978) Imperialism at Bay: The United States and the Decolonization of the British Empire, 1941-1945. New York: Oxford Univ. Press.
McCLELLAND, C. A. (1977) "The anticipation of international crises: prospects for theory and research." International Studies Quarterly 21: 15-38.
-----, P. J. McGOWAN, and W. R. MARTIN (1976) Threat, Conflict, and Committment: Final Report of the Threat Recognition and Analysis Project. Los Angeles: International Relations Research Institute, University of Southern California.
MEE, C. L. (1975) Meeting at Potsdam. New York: Dell.
MENAUL, S.W.B. and B. GUNSTON (1977) Soviet War Planes. New York: Paradise Press.
OSTROM, C. W. (1978) "A reactive linkage model of the U.S. defense expenditure policy-making process." American Political Science Review, 72, 3: 941-958.
----- (1977) "Evaluating alternative foreign policy decision-making models." Journal of Conflict Resolution 21, 2: 235-266.
PAUL, R. A. (1973) American Military Commitments Abroad. New Brunswick, NJ: Rutgers Univ. Press.

PAYNE, J. L. (1970) The American Threat: The Fear of War as an Instrument of Foreign Policy. Chicago: Markham.

PECHMAN, J. A. [ed.] (n.d.) Setting National priorities: The 1980 Budget. Washington, DC: Brookings Institution.

PIPES, R. E. (1978) "Nuclear weapons policy questioned." Aviation Week and Space Technology (November 6): 62-63.

RATTINGER, H. (1975) "Armaments, detente, and bureaucracy: the case of the arms race in Europe." Journal of Conflict Resolution 19, 4: 571-595.

RICE, D. B. (1979) Defense Resource Management Study: A Report Requested by the President and Submitted to the Secretary of Defense. Washington, DC: U.S. Government Printing Office.

RICHARDSON, L. F. (1960) Arms and Insecurity. Chicago: Quadrangle.

RIELLY, J. E. (1979) "The American mood: a foreign policy of self-interest." Foreign Policy 34: 74-86.

RUMMEL, R. J. (1976) Peace Endangered: The Reality of Detente. Beverly Hills: Sage Publications.

RUSSETT, B. (1975) "The Americans' retreat from world power." Political Science Quarterly 90, 1: 1-23.

——— (1974) "The revolt of the masses: public opinion on military expenditures," in J. P. Lovell and P. S. Kronenberg (eds.) New Civil-Military Relations: The agonies of Adjustment to Post-Vietnam Realities. New Brunswick, NJ: Transaction Books.

——— (1972a) "The revolt of the masses: public opinion on military expenditures," in Russett (ed.) Peace, War and Numbers Beverly Hills: Sage Publications.

——— (1972b) No Clear and Present Danger. New York: Harper & Row.

——— (1970) What Price Vigilance? The Burdens of National Defense. New Haven, CT: Yale Univ. Press.

SCOTT, W. S. (1979) "Tightening the reins on contract costs and schedules." Defense Management Journal 15, 2: 28-33.

SINGH, S., J. de VRIES, J.C.L. HULLEY, and P. YEUNG (1977) Coffee, Tea, and Cocoa: Market Prospects and Development Lending. Washington, DC: World Bank.

SIVACHEV, N. V. and N. N. YAKOVLEV (1979) Russia and the United States: U.S.-Soviet Relations from the Soviet Point of View. Chicago: Univ. of Chicago Press.

SORRELS, C. A. (1976) SALT and the U.S. Strategic Forces Budget. Washington, DC: Congressional Budget Office.

STAHL, I. (1978) "Expansion of the public sector." Skandinaviska Enskilda, Quarterly Review 3, 4: 98-104.

STEADMAN, R. C. (1978) Report to the Secretary of Defense on the National Military Command Structure. Washington, DC: Department of Defense.

STRAUSS, R. P. (1972) "An adaptive expectations model of East-West arms race." Peace Research Society (International) Papers 19: 28-34.

TAYLOR, L. B. (1974) Financial Management of the Vietnam Conflict, 1962-1972. Washington, DC: U.S. Government Printing Office.

TRUMAN, H. S (1965) Years of Trial and Hope: Memoirs by Harry S Truman, Vol. 2. New York: Signet.

TUCKER, R. W. (1972) A New Isolationism: Threat or Promise? Washington, DC: Potomac Associates.

U.S. Department of Commerce (1978) Statistical abstract of the United States 1977. Washington, DC: U.S. Government Printing Office.

――― (1975) Historical Statistics of the United States—Colonial Times to 1970. Washington, DC: U.S. Government Printing Office.
U.S. Department of Defense (1979) Department of Defense Annual Report, Fiscal Year 1980. Washington, DC: U.S. Department of Defense.
――― U.S. Department of Defense (1979) Department of Defense Annual Report, Fiscal Year 1980. Washington, DC: U.S. Department of Defense.
――― (1978) Department of Defense Annual Report, Fiscal Year 1979. Washington, DC: U.S. Department of Defense.
WALTON, R. J. (1973) Cold War and Counter-Revolution: The Foreign Policy of John F. Kennedy. Baltimore, MD: Penguin.
WATTS, W. and L. A. FREE (1976) "Nationalism not isolationism: a new national survey." Foreign Policy 24: 3-26.

PART II

WEAPONS AND FOREIGN POLICY

Chapter 4

DETERMINANTS OF FRENCH ARMS SALES: SECURITY IMPLICATIONS

EDWARD A. KOLODZIEJ
University of Illinois

This chapter has two general purposes. The first, discussed in the first section below, is to demonstrate the increasing dependency of the French economy and military policy on arms transfers and it challenges widely held assumptions among analysts of arms transfers who minimize French dependence (BDM Corporation, 1977; 11; Cahn et al., 1977: 64-65; Farley et al., 1978: 12-13; Cauchie, 1977: 23-27; U.S., Congressional Research Service, 1977: 65-67). The second purpose, which the remainder of this chapter addresses, is to explore the implications of the French case for policy-makers and students of international relations interested in

EDITORS' NOTE: This chapter was first received for review on May 7, 1979. The version published here was received July 6, 1979.

AUTHOR'S NOTE: Data for this chapter are drawn principally from original French sources. These primarily comprise parliamentary reports since administrative and bureaucratic materials, like the annual review of defense expenditures and military transfers published by the Arms Control and Disarmament Agency, are not readily available in France.
 The materials cited in the chapter are available in the United States at depository libraries of French governmental publications. The Library of Congress is likely to be the most reliable source for interlibrary loan. In France, the parliamentary reports can be purchased or photocopied at the *Journal Officiel,* 26 rue Desaix, Paris 75732. Also helpful for statistical materials on the economy and industry is Documentation Française, 31 Quai Voltaire, Paris 75340.
 Materials cited in this chapter are available by writing the author.

developing a theoretical framework to explain arms transfers as a subsystem of the international system.

ARMS TRANSFERS AND DEPENDENCY

Exports, Arms Sales, and Growing Economic Dependency on Foreign Commerce

French Adaptation to Systemic Change. The significance of arms sales for the French economy, including continued growth, technological development, balance of payments equilibrium, access to raw materials, and high employment can be better understood if the sale of arms is viewed against the revolutionary changes that have occurred in the structure and composition of the French economy since World War II. Most prominent among these have been the rapid modernization and industrialization of the French economy and its progressive, but relentless, opening to world competition. The Fourth and Fifth Republics have consistently nurtured these changes. They are presently central to the economic reform policies of the Barre government. Agriculture was mechanized and holdings consolidated to increase efficiency in production, making French agriculture competitive in world markets. Underutilized farm labor was attracted to the cities to fuel the industrial expansion. The proportion of the population engaged in agriculture fell from approximately one-fifth of the population at the end of World War II to 7.3% in 1977. Foreign workers, encouraged by the economic expansion, swelled the labor force, reaching a total of 1.9 million workers by the start of 1978 (*Le Monde*, 1977: 48).[1]

French economic growth in the 1960s was the highest in Western Europe. Average growth between 1960 and 1972 was 5.8%. Respective growth rates during the same period for the United States, the Federal Republic of Germany, and Great Britain were 4.1, 4.5, and 2.7% (France, INSEE, 1976: 81). French acceptance of the European Economic Community, as President Charles de Gaulle repeatedly observed (DeGaulle, 1970: 139-210), marked a sharp departure from centuries of protectionist policies. If French agriculture received privileged status within the EEC through protective tariffs and special levies on community states (like Germany, which imported agricultural foodstuffs on the world market), French industry was also forced to face heightened competition from within the community, most pointedly from Germany, as compensation for its support of the common agricultural policy and, gradually, with the decrease of world customs duties, from outside the EEC.

Based on figures supplied by France to the International Monetary Fund, the ratio of imports and exports to GNP has progressively grown. Table 4.1 presents selected figures over the twenty-year period from 1955

TABLE 4.1   Ratio of French Imports and Exports
to Gross National Product, 1955, 1965, 1975

(in billions of francs)

		1955	1965	1975
(a)	Exports	17.36	50.24	227.2
(b)	Imports	16.74	51.27	231.18
(c)	Gnp	172.2	489.8	1,442.4
*RATIO in %: (a) + (b) / (c)		20	21	32

*Rounded to nearest 1%.
Source: International Monetary Fund, *International Financial Statistics: 1977, Supplement, Annual Data: 1952-1976* XXI, 5 (May 1977): 132.

to 1975. In 1955 exports and imports were 20% of GNP. This percentage slightly increased to 21% a decade later, but jumped to almost one-third of GNP in 1975, a significant increase in the volume of exchanges relative to national production. The volume of exports and imports increased, respectively, 57.2 and 58.8% between 1970 and 1976. Exports increased an average of 17% each year.

Since the oil crisis of late 1973, however, the French economy has faced increasing difficulty in maintaining its previous momentum. It is within this context of a weakening world competitive position that, as the discussion below suggests, France's success in selling arms assumes importance. Economic growth, measured in gross interior product,* slowed to 4.8% in 1975 and slipped to 3% in 1976 (*Le Monde*, 1977: 46). Meanwhile, consumer prices based on 1970 prices increased 16 points on the index between 1974 and 1975 and 14 points a year later (IMF, 1977: 131-132). Unemployment reached its highest level in the 1970s in the second half of 1977, topping the one million mark (*Le Monde*, 1977: 50).

A worsening trade posture aggravated these symptoms of stagflation—lower economic growth, inflation, and high unemployment. The price of oil, on which more than two-thirds of France's energy needs depend, quadrupled between 1973 and 1976. France's energy deficit in 1976 was 60 billion francs. This contrasted with a deficit of 18 billion francs in 1973 (France, INSEE, 1977a: 3-58). The value of oil imports was 9.4% of French imports in 1973; it rose to 18% three years later although the monthly volume of oil imports increased by only 12.7% due to stringent conservation measures instituted by the government and private industry (France, INSEE, 1976: 6). To offset these charges efforts were increased by the government to stimulate exports. Results were mixed. Exports expanded spectacularly by 36.7% from 1973 to 1974. This was the highest

*Refers to a French measure that roughly corresponds to GNT.

increase in one year in over a decade. Increased competition from abroad and an emerging world recession narrowed, however, the possibility of expanding exports and of achieving a positive balance of payments position. Exports grew only 2.3% in 1975 and 20.5% in 1976. The commercial deficits for 1974 and 1976 reached record highs of 32.13 billion francs and 34.88 billion francs, respectively (IMF, 1977: 132).

The poor showing in the previously strong sectors of agricultural products and consumer goods partly explained these deficits. Surpluses of six billion francs and two billion francs in 1974 and 1975 were transformed into deficits of 600 million francs in 1976 and 4.4 billion francs in the first half of 1977 (France, INSEE, 1977a: 7). Except for automobile sales that increased by 53% for 1974 and 1976, consumer goods exports that had before held strong against foreign competition stagnated, especially for textiles, wood, and paper products (France, Douanes, 1976). Normally a supplier of consumer goods to Italy and Germany, France found itself in stiff competition with these states in sectors that had once contributed substantially to its commercial balance. Deficits in various financial transactions, including salary transfers of foreign workers, licenses, and royalties on patents held abroad, also doubled from 5,665 million francs in 1972 to 11,947 and 11,204, respectively, in 1974 and 1975. To finance these deficits and to encourage the expansion of exports, while holding domestic demand and wages down under a retrenchment plan articulated by Prime Minister Raymond Barre, the government encouraged the advancement of credits to foreign clients and borrowing by private companies to cover the nation's balance of payments deficit. Between 1970 and 1974 foreign credits amounted to 3 billion francs. These rose to 10 billion francs in 1975 and nearly 16 billion francs a year later. Borrowing followed a similar upward trend, amounting to 13 billion francs in 1974, 11.6 billion in 1975, and 21.5 billion francs in 1976 (France, INSEE, 1977a: 16). This deteriorating position led one analyst to conclude that "a systematic recourse to indebtedness cannot be perpetuated ... without a loss of independence.... [I]n the face of strong multinational interdependence, it is a question ... of being aware of the new conditions of the world economy in order to analyze the mechanisms of disorder and to define remedies. This calls for a psychological leap and a mutation of modes of thought" (*Le Monde*, December 13, 1977).

Some clear steps, if not a leap, in restructuring French foreign commerce can be detected in the advances made in exports of capital goods and in the nurturing of new partners in the Third World, two areas where arms sales have played an important role. Between 1974 and 1976, capital exports increased by 48% from 51.2 billion francs to 76 billion francs. The geographic structure of France's commercial transactions was also perceptibly modified as it widened the base of its commercial transactions. As Table 4.2 reveals, losses in trade with OECD and EEC states were partly offset by augmenting sales, especially of capital goods and arms, to OPEC countries in the Middle East. Slight increases were also recorded for the socialist states of Eastern Europe and the Third World. It is largely in these areas that many experts have argued that French trading relations should be redirected (Garcia, 1977). While the proportion of trade with OECD and EEC states fell from 73.8% in 1970 to 69.7% in 1976, trade with other states grew from 26.2 to 30.2%.

Arms Sales and French Economic Dependence. The significance of French arms transfers can now be more clearly understood against the background of the steady economic growth of the 1960s and the more erratic expansion of the 1970s. Table 4.3 presents figures for the delivery of French air, ground, naval, and electrical equipment.[2] Only military transfers are included. Excluded are associated materials of war, largely composed of civilian aviation materials, that must also be authorized for export under French law as materials of war. Arms exports increased from 2,081 million francs in 1965 to 11,640 in 1976, that is, from $421.50 million to $2,435.35 million. Air equipment accounted for two-thirds of all sales. Ground, electrical, and naval sales followed in order, representing on the average 18, 9, and 6% of all sales, respectively. Aeronautical sales averaged 20% each year; ground, 22%; and electronics, 24%. Average growth of naval equipment is more difficult to assess. Naval exports and production oscillated widely. The average growth rate of 97% is deceptive, obscuring chronic underemployment of capital and labor in naval construction works and the presence of increased world competition. The growth of military exports was 18%. This average approximated not only the average of over-all exports of 17%, noted above, but also the average increase in capital goods of 20% during the period. The correlation

TABLE 4.2 Structure of French Exports by Geographic Areas as a Percentage of the Total

	1970	*1972*	*1974*	*1976*
OECD of which EEC	73.8	76.9	75.2	69.7
	53.6	56.0	53.2	50.5
Others of which OPEC	26.2	23.1	24.8	30.2
	5.3	4.4	5.9	8.0
Socialist states	4.1	3.9	4.1	5.6
Developing states	16.8	14.8	14.8	16.6

Source: OCDE, *Etudes Economiques, France,* (December 1977): 24.

between total exports and arms sales between 1965 and 1976 is particularly striking; it is .92, within a probability of error of less than 1%. The rates of growth of each moved in almost lockstep in this period, suggesting an interdependency and structural relation between them.

Table 4.4 presents figures from 1965 to 1976 for French exports and imports and commercial balances as well as additional information on oil imports and exports of capital goods. It also relates the impact of arms sales on these areas of foreign commercial activity. Arms exports as a percentage of total imports were greatest in 1965 and 1967. They dropped below 3.0% in the period 1969-1973. Arms exports as a percentage of total exports reached their highest period in 1976 at 4.3%. The percentage, however, was only slightly higher than the 4.2% levels reached in 1965 and 1967. The lowest period was between 1969 and 1971 when arms exports fell to 2.6% in the final year of this period. It was precisely in this middle period that a renewed drive to expand arms exports was launched under Minister of Defense Michel Debré (Debré, 1972). This resurgence bore fruit in 1972 and thereafter. It occurred, moreover, at a time when French balances and terms of trade were about to enter a period of deterioration. What has not been generally recognized, however, is that this resurgence of French arms exports brought French sales, as a percentage of total exports, to the level of a decade earlier. The implications of this point will be discussed in the second section below.

The weight added to the French commercial position by arms sales, while not predominant, was nevertheless an important buttress for the structure of French exports. France's commercial deficits, which averaged 9.5 billion francs between 1968 and 1976, would theoretically have been greater by an average of 4.43 billion francs over this period if foreign currency had not been earned through arms sales. The successful run of six consecutive months of positive trade balances registered in the first half of 1978 may also be inferred to be due to continued high arms deliveries. The principal factor explaining France's improved 1978 position were capital exports which include military goods. These amounted to a favorable balance of 1.4 billion francs in the first six months of 1978 against 2 billion francs for 1977.[3] In the three years succeeding the oil crisis of 1973, arms sales covered less than one-fifth of France's oil imports. According to unofficial French estimates,[4] arms deliveries balanced one-third of France's oil bill in 1977. While this brought the proportion of arms deliveries to oil imports to the pre-1973 level (see Table 4.4), more arms had to be sold to reach levels of a decade ago. To cover a growing oil bill, France may be tempted to sell more arms than ever before unless it can find alternative export outlets, which are as profitable.

The geographic division of French arms sales should also be noted.

TABLE 4.3 French Arms Transfer Deliveries, 1965–1976 (in millions of current francs)[a]

Materials Delivered	1965	1966	1967	1968	1969	1970	1971	1972	1973	1974	1975	1976	Average
Air	1213	1406	1418	1753	1656	1769	2080	3060	3862	4189	5000	8101	2959
% of total[b]	58	66	58	68	71	66	70	76	74	63	60	70	67
% annual change		16	—	24	-5	7	18	47	26	8	19	62	20
Ground	516[1]	534[1]	456[1]	322[1]	427[1]	4372	5722	5183[3]	774[3]	1293[4]	1353[5]	2456[6]	809
% of total	27	25	19	12	18	16	19	13	15	19	16	21	18
% annual change		-6	-15	-29	33	2	31	-9	49	67	5	82	22
Naval	23	41	280	403	101	279	94	114	284	561	838	175	266
% of total	1	2	11	16	4	10	3	3	5	8	10	2	6
% annual change		78	583	44	-75	176	-66	21	149	98	49	-79	97
Electronics	278	144	289	126	159	188	235	345	313	625	1141	908	396
% of total	13	7	12	5	7	7	8	9	6	9	14	8	9
% annual change		-48	101	-56	26	18	25	47	-9	100	82	-20	24
Total	2081	2125	2443	2594	2343	2673	2981	4037	5233	6668	8332	11640	4430
% annual change		2	15	6	-10	14	12	35	30	27	25	40	18

a. Rounded to nearest one million.
b. All percentages rounded to nearest 1%; differences due to rounding.

Sources:
1. France, ANCF (1970:12).
2. France, Senat, Commission des Finances (1972:17); Dubos (1974:134).
3. France, Senat, Commission des Finances (1974:17).
4. France, Senat, Commission des Finances (1975:27-28)
5. France, ANCDN (1976:57).
6. France, ANCDN (1977:102-103).

TABLE 4.4 French Exports and Imports, Oil Imports, and Commercial Balances Related to Arms Sales, 1965–1976 (in billions of francs)

	1965	1966	1967	1968	1969	1970	1971	1972	1973	1974	1975	1976	Average
Exports	50.24	54.22	57.01	63.70	78.81	100.52	115.25	133.39	162.46	222.07	227.20	273.24	
annual % increase		7.9	5.1	11.7	23.7	27.5	14.7	15.7	21.8	36.7	2.3	20.3	17
arms sales/exports	4.2	3.9	4.2	4.0	3.0	2.7	2.6	3.0	3.2	3.0	3.7	4.3	3.5
Imports	51.27	58.22	61.43	69.21	90.06	106.26	118.15	136.19	167.25	254.20	231.18	308.12	
annual % increase		13.6	5.5	12.7	30.0	18.0	11.2	15.3	22.8	52.0	-9.1	33.3	18.7
arms sales/imports	4.0	3.6	4.0	3.7	2.6	2.5	2.5	2.7	3.1	2.6	3.6	3.8	3.2
Oil Imports	5.37	5.43	6.45	6.85	7.44	9.31	11.98	13.60	15.77	47.20	41.61	55.20	
annual % increase		1.1	18.8	6.2	11.6	25.1	28.7	13.5	16.0	200.0	-11.8	32.7	31.1
arms sales/oil imports	.3875	.3913	.3788	.3787	.3149	.2871	.2488	.2968	.3318	.1413	.2002	.2002	
commercial balance	-1.03	-4.0	-4.42	-5.51	-11.25	-5.74	-2.9	-2.8	-4.79	-32.13	-3.98	-34.88	-9.4525
arms sales	2.081	2.125	2.443	2.594	2.343	2.673	2.981	4.037	5.344	6.668	8.332	11.64	4.430
Deficit w/out arms sales	-3.111	-6.125	-6.863	-8.104	-13.593	-8.413	-5.88	-6.837	-10.023	-38.798	-12.312	-46.520	-13.8825

Source: International Monetary Fund, *International Financial Statistics, Supplement Annual Data: 1952–1976* XXI 5 (May 1977): 131–132.

Selling weapons has been one of the principal mechanisms for reorienting trade from the developing states, especially the Middle East states of OPEC, like Saudi Arabia, Libya, and Iraq. Also included are states like the Republic of Yemen and Egypt, which have been able to draw on Saudi Arabian capital to purchase French aircraft and ground equipment. Table 4.5 groups deliveries and orders of arms from the countries of the EEC, the United States, and the rest of the world. In 1970, deliveries to European states and the United States amounted to 57% of arms exports; orders were recorded at 37%. By 1976, the spread between developed and developing states increased. Deliveries to the European states of the EEC and the United States accounted for approximately 15% of deliveries and 17% of orders. The rest of the world absorbed 85% of deliveries and 83% of the orders. Middle East orders that totaled 37% of all orders in 1970 and 17% in 1971 grew to 54% in 1974 (Pinatel, 1976: 63; Crespin and Besancon, 1977: 45-53; *LeMonde,* January 30, 1976). The increased demand for French arms by Middle East and Arab states is further suggested by the export orders recorded in 1976 by the production plants organized under the Groupement Industriel des Armements Terrestres (GIAT), which is under the authority of the Direction Technique des Armes Terrestres (DTAT). Of 1,172 million francs in orders in 1976, 922 million francs or 78.7% was earmarked for four Arab states, Morocco, Qatar, Saudi Arabia, and Yemen.

French arms sales, if measured in constant francs, also evidence real growth. The value of deliveries has increased faster than the index for industrial prices. Figure 4.1 summarizes the evolution of arms deliveries in current and constant francs. The upward curves suggest real growth in the value or production and export of arms.

The proportion of arms sales to the export of capital goods and to the capital expenditures of the armed forces, presented in Figure 4.2, also provides useful measures of the significance of arms sales for the French economy. Arms sales have recently supplied much of the momentum for the success within this sector. If capital goods exports increased 48% between 1974 and 1976, arms sales expanded by 75%. Arms exports have been at the cutting edge of the expansion of capital goods exports. On the other hand, a striking feature of Figure 4.2 is the greater role that arms sales played in capital goods exports in 1965 and 1966 than a decade later. The French economy for almost a decade was able to increase exports of nonmilitary capital goods at a faster rate than its military sales. The downturn in the economy in the middle 1970s and difficulties with agricultural products and consumer goods again accented the contribution made by arms sales to the growth and solvency of the French economy. Increased governmental efforts to expand arms exports in the late 1960s

TABLE 4.5 Percentage of Distribution of French Arms Deliveries and Orders by Geographic Region for Selected Years

	Deliveries					Orders		
	1970	1971	1974	1975	1976	1970	1971	1974	1975	1976
EEC	49	58	30.7	23.93	14.65	33	30	8.69	10.44	16.65
United States	8	–	3.7	3.25	.25	4	–	2.06	1.15	.13
Remainder of world	43	42	65.4	72.93	85.1	64	70	89.15	88.41	83.22

Source: See Table 4.3, notes 1–6.

had merely the effect up to 1976 of returning the export of arms to the levels enjoyed by the French arms industry in the middle 1960s when the production, scientific, and technological base of the industry was much less developed and purchases were heavily dependent on so-called pariah states, like Israel and South Africa. Over the twelve-year period covered by Figure 4.2, military exports averaged 14.5% of capital goods exports. If those civilian capital goods which must also be authorized for export as materials of war are included, expanded arms sales averaged 17.6% of capital exports.

When arms sales are related to the capital exports of the French defense budget, the growing divergence between France's arms production for French needs and for global demand becomes clearer. This ratio provides some measure of dependency of the French arms industry on domestic and foreign demand. Between 1965 and 1976, the trend has clearly been in the direction of greater export dependency. In 1965, French arms sales were approximately 20% of capital expenditures. The proportion shifted sharply after 1971 and reached 54.1% in 1976.

The French military budget has not been able to assure the expansion of the arms industry, a point elaborated upon below; much less has it been able to maintain the level of spending in constant francs that was reached at the end of 1960, culminating in 1968 when student and worker protests forced a reordering of governmental priorities and a reduction of resources devoted to military expenditures. Expenditures for defense fell from 4.3% of GNP to 3.1% between 1965 and 1976. The proportion of the government's budget devoted to defense also fell from an average of 20.1% in the decade between 1958 and 1967 to 19.6% during the following decade.

More significantly, expenditures for operations absorbed an increasingly greater percentage of the defense budget, largely in response to heightened demands from army conscripts and professional cadres for better social and living conditions. In 1965, when a state of normalcy had returned to the French army after the withdrawal from Algeria, the operational and capital sectors of the defense budget were divided almost equally. Thereafter, and particularly after the May 1968 events, the operational budget grew, rising to 59% of the defense budget in 1977 with capital expenditures falling correspondingly to 41%. In terms of 1970 constant francs, the capital budget has also fallen. In the six-year period from 1965 to 1970, military capital expenditures averaged 13.7 billion francs each year; in the second six-year period, they average 12.9 billion francs (France, ANCON, 1977: 5-6; IMF, 1977: 131-132).

The dependency of the French aircraft industry on foreign military exports is particularly marked. In 1976, 53% or 10,400 million francs of the business affairs of the industry were attributable to exports. Military

FIGURE 4.1 French Arms Deliveries, 1965-1977, Measured in Current and Constant Francs (in billions of francs)

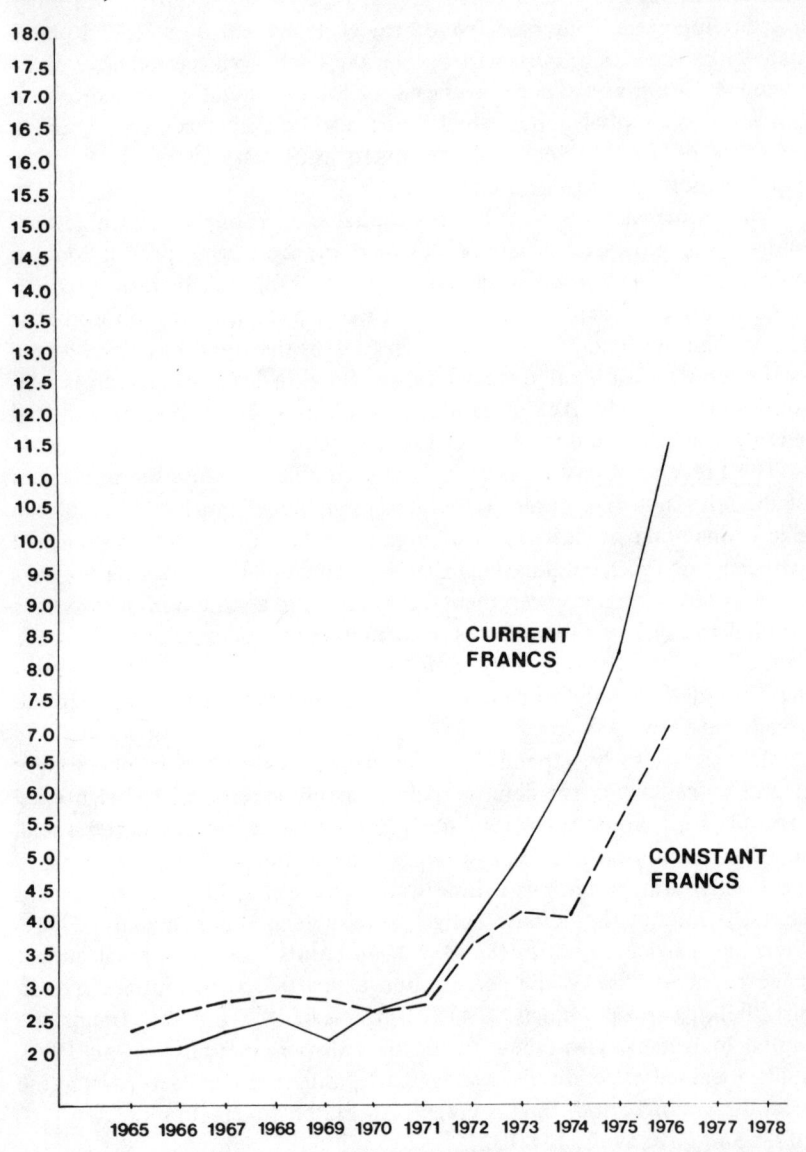

148

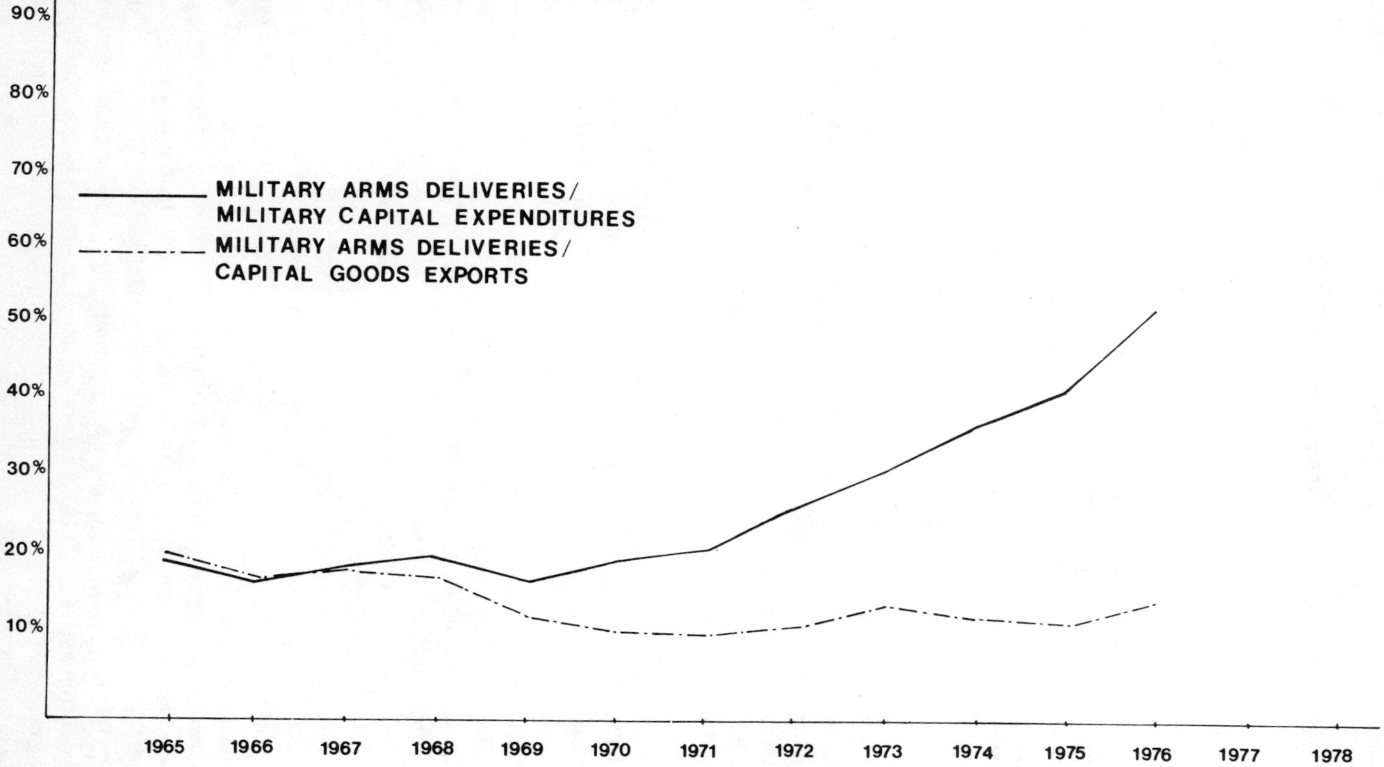

FIGURE 4.2 Ratios (1) of Military Arms Deliveries to Military Capital Expenditures and (2) of Military Arms Deliveries to Capital Goods Exports, 1965-1977

exports composed 78% of these exports or 8,112 million francs (*Le Monde* April 14, 1977). The average of military to civilian exports was 76% between 1965 and 1976. The business receipts of each of the four principal components of the aviation industry reflected the emphasis on exports. In 1975, for example, military sales accounted for 1,974.8 million francs or 27% of Aérospatiale's business affairs. SNECMA and its affiliates, the major producer of airplane engines, registered 630 million francs in exports or 33% of its business affairs. Almost all of exports of Matra, a private firm specializing in tactical missiles and electronic equipment, were for military equipment. These amounted to 85% of its exports of 234 million francs or 199 million francs (France, ASCF, 1977: 95-97; France, ANCON, 1976: 50-52).

The Dassault-Bréguet group, which is the most important producer of advanced military equipment, presents the most interesting case. As Table 4.6 suggests, the ratio of military exports to total business affairs has never fallen below 38% (1971) and has topped 60% in three of the six years since 1971. In 1975 and 1976, 60 and 77%, respectively, of the business affairs of Dassault-Bréguet arose from exports.

The employment provided by the armaments industry further suggests its importance to the French economy and to the social and political stability of the nation. Official estimates place employment between 270,000 and 280,000 (France, ANCD, 1977: 95-97; France, ANCON, 1976: 50-52). Personnel may be divided into one of three industrial and management groupings, including state-run or -administered units under the over-all control of the Délégation Général pour l'Armement (formerly Délégation Ministerielle pour l'Armement), nationalized associations (SNIAS, SNECMA, and SNPE), and private firms. The major producers among the latter include Aviations Dassault-Bréguet, Matra, Thomson-Hotchkiss-Brandt (and affiliate Thomson-CSF), Panhard and Levassor, Creusot-Loire, Turbomeca, and Berliet.[5]

A recent parliamentary report cites approximately 75,000 persons working for DGA. Of these, most were concentrated in four directorates. Direction Techniques des Armaments Terrestres (DTAT, 22,222), Direction Techniques des Construction Navale (DTCN, 33,093), Direction des Recherches et Moyens d'Essais (DRME, 4,217). Another 164,000 were distributed among a number of industrial sectors, including aerospace (78,000), electronics (40,000), mechanical and metallurgical materials (40,000), navel construction other than DTCN (3,000), and munitions (3,000). Finally, 12,000 were organized into the nuclear armaments industry and 20,000 others were scattered in diverse fields. This total of approximately 270,000 personnel does not include an estimated 35,000 workers in small subcontracting firms that service the armaments industry.

TABLE 4.6 Ratio of Civil and Military Exports to
Business Affairs of Aviations Marcel Dassault-Bréguet
Aviation, 1971–1976 (in millions of francs)

	Business Affairs	Civilian Exports	Percentage	Military Exports	Percentage
1971	1756	105	6.0	680	38.7
1972	2173	142	6.5	1363	62.7
1973	3460	225	6.5	2155	62.3
1974	3655	357	10.2	1583	43.3
1975	4258	409	9.6	2153	50.6
1976	5928	428	7.2	4121	69.5

Source: France, Assemblée Nationale, Commission des Finances de l'Economie Générale, *Rapport sur le projet de loi de finances pour 1978*. No. 3131 Annexe 50, Defense (Rapporteur: M. Le Theule), p. 97 and A.M. Dassault-Bréguet, *Bilans 1973, 1974, 1975*.

If these are added to the large groupings of personnel already mentioned, the present size of the French armaments industry would appear to be closer to 300,000 than to 270,000 (France, ANCD, 1976: 67, 72-73; France, ANCDN, 1975: 46-47).

The geographic distribution of the armaments industry should also be appreciated as a factor adding to the industry's political weight. It is widely decentralized throughout France. Sites, public and private, are roughly distributed along three axes. The first two stretch along the western and southern coasts of France where many of the naval construction works are found, such as Cherbourg, Brest, Lorient, and Toulon. The third axis cuts the country in half, starting slightly north of Paris and moving south toward Toulouse and Tarbes.[6] Approximately one-third of the personnel in the armaments industry is concentrated in the Paris region. Aside from the major producers, noted above, who also have their operations decentralized throughout France, over 1,000 other smaller firms are estimated to be engaged in varying proportions in armaments production (C.L.I.C.A.N., 1977: 53). The decentralization of firms, personnel, and communities associated with the defense industry creates a broad base of interest and potential support for the arms industry and pressure for a strong export policy.

The precise number of personnel working for exports is more difficult to determine than the number working within the arms industry since the size of the industry has not grown substantially in the past decade. The proportion of labor, capital, and state investment devoted to the export of arms has, however, shifted. Varying estimates confuse the picture. These range from a low of 50,000 to a high of approximately 93,000; others fall within these figures.[7] These estimates would appear to underestimate the recent reexpansion of French arms sales abroad. The ratio of military exports to the business affairs of the industry was calculated to be 32% in 1975, 36% in 1976, and approximately 40% in 1977 (France, ANCDN, 1977: 102). These percentages would suggest that personnel working for exports were closer in number to 110,000 to 120,000 when the figures noted in public statements by officials or in governmental reports. This is not a negligible number when viewed against the background of relatively high unemployment.

The structure of arms orders, especially those recorded in the past three years, also indicates that France's arms policy can be restricted in the immediate future only if the government is willing to accept the serious negative economic consequences of such a decision and the political liabilities of broken contracts with foreign clients. President Giscard d'Estaing hinted on taking office that he would curb arms sales. Since then he has discreetely backed away from such a commitment as the economic difficulties of the nation have multiplied and as employment has become a major problem.

Figures 4.3A and 4.3B present arms orders for air, ground, electronic, and naval equipment between 1965 and 1977. Orders between 1972 and 1977 multiplied seven-fold from 3,867 million francs to 27,100 million francs. After a drop to 14,658 million francs in 1975, a 20% decrease, orders in 1976 again topped the previous record of 1974 and reached 18,483 million francs. Orders for 27.1 billion francs in 1977 or approximately $6 billion represent a 50% increase in military orders over the previous year. Deliveries of these weapons will require the next half decade to complete and will necessarily limit the possibility of the French government entering seriously into arms transfer negotiations that would hamper execution of these contracts. Meanwhile, arms production for export will assume a growing importance in the structure of the French economy. As suggested below, the success of French arms sales is not without its problems.

Can France Afford Success?

The French arms industry is in a seemingly paradoxical situation. On the one hand, the industry has contributed less to French GNP and exports in 1976 than a decade ago, yet the real value of its productivity, business affairs, and exports has grown. Like other export sectors of the French economy, the industry has had to run harder to keep pace with competitors and the demands made upon it. The rate of trade exchanges has accelerated, while France's balance of payments position remains precarious and its employment situation had deteriorated.

FIGURE 4.3A Orders for Military Equipment,
1965-1977: Sales of Ground, Naval, and Electronic
Equipment (in millions of current francs)

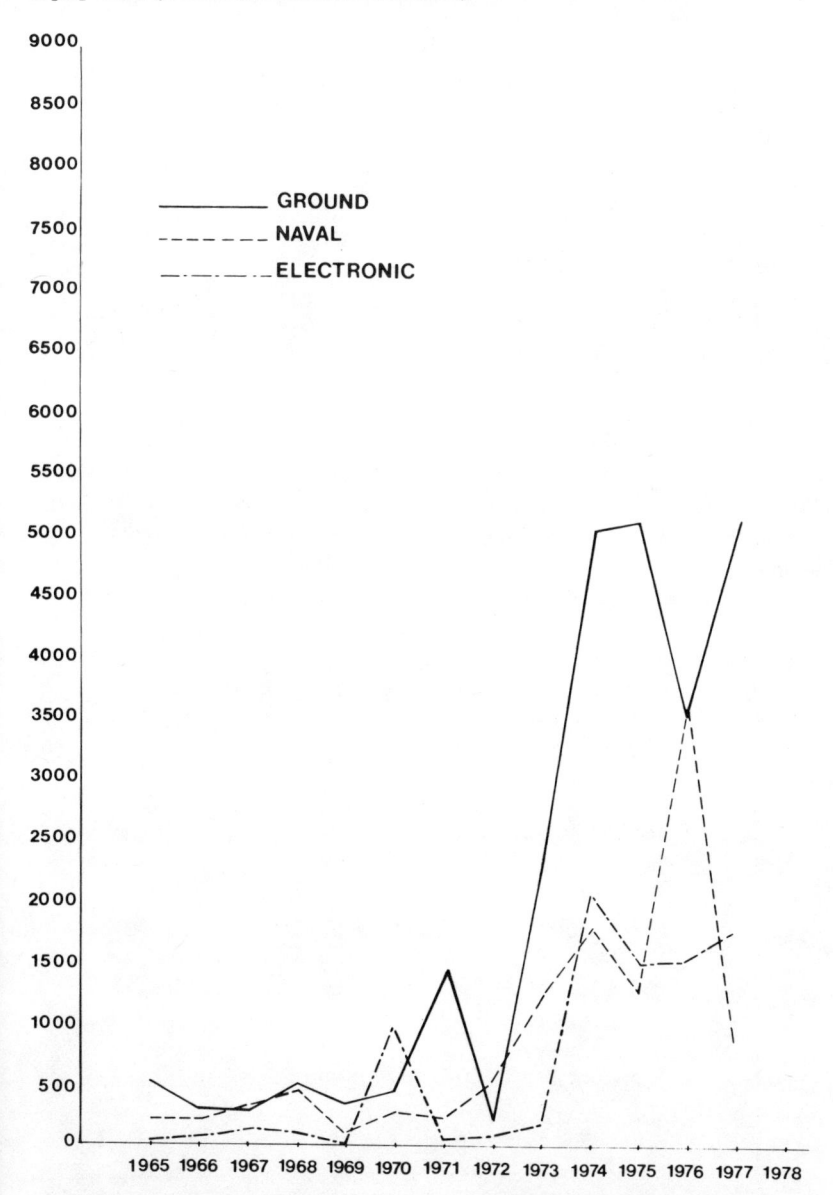

Sources: For 1965-1969, see Pinatel (1976: 161) and Klein (1976: 563-586). Since Klein combines civil and military sales, Pinatel's lower figures are used. For 1971-1973, see n. 3, Table 4.3. For 1974, see n. 4, Table 4.3. For 1975, see n. 5, Table 4.3. For 1977, see France, ANCDN (1978: 149-150).

FIGURE 4.3B Orders for Military Equipment, 1965-1977: Sales of Air Equipment and Total Sales (in millions of current francs)

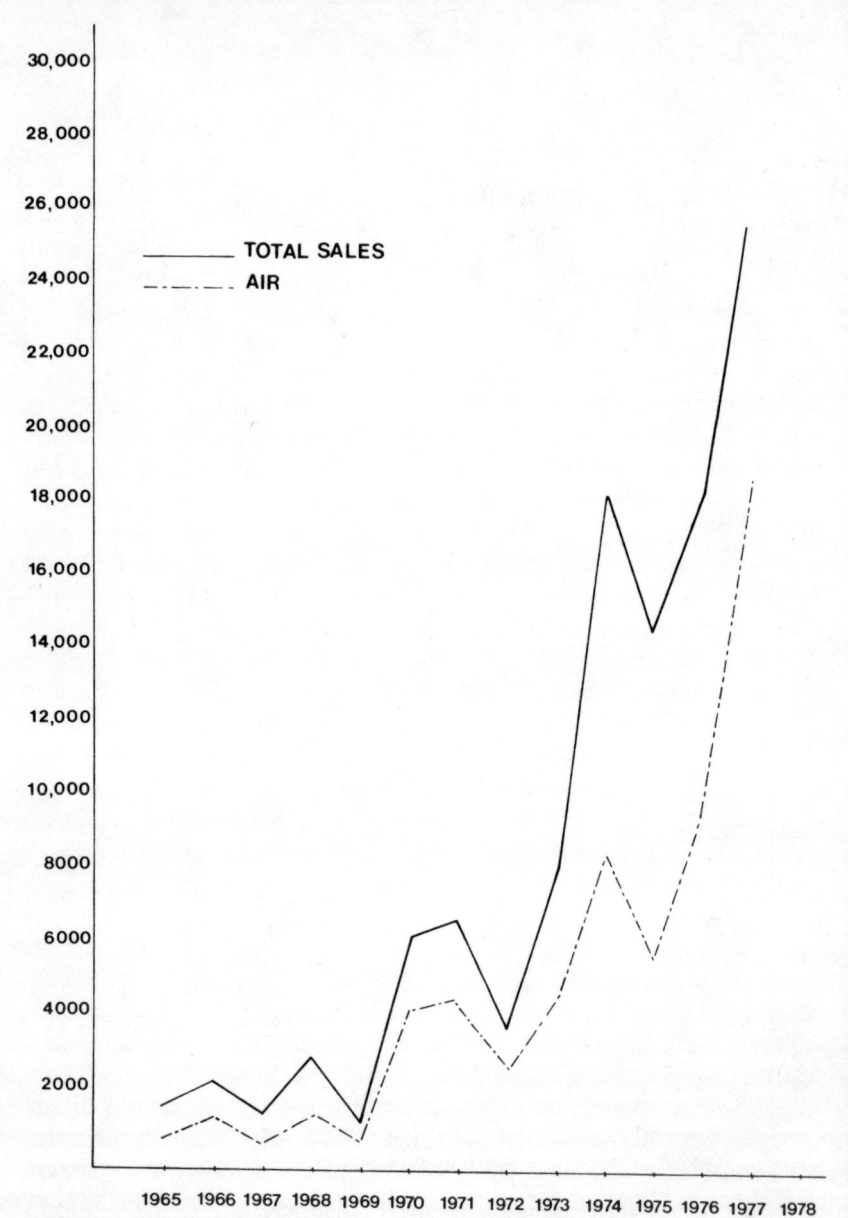

Sources: For 1965-1969, see Pinatel (1976: 161) and Klein (1976: 563-586). Since Klein combines civil and military sales, Pinatel's lower figures are used. For 1971-1973, see n. 3, Table 4.3. For 1974, see n. 4, Table 4.3. For 1975, see n. 5, Table 4.3. For 1977, see France, ANCDN (1978: 149-150).

On the other hand, the arms industry has never been more important to the French economy given an increased dependency on exports. Recent, unfavorable economic conditions further underline the significance of arms sales. They are one of the few bright spots in France's export picture. Except for naval construction the record annual orders registered between 1974 and 1976 that reportedly will be sustained in 1977 and 1978 assure continued high production and employment for almost all segments of the industry for the next three to four years (France, ANCDN, 1977: 102-103). The success of French arms sales occurs at a time when a series of economic forces are encouraging a restructuring of world trade and investment and forcing increased specialization on producing centers. The conjuncture of these factors—the success of arms sales in the context of French economic recession, high inflation, and unemployment, the quadrupling of oil prices—presents a dilemma for French planners: whether to attempt to broaden the base of France's competitive position or whether to tie itself increasingly to an industry whose future is uncertain while seeing the nation's ability to launch new initiatives or to keep pace with, much less overtake, competitors in other economic areas being eroded because of its increasing commitment of resources and investment to foreign export of military equipment.

Like the economies of West Germany and Japan, the French economy depends on increased exports. Unlike them, however, it has maintained its balance of payments and commercial position by selling arms rather than basing its stability principally on civilian goods and services.[8] Strategic and foreign policy considerations initially justified this dependence. Arms sales were believed to reduce the cost of new weapons by spreading research, development, and industrial expenditures over as large a number of units as possible. Foreign sales were also relied upon to advance France's technological capability and to support an independent military and diplomatic policy. Sales were consciously subordinated to strategic and foreign policy objectives. Since then, the evolution of France's arms industry and its current and increasing dependence on exports suggest that this idealized version of the factors and process shaping France's arms sales behavior is somewhat removed from the facts.

If France's arms and commercial policy had once been primarily defined by foreign and security considerations, the reverse is now the case although French policy-makers are chary of openly admitting the problem. President Giscard d'Estaing intimated on assuming office in 1974 that arms sales would be deemphasized during his tenure. He retreated from this position as France's economic problems resisted abatement and unemployment grew. Sales reached unprecedented levels. Moreover, the problem has been assigned secondary priority in the French President's disarmament strategy. Accent has been placed on the reconstitution of the Geneva disarmament conference to enlarge its representation and to increase the influence of smaller powers, on the creation of a satellite control agency, and on a European conference on conventional disarmament.[9] Negotiations to decrease arms sales among suppliers were made contingent on at least three conditions: progress on the disarmament proposals advanced by the French President, limits on sellers *and* buyers of arms, and the presence of the Soviet Union at arms transfer control negotiations.[10] More, not fewer, obstacles were placed in the path of international negotiations on arms transfers.

There is, of course, evidence that the French government has tried, and is still trying, in certain selected sectors to redirect the arms industry to civil purposes. The prospects of success are not immediately apparent. The Airbus and Falcon programs have made headway—both have penetrated the American market—but the Concorde remains a financial albatross. In any event, France's ability to increase its share of civilian air exports to compensate for decreased dependency on the sale of military aircraft hinges significantly on the willingness of the American aircraft industry and government to share a greater portion of the civilian air market with France—a doubtful possibility—and on the commitment of France's European partners to cooperate on joint European projects. The accord between Paris and Bonn of February 1978 to launch the B-10 medium-range civilian carrier is auspicious but not conclusive.[11] France is too deeply ensnared in arms sales to expect any one program to extricate it from its dependency.

What began after World War II, and especially after the formation of the Fifth Republic, as an effort to develop an independent weapons production capability has assumed a life of its own, progressively detached from the strategic considerations that initially animated its creation. Arms transfers have been banalized. They are increasingly merchandized like other conventional capital and consumer products. The naval, ground, and air shows held every two years at Satory and Bourget evidence this promotional effort.[12] Arms are presented as goods and services, like machine tools or automobiles, to be bought and sold rather than as instruments of the nation's defense and security. Military and merchant roles are progressively being merged. The military career ladder no longer culminates exclusively in the discharge or increasingly higher operational responsibilities. Many officers can now look forward to the rewards of well-paid posts in the industrial-scientific-technological complex that has been constructed to support the military establishment.[13] A prominent example is Hugues de l'Estoile, a "polytechnicien," who spearheaded, as head of the Direction des Affaires Internationales, France's arms sales expansion in the early 1970s and now holds a top post at Dassault although his transfer from the public to the private sector was accomplished before the grace period prescribed by French law. The growth of arms exports has also affected the role of the Minister of Defense. Jean-Laurens Delpech, former head of DMA, was quite candid about the shift in the role played by the Minister of Defense: "The trademark of our minister of defense is undergoing a radical change. From a minister of expenditures ... the minister of defense is becoming a minister of receipts who produces, moreover, foreign exchange indispensable for our foreign trade" (*Le Monde,* January 11, 1977). Problems of defense risk being reduced to commercial problems of promotion, marketing, and production.

But there are still other problems associated with the sale of arms. There is the worry, shrouded in secrecy within the French arms community, that arms sold to Libya might be used by rebel forces fighting French forces in Chad since Tripoli supports and supplies arms to insurgents against the Paris-backed government.[14] There is also the danger that some technical advances will fall into the hands of hostile powers in transferring weapons to third countries. The possibility of advanced equipment falling into the hands of Russian advisers attracted attention in the request of the Iraqi military to purchase aircraft and naval vessels equipped with advanced radar and electronic devices for evasion and countermeasures.[15] The French contend that they are able to devise black boxes that conceal key operating components of a weapon system, but it is not clear how these components can long remain secret since France has little or no control over weapons once they are transferred to a foreign government. Indeed, one of the promotional attractions of buying from France is that, in contrast to superpower or Swedish practice, there are normally a minimum number of political strings attached to the sale.

Technological transfers may also lead to the creation of competitors. The Israeli Kfir fighter draws on the design of the Mirage III.[16] Similarly, the Roland ground-to-air missile, sold under license to the United States, has now returned to the world market in a more sophisticated form and poses a competitive threat to French sales.[17] The French military may also find itself becoming a dumping ground for excess inventory or newly produced arms because of a lack of foreign buyers. The fifty Mirage V aircraft embargoed to Israel were eventually absorbed by the French Air Force. The same was true of an excess of Nord 262, which had to be bought by the French Navy when foreign buyers were unavailable (Dubos, 1974: 140). On the other hand, given the large amount of orders outstanding for military equipment, the immediate problem facing French planners is how to maintain the operational readiness of French armed forces and fill arms contracts without drawing on the equipment available to French troops.

Servicing sold equipment and training foreign military to use it also cost the armed forces the availability of valuable personnel. The sale of a submarine, for example, requires a year of training that absorbs much of the time of a regular French submarine crew and detracts from other mission responsibilities (Crespin and Besançon, 1977: 49). The ability of the military to shift these burdens or acquire the needed resources to discharge them appears more and more problematic. Given the pressures to export, the tendency in political circles, reflected in reports of the National Assembly, is to recommend more, not less, military involvement in the *après vente* phase of arms sales.

Nor do weapons programs necessarily derive logically from the mission requirements generated by the nation's strategic position and policy. The tergiversations surrounding the acquisition of the F1 do not appear to fit the textbook description of the weapons acquisition process (Sterling, 1974). Powerful economic forces were at play that threatened the French Air Force's future as an effective combat arm. New aircraft and weapons for the French Air Force are supposed to be developed initially through a series of operational and engineering studies indicating mission and technological requirements of weapon systems capable of discharging the missions assigned to the military. The French Air Force had been working since the 1960s on an *avion de combat future* (ACF), a bi-motor, high performance aircraft for air defense. Parallel to this development, Dassault, partly in collaboration with the Air Force and partly in response to export opportunities, was also working on the F1, powered by an Atar engine. Differences over these two programs came to a head over the "sale of the Century," a contract to replace the aging air defense fighters of the Belgian, Dutch, Danish, and Norwegian air forces. Working in close cooperation with governmental authorities, Dassault proposed a modified version of the F1, with a more powerful M 53 engine, as France's entry into the competition. To support this proposal, the French Air Force was obliged to commit itself to the purchase of the F1 M 53. Forcing the Air Force's hand on the F1 M 53 threatened the ACF program while posing the possibility of increasing the costs of logistics, operations, and maintenance. The Air Force did not necessarily object to an F1 aircraft powered by the weaker Atar engine. There was a clear need to replace the Mirage III force. What prompted concern was the substitution of the F1 M 53 as the follow-on air defense aircraft for the 1980s rather than as a transition to the ACF.[18] The award of the contract to General Dynamics for the F-16 relaxed some of the constraints placed on the French Air Force. The F1 M 53 proposal was dropped, and the F1 with the Atar engine was ordered as a satisfactory transition aircraft pending the development of the Mirage 2000, a program with its own special problems. The ACF program had to be canceled in favor of the single-motor Mirage 2000 when cost estimates for the development of the aircraft were estimated to exceed that of the Concorde.

The history of the F1 and the F1 M 53 programs raises legitimate doubts about the ability of the French arms industry and even the French nation to marshall the resources and technical capabilities to develop arms that are simultaneously responsive to the nation's strategic and economic imperatives. In question is not only the viability of the French arms industry but also the future of an independent French foreign and security policy, even one defined in more modest and marginal terms than that which prevailed during the tenure of President Charles de Gaulle. The French defense budget is presently unable to meet the nation's equipment needs. At the same time the Ministry of Defense has had to rely on increased arms sales to generate the resources needed to meet the material needs set out in the fourth *loi-programme* for the military establishment.

Only 55% of the Army's equipment requirements will be met by 1982. The construction of a sixth nuclear submarine and an aircraft carrier has also been arrested pending further study. Previous plans to increase the number of missiles on the Albion Plateau and to create a sixth Pluton regiment have been dropped. Purchases of military aircraft will remain at current levels, with some backsliding in the acquisition of aircraft, like the Jaguar. The Mirage 2000 is scheduled to enter French inventories in the middle 1980s.[19] It is expected to meet French needs for the remainder of much of the century although American planning already envisions follow-on aircraft in the 1990s for the F-16s and F-15s that will compose much of the backbone of American air forces for the 1980s.

More ominous for the future of the French arms industry and its competitiveness is the stagnating trend in expenditures for research and development. Expenditures in constant francs in 1978 will just reach the levels attained in 1967 and 1968 or just before the oil crisis in 1973. Credits for basic research and study will actually go down in constant francs from 310 million francs in 1971 to 184 million in 1978 (France, ANCDN, 1977: 80-85). This force remains the key to France's nuclear striking power given the aging Mirage IV force and the vulnerability of the missiles on the Albion Plateau, increasingly more a target than a deterrent. Pluton units are also hampered by their small number, vulnerability, limited range, the absence of adequate accords for their use on foreign, especially German, territory, the difficulty of deploying them under crisis conditions, and the problems of accurate firing to maximize the precise destruction of desired military targets while minimizing collateral civilian damage and casualties. The ambiguity that persists with respect to the circumstances under which these tactical nuclear weapons would be used advised curtailment of the program. This point should not obscure a still larger one, viz., the lack of adequate resources available to France to create an effective force comparable to American and Soviet capabilities.

Only one new program, the Mirage 2000, was launched by the military *loi-programme* of 1977-1982. The Air Force showed little interest in a follow-on for the Mirage IV. The Mirage 4000, a bi-motor aircraft, is a dassault venture intended to compete for the market already dominated by the F-15. The French Air Force sidestepped direct support for the program. Its eggs are in the Mirage 2000 basket. However, the future of this program, either as a response to France's strategic needs or to expanded arms sales, is not fully assured since it has yet to be developed with its supporting equipment. Plans for engine design are not new. Indeed, there were no funds allocated as late as 1978, for example, for the development of a more powerful engine, the M 53-7, to give greater thrust (approximately 10,000 pounds) and range to the aircraft. There were few funds, moreover, for such new areas of concern as cruise missiles or military satellites (France, ANCF, 1977: 107).

Meanwhile, the American aerospace industry offers a panoply of aircraft, like the F-16 and F-15, that, respectively, promise lower cost and greater technical performance, covering maneuverability, acceleration, high and low altitude radar, and weapon firing than the Mirage 2000 or the Mirage 4000. It is already producing aerospace equipment that has yet to be developed by French industry, signaling the increasing gap between French technological development and the military and economic challenges that it confronts from allies and opponents. This is not to suggest that within the resources provided by the French government that French military aircraft are of questionable quality. The Mirage III and V have acquitted themselves in Middle East wars. Despite the drawbacks of the F1 in low altitude radar, it is widely valued as a fighter aircraft. What is at issue is the accelerated pace and increasing cost of developing new weapons, especially in the aerospace field and the receding capacity of a country of France's size to keep itself in the race. The dilemma deepens when a policy of unbridled arms sales aggravates an already delicate situation of remaining abreast of technical improvements and of responding to strategic threats.

In the immediate future France finds itself in the throes of a vicious circle. If exports represented 35% of the business affairs of the ground sector of the arms industry in 1975, they will have to rise to 40 or 50% by the end of the fourth military *loi-programme* to keep private industry and GIAT arsenals in full operation. The suspension of a sixth nuclear submarine and an aircraft carrier nullified 18 million hours of work for naval construction sites. Naval planning foresees the gradual diminution of new building through the 1970s, resulting in production levels that will be 20% lower at the end of the planning period than that of 1975. As naval production goes down and the demand for exports increase on an industry that has been the weakest link in the French arms industrial chain, French naval requirements and missions have been expanded not only because of the increased Soviet naval threat but also because of the institution of the 200-mile limit that must be surveyed. Finally, by 1980, government purchases of helicopters on which Aerospatiale depends will represent only 5% of the division's business affairs contrasted with 42% in 1971.[20] The observations of M. Joel Le Theule, presented in the spring of 1976 before the Commission de la Défense Nationale et des Forces Armées still appears prophetic: "For the next three years our arms industry will be largely tributary to exports for its production program. This situation is not without its risks. One should hope that it can pass through this difficult period without too much damage and that it can preserve a potential and a technological level capable of confronting later the new needs engendered by technological change" (France, ANCDN, 1976a: 107). This hope may be somewhat exaggerated if the forecast made by M. Delpech, while he was the Délégue Ministeriel pour l'Armement, can be given credence: "Unless there is a reverse of the trend in appropriations for the armed forces, one can expect certain difficulties because one can fear a saturation" (*Le Monde,* December 12, 1975).

Partly because of this pessimistic prediction and partly because of the heavy proportion of arms exports to total deliveries, the French DGA and, specifically, its sales arm, the Direction des Affaires Internationales, have increased efforts to sell to Asian and Latin American countries with some success as evidenced in the sale of nineteen F1 fighters to Ecuador (*Le Monde,* November 19, 1977). They are fully aware that weapons decisions are not made solely on the technical merits of the products France sells, but on political grounds that may, indeed, be in conflict with foreign military requirements. If there are signs that the French arms makers, principally in the private sector, are developing their civilian markets,[21] there is no evidence of a cutback in productive capacity devoted to arms or to reconversion. Dassault, Thomson-Brandt-CSF, and Matra, leading arms producers in the private sector, still devote much of their production to military items. The arsenals run by the government are actually producing below capacity.

In the short run the French arms industry may very well be responding to world demand for French arms, often simpler and more easily serviceable in the field than those of other developed states, but it is not at all certain that it is able, given the strictures of French national resources, to meet simultaneously the strategic and economic imperatives facing the French nation without encouraging the spread of weapons and weapons production know-how around the world. The arms industry threatens to float increasingly away from its initial moorings in French strategic and diplomatic policy. In servicing legitimate enough national economic objectives and less estimable bureaucratic, industrial, and private professional interests, the arms industry acts with increasing independence, justified partly by its very success in selling arms. But, meanwhile what of France's national interests? Government authorities confront a paradoxical question that has not had to be posed before: Can France really afford the success of its arms sales? The answer is neither as simple nor as obvious as arms sales advocates and opponents would lead one to believe.

The French case has also important implications for foreign policy-makers and policy analysts concerned with arms transfers and for students of international relations interested in explaining the arms transfer regime as a sybsystem of the international system and in exploring its ramifications for international relations theory. These audiences are successively addressed in the sections below.

POLICY AND THEORETICAL IMPLICATIONS OF THE FRENCH CASE

Policy Implications of the French Case for International Security

The growing economic dependency of France on arms transfers raises serious questions about efforts to control the flow of arms and arms technology across national borders. As the third largest arms supplier, France has a critical role to play in any international control scheme. In light of the preceding analysis, it becomes apparent that there is little French interest in cooperating with other states in controlling the quantity and sophistication of the arms and arms technologies being transferred. The Carter administration's arms transfer policies were most immediately challenged. During his election campaign President Carter pledged that his administration would follow a policy of sales restraint and would press for greater international control of arms shipments. The President reiterated his concern in his statement on conventional arms transfer policy of May 19, 1977: "Because of the threat to world peace embodied in this spiralling arms traffic; and because of the special responsibilities we bear as the largest arms seller, I believe that the United States must take steps to restrain its arms transfers" (U.S., Committee on International Relations, 1977: 43-44).

The President's policy statement defined guidelines for unilateral American initiatives to slow arms transfers and to set an example for other states to follow. These steps included a monetary ceiling on arms sales agreements, discouragement of arms design and production solely for export, prohibition of "coproduction agreements for significant weapons equipment and major components," greater restrictions on third party transfers, tighter governmental rein on corporate promotion of arms sales, and a no-first policy on introducing "into a region newly-developed, advanced weapon systems which could create a new or significantly higher combat capability" (U.S., Committee on International Relations, 1977: 43-44).

These self-restraining measures, however important in themselves, were also designed to influence the behavior of other suppliers, like France and the Soviet Union. American example was viewed as a means "to alter the intensity of the competitive atmosphere surrounding the arms trade" and as a prerequisite for American efforts, aimed at other major suppliers, to "seek their active cooperation and try to convince allies and adversaries that restraint is in everyone's interest" (U.S., Congressional Research Service, 1977: 60). Administration spokesmen reasoned that the President's call for cooperation from suppliers to restrain arms flows would lack credibility unless American transfers were first cut as a show of good faith and resolve.

On the other hand, continued American restraint was premised on a cooperative response from other suppliers, like France. Three conditions were implicitly applied as a kind of litmus test of cooperation: other suppliers were expected to consult with the United States before agreeing to sell arms; they were to resist filling voids left by United States rejection of requests from third states for arms; and they were to restrict the sophistication of the material transferred.

France has shown little enthusiasm for the Carter administration's proposals. For its part, the administration has consistently depreciated French dependency on arms sales. Administration and analyst optimism about the prospects of French cooperation is partly rooted in the systematic understatement of French arms deliveries by the intelligence community of the federal government whose findings are published annually in ACDA's World Military Expenditures and Arms Transfers. Figures for the period 1966-1975 contrast sharply with those cited earlier based on official French sources. For example, during this period ACDA data have estimated French deliveries on the average at a rate of $500 million below French figures (Kolodziej, 1979a). This gap appears to be widening. In figures published for 1976, ACDA estimates French deliveries at $840 million or approximately one percent of total exports (U.S., ACDA, 1978: 130). French parliamentary reports place French deliveries at approximately $2.6 billion, a difference of more than three to one relative to ACDA estimates. French export dependency also significantly changes, as noted above, to 4.3%.[22] ACDA's underestimations have been echoed in other governmental and nongovernmental analyses in support for the view that the French government could decrease its arms transfers without harm to the French economy or to regime political needs for growth, markets, balance of payments stability, and employment.[23]

What is also obscured in these analyses are the larger rationale and socioeconomic-political framework within which the growth of French arms transfers have occurred. This evolution has not been the product of chance or happenstance. Whatever the distorting effects of rising arms transfers on France's economy and military posture might be, as sketched above, the central government and the arms production bureaucracy have pursued a vigorous sales policy based on a subtle and complicated set of considerations. Impetus for increased arms sales, as a broad economic and developmental strategy, has been particularly marked since the upheavals of 1968 in whose wake defense expenditures were cut to meet social welfare needs. As the analysis earlier demonstrates, defense spending now claims a smaller percentage of the government's budget and of GNP, and spending within the defense budget has shifted dramatically in favor of expenditures on personnel over equipment.[24] The fourth *loi-programme*, the basic military planning document approved by the National Assembly in 1976 for the period 1977-1982, projects a modest reversal of these trends. Defense spending is expected to climb to 20% of the government's budget, and the proportion of resources devoted to personnel and equipment is expected to shift in favor of the latter. Spending for personnel and operations are set at 58.8% in 1977; this level is scheduled to fall to 52.2% in 1982. Correspondingly, at the end of five years spending for military capital expenditures is supposed to climb from 41.2% of the defense budget to 47.8% (France, ANCDN, 1976a: 17-20). This increase responds to French commitments within the Atlantic Alliance and to leadership perceptions of the need for increased defense preparedness. However, these increases in spending for equipment will result in no appreciable change in French export dependency on arms transfers. Nor do they lessen incentives for French use of this strategy to serve a variety of other associated purposes. These broad goals were spelled out in the French White Paper issue in 1972 by the Ministry of Defense under the inspiration of Michel Debré, a life-long supporter of President Charles de Gaulle's nationalist policies of independence:

> Our military industrial policy should in the first place guarantee the realization, today and tomorrow, of the arms programs which the [nation's] defense needs. It should also be harmoniously related to the Government's industrial, economic, and social policy.
>
> In other words, it is necessary, on the one hand, to maintain and modernize an industrial potential which assures us in the area of

armament a sufficient independence in order that the effectiveness of our defense is not tributary to foreign industrial constraints which would compromise our liberty of decision; it is necessary, on the other hand, to contribute to economic development without weighing on the balance of payments, to enrich the general economy by applying useful scientific and technical progress to other purposes than defense, and to relate our [arms production] policy to internal development [Debre, 1972: 44-45].

It would be misleading to reduce French arms transfer behavior entirely to purely economic motives. They serve a larger array of national and particular subnational interests.[25] The search for independence and an autonomous weapons production capacity, a distinguishing mark of successive Fourth and Fifth Republic governments since World War II,[26] continues undiminished as a national goal (Méry, 1976). French arms transfer behavior reflects a more basic demand for an independent arms production capability as a means by which to provide some maneuver and leverage in bargaining with other states, particularly the superpowers. The need to transfer arms is sequentially and causally the result of a preceding commitment to national self-determination whose roots lie deep in the development of the French state.[27] These security and diplomatic functions have been progressively extended to economic growth and development. Arms transfers thus link the welfare and security functions of the government. The military industrial administrative-techno-scientific complex that responds to these functions—as well as its own self-serving bureaucratic interests—is viewed as a beneficial instrument of national policy, and not necessarily as a threat to either national preparedness or economic progress and job security. Criticism of this complex has largely come from outside the framework of the political process. There is widespread agreement on the Right and on the Left that the arms production system is a mechanism of modernization by which the French nation stays abreast of its European and Atlantic competitors.

Support on the Right is well known since, under its political rule, French arms sales have steadily grown. Less appreciated is the support accorded by the opposition parties on the Left and their allies in labor for continued sale of arms abroad. During the legislative election campaign of fall and winter of 1977-1978, the Socialist and Communist parties attacked more the direction of the arms trade and the internal organization and control of arms production than the existence of an independent arms production capacity. No major leader advocated significant cutbacks in arms production or sales. Socialist party head, François Mitterrand, condemned French shipments to Chile, Argentina, and Brazil and suggested a lessened accent on arms sales as a governmental policy, but there was no wholesale rejection of an active French effort (*Le Monde*, December 1, 1977). There was agreement with the Right that France's independence rested on an autonomous military industrial base. France's supply of arms to Third World states is also considered a counterweight to American and superpower domination, particularly the United States as the major arms supplier (Leitenberg and Ball, 1979: 35). The flow of arms abroad would be presumably denied to regimes opposed to Left preferences, and arms to ideologically compatible and revolutionary movements would be assured. The job security of arms workers organized by unions aligned with the Left parties would also be guaranteed by the state, and not subject to market fluctuations. A major objection of these groups to arms production is that the privately managed segments of the arms industry have too much control over salaries, working conditions, and job tenure. What is done with the arms produced is a lesser question than that current levels of production be maintained by any means, whether through increased domestic demand or exports.[28] The Right and Left could agree, although for divergent reasons, that France needs to protect and even extend its arms supply option to play an independent role in international politics as critic and counterweight of the strong on behalf of the weak.

Where Left and Right part is on the question of the internal control of arms production. Both Socialists and Communists press for nationalization of the remaining private components of the arms industry, a traditional goal of the Left.[29] Particular attention has centered on nationalization of Dassault-Bréguet. Through nationalization a major contributor to the Gaullist party, Marcel Dassault, would be directly attacked and the most successful branch of the French aerospace industry would be placed under governmental control. Victory of the Left at the polls would then place the direction of this vital industry in its hands. The Left critique focused specifically on the alleged excess profits of the Dassault firm as a consequence of unwarranted governmental subsidies.[30] Except for the pacifist wing of the Socialist party, there were few who attacked the proposition that Dassault-Bréguet continue to produce military aircraft for sale abroad. Job security and a more equitable distribution of economic benefits from production were the dominant concerns. Left control under the aegis of nationalization would presumably assure these objectives. Specifically opposed were governmental efforts to decrease reliance on its arsenals and to increase the use of the private sector, including seminationalized corporations, like Aérospatiale. The unions and their political party allies resisted the play of market forces, including the demand for arms, as a determinant of employment levels. These same considerations underlay the strikes at governmental ship construction facilities in spring 1978, the largest since the 1950s.

If the enlarging economic dependency of French arms transfers is related to the security, diplomacy, and domestic policy dimensions of arms transfers, it becomes clear that any French government would have strong reservations about cooperating with other suppliers on international arms transfers controls. These reservations multiply if, as in the Carter approach, they imply bilateral accords with the United States. None of the principal political parties has much to gain domestically by supporting the Carter administration's proposals. From this perspective the sale of nineteen French F-1 fighters to Ecuador in fall 1977 is not surprising although it directly conflicts with Washington's expectations of allied cooperation. The United States had earlier refused to sell F-4's to Ecuador and had subsequently vetoed an Israeli request to fill this order with Kfir fighters equipped with GE motors.[31] President Giscard d'Estaing was also explicit about the conditions under which the French government would enter into talks with the United States and other suppliers. Not only would the Soviet Union be required to participate but recipient states were to be included to assuage Third World fears of a suppliers' cartel (*Le Monde*, May 27, 1978). Even if the United States and the Soviet Union were to make progress on Conventional Arms Talks (CAT)—which they have not to date—meeting a test of recipient consent would still be a formidable obstacle to French participation. Moreover, increasing the number of states widens the number of divergent perspectives and interests at play. Accord becomes more difficult and progress slower.

The standardization issue raised by the United States within NATO reinforces French skepticism about the feasibility of arms cooperation with supplier states and, specifically, with the United States. The French view American proposals for standardization within the Alliance as more an attempt by Washington to consolidate its arms sales position within the Atlantic Alliance than as a means to resolve the problem of NATO force readiness arising from the multiplicity of equipment used by NATO units. Not unlike other West European arms producers, the French government sees virtues in the production of multiple weapon systems for similar tasks. They confound enemy planning; stimulate competition in weapons design; and are more adaptive to different environmental settings (Freedman, 1978). European producers are also concerned that they not be reduced to subcontractors for American firms. French experience with the Roland missile holds little promise that much benefit, economic or strategic, lies in close European-American cooperation in arms development, production, or sales.

Implications of the French Case for Students of International Security

The French experience, and similar cases in the developed and developing world, have interest for students of international politics at several levels of analysis. First, they are critical to the development of a theory of arms transfers or, more broadly, the diffusion of military technology and the creation of arms production centers. Close examination of French relations with the international environment and the incentives at play in French governmental arms transfers behavior suggests at least four sets of actor relations and appropriate incentives within each set of relations that, together, form a nexus of self-sustaining relations and creates a subsystem of the international system. This subsystem is composed of national, subnational, transnational, and international components. The first refers to the nation state; the second to the military-industrial-administrative-technoscientific complex within each state; the third to the growing multilaterization of arms manufacture, linking subnational actors in a common interest to keep arms production and transfers flowing; and the fourth to security pacts, like NATO and the Warsaw Pact, that encourage intra-alliance arms exchanges. French arms supply behavior can be viewed from each of these levels of actor activity. Each contributes to the maintenance of the arms transfer subsystem at the global level.

The French experience reveals much about the workings of nation-state security relations and about the dynamics of arms technology motored by national interest. Conflict, competition, and cooperation among states in security and arms control domains conspire, paradoxically, to reinforce the arms traffic subsystem. The search for military independence as a function of national-state conflict encourages national arms production; the competition for markets and access to raw materials reinforces already strong incentives to sell arms; cooperative programs to cut the costs of research and development and to assure outlets creates a web of transnational relations that resist efforts to reduce weapons production or sales.

These incentives, operating at the nation-state level, tend to become institutionalized in the form of the production complexes created to respond to security, foreign policy, and economic imperatives. These bureaucratic organizations develop an interest in their own survival. Their health is defined by the level of arms production and the growth of sales of arms abroad. These structures yield still more complex multinational organizations. These bind national centers of production together and, accordingly, strengthen the structure and process of arms transfers as a subsystem of international relations.[32]

To explain the structure and operation of the arms transfer subsystem a series of case studies of specific national arms production centers is needed in which the four levels of analysis stipulated above are applied to each case. The approach would be similar to that developed by Alexander George and Richard Smoke in their *Deterrence in American Foreign Policy: Theory and Practice* (George and Smoke, 1974) Case studies by themselves do not lead to an accumulation of data. Nor can generalizations be made across cases. Comparisons can be made meaningful by "employing the same variables, while accounting explicitly for the variation in these factors from case to case" (George and Smoke, 1974: 95). Space limits have required concentration in this chapter on economic variables, but as the discussion above suggests, other factors have also shaped French practice. The kind of analysis applied to the French experience could well be applied to other national cases to foster generalization across cases about the structure and operation of arms transfers at a systemic level.[33]

A comparative approach based on discrete but similar cases cast within a common framework of analysis promises to join the perspectives of comparative and international politics and to draw on both to illuminate and explain the arms transfer subsystem. Moreover, the artificial wall between policy-makers and policy researchers, on the one hand, and students of international politics and international relations theory, on the other, would be broken down. The arms transfer subsystem resting on four sets of actor relations can be helpful in explaining the persistence of arms transfers despite changes in the actor relations composing the subsystem. Clearer delineation of the input of key actors of the subsystem can aid the prediction of individual actor behavior, either of suppliers, producers, or recipients. Detailed studies of the specific factors shaping actor behavior are critical to progress in explaining subsystem and specific actor behavior. Knowledge of these two levels—the subsystemic and the specific—is crucial if we are to better answer two other questions, viz., the impact of arms transfers on international security and on economic development and growth. In the first instance, absence of specific knowledge about actor behavior, especially at the nation-state level, precludes making an evaluation of the stability of instability of current international security arrangements tied to an increasingly interdependent weapons production system, driven, paradoxically, by the pursuit of national independence. We do not know enough about the incentives prompting national and subnational actors and the impact of each within their *milieux*. An accumulation of specific studies can provide the foundation on which such questions can be more comprehensively answered. In the absence of such studies we will not be able to assess whether increased spending on arms increases and decreases economic growth and modernization since we will not have developed the conceptual framework and data to make such evaluations at a subsystemwide or a country-specific level.

The French case, viewed from the perspective of the elite in control of the decision-making process on arms transfers, challenges two widely held propositions. The first asserts that spending on arms necessarily decreases economic growth. This proposition is partially based on the assumption that the production of military goods is inherently a waste of resources (SIPRI, 1975). Little credence is given the assumption underlying French behavior that transfers serve national needs for full employment, especially of skilled personnel, balance of payments equilibrium, and access to markets and raw materials. However, for French elites there is no necessary contradiction between national welfare and security. An independent weapons production capacity and increased arms transfers are viewed simultaneously as a response to security and welfare imperatives. The choice is not between guns and butter, but making guns in order to have butter. The critics of increasing arms transfers and arms production may well be correct at a global level; increasing expenditures on military power may have a negative systemic impact on the beneficial development of the economic resources available to what might be termed the international community. However, this approach takes little account of the authoritative structure of the nation-state through which this allocation process is made. To assume the view of critics is ultimately to deny or denigrate the security function of nation-states. The disturbing implication of the French case is that, at least in the short run, a state *can* improve its economic position by arms transfers. Or, at the very least, it can cut its losses by an active arms transfer policy. Unless theorists can address the dichotomy between subsystemic loss but specific actor gain and the incentives that operate on actors to transfer arms for specified gains, there is little likelihood that those favoring transfers will be very much persuaded to accept constraints by criticisms pitched at a systemic level. Gains at a national and subnational level will be more persuasive whatever the adverse impact on global or regional security and economic relations.

The need for focusing at the level of specific actor behavior in order to illuminate the subsystem effects of that behavior opens another fruitful line of inquiry that remains to be explored at a comparative level. If the literature on the military-industrial complex is expansive with regard to United States practice, much needs to be done regarding other systems, like Britain, Germany, or the Soviet Union. The French military-industrial-administrative-technoscientific complex contrasts with the American model since the principal thrust for weapons production and sales has come from *within* the government. Parties on the Left which advocate nationalization are still prepared to sell arms although they differ with the Right on the magnitude and the direction of trade, the kinds of weapons to be sold, and the controls that might be applied. An analysis of arms transfers, based on market or capitalist sources, has to be complemented by the institutional impact of an arms production system whose interests are interposed between national claims for maximum security and economic growth and equitable distribution of economic benefits within the nation among individuals and groups. Too great a share of national wealth may well be devoted to servicing bureaucratic interests at the expense of national welfare and security. The transnational development of the arms industry and the growth of national arms production centers suggest that these national and transnational production systems may play a greater role in determining the allocation of global resources for arms and economic development than available findings would seem to substantiate. The concerns of critics of arms transfers need to be focused at the nation-state level but in a comparative framework linked to international political issues of global and national security and economic and political development. The French case expanded along the lines sketched above and applied to other suppliers and recipients is one promising way of approaching the issues posed by arms transfers and the diffusion of military technology.

A final word should also be addressed to the problem of data collection. The French case indicates the need for more comprehensive and reliable information about the value of arms deliveries and sales. The figures used in this study contrast sharply with those published by ACDA or SIPRI (U.S., ACDA, 1978; SIPRI, 1975). Other studies show similar disparities for other arms producing centers (Freedman, 1978). It would appear that both ACDA and SIPRI err significantly in underestimating the actual value of global arms transfers. One result has been to discount the economic significance of arms transfers and, concomitantly, to be too optimistic about finding economic alternatives to arms transfers as a response to national economic, foreign policy, and security imperatives. Carter administration policies appear to be based on such optimistic notions of economic feasibility of reduced arms transfers and to have placed too high a premium on American example as an instrument of inducing other states to restrain their transfer of arms and military technology. Better data would provide a "better picture of the world" and a sounder foundation on which to advance propositions about the arms transfer regime including its structure, processes, and linkages to other international subsystems and about the likely consequences of different proposals to control arms transfers and the military diffusion process. This chapter has tried to show how the French case can serve as a guide for better data gathering and, more importantly, as a model for a comparative approach to a significant problem of contemporary international politics, the control of arms transfers and the diffusion of military technology.

NOTES

1. The key works on economic growth are Carré et al. (1972); for a useful oversight of current French economic problems, consult De Lattre and Deguen (1976).

2. The figures provided by ACDA have become widely used and quoted, although they seriously underestimate not only the actual level of French arms exports but also the impact of arms exports on the French economy. See the following sources that repeat and therefore reinforce the general acceptance of ACDA underestimations: BDM Corporation (1977); Cahn et al. (1977); Farley et al. (1978); Cauchie, (1977); U.S., Congressional Research Service, (1977). ACDA figures are evaluated in the author's *Journal of Conflict Resolution* article, forthcoming, 1979).

3. *Le Monde,* August 24, 1978. See below for further discussions of the relation of capital goods to arms deliveries.

4. Interviews, Paris, 1978.

5. For a general discussion of the military industrial complex in France, see Dubos (1974); C.L.I.C.A.N. (1977): Sirjacques (1977); Cerdan (1975); and Menahem (1976).

6. C.L.I.C.A.N. (1977): 41ff. The figures given above for the distribution of employment differ slightly from a recent publication of the Minister of Defense. See France, SIRPA (1977): 10.

7. These figures are drawn from several sources which should be compared: FRANCE, ANCF (1977): 40, *Le Monde,* November 9, 1976; ibid., January 14, 1976; FRANCE, ANCDN (1975): 46.

8. Recent trends in German arms transfer behavior suggest growing reliance on arms sales to bolster employment in lagging sectors, like navel construction, and to place Germany in a more competitive position in the aeronautics and electrical equipment industries. Note the signing of what was reported as over a billion dollars in naval contracts with Iran (Interviews, Germany, 1978). These have been since suspended in the wake of the Iranian revolution. West Germany is now listed as the fourth largest arms supplier (U.S., ACDA [1978]: 131, 153).

9. *Le Monde,* January 27, 1978, publishes a transcript of the President's proposal.

10. See ibid., February 11, 1978, for President Giscard d'Estaing's news conference.

11. Ibid.

12. The most recent Satory show for military ground equipment is described, for example, in *Internationale Wehrrevue* (1977: 916-925. The budget for the promotion of arms is also covered in Dubos (1974): 108-114; and *Le Monde* September 18, 1976.

13. Ibid., January 11, 1977.

14. Interviews, Paris, 1978.

15. See the following sources: *Le Monde,* November 18, 1976; ibid., November 19, 1976.

16. Relevant are *Le Monde,* March 15, 1977; and ibid., November 19, 1977.

17. Interviews, Paris, 1978.

18. Interviews in Paris and Washington, 1977-1978. For a brief review of the ACF program, see France, ANCDN (1975): 74-76.

19. The fourth military *loi-programme* is evaluated in France, ANCDN (1976a).

20. See n. 19 above especially Vol. 2, pp. 23-27.

21. See annual reports of Matra, Thomson-CSF and Table 4. In 1977, over half of the production of Dassault and Matra were for military equipment; approximately 35% of Thomson-Brandt were devoted to military production, the bulk of which was concentrated in Thomson-CSF, a major affiliate. Interviews, Paris, 1978.

22. See Table 4.4. The exchange rate for 1976 is 4.7796.
23. See n. 2.
24. See p. 10.
25. These varied purposes are rationalized in a remarkable statement published in *Le Monde*. For a rejoinder, see *Le Monde* (June 12, 1976).
26. Various sources should be consulted: Kolodziej (1974); Kohl (1971); Scheinman (1965).
27. The tradition of France in production of arms is recounted in Jacomet (1945); Bigaut (1939); Le Marquand (1923).
28. Interviews with officials of the Conféderation Francaise Démocratique du Travail (CFDT), Congrès Général des Travailleurs (CGT), and Force Ouvrière, April-May, 1978. See, e.g., *L'Action Syndicale* January through May 1978 for articles criticizing reorganization and cutbacks in selected parts of the arms industry, primarily in the arsenal system.
29. See n. 27.
30. The Dassault-Bréguet governmental relation is explored in a special legislative investigation. See France, Commission d'Enquête (1977).
31. U.S., Congressional Research Service (1977): 63-64. Also useful for a review of American arms policy and international cooperation is U.S., Committee on Foreign Relations (1979).
32. For an elaboration of these relations, see Kolodziej (1979).
33. The author is presently working on a manuscript that identifies and describes the various dimensions of each of these variables.

REFERENCES

BDM Corporation (1977) A Study of U.S. Arms Sales to Foreign countries. Vienna, VA.
BIGAUT, A. (1939) La nationalization et le contrôle des usines de guerre. Paris: Domat-Montchristien.
CAHN, A., J. KRUZEL, P. DAWKINS, and J. HUNTZINGER (1977) Controlling Future Arms Trade. New York: McGraw-Hill.
CARRE, J.-J., P. DUBOIS, and E. MALINVAUD (1972). Abrégé de la croissance française. Paris: Seuil.
CAUCHIE, N. (1977) "La politique française en matière d'armements et l'interopèrabilité." Colloque: une politique européenne d'armement. Paris.
CERDAN, E. (1975) Dossier A . . . comme armes. Paris: Alain Moreau.
CHOFFEL, J. (1976) Le problème petrolier français. Paris: La Documentation Française.
C.L.I.C.A.N. (1977) Les trafics d'armes de la France: L'engrenage de la militarism. Paris: Maspéro.
CRESPIN R. and J. BESANÇON. (1977) "Ventes d'armements et relations entre pays industrialisés et pays en voie de développement." Défense 9 (May), Paris.
DEBRE, M. (1972) Livre blanc sur défense nationale. Paris.
DE GAULLE, C. (1970) Mémoires d'espoir: Le renouveau, 1958-1962. Paris: Plon.
DE LATTRE A. and D. DEGUEN (1976) Politique economique de la France. Paris: Institute d'Etudes Politiques de Paris, 3 vols.
DUBOS, J.-F. (1974) Ventes d'armes: Une politique. Paris: Gallimard.
FARLEY P., S. KAPLAN, and W. LEWIS. (1978) Arms Across the Sea. Washington, DC: Brookings Institution.

*France, Assemblée Nationale, Commission des Finances (1970) Rapport sur le projet de loi de finances pour 1971. No. 1395, Annexe 44, Défense nationale: Dépenses en capital.

*France, Assemblée Nationale, Commission des Finances (1976) Rapport sur le projet de loi de finances pour 1977. No. 2525, Défense: Dépenses en capital.

*France, Assemblée Nationale, Commission des Finances (1977) Rapport sur le projet de loi de finances pour 1978. No. 3131, Annexe 50, Défense: Dépenses en Capital.

France, Assemblée Nationale, Commission d'Enquête (1977) Rapport sur l'utilisation des fonds publiques alloués aux enterprises privées ou publiques de construction aéronautiques. No. 2815, Vols. 1-2.

**France, Assemblée Nationale, Commission de la Défense Nationale et des Forces Armées (1975) Avis sur le projet de loi de finances pour 1976. No. 1919, Défense: Dépenses en capital, Vol. 1.

**France, Assemblée Nationale, Commission de la Défense Nationale et des Force Armées (1976) Avis sur le projet de loi de finances pour 1977. No. 2532, Défense: Dépenses en capital, Vol. 1.

** France, Assemblée Nationale, Commission de la Défense Nationale et des Forces Armées (1976a) Rapport sur le projet de loi portant approbation de la programmation militaire pour les armées 1977-1982. No. 2292, Vols. 1-2.

**France, Assemblée Nationale, Commission de la Défense Nationale et des Forces Armées (1977) Avis sur le projet de loi de finances pour 1978. No. 3150, Défense: Dépenses en capital, Vol. 1.

France, Assemblée Nationale, Commission de la Défense Nationale et des Forces Armées (1978) Avis sur le projet de loi finances pour 1979. No. 573, Défense, Dépenses en Capital, Vol. 1.

France, Sénat, Commission des Finances (1972) Rapport général sur le projet de loi de finances pour 1973. No. 66, III, Annexe 37, Défense nationale: Dépenses en capital.

France, Sénat, Commission des Finances (1974). Rapport général sur le projet de loi de finances pour 1975. No. 99, III, Annexe 40, Défense: Dépenses en capital.

France, Sénat, Commission des Finances (1975). Rapport général sur le projet de finances pour 1976. No. 62, III, Annexe 43.

France, French Embassy, Press and Information Division (1977) France's Position on the Sale of Arms. New York.

France, Institut National de la Statistique et des Etudes Economiques (INSEE) (1976) Tableaux de L'Economie Française. Paris.

France, Institut National de la Statistique et des Etudes Economiques (1977) Economie & Statistique 91 (July-August).

――― (1977a) Economie & Statistique 94 (November).

France, Ministère de l'Economie et des Finances, Direction Générale des Douanes (1976) Statistiques de Commerce Extérieur de la France. Paris.

France, Service d'Information et de Relations Publiques des Armées (SIRPA) (1976) Dossier d'information, les armées françaises de demain. No. 49, Paris.

France, Service d'Information et de Relations Publiques des Armées (SIRPA) (1977) Dossier d'Information, La délégation générale pour l'armement. Paris.

FREEDMAN, L. (1978) Arms Production in the United Kingdom: Problems and Prospects. London: Royal Institute of International Affairs.

GARCIA, A. (1977) Les Instruments de la politique française du commerce extérieur. Paris: Documentation Française.

---

*Cited as France, ANCF. **Cited as France, ANCDN.

GEORGE, S. and R. SMOKE (1974) Deterrence in American Foreign Policy: Theory and Practice. New York: Columbia Univ. Press.
International Monetary Fund (1977) International financial Statistics, Supplement, Annual Data: 1952-1976 21 (May), Washington, DC.
Internationale Wehrrevue (1977).
JACOMET, R. (1945) L'Armement de la France. Paris: Lajeunesse.
KLEIN, J. (1976) "Commerce des armes et politique: le cas français." Politique Etrangère 41, 5.
KOHL, W. (1971) French Nuclear Diplomacy. Princeton, NJ: Princeton Univ. Press.
KOLODZIEJ, E. (1974) French International Policy under De Gaulle and Pompidou: The Politics of Grandeur. Ithaca, NY: Cornell Univ. Press.
KOLODZIEJ, E. (forthcoming, 1979) "Arms transfers and international politics: the interdependence of independence," in S. Neuman and R. Harkavy (eds.) Arms Transfers and International Politics. New York: Praeger.
KOLODZIEJ, E. (forthcoming, 1979a) "Measuring French arms transfers: a problem of sources and some sources of problems with ACDA data." Journal of Conflict Resolution (June).
LEITENBERG, M. and N. BALL (1979) "The foreign arms sales of the Carter administration." Bulletin of the Atomic Scientists 35 (February): 31-35.
LE MARQUAND (1923) La question des arsenaux (guerre et marine) par le controlleur général. Paris.
Le Monde (1977) L'Année économique et sociale. Paris.
MENAHEM, G. (1976) La Science et la militaire. Paris: Seuil.
MERY, G. (1976) "Une Armée pour quoi faire et comment?" Défense Nationale 32 (June).
PINATEL, J.-B. (1976) L'Economie des Forces. Les Cahiers de la Fondation pur les Etudes de Défense Nationale. Paris.
Scandinavian International Peace Research Institute (1975) World Armaments and Disarmament: SIPRI Yearbook. Cambridge, MA: MIT Press.
SCHEINMAN, L. (1965) Atomic Energy Policy in France under the Fourth Republic. Princeton, NJ: Princeton Univ. Press.
SIRJACQUES, F. (1977) Determinanten der französischen Rüstungspolitik: Ein Beitrag zur Analyse von Rüstungsdynamik. Frankfurt: Peter Lang.
STERLING, J. (1974) The French Weapon Acquisition Process. Washington, DC: Army Foreign and Technology Center.
United States, Congress, House, Committee on International Relations (1978) Conventional Arms Transfer Policy. Washington, DC: U.S. Government Printing Office.
United States, Congress, Senate, Committee on Foreign Relations (1979) Prospects Multilateral Arms Export Restraint. Washington, DC: U.S. Government Printing Office.
United States, Congressional Research Service (1977) Implications of President Carter's Conventional Arms Transfer Policy. Washington, DC.
United States, Arms Control and Disarmament Agency (1978) Expenditures and Arms Transfers: 1967-1976. Washington, DC: U.S. Government Printing Office.

Chapter 5

LEGISLATIVE CONTROL OF WEAPONS SYSTEM ACQUISITION: A COMPARATIVE ANALYSIS OF THE UNITED KINGDOM AND THE UNITED STATES

NORMAN A. GRAHAM
Columbia University

DAVID J. LOUSCHER
University of Akron

The purpose of this study is two-fold: (1) to compare and assess the relationship between legislators and technical experts in the evaluation and appraisal of weapon systems in two legislative environments, the United

EDITORS' NOTE: This chapter was first submitted for review May 1, 1979. The version published here was received July 11, 1979. The authors report that the data studied here are available to others from them at Department of Political Science, University of Akron, Akron, Ohio 44325

AUTHORS' NOTE: We would like to express appreciation for financial support provided by grants from the Institute for the Study of World Politics, which enabled completion of the research on legislative control in the United Kingdom, and from the Faculty Research Committee of The University of Akron, to complete interviews in the American legislature.

The data generated for this study are available to others without restriction from the authors. The data were made by coding public records available to all. The authors feel the method utilized in the paper can be used by others to generate further data or to conduct replication studies.

States and the United Kingdom, and (2) to attempt methodological innovation in the comparative analysis of foreign policy behavior. The United States House Armed Services Committee (HASC) is compared to its closest functional equivalent in the U.K., The Defense and External Affairs Subcommittee (DEASC) of the British House of Commons Expenditure Committee. The authors have utilized a truly comparative research design and field study program. Data on perception and behavior were obtained through a common interviewing schedule. In addition, the authors have attempted to confirm legislator perceptions of their roles and constraints on their roles by examining legislative behavior in one area where legislators interact the most with defense experts, namely hearings. The principal instrument used to assess actual behavior was a modified form of content analysis.

Increasingly, scholars have turned to an examination of domestic influences in attempting to explain huge arms expenditures or defense system choices. A major debate has centered on how domestic influences may determine defense systems or international arms competition. Usually, attention is directed toward the role or advantages of certain interest groups; scarcely any attention is focused on the role of the legislature. There are few studies that consider a legislature as an independent or key actor in defense systems decision-making, and there are practically no comparative treatments. However, it is a cardinal assertion of this study that the way legislatures organize themselves for evaluating defense systems and that the way individual legislators define their function in dealing with defense systems are important areas for research in considering the broad issues of threats, weapons, and foreign policy behavior.

RESEARCH AND HYPOTHESES

The literature on legislative control over defense issues and choices may, as Korb (1973) has indicated, be divided into three basic positions or hypotheses: fiscal, programmatic, or negligible. The fiscal or budgetary hypothesis focuses on congressional efforts to control the level of defense spending. Huntington (1961), in particular, argued that issues developed on monetary terms ("structural") were of most concern and best controlled by Congress. Legislators, then, feel most confident when focusing on eliminating waste or inefficiencies in defense budgets (Fenno, 1966 and Wildavsky, 1964). Influence or control is in the form of "across-the-board reductions or extending spending programs over longer periods" (Korb 1973).

The programmatic hypothesis asserts that Congress controls the defense budget in policy terms and uses its primary interest, "the power of the purse," to shape defense policy, programs and strategy. Kanter (1972), in a quantitative analysis of the distribution of congressional changes of the defense budget, concluded that Congress has a programmatic impact on defense issues. Laurance (1976) also concluded that Congress performed more of a policy role than a fiscal role. Since 1974, increased legislative resources, argued Bledsoe and Handberg (1977), have permitted committees to have greater policy impact on defense issues.

The third position asserts that while Congress often makes concerted attempts to influence both the budget and programs, the general impact is negligible. Vast numbers of scholars and legislators subscribe to this position. Kolodziej (1966), Goss (1970), Robinson (1962), Dexter (1963), Scher (1963), Neustadt (1955), Schlesinger (1972), Korb (1973), and Salisbury and Louscher (1974), Aspin (1974), and Liske (1975) have, among others, documented the passive but sometimes fretful role Congress has in the making of defense policy. According to this group, congressional activities in defense policy making are more "shadow than substance," more reaction than action, more response than initiative, more stagnation than innovation, more spasmodic and fretful than constant and routine, more ratification than decision.

Among scholars searching for the causes of limited legislative control over defense issues or weapons acquisition, considerable attention has been devoted to legislative information problems. These information problems have been, for the most part, defined as depending upon the agencies for the information needed to make decisions about defense (Robinson, 1962; Dexter, 1963). The assumption on the part of the executive of the power to withhold information from the Congress through the use of such practices as "executive privilege," overclassification, extended use of "executive agreements," lying and deliberate deception are often cited as the reason Congress has limited control. At a 1973 conference of about thirty-five congressmen and twenty diplomats, scholars, and former officials, the congressional participants constatly stressed that large amounts of time and energy were expended attempting to gain access to information the executive possessed (Salisbury and Louscher, 1974). Similarly, the Committee on Government Operations (U.S. House of Representatives, 1972) attempted to document the problems of Congress in obtaining information from the executive branch. Congressional witnesses emphasized their efforts to avoid ignorance by battling agencies. Though there are exceptions (Aspin, 1974), many congressmen perceive the information problem as one in which legislators are eager "to know" but are kept ignorant by others, specifically, the agencies.

As the above suggests, most of the literature on legislature control primarily deals with the U.S. Congress. This raises the question, is the

United States pattern unique? Are there similarities in committee hearing behavior and information processing with other national legislatures, and what are the key differences? Unfortunately, previous research related to these questions on defense issues is quite sparse—indeed, practically nonexistent.

There is of course considerable variation in structure and function among the legislatures of the world. Jean Blondel (1973: 137-140) suggests four distinct types. First, and lowest on his scale of role and influence is a type where activities are almost nonexistent and where influence is limited primarily to detailed matters. The legislature of East Germany provides the best example of this type. Second is a type where bills and sometimes general policies are discussed; the legislature has influence but not in some of the most important concerns of the country. Many African legislatures, particularly in French-speaking countries, fall within this category. Third is a type of legislature which discusses all matters of government, but does not, for various reasons, have the means for influencing the executive to any considerable extent. Blondel classifies the legislatures of Uruguay and Venezuela as well as that of France under the Fifth Republic in this category. The final types includes the U.S. Congress and the British Parliament, indeed most Western European legislatures, which "can be said to fulfill in a generally adequate way the functions of channeling demands and discussing general problems as well as having various means of intervention in order to veto some of the more exaggerated suggestions of the executive or in order to initiate a number of new ideas, even in the field of general matters" (Blondel, 1973: 139).

However, the fact remains that there are important structural differences among the legislatures which fall within Blondel's fourth type, and many questions about patterns of executive-legislative relations remain to be explored. To date, comparative studies of these legislatures have largely consisted of descriptions of the composition of their membership or rather general treatments of their functions and patterns of behavior (see Kornberg, 1973).

Examinations of the role of Western European legislatures in foreign and defense policy have been for the most part limited to portions of more general treatments of foreign policy making, as in the works of Richards (1973), Snyder (1964), Vital (1968), Wallace (1977), or have been rather general case studies of the parliamentary influence on the policy of one country, as in Baehr (1974) and Richards (1967). The comparative studies which look into patterns of executive-legislative relations either have not focused specifically on defense issues, as in the recent study by King (1976), or have examined such patterns only as a rather limited concern of the inquiry, as in Burt (1975).

As the above summary of the principal literature of scholarly and legislator concerns about legislative control of defense policy reveals, analysis of the problems and explanation of causes may be reviewed at two levels. The first may be called the macrolevel, which focuses primarily on plenary voting behavior concerning budgets and programs. The second may be called the microlevel, which focuses on individual legislative perceptions, roles, and personal problems or on the impact or problems of committees.

The present study focuses on committee behavior as an important area for assessing the constraints placed upon legislators and in understanding certain weapons acquisition decisions. In the past, committee behavior has not been given enough attention in understanding defense decision-making. In particular, this study focuses on hearings as an important arena of interaction between legislators and defense experts concerning choices of weapons systems and problems of defense.

Hearings are an ideal domain in which to assess legislative use of information or to evaluate a legislator's interaction with experts. A hearing is a recorded form of interaction. Moreover, especially U.S. legislators among our respondents reported that limited time to read or study defense matters compels them to use the hearings as their major information source. While contacts with government defense experts are varied (personal and social contact, departmental briefings, field trips, interaction between staff and experts, personal letters and phone calls, indirect interaction through the press, etc.), many legislators reported that their most significant contact with defense experts occurred during hearings. Thus, not only is the hearing a recorded form of interaction, it is also a primary form. The annual hearings on military posture in the U.S. Congress have long been heralded as a primary means for legislative evaluation of major weapons systems. Indeed, in 1959 the House Armed Services Committee, in what was considered a major innovation in defense oversight, instituted annual review and authorization of major weapon systems through an amendment (Section 412b) to the Military Construction Authorization Act of FY 1960. Writing about that amendment, Raymond Dawson (1962: 57) predicted annual posture hearings would have a major impact for the House Armed Services Committee:

> The innovation embodied in Section 412 opens the door to the fulfillment of a vital need in the processes of defense policy-making in the United States: *effective searching debate of strategic issues and choices* [Emphasis added].

Most members of HASC report that the posture hearings were a central point of interaction with experts. Said one:

> The posture hearings are the best learning instrument we have; they are the one way people who aren't experts can get a total picture of military needs.

Commented another about the importance of hearings:

> This job is an up-hill battle with paper. The posture briefs alone are thousands of pages. All I can do is flip through them. If everyone were honest with you they would probably admit they don't read this stuff. They rely on what they hear in committee.

In the case of the British Parliament, there are also several means by which Members of Parliament (MPs) interact with government defense experts. These include formal hearings of the Defence and External Affairs Subcommittee of the Select Committee on Expenditure of the House of Commons. This Committee was created in 1972 to replace and expand the purview of the Estimates Committee. Second, there are full-House debates of defense white papers, usually presented each year to Parliament by the government. Finally, there are sporadic interactions during the "question period" and during visits to the Ministry of Defence on matters of concern to individual MPs. While expert-MP interaction is not nearly as formalized through committee hearings as in the United States, British legislators have made a concerted effort in the last six years to develop a formal structure of interaction similar to that of the Congress.

Second, hearings provide a medium by which propositions related to the relationship between experts and nonexperts as they exchange information may be assessed. A growing body of literature focuses on dilemmas of the knowledge gap—the gap between what one knows and what is available to be learned (Lerner 1976). Increasingly, many legislatures are confronting the irony of greater social responsibility but increased dependence upon experts (Brewer, 1973; Lieberman, 1970). Legislators increasingly depend upon experts for technical judgment. The legislators' dilemma is how to use the expert without becoming a captive of the expert or abrogating all responsibility to the expert.

In any interchange between an expert and nonexpert there are two basic strategies open to the nonexpert concerning the information to be received. He can permit the expert to determine the content of the exchange or he can attempt to influence the choices of information exchanged. The quantity and quality of the questions asked of or comments made to an expert during hearings are two dimensions of the nonexperts' effort to shape the exchange. The number of questions or comments or the type of questions or comments made by the nonexpert may be viewed as means of controlling information received.

Third, an analysis of hearing behavior of legislators provides an opportunity to explore the role of seniority. Among others, Matthews (1960), White (1956), and Fenno (1966) have found that legislators often attribute great weight to seniority as a definer of influence. Hearings provide a record of behavior that may be useful for assessing the importance of seniority for defense issues.

Fourth, hearings may provide a device to consider an important proposition suggested by Huntington in his classic, *The Common Defense* (1961): on strategic decisions "the United States almost has a form of semi-parliamentary government" (1961: 180). It is assumed under a parliamentary pattern that the opposition party opposes the position of the governing party. Huntington's proposition was assessed by Liske (1975) with regard to plenary voting in the Senate. Hearings provide an opportunity to test further dimensions of the proposition by focusing on "opposition" and "support" behavior of members of a committee as they interact with government witnesses. Voting behavior does not seem to be highly influenced by party affiliation. But is party affiliation a factor in opposing government defense policies during hearings? This is an important question, since administrators frequently adjust their programs as a consequence of feedback from congressional action or views (Laurance, 1976; Bledsoe and Handberg, 1977).

Fifth, an analysis of hearing behavior may provide an opportunity to assess the supporting value of legislative staff, particularly, professional staff. U.S. legislators frequently have a personal staff of fifteen or more each, many of which have professional training. In addition, in varying degrees, they have the use of the committee staff, often consisting of ten to fifteen professionals in the House and often more in the Senate. British legislators, however, have little staff support. MPs generally have no paid personal staff and the staff for a committee usually is no larger than three professionals. Wallace (1977: 96) argued that limited staff was a serious detriment to parliamentary control of foreign affairs. Does staff support affect the type of interaction legislators have with government witnesses? Bledsoe and Handberg (1977) offered the greater number of staff as an explanation for their finding that Congress exerted considerably greater policy impact. The types and quantities of questions asked during hearings may provide tools to evaluate the utility of staff.

Sixth, a comparative analysis of hearings provides an opportunity to consider the impact of differences in function between the two committees. While in general the Defence and External Affairs Subcommittee does represent the closest functional equivalent in the U.K. to the House Armed Services Committee, it should be noted that the two committees do have rather different levels of responsibility in defense decision-making. Since the 412(b) legislation of Fiscal Year 1960, all major weapons systems must be authorized on an annual basis by Congress. HASC recommendations to Congress on the basis of its posture hearings are critical to final authorization. DEASC, on the other hand, plays no such regular role in defense authorization. Rather its major function is to publish the findings of its inquiries on various defense-related topics so as to inform or "educate" the rest of the House of Commons membership on defense issues and problems. The subcommittee does not control defense expenditures nor does it directly influence major defense policy. Whereas HASC's influence is direct and extensive, the influence of DEASC is indirect and limited. Do these differences in function have an impact on differences in committee behavior, as members interact with defense experts?

The following represent six hypotheses that derive from our assessment of the uses of hearings:

H_1: Frequent legislative hearings provide a forum for "effective searching debate of strategic issues and choices."

H_2: A legislator will be reluctant to challenge an expert witness in an information exchange that is highly technical.

H_3: Legislators with the most legislative experience will play the largest role in the information exchange with defense experts.

H_4: Information exchanges between legislators and defense experts will resemble the "parliamentary pattern" in which the "non-governing" party will be more inclined to challenge government defense experts.

H_5: As a function of less staff support, British MPs will be less effective in controlling the information exchange with defense experts.

H_6: As a consequence of clear distinctions in committee function in the defense decision process, DEASC and HASC interaction with defense experts will differ.

METHOD

Interviews

In the period from 1973 to 1979, interviews were conducted with thirty U.S. congressmen who were either current or former members of the Armed Services Committee and with fifteen Members of Parliament principally involved in overseeing defense issues. In addition, seventy-five staff assistants and administrators in both countries who were connected with legislative oversight of defense issues were interviewed. The interviews were open-ended but dealt with a specific list of concerns: (1) the amount of time legislators could devote to evaluating defense issues; (2) legislators' areas of specialization in defense matters; (3) difficulties in becoming informed generally about defense; (4) difficulties in becoming a specialist; (5) executive agency willingness to provide information to legislators; (6) the impact of technical change upon legislators' feelings of confidence in making decisions about weapon systems; (7) legislators' perception of what their role is in defense policy-making. The interviews, focusing on these common sets of concerns provided a basis for systematic analysis of committee hearing behavior through the use of content analysis.

Content Analysis

The authors created a form of content analysis modified for the evaluation of interaction between legislators and defense experts. The main characteristics of the tool are the following: The interactions between legislators and defense witnesses at hearings are differentiated into six distinct categories, with a discrete interaction placed in a specific category only if it met the criteria determined for that category. The six categories constitute an ordinal scale of legislator intervention:

(I) A Statement of Agreement;
(II) A Clarification Question or Information Request;
(III) A Waste, Cost or Budgetary Question;
(IV) A Position or Action Challenge Question;
(V) A Statement of Disagreement with the Witness's Proposed Action or Program;
(VI) A Proposal to the Witness.

Questions asked of the witnesses or comments made to the witnesses were assigned a code in accordance with criteria established for each category. The criteria used as well as examples of each type are presented in the following:

Type I: Statement of Agreement. The coding rule for this type is that the legislator voices his opinion in the affirmative about the experts statement on a given subject. Some examples include:

> Mr. Brinkley. I couldn't possibly, Mr. Chairman, agree with any statement more than the one the General has just made.

> Mr. Whitehurst. Well, I would just say I am very much in favor of your proposal.

Type II: Clarification Question or Request for Descriptive Information. The coding rule for this type is that the legislator requests the witness to inform him about or describe to him a program proposal, item or event. Some examples include:

> Mr. Downey. The ECM systems being developed can they be put on the B-52 or the FB-111?
>
> Mr. Stratton. Which aircraft utilized the Sidewinder?
>
> Mr. Roper (MP). In your paper you talk about the modular basis for developing new systems. How far are these modules common to missiles which may operate in different environments?
>
> Mr. Badham. What is the design fuel use of CVV as far as quantity? How much oil do they use?

Type III: Waste, Cost or Budgetary Question or Statement. The coding rules for this type are: (a) The legislator asks the witness to explain or respond in monetary terms; or (b) the legislator is critical of the expenditures connected with a given program. Some examples include:

> Mr. Carr. Mr. Chairman, I just have a question about the slide in the first column of the budget there, at the bottom of the first column. How does four and two equal seven?
>
> Mr. Bennett. You already said it cost $1-1/2 billion this morning; that is half billion more than I thought it was. Do you have any figures for that?

Type IV: Position or Action Challenge Questions (Nonmonetary). The coding rules for this type are: (a) The legislator requests the witness *to justify* his action or proposal; (b) the legislator refers to an opposing view and asks the witness to explain why he differs; (c) an action, program or proposed program does not meet the legislators expectations or he requests an explanation as to why the witness or his agency acted in this way. Here are some examples from hearings:

> Mr. Whitehurst. Standardization reminds me of the weather, everybody talks about it but nobody does anything about. My question is what are we doing about it besides talking about it? What positive steps is this administration, you in particular, taking to get off dead center and really make some progress?
>
> Mr. Conlan (MP). Why do we appear in almost every single instance, with the exception of MRCA, to be pulling at the coattails of manufacturers In Europe as far as advanced weapons systems are concerned?
>
> Mr. Pike. Dr. Foster, are you firmly convinced that the system which you sold to us so eloquently last year should now be abandoned in favor of the system which you are selling to us with equal eloquence this year?

Type V: Statement of Disagreement. The coding rule is that the legislator does not agree with the defense expert with respect either to his proposal or his interpretation of the facts. Some examples include:

Mr. Lloyd. In response to that, I don't agree with you.... The point that I make is that I think this airplane is a better maneuvering airplane than you will give it credit for.

Mr. Stratton. You really don't expect me to believe that, now General, that you are having twice the number of these planes forced on you than you really wanted?

Mr. Conlan (MP). Mr. Green, do you appreciate that your answers to previous questions lack a great deal of conviction?

Mr. Stratton. Admiral, I think you are whistling in the dark!

Type VI: Proposal to the Witness. The coding rules for this type are: (a) The legislator offers advice as to the "proper" way of performing a given function; (b) the legislator offers a proposal for an "effective" program or policy. Some examples include:

Mr. Cohelan. Why do we have to have all these things [missiles] in continental United States? Why, for example, can't we deploy the Minutemen in Alaska? ... it would seem to me that would be a very fine place to have a delivery system.

Mr. Arends. Just take one of the ICBMs, intermediaries or whatever you want to do, and touch it off someplace at a given target at some spot, for the psychological effect or whatever it might be, to let these people know that we are really in business when that time comes. I think this is one of the things that would help, sometime. So—now I am expressing one man's opinion.

Mr. Harrison (MP). Reading this very much as a layman, I am wondering whether Poseidon is really so practical or so necessary. One is almost led to think that possibly a fifth Polaris boat might do whilst waiting for ULMS-1, which I understand could be fitted to our Polaris boats.

These six categories permit the researchers to differentiate patterns of interaction between legislators and defense experts. They also represent an ordinal ranking of the means by which legislators attempt to manage the information they receive from experts. Each category indicates an increasing willingness to challenge the witness.

Of course the validity of the generalizations to be made from the coding is directly related to the effectiveness of the coding procedure. To determine this, after development and pretesting of the scheme, the authors conducted a pilot study of 325 interactions, selected on the basis of a systematic random sample from U.S. House Armed Services Committee Posture Hearings. The authors independently coded the sample of 325 interactions. The Louscher codes on each interaction were correlated with the Graham codes on each interaction. The authors were pleased to discover that several measures of intercoder agreement were quite high, for example:

Kendall's Tau = .90

Contingency Coefficient = .91

These high intercoder agreement scores suggest, first, that the coding rules displayed in the six categories are clear enough to permit reproducibility of the data generated by any one researcher using the technique. Secondly, the high intercoder agreement scores suggest that several scholars could engage in this form of content analysis with fairly high assurance of comparable data (North, 1963).

Legislative Interactions Selected for Analysis

In the United States, the Military Posture Hearings for FY 1976, FY 1977, and FY 1978 were selected to assess legislator-government defense expert interaction. The interactions coded were limited to the House Committee on Armed Services (HASC). The authors coded all interactions of the members and government defense experts during full committee hearings on military posture. The number of coded interactions for the three hearings was 6,070.

For the British Parliament the authors selected for analysis three sets of hearings from the Defence and External Affairs subcommittee (DEASC) of the Expenditure Committee. These three hearings broadly represent the nature of probing that subcommittee members are able to undertake on defense questions: the 1973 Hearings on the Nuclear Weapon Programme (NWP 1973), the 1976 Hearings on Guided Weapons (GW 1976), and the 1978 Hearings on British Forces Germany (BFG 1978). In addition, the parliamentary debates on the 1978 defense white paper (Cmnd. 7099) were also subjected to content analysis. All interactions between British legislators and defense experts during these hearings and debates were coded as described above. The total number of interactions was 967.

DESCRIPTION OF THE DATA

Figures 5.1 and 5.2 display the amount of member interaction with defense witnesses. They demonstrate that limited participation is quite prevalent in HASC hearings but not nearly as prevalent in DEASC hearings. While interaction varies from year to year it is apparent that large percentages of HASC members do not actively interact with witnesses. For example, in FY 1976 hearings 25% of the members of the committee asked less than 1% of the total questions posed by the committee. In FY 1977 and FY 1978 the figures were even higher, 35% and 32%. Limited participation among DEASC members was less prevalent especially after the 1973 hearing. In 1976, 11% of the committee asked less than 1% of the total questions asked by the committee. For 1978 limited participation was very low.

Conversely, few members were highly active in interacting with defense witnesses in HASC. In the FY 1976 and the FY 1977 hearings, less than 5% of the committee members asked more than 10% of the questions. On the other hand, in DEASC hearings from 35% to 45% of the members asked more than 10% of the questions. It should be stressed that the adoption of active versus passive roles did not seem to be a function of seniority or experience on the committee and was not apparently related to party identification in either country.

As stated earlier, in any interchange between an expert and a nonexpert there are two basic strategies open to the nonexpert concerning the information to be received. He can permit the expert to determine the content of the exchange, or he can attempt to influence the choices of information exchanged. The quantity and quality of the questions asked of an expert are two dimensions of the nonexperts effort to shape the exchange.

Asking questions may be perceived as a means of controlling information received. Yet, committee members differ markedly in their use of questions as a means of controlling the information exchanged with witnesses. Some play very passive roles permitting, for the most part, the

FIGURE 5.1 Amount of Member Participation in Committee Hearings, HASC (percentage distributions)

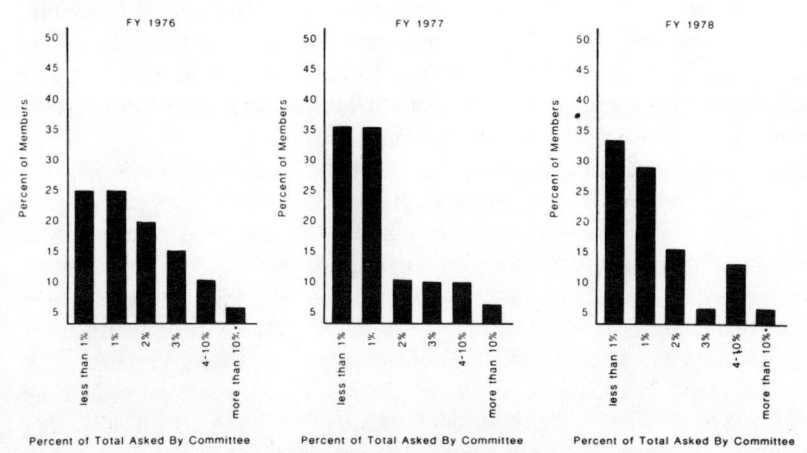

*In FY 1976, Samuel Stratton asked 23% of the questions; in FY 1978, he asked 21% of the questions.

FIGURE 5.2 Amount of Member Participation in Committee Hearings, DEASC (percentage distributions)

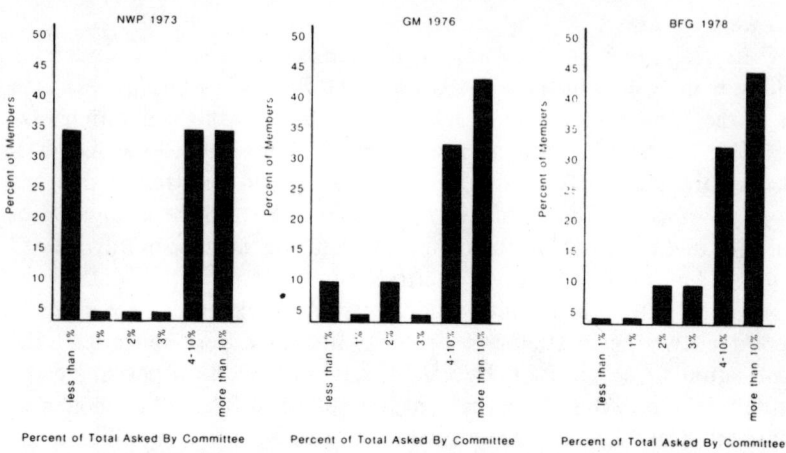

witness and others to determine what will be discussed. Others occasionally intervene. A third group is quite active. But a fourth group, generally, constituting a small percentage of the committee membership interact extensively with witnesses and perform a dominant role within the committee in shaping the information exchange agenda.

Table 5.1 reveals these marked committee room behaviors. The table depicts four information exchange roles found in HASC and DEASC hearings. As shown, in HASC frequently up to 35% of the members ask fewer than 1% of the questions posed during an annual posture hearing. No more than 10% to 15% of the members will each ask 4% to 6% of the questions. One member, Representative Samuel Stratton in FY 1976 and again in FY 1978, posed over 20% of all the questions asked those years during the full committee posture hearings.

Our analysis of British hearings revealed similar patterns of committee behavior. However, the percentages performing each role are different. A much higher percentage of legislators in DEASC perform Active Participant and Dominant Participant roles. Indeed, while Active Participants may constitute less than one-fifth of the committee in HASC they equal more than a third in DEASC. Moreover, few Dominant Participants exist in HASC while in DEASC one-third of the members of the committee may be Dominant Participants. However, committee dynamics should be expected to differ as a function of the disparities in size. HASC generally has thirty-nine members while DEASC always has nine.

A second strategy for nonexperts who are attempting to shape the

TABLE 5.1 Information Exchange Roles of HASC and DEASC Committee Members

Role	Percentage of Committee Members	
	USA	U.K.
1. Passive (Interactions with defense experts limited to less than 1% of total committee interactions)	31–35%	15% or less
2. Minimal Participation (Interactions with defense witnesses range from 1% through 2% of total committee interactions)	18–35%	10–15%
3. Active Participant (Interaction with expert witnesses range from 3% through 10% of total committee interactions)	18–23%	33–35%
4. Dominant Participant (Interaction with witnesses are in excess of 10% of the total committee interactions)	5%	33%

nature of the information exchange relates to the type of interactions chosen. Tables 5.2, 5.3, and 5.4 present data on the types of interaction. No table was created for Type I interactions as agreeing with defense experts is an interaction rarely engaged in by legislators during hearings. Table 5.2 reveals the extent to which Type II interactions (clarification questions or information requests) tend to be the dominant form of interaction between committee members and defense experts in both the U.S. and U.K. committee hearings examined. For example, for 31% of HASC members asking questions during the FY 1976 posture hearings, over 80% of their total interactions were Type II questions. Indeed, for 59% of HASC members asking questions during those hearings, over 60% of their total interactions were Type II questions.

The picture is somewhat different in the case of the U.K. DEASC hearings. Type II questions were posed with considerably less frequency for the 1973 and 1976 hearings. However, the 1978 hearings on British Forces in Germany, the hearings which seem most closely to approximate the nature of the U.S. HASC posture hearings, reveal very high percentages

TABLE 5.2 Percentages of Type II Interactions of
HASC and DEASC Members (as a percentage of total
interactions)

	Percentage Groupings of Type II Questions Asked						
	0	1–19%	20–39%	40–59%	60–79%	80–100%	N
U.S. – HASC (Percentages of Members by Hearing)							
FY 1976	0	3%	5%	33%	28%	31%[a]	39
FY 1977	3%	0	0	20%	49%	29%	35
FY 1978	0	10%	8%	31%	41%	10%	39
U.K. – DEASC (Percentages of Members by Hearing)							
NWP 1973	17%	0	50%	33%	0	0	6
GW 1976	0	0	50%	38%	13%	0	8
BFG 1978	0	0	0	0	56%	44%	9

a. The breakdown here is of groupings of percentages of questions asked by members during hearings. For example, for 31% of HASC members asking questions during FY 1976 posture hearings, at least 80% of their total interactions were Type II questions.

of Type II questions. It should be emphasized that the nature of the DEASC hearings varies more extensively than HASC in terms of substance, witnesses and purpose.

Moving up our scale of legislator intervention, Table 5.3 provides a complementary presentation of the distribution of Type III interactions (waste, cost or budgetary questions or statements). Here we find in general much lower percentages of this type posed by HASC and DEASC members. Indeed, for a very large proportion of committee members, less than 20% of their total interactions were Type III. The 1973 DEASC hearings on the Nuclear Weapon Programme do display some deviation from this trend. However, one can readily accept that hearings focusing on the question of maintaining or upgrading the British Polaris nuclear force would likely tend to raise important budgetary and cost issues.

Table 5.4 continues this presentation with respect to Type IV interactions (position or action challenge questions). Here we have rather different findings for the two committees. The British DEASC hearings seem to be characterized by larger percentages of committee members posing more questions which constitute challenges to the government

TABLE 5.3 Percentages of Type III Interactions of HASC and DEASC Members (as a percentage of total interactions)

	\multicolumn{6}{c}{Percentage Groupings of Type III Questions Asked}	
	0	1-19%	20-39%	40-59%	60-79%	80-100%	N
U.S. – HASC (Percentages of Members by Hearing)							
FY 1976	8%	46%	28%	13%	3%	0%	39
FY 1977	9%	50%	29%	6%	3%	3%	35
FY 1978	10%	49%[a]	23%	8%	5%	5%	39
U.K. – DEASC (Percentages of Members by Hearing)							
NWP 1973	0%	17%	50%	17%	17%	0	6
GW 1976	25%	75%	0	0	0	0	8
BFG 1978	22%	78%	0	0	0	0	9

a. The breakdown here is of groupings of percentages of questions asked by members during hearings. For example, for 49% of HASC members asking questions during FY 1978 hearings, from 1 to 19% of their total interactions were Type III.

defense experts. Again, however, this difference is less apparent in the case of the 1978 hearings on British Forces in Germany.

As one might expect from Tables 5.2, 5.3, and 5.4 the proportions of Type V and Type VI interactions by committee members were quite small for both HASC and DEASC. This in itself is an important finding, because it indicates a reluctance of both congressmen and MPs to challenge witnesses in any way other than to request them to provide descriptive or explanatory information.

While Tables 5.2, 5.3, and 5.4 display the interaction behavior of the entire membership of HASC and DEASC, Tables 5.5 and 5.6 focus on those members who play active roles in the hearings. Table 5.5 and Table 5.6 display the individual profiles of Active and Dominant Participants in HASC and DEASC hearings. As indicated, in HASC most of the interactions with defense experts are information type questions. Six of the nine HASC members who perform Active or Dominant Participant roles asked 50% or more Type II questions of all their interactions. Large percentages of budgetary questions were asked by six of the nine.

Type IV questions or statements ranged from 2% to 25% among those

TABLE 5.4 Percentages of Type IV Interactions of
HASC and DEASC Members (as a percentage of
total interactions)

	\multicolumn{7}{c}{*Percentage Groupings of Type IV Questions Asked*}
	0	1–19%	20–39%	40–59%	60–79%	80–100%	N
U.S. – HASC (Percentages of Members by Hearing)							
FY 1976	13%	77%[a]	10%	0	0	0	39
FY 1977	23%	77%	0	0	0	0	35
FY 1978	10%	67%	21%	3%	0	0	39
U.K. – DEASC (Percentages of Members by Hearing)							
NWP 1973	17%	0	50%	17%	0	17%	6
GW 1976	0	13%	25%	38%	25%	0	8
BFG 1978	0	78%	22%	0	0	0	9

a. The breakdown here is of groupings of percentages of questions asked by members during hearings. For example, for 77% of HASC members asking questions during FY 1976 hearings, from 1 to 19% of their total interactions were Type IV.

members performing active roles in HASC. This form of challenge to defense witnesses constituted at least 10% of all interactions, seven of the nine Active Participants had with such witnesses. Yet, it is apparent that statements of disagreement with witnesses or proposals to witnesses represented a small proportion of total interactions.

Table 5.6 depicts individual profiles for Active and Dominant Participants in DEASC. In 1973 and 1976, Type II or information questions represent a smaller percentage of all the interactions each had than in HASC. However, in 1978, the active groups' proportions of Type II questions more closely resemble the proportions of Type II questions among the active HASC group. It should be noted that DEASC activists disagree with witnesses or present alternative proposals to them even less than do HASC activists.

Each table includes an Intervention Index. This device is useful as a summary statistic to compare committees and individuals. It is a mean score of all interaction of each individual. It was calculated by multiplying the frequency of each type of question asked by the ordinal rank of the question type and dividing the product by the number of total interactions of the member. The higher the Intervention Index score, the greater the

TABLE 5.5 U.S. – HASC: Individual Profiles of Active and Dominant Participants, FY 1978 Posture Hearings

Member	Type I	Type II	Type III	Type IV	Type V	Type VI	(N)	Intervention Index[a]
Jim Lloyd (D)[b]	22[c]	3%	43%	21%	18%	7	8	(118)	3.08
Thomas Downey (D)	24	0	57	10	25	1	6	(87)	2.87
Samuel Stratton (D)	3	1	51	27	16	4	2	(364)	2.78
Richard Ichord (D)	4	1	33	49	15	2	2	(111)	2.73
Robin Beard (R)	6	2	69	5	14	6	6	(86)	2.68
Charles Bennett (D)	2	6	40	23	24	3	3	(62)	2.52
Mendel J. Davis (D)	17	1	67	17	11	3	1	(76)	2.50
Floyd Spence (R)	4	2	92	2	2	3	0	(66)	2.12

a. The Intervention Index was calculated by multiplying the frequency for each type of question asked by a member by the ordinal rank of the question by a member of the ordinal rank of the question type, the product is then divided by the number of total interactions of the member.
b. Indicates party identification: R = Republican; D = Democrat.
c. Indicates seniority ranking in committee.

TABLE 5.6 U.K. – DEASC: Individual Profiles of Active and Dominant Participants

Member		Type I	Type II	Type III	Type IV	Type V	Type VI	(N)	Intervention Index[a]
NWP 1973									
James Boyden (L)[b]	4[c]	0	20%	50%	30%	0	0	(10)	3.10
Sir John Tilney (C)	1	0	0	20	80	0	0	(5)	3.00
David Owen (L)	5	0	39	36	21	0	4	(28)	2.93
Sir Harwood Harrison (C)	2	0	29	64	0	0	7	(14)	2.93
Sir Henry d'Avigdor-Goldsmid (C)	3	0	40	20	40	0	0	(5)	2.60
Sir James d'Avigdor-Goldsmid (C)	6	0	50	17	33	0	0	(6)	2.50
GM 1976									
Bernard Conlan (L)	4	0	27%	8%	60%	5%	0	(66)	3.42
Geoffrey Finsberg (C)	6	0	33	8	56	1	0	(48)	3.27
Anthony Kershaw (C)	3	0	37	0	63	0	0	(19)	3.26
Sir Frederic Bennett (C)	2	0	33	10	57	0	0	(21)	3.24
Maurice Miller (L)	5	0	44	13	38	0	6	(16)	3.13
John Roper (L & Coop.)	7	0	55	3	42	0	0	(88)	2.88
Sir Harwood Harrison (C)	1	6	55	2	38	0	0	(55)	2.73
BFG 1978									
Geoffrey Finsberg (C)	6	0	61%	13%	26%	0	0	(163)	2.66
John Roper (L & Coop.)	7	0	67	11	19	0	1	(105)	2.53
Anthony Kershaw (C)	2	0	75	5	19	0	1	(105)	2.47
Maurice Miller (L)	5	0	82	0	14	0	5	(22)	2.46
Sir Harwood Harrison (C)	1	2	74	13	11	0	0	(62)	2.34
Bernard Conlan (L)	4	0	83	6	11	0	0	(18)	2.28
James Boyden (L)	3	4	64	16	16	0	0	(25)	2.28
Neville Sandelson (L)	8	0	88	4	8	0	0	(24)	2.21

a. The Intervention Index is calculated as in Table 5.5.
b. (L) Indicates member of Labour Party; (C) indicates member of Conservative Party; (L & Coop.) indicates member of Labour and Cooperative Group.
c. Seniority ranking in committee based upon House of Commons service.

"challenge" to the witness. A comparison of such scores among the activists reveals quite marked variation in both committees. A comparison of the committees reveals higher scores among DEASC members in 1973 and 1976 than among HASC members in FY 1978 but somewhat similar scores in the 1978 hearings. It is the 1978 DEASC hearing as noted earlier which appear to be most analogous in substance to posture hearings.

Table 5.7 compares the Intervention Index scores of active and passive members of HASC during the FY 1978 hearings. It clearly shows that there is little relationship between the type of role assumed in the hearings and the type of questions asked. Active Participants do not have Intervention Index scores that are any higher than those members who assume a Passive role. Active Participants clearly manage the information exchange over weapons choices more extensively than Passive members simply because they do not permit the witness to unilaterally determine the nature or content of the exchange. They ask a great many information type questions. However, they do not appear to force the witness to justify weapons choices, do not disagree with witnesses about defense policy and do not present alternative choices to defense experts in any higher proportions than do Passive members of the committee.

Finally, Table 5.8 presents the results of a content analysis of the parliamentary debate of the 1978 defense white paper during full meetings of the House of Commons. Since such debates constitute an important

TABLE 5.7 Comparison of Intervention Index of Active and Passive Members of HASC, FY 1978 Hearings

Active Participant Roles			*Passive Roles*[a]		
Member		Intervention Index	Member		Intervention Index
Jim Lloyd (D)[b]	22[c]	3.08	Jack Brinkley (D)	10	3.87
Thomas Downey	24	2.87	Elwood Hillis (R)	10	2.80
Samuel Stratton (D)	3	2.78	G. V. Montgomery (D)	13	2.74
Richard Ichord (D)	4	2.73	Les Aspin (D)	15	2.70
Robin Beard (R)	6	2.68	David Emery (R)	11	2.57
Charles Bennett (D)	2	2.62	David Treen (R)	5	2.55
Dan Daniel (D)	12	2.52	Pat Schroeder (D)	18	2.52
Mendel J. Davis (D)	17	2.50	Antonio Won Pat (D)	20	2.36
Floyd Spence (R)	4	2.12	Bill Nichols (D)	9	2.15
			Robert Mollohan (D)	11	2.07

a. Intervention Index scores were not calculated for passive members who asked fewer than 10 questions; four members present asked fewer than 10 questions in FY 1978 Posture Hearings.
b. Indicates party identification: R = Republican; D = Democrat.
c. Indicates seniority ranking.

point of interaction between legislators and government defense experts (here essentially government ministers), indeed the only opportunity for such interaction for the vast majority of MPs, it seems appropriate to examine the nature of that interaction. It can readily be seen that Type IV interactions are predominant, accounting for more than 50% of the total interactions. This is as one would expect in highly partisan debates during which the Labour Government position is likely to be challenged both by the Conservative opposition and the left wing of the government's own party.

EVALUATION OF HYPOTHESES

Congressional behavior during posture hearings suggests that, contrary to Dawson's (1962) expectations, annual review of major weapons systems does not appear to generate "effective searching debate of strategic issues and choices." While this study focused on committee hearing behavior alone, it should be expected that if major debate was to take place between defense experts or officials and legislators, it would be revealed in this forum. Certainly, posture hearings are not without debates, system challenges, disagreements, and alternative proposals. But as our description of the data reveals, these types of interaction are fairly limited.

First, the information exchange roles in Table 5.1 reveal that a limited number of the committee play active roles in attempting to shape the nature of the information presented. Scarcely more than 20% of HASC members can be considered active. Yet, we could expect that, at a minimum, "effective searching debate" would require an extensive effort by committee members to shape and control the information exchange between government witnesses and themselves.

TABLE 5.8 U.K.: Percentage of Each Type of Question Asked During Full Parliamentary Debate of the 1978 Defense White Paper

		Type of Question					
I	II	III	IV	V	VI	(N)	Intervention Index
11%	15%	7%	54%	4%	9%	46[a]	3.52

a. It should be noted that the parliamentary debate of defense white papers normally also includes a large proportion of interactions between backbench MPs. However, these interactions were not included in the content analysis, as the focus of this study is solely on legislator-government defense expert interactions.

Second, our description of Tables 5.2 through 5.6 reveals very limited frequencies in which members of the committee "challenged" defense experts by requiring justification of cost or rationale for programs, by disagreeing or presenting alternative proposals. Table 5.2, in particular, clearly shows that most members of HASC limit their information exchange to questions which only demand a description of a weapon, program or event.

Table 5.4 reveals that system or action challenges are not frequent during hearings. Type IV interactions represent less than 19% of total interactions for more than 75% of the committee. Even when focusing on Active and Dominant Participants it is apparent Type IV interactions are limited. For example, Table 5.5 shows that only two members of the committee, Thomas Downey and Charles Bennett, extensively challenged witnesses. About 25% of their total interactions were Type IV interactions. Table 5.5 further illustrates that disagreeing with a witness or presenting alternative proposals to a witness constitutes very small percentages of the total interactions of even active members of HASC.

Finally, our comparison of the two committees also does not substantiate Dawson's expectation. Hearings on strategic questions are not as regular in the British case. Dawson predicted that annual hearings would give committee members the experience necessary for critical review of weapons choices. Yet, even though HASC members have much more committee hearing experience and on a more regular basis, they do not challenge witnesses any more than DEASC members. Indeed, a comparison of Tables 5.5 and 5.6 indicates that Active and Dominant Participants in DEASC have much higher percentages of Type IV interactions than do their counterparts in HASC. It does appear, however, that Active and Dominant HASC members are more willing to disagree or present alternatives to witnesses than DEASC Active and Dominant Participants.

It would appear from the above review of the data that whatever the uses of annual posture hearings, they do not seem to be a forum for the kind of debate Dawson expected when the innovation was instituted in FY 1960.

Our data from the content analysis do not categorically confirm or falsify the second hypothesis regarding reluctance to challenge a witness to the technical level of the information exchange. Our interviews with legislators, as will be shown, do confirm the hypothesis. Using content analysis the hypothesis could be effectively tested by creating a typology of subjects ranged in order of technical difficulty. Types of questions could then be correlated with types of issues. The authors have not yet created a technical information range instrument. Moreover, it may be very difficult to create one because feelings of expertise or competence to deal with a technical matter will vary from one legislator to another, reflecting experience and personality characteristics. Moreover, a legislator might specialize on a single technical question, feel confident about his position on the subject, but the subject might rarely emerge as a serious item on the hearing agenda. Thus, the researcher may reach erroneous conclusions.

These serious reservations aside, the content analysis data do suggest that legislators are reluctant to challenge technical experts during hearings on major weapons systems. From interviews conducted in the mid-1950s, Dexter (1963) concluded that legislators overseeing weapons choices were the victims of "the tyranny of information and ideas." An element of this tyranny is a reluctance to challenge experts. The annual posture hearings of HASC and the fairly frequent hearings of DEASC are opportunities to have influence if in no other way than to compel government witnesses to provide rationale for the weapons choices made. Yet, as was shown, few members attempt to shape the nature of the information exchange. Only limited numbers are active, only a few ask why a weapons choice should be made, disagree with a witness, or present a witness with an alternative. As will be indicated in our discussion of probable causes of this pattern, many legislators admit in interviews a lack of confidence in dealing with technical experts.

Seniority does not appear to relate either to participation roles or to types of interactions. Tables 5.5, 5.6, and 5.7 display seniority ranking. It is difficult to assess the impact of seniority in the British case as DEASC has been in existence only since 1973. The seniority figures in Table 5.6 are calculated on relative rank in the House of Commons, not years on the committee. Among the Active and Dominant participants on the committee there is no clear relationship between seniority and the types of interaction MPs had with witnesses. For example, one of the lowest ranking members of the committee, Geoffrey Finsberg asked the greatest proportion of challenging questions.

As indicated in Table 5.5, seniority does not appear to influence participation in HASC either. Four of the nine active or dominant participants during posture hearings had minimal committee experience. For example, Jim Lloyd and Thomas Downey are among the lowest-ranking Democrats on the committee, yet, they have the highest Intervention Index scores. Despite this finding a number of low-ranking members told us that seniority did shape their hearing behavior. Said a junior member:

> The chairman calls on members in order of seniority of those present. By the time he gets to me all the good questions have been asked.

Congressmen Lloyd, Downey, and Davies did not find seniority inhibiting. Moreover, it is interesting to note that the most passive members of the committee, as revealed in Table 5.7, are mostly middle-ranking members, not low-ranking members as the seniority hypothesis would suggest.

As suggested earlier, the findings of our content analysis have interesting implications as we compare American and British legislators. Tables 5.1 through 5.8 do reveal important differences in intervention behavior during committee hearings. However, some of these differences run contrary to the expectations of our hypotheses.

Stemming from an argument made by Huntington (1961), Hypothesis 4 suggests that in both countries, we should expect committee members from "nongoverning" parties to challenge government defense experts more than members from "governing" parties. This is clearly not the case; there is no consistent pattern of partisan committee behavior, even in the U.K. "parliamentary" system. Tables 5.5 and 5.6 indicate that committee members from the major political parties in each country comprise the active or dominant participant groups, and Table 5.7 indicates party balance among passive HASC members. Since change in the "governing" party took place in both countries during the period we examined—Republican president (FY 1976) to a Democratic president (FY 1977 and FY 1978) in the United States; and Conservative government (NWP 1973) to a Labour government (GW 1976 and BFG 1978) in the U.K.—our findings clearly suggest that the Huntington proposition, supported by Liske's findings (1975) for Senate plenary voting, does not hold for committee hearing behavior. Differences in questioning or intervention strategies may better be explained by role conceptions and personality differences than by party identification.

Hypothesis 5.5 is also not supported by the data. Despite inferior staff support, British MPs were if anything more effective in controlling the information exchange with defense experts, at least to the extent that national security constraints were not an issue. Tables 5.1-5.7 reveal that British members of DEASC were somewhat more active and made more challenging interventions than their HASC counterparts.

It is clear, however, that there are some differences between HASC and DEASC committee member interactions with defense experts. Moreover, the impact of clear distinctions in committee function, as suggested in Hypothesis 6, seems to offer the beginnings of a plausible explanation. This will be discussed in the next section.

POSSIBLE CAUSES OF COMMITTEE HEARING BEHAVIOR PATTERNS

This content analysis of legislative behavior in evaluating defense policy and weapons systems reveals that generally legislators are reluctant to challenge defense experts in ways other than to request descriptions of weapons, policies or actions. This behavior is confirmed by interviews. This is especially the case among members of the Armed Services Committee.

Why are their such variations in roles of legislators in interacting with witnesses? Why do even active members ask predominantly information questions? Our interviews suggest some plausible explanations.

From interviews conducted in the mid-1950s, Dexter (1963) concluded that legislators overseeing weapons choices were the victims of "the tyranny of information and ideas." As an experienced committee member reported to Dexter (1963: 313), "The whole problem is that we are not military experts and have to rely upon what the military people tell us." Despite a number of procedural innovations, including annual authorization and review of major weapons systems, legislators have similar views today. Said a senior member of HASC:

> We try to specialize in order to handle this stuff. Some members have good reputations. I feel good about my knowledge of force levels when talking on the floor. But I don't feel confident about these weapons.

Congressional perceptions of the reasons why they lack confidence in deciding about weapons systems are several. First, some are disturbed by the responsibility. Said a ranking member of HASC:

> It is often frightening that we are compelled to make major decisions about the nation's security, yet we just don't have a handle on many of these weapons systems.

A subcommittee chairman commented on the broad scope of the committee's work:

> You have to keep in mind that this committee has one of the toughest jobs in Congress. We oversee the largest organization in the world. We have to deal with experiments—with technologies that are in the experimental stage. We have to make decisions on weapons and instruments that have never been used before.

Clearly, U.S. legislators are frustrated by the increasing technological dimensions of defense choices. Many complained that while they were able to comprehend some subjects, such as manpower, others were too technical to understand. Said one of the more experienced members of the committee:

> Sometimes on long term programs we know more than the people who testify. They have high turnover. On technical weapons questions, however, they have the advantage. We can't keep up.

Said a relatively new member of the committee:

> When I came to Congress I thought we were supposed to be a devil's advocate. These weapons and systems are so sophisticated its hard to know what a devil's advocate should do.

A legislator who left the committee explained why:

> This committee is frustrating. I didn't come to Congress to be a technician. I want to be a policy-maker. Yet, all this stuff is too technical.

A serious problem for many members in becoming confident about defense issues is the multiple responsibilities of congressmen. Several pointed out that they have three jobs: (1) legislation on the floor, (2) committee work, and (3) district work. Each is a full-time job. With the exception of subcommittee chairmen most members reported they could not devote more than two hours a day on the average to defense questions.

> We don't have time to really probe the witnesses, that requires too much homework. I can only devote about 10% of my time to Armed Services Committee work.

Frequently the sheer volume of information itself was cited as an obstacle to searching review of proposed weapons systems:

> In R&D we get five books twelve inches thick we are supposed to read before the hearing. I don't have time to read them. Thus, I have to rely on Defense witnesses to tell me. I don't have time to do it any other way.

For HASC members, obtaining information has not been a problem. Frequently, the major problem was finding some means of reducing the information to usable proportions or assimilating it. A few members complained that the agencies withheld important information from them. Some referred to the necessity of "harassing" the agencies. But HASC members had few complaints about the willingness of agencies to provide them necessary information. Their essential problem was knowing what to do with it. As a member who often votes against the majority of the committee noted:

> We really have an information problem, but it's not that DOD withholds it; they are better than most agencies. The problem really is that the technology changes so fast it is difficult for us to get command of it so we can feel competent in talking with Defense people.

Feelings of inadequacy about one's expertise in dealing with weapons decisions do not seem to be as prominent among British MPs. Indeed, in interviews with us and in published articles, the Expenditure Committee and DEASC subcommittee chairmen have gone to some length to underline the expertise of committee members, both in terms of previous defense experience within the Ministry of Defense (MOD)—several held very responsible defense positions in previous governments—and with organizations such as the Western European Union and the NATO assembly (see Harrison, 1972). Members of DEASC also cited their long experience on the committee as another factor for their expertise. (Paradoxically, many members of HASC have been on the committee for over twenty years, yet they still have major reservations about their expertise.)

Rather, the major concern among DEASC members about their ability to perform an effective legislative review function relates to the problem of gaining adequate information (in contrast to HASC). The DEASC was initially viewed with considerable suspicion by the Defence Ministry. It was necessary for the subcommittee to gain MOD confidence and develop a good relationship through time ("without being in their pocket"). There have been important problems in gaining data which was viewed by the MOD as essential to the national security. This may account for the intense nature of many of the questions during the hearings; extensive probing and cross-examining of reluctant witnesses in order to extract the desired information. Member frustration is often evident in attempting to determine the future policy directions that the government is considering. This frustration was rarely expressed by HASC and may account for differences in questioning style.

A related difficulty here is the question of being able to publish the committee's findings without extensive censorship by the MOD. This problem has improved somewhat recently through the development of new MOD review procedures, but it remains an important threat to perhaps the main function of the subcommittee. This function is to inform or "educate" the rest of the House membership on defense issues and problems through its reports. The subcommittee does not control defense expenditure nor directly influence major policy; its influence is indirect and limited.

This question of the subcommittee's function may also help to explain differences between DEASC and HASC members on feelings about their expertise as well as differences in activity during committee hearings. It is certainly true that HASC has much more direct responsibility in defense decision-making. Feelings of lack of expertise and subsequent reluctance to challenge may stem from this heavy responsibility as well as the size of the U.S. defense effort and the complex technology of many of its weapons systems. DEASC, on the other hand, has a little more freedom to be in error. The consequences of a mistake for this subcommittee in stating its views or taking a position are less directly felt.

CONCLUSIONS

The foregoing appears to have important theoretical and policy implications. Our technique of assessing hearing behavior appears to have provided further insights into the literature on defense decision-making. Much of the literature dealing with the role of legislators focuses on plenary voting. Committee behavior and committee information problems have not been given much attention. Our research suggests, however, that greater attention should be given to the ways legislators gather information.

The literature that does focus on legislative information problems argues that executive control of information is a major reason legislatures have limited influence on defense decision-making. Our research suggests that legislative information problems or the "tyranny of information" may be explained as much by legislative behavior patterns, the roles assumed during hearings, as by executive practices.

Speaking about practical policy questions, Schlesinger (1973: 112) stated:

> If Congress really wants to reclaim its lost authority, it can do little more effective than to assure itself a steady and disinterested flow of information about foreign affairs. More than ever, information is the key to power.

The policy implications of our research seem to be that the legislative committees overseeing defense may need to review the instruments they use for gathering information. The information gathering process is not very effective. Moreover, it is not just information that is needed for power, but rather certain types of information. We have shown that certain types of questions are rarely asked by a vast majority of the two committees assessed. For example, vast amounts of descriptive technical information in the hands of a legislator may not be a "key to power" as to whether or not to deploy the MX missile. Rather, the key may be improved and expanded tools for demanding justification and explanations as to why the MX should be deployed.

Our experience with the content analysis methodology used in this study has been encouraging. This approach to comparing legislative behavior seems to work effectively in different national settings, although one must be very sensitive to differences in political and governmental structure in general, as well as to the particular role or functions of committee hearings in each legislative system.

Content analysis appears to be a fairly objective method of assessing the efficacy of committee hearings as a means to legislative influence in defense decision-making. It also has potential for application in other issue areas and other substantive questions of interest to scholars in comparative foreign policy behavior. With recent efforts in the British House of Commons to expand the extent to which government ministries are scrutinized by parliamentary select committees, the utility of this method of analysis can only increase.

Finally, this adaptation of content analysis is replicable, suggesting the possibility of cumulation and refinement of findings through future studies. It is also a fairly manageable approach, although the coding can be tedious; but with a clear set of instructions, the data gathering can be performed by several coders with acceptable levels of intercoder agreement.

REFERENCES

ASPIN, L. (1974) "Why doesn't Congress do something?" Foreign Policy 15: 70-82.
BAEHR, P. R. (1974) "Parliamentary control over foreign policy in the Netherlands." Government and Opposition 9: 165-188.
BLEDSOE, R. L. and R. B. HANDBERG (1977) "Congressional decisions on defense programs: FY 1972-FY 1978." Delivered at the 1977 Annual Meeting of the Southern Political Science Association, New Orleans, November.
BLONDEL, J. (1973) Comparative Legislatures. Englewood Cliffs, NJ: Prentice-Hall.
BREWER, G. D. (1973) Politicians, Bureaucrats, and the Consultant. New York: Basic Books.
BURT, R. (1975) "Defense budgeting: the British and American cases." Adelphi Papers 112.
DAWSON, R. H. (1962) "Congressional innovation and intervention." American Political Science Review 56: 42-57.
DEXTER, L. A. (1963) "Congressmen and the making of military policy," in R. L. Peabody and N. W. Polsby (eds.) New Perspectives on the House of Representatives. Chicago: Rand McNally.
FENNO, R. (1966) The Power of the Purse: Appropriations Politics in Congress. Boston: Little, Brown.
GOSS, C. F. (1972) "Military committee membership and defense-related benefits in the House of Representatives." Western Political Quarterly 25: 215-233.
HARRISON, Sir H. (1972) "Parliament and defence." RUSI 117, 4.
HUNTINGTON, S. P. (1961) The Common Defense: Strategic Programs in National Politics. New York: Columbia Univ. Press.
KANTER, A. (1972) "Congress and defense policy, 1960-1970." American Political Science Review (March).
KING, A. (1976) "Modes of executive-legislative relations." Legislative Studies Quarterly (February).
KOLODZIEJ, E. A. (1966) The Uncommon Defense and Congress 1945-1961. Columbus: Ohio State Univ. Press.
KORB, L. J. (1973) "Congressional impact on defense spending, 1962-1973: the programatic and fiscal hypotheses." Naval War College Review (November).
KORNBERG, A. [ed.] (1973) Legislatures in Comparative Perspective. New York: David McKay.
LAURANCE, E. J. (1976) "The changing role of congress in defense policy making."

Journal of Conflict Resolution 20: 213-253.
LERNER, A. W. (1976) "Experts, politicians, and decision making in the technological society." University Programs Modular Studies. Morristown, NJ: General Learning Press.
LIEBERMAN, J. K. (1970) The Tyranny of the Experts. New York: Walker.
LISKE, C. (1975) "Changing patterns of partisanship in senate voting on defense and foreign policy, 1946-1969," in P. J. McGowan (ed.) Sage International Yearbook of Foreign Policy Studies, Volume 3. Beverly Hills: Sage Publications.
MATTHEWS, D. R. (1960) U.S. Senators and Their World. Chapel Hill: Univ. of North Carolina Press.
NEUSTADT, R. (1955) "Presidency and legislation: planning the president's program." American Political Science Review 49: 980-1021.
NORTH, R. (1963) Content Analysis. Evanston, IL: Northwestern Univ. Press.
RICHARDS, P. G. (1973) "Parliament and the parties," in R. Boardman and A.J.R. Groom (eds.) The Management of Britain's External Relations. London: Macmillan.
--- (1967) Parliament and Foreign Affairs. London: Allen & Unwin.
ROBINSON, J. A. (1962) Congress and Foreign Policy Making. Homewood, IL: Dorsey.
SALISBURY, R. and D. J. LOUSCHER (1974) "Congressional information problems in foreign affairs." Report submitted to the Foreign Affairs Task Force, Democratic Study Group of the U.S. House of Representatives (June).
SCHER, S. (1963) "Conditions of legislative control." Journal of Politics 25.
SCHLESINGER, A. J. (1972) "Congress and the making of American foreign policy." Foreign Affairs (October).
SNYDER, W. P. (1964) The Politics of Defence Policy, 1945-1962. Columbus: Ohio State Univ. Press.
U.S. House of Representatives, Committee on Government Operations (1972) Hearings on U.S. Government Information Policies Problems of Congress in Obtaining Information from the Executive. Washington, DC: U.S. Government Printing Office.
U.S. House of Representatives, Committee on Armed Services (1977) Hearings on Military Posture and H.R. 5068, Department of Defense Authorization for Appropriations for Fiscal Year 1978. Washington, DC: U.S. Government Printing Office.
--- (1976) Hearings on Military Posture and H.R. 11500, Department of Defense Authorization for Appropriations for Fiscal Year 1977. Washington, DC: U.S. Government Printing Office.
--- (1975) Hearings on Military Posture and H.R. 3689, Department of Defense Authorization for Appropriations for Fiscal Year 1976. Washington, DC: U.S. Government Printing Office.
United Kingdom, House of Commons, Twelfth Report from the Expenditure Committee, Session 1972-1973, Nuclear Weapon Programme.
--- Seventh Report from the Expenditure Committee, Session 1975-1976, Guided Weapons, Volume 2.
---, Tenth Report from the Expenditure Committee, Session 1977-1978, British Forces Germany, Volume 2.
VITAL, D. (1968) The Making of British Foreign Policy. New York: Praeger.
WALLACE, W. (1977) The Foreign Policy Process in Britain. London: Allen & Unwin.
WHITE, W. S. (1956) Citadel. New York: Harper & Row.
WILDAVSKY, A. (1964) The Politics of the Budgetary Process. Boston: Little, Brown.

Chapter 6

MILITARY PRODUCTION IN THIRD WORLD COUNTRIES: A POLITICAL STUDY

ILAN PELEG
Lafayette College

" ... those nations who can, manufacture [arms], and those who cannot, purchase." (Stanley and Pearton, *The International Trade in Arms,* 1972, p. 7)

The supply of arms to Third World countries is often associated with the political influence of the supplier over the recipient, either as an intended consequence or as a by-product. The supply reflects the multidimensional superiority of the supplier over the recipient in areas such as technological capacity, economic resources, and scientific potential. This superiority can be translated in a variety of ways into political influence. It is used as a diplomatic tool in order to cause changes in the behavior of other actors in the system, the recipients of arms. Weapons can be perceived as a threat to the independence of the recipient nation by their ability to cause changes in the foreign policy behavior of the nation.

EDITORS' NOTE: This chapter was first submitted for review May 7, 1979. The version published here was received July 1, 1979. The author reports that the data used in this study are available on IBM cards from him at Department of Government and Law, Lafayette College, Easton, PA 18042.

AUTHOR'S NOTE: The author would like to thank Lafayette College for financial support of this study. Thanks are also extended to James A. Caporaso of the University of Denver and to Amelia C. Leiss from the Center for International Studies at MIT, as well as to the editors of this volume.

Though weapons suppliers are frequently interested in influencing their clients, recipients strive to maintain their political independence, the freedom of acting according to what they consider to be their interests. From the point of view of the recipient there are a number of potential ways for eliminating, or at least minimizing, military—and therefore political—dependence on suppliers: (a) the recipient might look for substitutes, military items which can perform the same function that currently supplied items perform; (b) the recipient might look for alternative sources of supply, nations which have both the motivation and the ability to replace current suppliers; and (c) the recipient might decide to produce by itself the needed military items. The third alternative will be analyzed in this chapter.[1]

Self-production of arms is a course of action which might reduce the dependence of Third World countries on foreign suppliers. As with other courses of action, it has the potentiality of having important political meanings, that is, relevance in terms of the influence relationships between actors in the international system.

WEAPONS SELF-PRODUCTION: A POLITICAL INTERPRETATION

Self-production of arms by any Third World country invariably requires considerable sacrifices on the part of that state. As demonstrated by the SIPRI study (1971: 738) in the case of India,[2] the financial burden associated with domestic production is considerably heavier than that associated with the importation of arms.[3] Moreover, in the economic take-off stage the Third World Country is likely to rely heavily on financial assistance, technological know-how, and political cooperation of one or more industrialized nation(s). The assistance often takes the form of licensing production, codevelopment or coproduction, sending personnel, and other forms of close cooperation. Rarely can a take-off occur independently. These forms of cooperation create a measure of dependence—in order to achieve a measure of independence.

Nevertheless, in the last decade and a half we have witnessed a growing tendency among some Third World countries to become independent of outside sources by developing large weapon industries of their own. This chapter deals with this phenomenon empirically, by trying to identify trends of weapons self-production in the Third World, and theoretically, by trying to explain these developments as a politically significant phenomenon.

Self-production is hypothesized to be a function of two basic determinants: motivation and capacity. Within the context of this discussion, *motivation* relates to the desire of a potential self-producer to develop or to expand an independent or semiindependent weapons industry, in order to prevent other actors from taking advantage of his military dependency. *Capacity,* on the other hand, relates to the indigenous or purchasable capabilities of a potential self-producer, capabilities which determine its options in terms of developing an arms industry.

TRENDS AND DEVELOPMENTS[4]

Table 6.1 presents information regarding weapons producers in the Third World, the types of manufactured weapons, and the degree of production independence. It distinguishes between indigenous production (truly self-production), arms codevelopment (i.e., cooperation of the Third World country with a foreign country), and licensed production. Self-production scores for each of the Third World producers are then calculated. The scores reflect the ability of the Third World country to produce military equipment on her own, taking into account two dimensions: the variety of production in terms of manufactured items and the degree of production independence. Technically speaking, a country's score is the summation of "points" assigned to the country according to the following principles: 3 points for the indigenous production of an item, 2 points for codevelopment, and 1 point for licensed production. This scale reflects the assumption that indigenous production guarantees more independence to the producer than codevelopment with another, usually more powerful, nation, but that codevelopment, a process to which the Third World country contributes independently, is associated with more independence than licensed production.[5]

Table 6.1 reflects a distribution in which two groups of Third World self-producers are distinguishable. The first is a group of five relatively important self-producers: Argentina, Brazil, India, Israel, and South Africa. The second is a group of nations which produce some military items but are still almost totally dependent on foreign supply of weapons. We face a bimodal distribution of military self-producers in the Third World.[6] A third category of countries, those who do not produce at all, is larger than the two groups combined.

As for the degree of production sophistication, a qualitative review of the activity of the main producers is required. All of these have developed serious weapons industries in at least some of the areas of military production. Their ability to produce sophisticated weapons, independently or with foreign assistance, is constantly increasing.

Argentina is currently producing a light transport aircraft (IA-50 Guarani II), a COIN[7] fighter (IA-58 Pucará), and a jet trainer. Preparations,

TABLE 6.1 Arms Production in Third World Countries, 1950–1977[a]

Country	Military Aircraft a	b	c	Guided Missiles a	b	c	Armoured Fighting Vehicles a	b	c	Warships a	b	c	Military Electronics a	b	c	Aero-Engines a	b	c	Self-Production Score
Argentina	x	x	x	x			x			x	x						x		15
Bangladesh											x								3
Brazil	x	x	x	x	x			x		x	x		x	x			x		24
Burma											x								3
Chile		x									x								6
Colombia	x									x									2
Dominican Rep.											x								3
Gabon											x								3
India	x	x	x	x	x			x	x	x	x		x	x			x		26
Indonesia	x	x									x								7
Iran	x						x												2
Israel	x	x		x	x	x	x	x	x	x	x		x	x		x	x		25
Kuwait					x														3
Libya			x																2
Mexico		x																	6
North Korea	x										x								5
Pakistan	x				x		x				x								6
Peru										x	x								4
Phillipines	x				x		x			x	x		x						5
Singapore										x	x								4
South Africa	x	x			x	x	x	x		x	x			x		x	x		21
South Korea	x									x									2
South Vietnam	x																		1
Syria											x								3
Taiwan	x									x	x								5
Thailand	x									x	x								5
Venezuela	x									x									2

a. Countries not included have very limited or no production capacity.
Code: a = licensed production; b = indigenous production; c = weapon codevelopment
Sources: SIPRI Yearbooks, 1973–1978 editions. Self production scores calculated by author (see text).

however, are being made for the production of helicopters, 40-passenger STOL[8] transports, and an interceptor/ground-attack fighter. The assembling of some large naval systems in recent years (in cooperation with West Germany and Britain) indicates the development of another area of military production. The aircraft production, through licensing, is still mostly American.

Brazil is in a somewhat more advanced stage of military development than Argentina. While in terms of naval systems Brazil is still in the assembly phase, considerable progress has been made in the area of aircraft production.[9] By 1974 an unarmed and an armed jet trainer (Neiva N621 Universal and AT-26 Xavante), 12-passenger light transport (EMB-110 Bandeirante), and 6- and 2-seat basic trainers (Neiva Bi-Universal and AEROTEC 122 Uirapuru) had been developed and entered production. Brazil is currently interested in producing more sophisticated aircraft, such as the SA-341 Gazelle light utility helicopter, and a fighter. Oberg estimates the Brazilian aircraft production in 1976 at 500-600.[10] A missile industry has been developed in recent years, and the production of armoured fighting vehicles continues.

India became one of the first producers of arms in the Third World, but it has made its main progress only in the last decade. In 1964 India succeeded in obtaining the rights of production of the Soviet MiG-21 (HAL MiG-21 FL), the sophisticated interceptor/fighter bomber, including the engine, the missiles, and the electronics of this aircraft. In the production stage there is also a multipurpose version of the MiG-21. Before the historical agreement with the Soviets, the Indian aircraft industry concentrated on the production of different versions of the British-designed Marut as well as the British HAL HS-748 MF (military fighter/paratroop version). India has also produced two french-designed helicopters, and cooperated with France in the area of missile production. Though India cooperates with the Communist countries in producing armored fighting vehicles (India's OT-62 tracked armored personnel carrier is the Soviet BTR-50), its main project in this area is still the Vijayanta main battle tank, a modification of the British Chieftain.

The most successful self-producer in the Third World,[11] *Israel's* two main aircraft projects are the IAI 201 Arava (STOL light-transport/COIN fighter) and the IAI Kfir (supersonic Delta-winged multirole combat aircraft). Both aircraft were under intensive development in the early 1970s, and they are currently produced in the rate of four per month (each). Israel has also developed an impressive missile industry, and it is currently producing a surface-to-surface missile (MD. 660 Jericho), a ship-to-ship missile (Gabriel), air-to-air missile (Shafrir), and air-to-surface missile

(Luz). In 1971-1973 the production of the Sabra medium battle tank and the missile-carrying gunboats Saar and Reshef began.

South Africa made it self-production progress especially since the UN embargo resolution of 1963. At present, it is producing the armed jet trainer/ COIN fighter Atlas Impala, two versions of the French Mirage, and an advanced COIN fighter. A helicopter will be manufactured in the near future. Since the early 1960s a great number of armored cars have been produced, and entered production in 1976.

The record of military production in the Third World is almost entirely limited to these five nations. The contribution of other states has been modest, and in most cases nonexistent. All Third World countries, including the five major self-producers, are still far from military self-sufficiency.

CAPACITY FOR SELF-PRODUCTION

The ability of a Third World country to produce its own arms is dependent on the following components: (a) financial resources, (b) level of industrial development, (c) scientific and educational potential, (d) organizational and political abilities.

Limited economic and financial resources explain, at least partially, the difficulties of Third World countries to develop an independent weapons industry. The development of an arms industry, especially a totally independent one, requires very large amounts of financial resources. These are often beyond the abilities of most Third World states. It is well known that even some of the advanced industrial powers, such as Britain and France, have been compelled to cancel military production plans due to financial difficulties. Arms industries are often not profitable economically; under such circumstances only political and security considerations of high priority can induce a nation to develop an independent military production base. The interaction between capacity and motivation becomes very intensive.

Financial resources are often a crucial factor, not only in determining the success or the failure of weapons production, but sometimes in determining whether or not an attempt to establish a weapons industry is being made. Financial difficulties can bring about the cancellation of military projects, sometimes after actual production has begun. It is therefore not surprising to note that the five big producers are invariably the leading military spenders in their respective regions, and that they are generally among the main spenders in the Third World as a whole.

In the first place, it is important to remember that though labor in the nonindustrialized Third World is cheaper than in the industrialized countries, the final cost per military item produced in a Third World state is often higher. Other factors (see below) intervene. This holds in particular for the more sophisticated weapons, exactly the types of weapons that might enhance the producer's political-military independence. Hard data on the costs of domestically produced weapons versus the costs of the same weapons imported are difficult to obtain, but on the whole it seems that often it is cheaper to import weapons than to produce them oneself.

The experience of the Third World countries that have developed an arms industry indicates that financial problems stem from their general lack of industrial development. Many technical factors contribute to the high costs of weapons production in Third World countries: (a) the prices of imported industrial materials, (b) delays in importing materials, (c) the lack of technical facilities (compelling the use of such facilities abroad), (d) low capacity utilization, and (e) low productivity.[12]

But beyond these somewhat technical factors, there are basic economic conditions which make the production of modern arms in the Third World often impossible. First, the costs of military research and development are almost always beyond the reach of a Third World country.[13] Second, problems are likely to arise with the rate of production. This rate is very limited in all Third World countries, and the cost per manufactured unit is, therefore, very high. Economies of scale, the ideal solution for making production profitable, are difficult to achieve since the domestic demand for weapons in Third World countries is always limited and the export of weapons to industrialized and nonindustrialized countries alike is in its infancy. Exporting is dependent, in the final analysis, on the ability of the Third World producers to compete successfully with the industrialized producers, and mainly with the great powers.

The examination of the relationships between Gross National Product, as a crude indicator of economic capacity, and weapons production, can be useful. Though it is impossible to make any statement about casual relationships, it appears that GNP is positively correlated with self-production of arms in the Third World. Tables 6.2 and 6.3 indicate that the correlation is .58 for the group of weapons producers, and .72 for the whole Third World.

Examination of the scattergram reflecting the relationships between GNP and weapons production,[14] indicates that among the important weapons producers in the Third World only Israel is not included in the group of states with a relatively large Gross National Product (i.e., above $10 billions a year, 1965). Taking into account that Israel makes up for its own limited financial resources by a high level of foreign financial aid, its economic possibilities are still superior to those of most Third World countries. Among the seventy-three less important producers in our sample, only Mexico, Indonesia, and Pakistan, have a relatively large GNPs.

TABLE 6.2 National Attributes and Weapon Self-Production: Self-Producers Only

	var1	var2	var3	var4	var5	var6	var7	var8	var9	var10
var1	1.00									
var2	.83	1.00								
var3	.65	.85	1.00							
var4	.58	.52	.43	1.00						
var5	.30	.47	.55	.15	1.00					
var6	.43	.32	.36	−.16	.37	1.00				
var7	.13	.18	.21	−.20	.67	.61	1.00			
var8	.60	.52	.54	.80	.40	.26	.13	1.00		
var9	.73	.57	.38	.87	.06	−.17	−.26	.61	1.00	
var10	.16	.40	.36	.59	.24	−.20	−.13	.42	.45	1.00

N = 21

Variable list:

var1: weapon self-production, 1950–77 (author's index)
var2: embargo index, 1st version (author's index)
var3: embargo index, 2nd version (author's index)
var4: GNP 1965 $US million (Source: *World Handbook of Political and Social Indicators*, Vol. 2, 1972)
var5: level of conflict (author's index)
var6: defense expenditure per capita, 1965 ($US) (*World Handbook*)
var7: military expenditure as percentage of GNP, 1965 (*World Handbook*)
var8: contribution to world scientific authorship, 1965 (*World Handbook*)
var9: number of scientific journals, 1965 (*World Handbook*)
var10: number of students, engineering and natural sciences, 1965 (*UNESCO Statistical Yearbook*, 1976)

None of these states, however, is an important producer of arms. Though both Indonesia and Pakistan are militarily and politically motivated—both have been engaged in serious conflicts in the past—their scientific ability and industrial potential, additional relevant variables that will be later considered, are too limited to enable them the establishment of a large arms industry. The geographical proximity of Mexico to the United States might explain her own modest development of a weapons industry. Here the explanation is in terms of motivation rather than capacity.

The identification of outliers—observations that fall substantially away from the regression line—is, then, very interesting from the theoretical point of view of this study. In the group of Third World producers there are two distinguishable types of outliers: (a) states with relatively large GNP but limited weapons production, namely, outliers in the direction of the horizontal axis (GNP); (b) states with relatively small GNP but large weapons industry, namely, outliers in the direction of the vertical axis, weapons self-production. In the first category we find nations with large populations which are either scientifically and industrially underdeveloped, especially Indonesia and Pakistan, or politically very dependent on a foreign power, especially Mexico. Since the establishment of a

TABLE 6.3 National Attributes and Weapon
Self-Production: All Third World Countries[a]

	var1	var2	var3	var4	var5	var6	var7	var8	var9	var10
var1	1.00									
var2	.88	1.00								
var3	.69	.80	1.00							
var4	.72	.65	.56	1.00						
var5	.32	.38	.48	.22	1.00					
var6	.43	.36	.41	.03	.41	1.00				
var7	.22	.21	.34	.05	.67	.49	1.00			
var8	.64	.60	.55	.81	.32	.29	.15	1.00		
var9	.80	.68	.52	.90	.14	.02	.02	.66	1.00	
var10	.52	.59	.54	.71	.28	.03	.12	.51	.63	1.00

N = 78

a. For variable list, see Table 6.2.

weapons industry requires *both* industrial/scientific ability and political motivation (the model is multiplicative), these states are inferior to Third World states with an equal economic base.

In the second group of outliers we find South Africa and Israel. Their deviation from the regression line can be explained in terms of the theoretical interest of this study. Both countries are in an extreme situation of actual or potential conflict, and both were denied weapons in the past, sometimes by their political allies. Under these circumstances, the Israeli and the South African governments became determined to develop an arms industry of their own, relying on their considerable technological ability. In trying to explain the development of weapons industry in Israel and South Africa, then, factors such as technological ability, arms limitations' experience, and general diplomatic position seem to be far more relevant then the magnitude of the national economy, expressed in terms of GNP.

Usually it can be assumed that there is a strong positive correlation between a country's industrial development and its ability to produce modern weapons. A relatively large industrial base is a prerequisite for the establishment, maintenance, and development of a serious arms industry. Moreover, such a base is a prerequisite even for the absorption of modern weapons in a country's armed forces.

An additional factor is the scientific and the educational potential of a nation. Examining the importance of educational/scientific abilities in the Third World, Tables 6.2 and 6.3 support the hypothesis that these abilities are positively—and relatively strongly—associated with weapons self-production. In theoretical terms, these variables relate to the national capacity, as the size of the economy does.

Scientific ability is by all means a necessary condition for the development of a modern weapons industry.[15] Third World countries lacking considerable scientific potential must rely on foreign assistance also in this respect. Brazil, Argentina, India, Egypt, and other Third World countries developed their arms industries with the active assistance of foreign scientists, engineers, and technicians. This kind of dependence, however, is as dangerous for the recipient country as financial and industrial dependence are, and sometimes more so, especially when the assistance is given by individuals, foreign citizens, rather than by governments. Intergovernmental political alliances are more stable than *ad hoc* agreements between governments and foreign individuals, based usually upon the urgent needs of the governments and on the financial desires of the individuals. Moreover, such agreements between individuals and governments are extremely vulnerable. Israel, for example, contributed considerably to the departure of German scientists from Egypt by engaging in operations against these scientists, who were involved in arms production. West Germany contributed its share by deciding to cancel the citizenship of any German scientist who remained to work in Egypt. According to the SIPRI study (1971: 736), "the virtual disintegration of the Egyptian Defense program is mainly attributable to the departure of foreign scientists and engineers."

Though it is more difficult to evaluate and weigh, political and organizational capacity is also of some importance for the production of modern weapons in a Third World country. Political capacity has both internal and external aspects. Internationally, industrialized countries are often unwilling to share their technological knowledge with Third World countries, whatever the relationships between the nations are. Technology and knowledge are power, and power is often influence. It is important to note that the Soviet Union, for example, allows only one Third World state (india) to produce sophisticated Soviet-designed weapons, and even in that case the supply of knowledge is kept at a minimal level. No Third World state has been allowed to produce modern, complex American arms.

Other things being equal, a diplomatically powerful and politically important Third World country—such as India—can succeed where other Third World countries fail. However, even such a state will have to overcome political obstacles of international nature. One of these is the considerable difficulty of exporting weapons in the face of great power competition.

As far as international political considerations are concerned, it seems that the crucial aspect is the ability of a government to channel significant resources to military production from other areas of societal activity. Technical and scientific manpower, and financial means, are, of course, the sine qua non of weapons self-production. In an underdeveloped economy their shifting to military production could slow down the development of the civilian industries, at least at the short run. The existence of a relatively powerful and determined government is a prerequisite for the development of serious ability to produce modern weapons. Israel and South Africa are examples of the importance of the human factors in weapons production.

Some Third World countries have suffered from inadequate planning of their military production development. Considerations of political prestige rather than commercial profitability have led them to initiate ambitious and overly diversified projects which have often collapsed. Limited attention has been given to the goal of creating real self-sufficiency and to economic problems directly related to military production, such as the export of weapons. Long-range planning and an overall design have often been nonexistent. Political instability has been responsible for slowing down development in other cases (Argentina is an example).

MOTIVATION FOR SELF-PRODUCTION

Whatever its economic and scientific abilities, and these are extremely important, a Third World nation needs very strong motivation in order to establish, maintain, and develop a weapons industry. Motivation, in addition to economic-scientific-technological capacity, is a prerequisite for weapons self-production.

Two concrete factors can be identified as determinants of the national motivation in developing an arms industry. The first factor is the level of conflict in which the nation is involved (the local determinant); the second is the military foreign-aid possibilities open to the nation (the global determinant). The identification and measurement of other factors of relevance for motivation are much harder.

The level of conflict relates to the intensity of actual or potential violent conflict in which the nation is involved. Some important self-producers are hardly engaged in actual large-scale military activity, but they are acting under the assumption that a major violent conflict between themselves and other nations is a distinct possibility. Other important self-producers operate in the environment of either sporadic (e.g., India) or continuous (Israel) international violence.[16] For these countries the necessity of continuous weapon supply is self-evident, and self-production is a relatively reliable way of guaranteeing that supply. Tables 6.2 and 6.3 demonstrate that the level of conflict and self-production are positively correlated, as expected, though the correlation is not very strong. Adding capacity indicators should enhance the explanatory power considerably (see below).

Military foreign-aid possibilities is the second element determining the motivation for self-production. This factor relates to self-production in a more direct way than does conflict level. The military aid possibilities influence the degree to which a Third World country has to satisfy the needs for military equipment through its own production efforts. Included in this concept of aid possibilities are the conditions attached to the supply, but a country's prior experience of arms supply limitations is of the greatest relevance. The diplomatic position of a nation, especially its relationships with potential suppliers (U.S., USSR, France, or Britain, in most cases) is surely a crucial factor for the determination of national motivation concerning self-production, but the national experience of past embargoes is just as important. The two are strongly connected, an important fact to remember while deciding upon the question of how to measure the motivation for self-production (see below).

Tables 6.2 and 6.3 include interesting information concerning the relationship between foreign-aid possibilities and weapons self-production in the Third World. These relationships are crucial for substantiating the main argument of this chapter. The argument is that Third World countries, when denied military assistance by outside sources, will feel themselves forced to develop their own military industries, in order to prevent the total loss of the ability to act independently in their relationships with other nations.[17] If this argument is correct, the correlation between weapons self-production and the degree to which a nation was exposed to arms supply limitations in the past should be strong and positive. The correlation matrices examine this hypothesis.

Two indices of arms supply limitations were constructed to measure the experience of Third World countries as targets of outside weapons embargoes. *EMBARGO 1,* the more simple index, evaluates whether the nation has been exposed to limitations of military supply or not. It is a binary index, insensitive to variations in the seriousness of the limitations. *EMBARGO 2,* the more complicated index, distinguishes three categories of nations: those which had no experience of supply limitations, those which had some experience of supply limitations, and those which had a severe experience of military limitations. Tables 6.2 and 6.3 indicate that, as hypothesized, the relationships between embargo experience and arms production, are not only positive, but also quite strong (for both Third World producers and the Third World as a whole). The relationships vary between .65 and .88. An analysis of the equivalent scattergram revealed that with the exception of Pakistan all countries previously exposed to severe arms limitations have become major weapons producers. Pakistan's position as an unimportant producer can be explained by its lack of advanced technological ability.

It seems that motivation for self-production is positively associated with, and probably causally linked to both conflict and arms supply limitation. National military motivation, to which weapon production is only one outlet, can be, however, estimated not only by its determinants but also by its indicators. Two indicators were selected in order to evaluate the national motivation of Third World countries: (a) defense expenditure per capita, (b) military expenditure as percentage of GNP. As indicated in Tables 6.2 and 6.3, self-production is more strongly associated with defense expenditure per capita as an indicator of motivation than with defense expenditure as percentage of GNP. It is positively related to both indicators. The indicators of military motivation are strongly correlated with level of conflict, as described in the model: $r = .37$ for conflict with defense expenditure per capita, and .67 for conflict with military expenditure as percentage of GNP, both results for the group of weapons producers. For the whole Third World the respective results are .41 and .67. The indicators are less strongly correlated with arms limitation experience as measured by the two embargo indices.

EMPIRICAL EVALUATION

In previous sections motivational and capacity factors associated with weapons self-production in the Third World were identified. These factors were evaluated mainly qualitatively, but their quantitative bivariate relationships with weapons self production were also estimated (Tables 6.2 and 6.3). A more complete and comprehensive evaluation of the determinants of self-production is needed. This evaluation should deal with the relationships between the motivational and capacity factors, and try mainly to assess the validity of the basic theoretical model which argues that weapons self-production is determined, and can be interpreted as a function of the relationships between motivation and capacity to act in areas relevant to such behavior.

Tables 6.2-6.5 and Figure 6.1 supply us with the data needed for at least partial evaluation of the model. This figure and tables include the ten variables specified in Table 6.2. Four of the variables are considered measures of capacity (4,8,9,10), four as measures of motivation (2/3, which are two alternatives for measuring arms supply limitations, and 5,6,7), and one is the dependent variable (Variable 1). Variables 1, 2/3, and 5 are based upon the author's evaluation, 4 and 6-9 on the World Handbook II, and 10 on the UNESCO Yearbook. Variable 1 is the summary of a period of time (1950-1977), and so are variables 2/3, and 5. Others relate to the year 1965 which represents the middle point of the period studied in this research, the period stretching between the early

FIGURE 6.1 Determinants of Weapons Self-Production in the Third World: Theoretical Model and Bivariate Relationships

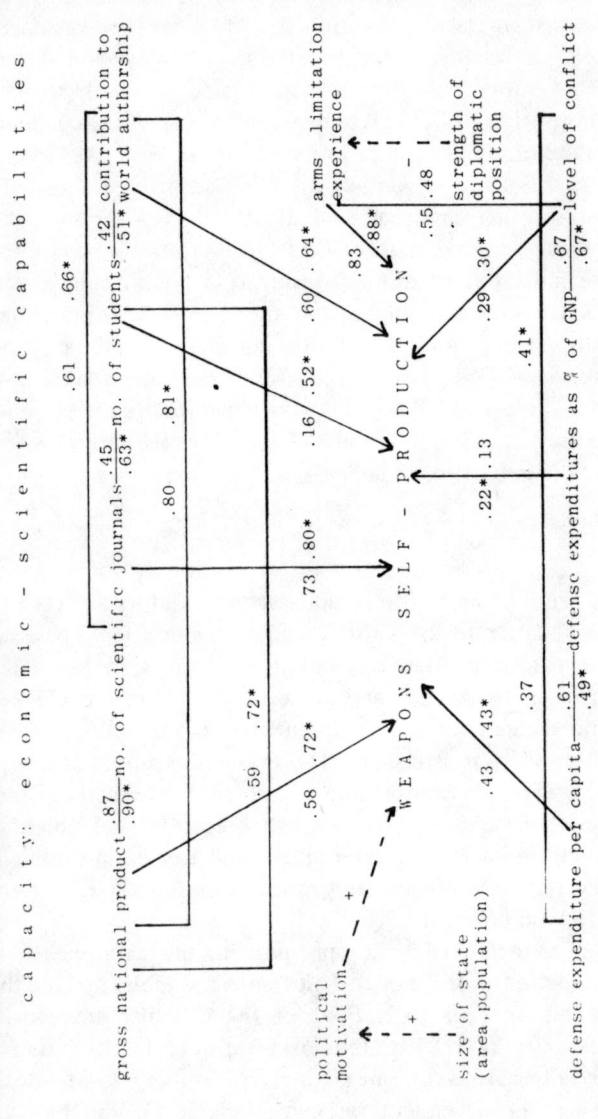

Code: For specifications of variables see text. * = correlations for the whole Third World; no * = correlations for weapons producers only; ——— tested relationships; - - - - hypothetical relationships; + = positive relationships; − = negative relationships.

TABLE 6.4 Weapons Self-Production in the Third World: Estimation of Determinants (stepwise regression)[a]

Case Description	R^2	N	F	Sig.	Estimated Equation
Third World producers, embargo1 index	.90	21	48.69	.001	var1=1.47+4.82var2+.02var9+.09var6 1.69[b] .004 .02
Third World producers, embargo2 index	.87	21	35.94	.001	var1=1.08+.03var9+.11var6+1.50var3 .003 .02 .96
All Third World countries, embargo1 index	.88	78	181.21	.001	var1=−.25+7.86var2+.02var9+.07var6 1.12 .002 .01
All Third World countries, embargo2 index	.82	78	110.08	.001	var1=−.59+.03var9+.09var6+1.60var3 .002 .01 .60

a. For explanations concerning the 2 Embargo indeces, see text.
b. Standard error.
Variable list:
 1: weapons self-production
 2: embargo index, 1st version (embargo1)
 3: embargo index, 2nd version (embargo2)
 9: number of scientific journals (capacity measure)
 6: defense expenditure per capita (motivation measure)

TABLE 6.5 National Attributes and Weapon Self-Production: Correlation Between Weapon Self-Production, 1950–1977 (variable 1) and Multiplication of a Motivation Indicator and a Capacity Indicator

	G.N.P. with Motivation Factors		Contribution to World Scientific Authorship with Motivation Factors		Number of Scientific Journals with Motivation Factors		Number of Students with Motivation Factors	
Sample	var.	r	var.	r	var.	r	var.	r
All Third World countries	4 x 2	.72[b]	8 x 2	.45	9 x 2	.81[b]	10 x 2	.56[b]
	4 x 3	.67[b]	8 x 3	.51	9 x 3	.78[b]	10 x 3	.52[b]
	4 x 5	.60[b]	8 x 5	.45[b]	9 x 5	.71[b]	10 x 5	.47[b]
	4 x 6	.78[a]	8 x 6	.48[b]	9 x 6	.86[a]	10 x 6	.67[a]
	4 x 7	.66[a]	8 x 7	.49[b]	9 x 7	.75[b]	10 x 7	.70[b]
Only weapon producers	4 x 2	.63[b]	8 x 2	.57	9 x 2	.77[b]	10 x 2	.28[b]
	4 x 3	.58[b]	8 x 3	.56	9 x 3	.74[b]	10 x 3	.24[b]
	4 x 5	.48[b]	8 x 5	.54[b]	9 x 5	.63[b]	10 x 5	.18[b]
	4 x 6	.76[a]	8 x 6	.47[b]	9 x 6	.89[a]	10 x 6	.51[a]
	4 x 7	.50[b]	8 x 7	.58[b]	9 x 7	.66[b]	10 x 7	.60[a]

a. The correlation is higher than the correlation between each of the variables (separately) with variable 1.
b. The correlation is higher than the correlation between one of the variables and variable 1 (but not the second variable).
Variable list:
var2: embargo, index 1
var3: embargo, index 2
var5: level of conflict
var6: defense expenditure per capita
var7: defense expenditure as percentage of GNP

1950s and the late 1970s. In any event, these indicators are not amenable to major intertemporal variation, nor has the relative position of different polities on them changed dramatically.

Figure 6.1 reflects both the positive and the relatively strong relationships between various independent variables (divided into a motivation group and a capacity group) and between these variables and weapons self-production, the dependent variable. Tables 6.2 and 6.3 are two correlation matrices, in which different national attributes, as well as weapons production, arms limitations experience and level of conflict, are correlated. Both correlation matrices reflect positive relationships between the amount of weapons produced by a Third World country, and its arms limitation experience, its economic and scientific capacity, the level of conflict in which it is involved, and its relative amount of expenditure on defense. The importance of these factors in determining weapons self-production in the Third World and their theoretical significance are fully explained in this chapter.

The matrices (Tables 6.2 and 6.3), however, test also partially the validity of the variables as indicators for the theoretical concepts. Three indicators, for example, were selected for measuring the scientific capacity of a country: the country's contribution to world scientific authorship, the number of scientific journals published in the country, and the number of engineering and natural sciences students in the country's universities. Tables 6.2 and 6.3 examine the interrelationships between these indicators and reveal that the Pearson's r fluctuates between .42 and .61 for the weapons producers group, and between .51 and .66 for the whole Third World. Similar results exist for the interrelationships of the indicators of motivation. Though convergent validity is achieved, the results are less satisfactory from the point of view of discriminant validity. Generally, the theoretical argument concerning the relationships between self-production and capacity-motivation is supported.

Table 6.4 estimates the relative importance of the independent variables associated with weapons self-production in the Third World. The technique used is that of stepwise regression. The table indicates that in each of the four cases examined (sample of the nations and Embargo Index manipulated) between 82 and 91% of the variance can be explained by only three variables, forming different combinations of capacity and motivation. The explanation of self-production is, then, quite parsimonious, and relatively powerful. Moreover, it includes elements theoretically interpretable in terms of the analytical scheme suggested here. The three variables which explain weapons production in each of the cases are:

(1) arms limitations experience (measured by either the EMBARGO 1 or the EMBARGO 2 indices), considered as a motivation factor;
(2) number of scientific journals (scientific capacity); and
(3) defense expenditure per capita (motivation).

Table 6.5 supplies additional evidence concerning the effectiveness of analyzing weapons production (actual international behavior) in terms of both capacity and motivation. It is a correlation matrix in which weapons self-production is correlated with different combinations of motivation and capacity factors (always one variable of each). The table identifies cases in which the multiplication of a motivation factor and a capacity factor is correlated with weapons self-production either higher than each of the factors separately or higher than at least one of these. An examination of the pattern reveals that in almost all cases (36 out of 40) *The multiplication of a motivation factor by a capacity factor contributes to our ability to predict weapons production.* In other words, the knowledge of not only both factors separately, but also their multiplicative function are important in explaining actual behavior, in this case weapons self production.

Additional analysis, that cannot be included here for lack of space, indicates that when motivation or capacity factors are taken *separately* as predictors of weapons self-production, they are usually less efficient than when they are taken together. This is exactly what the basic model predicts. There are very few exceptions to this rule.

THEORETICAL INTERPRETATION

The main argument that this chapter tried to evaluate empirically was that national motivations and abilities to self-produce arms as a viable solution for dissatisfaction with existing arms transfer patterns determine their self-production. This phenomenon is politically very important. Self-production of weapons gives a nation more freedom of action in its foreign affairs and makes it less dependent on other actors.

The focus of the empirical evaluation was on the relationships between motivation and capacity, on the one hand, and weapons self-production, as a form of behavior, on the other hand. It was found that weapons self-production can be predicted to a great extent by looking at motivation and capacity factors *together*. In other words, knowledge concerning national motivation to self-produce (factors such as conflict and embargo) and national capacity to self-produce (i.e., technoeconomic-scientific abilities) can lead to relatively accurate predictions concerning the nation's actual success in the area of arms production.

The *motivation* for self-production is determined by a perception of deprivation of some international actors concerning at least some aspects of their arms supply situation. This deprivation is a function of the difference between the existing and the desired arms supply patterns of the nation. The perception of such a difference might lead to the motivation of establishing independent or semiindependent sources of supply, especially when this supply is of the highest national priority, or when its continuation is very insecure. The structure and the content of both the actual pattern of weapons transfer and the desired pattern of weapons transfer are both, then, of great importance in determining the direction and the intensity of the national motivation concerning the production of arms. Many factors are relevant in this connection. As the number of suppliers of weapons to a state increases, for example, its motivation to develop its own arms industry should decrease, especially when this development is economically costly. The experience of arms supply limitations, on the other hand, must influence the national decision-makers in the opposite direction: a nation with an unstable foreign supply pattern will feel itself obliged to find alternatives, through self-production or other means. Another factor of comparable effect on motivation is that of violent conflict with foreign powers. As a conflict becomes more severe, a guaranteed secured source of supply becomes more critical.

It is important to understand that the development of an independent arms industry, in all these situations (conflict, embargo, etc.) is linked strongly to the desire of the Third World nation to prevent other actors in the system from influencing its behavior. Sizeable weapons industries in the Third World have always been the result of the combined pressure of conflict and embargo. Both violent activity directed against a nation and the limitation of arms supply to its armed forces, originate from the intention of other actors to influence the nation's behavior. Weapons production is, functionally, a device to guarantee the nation's freedom to act according to its perceived interests.

Motivation is behaviorally meaningless without the equivalent *capacity*: the desire to self-produce weapons must be complemented by the possession of relevant capabilities. These are mainly technological, scientific, and economic, but political variables are of some relevance. As was empirically proven, Third World producers have clearly greater abilities than Third World nonproducers.

The national capabilities determine the dependency balance of a nation (namely, the extent to which it has to rely on foreign sources), which, it has to rely on foreign sources), which, in turn, determines the country's capacity to develop its military ability independently. Empirical data indicate that every Third World nation is dependent to at least some extent on foreign powers in developing weapons industries. The intensity of the dependence, however, is not identical for all nations. It is a function not only of the level of production sophistication which the nation attempts to reach, but also, and mainly, of the basic capabilities which the nation can invest in its military projects. The dependence on foreign sources decreases as the country is better equipped technologically, scientifically, and economically. The usual result is a more developed military production capacity.

All in all, however, it is most important to understand that self-production is a function of the multiplicative interaction between national motivation and capacity, not of each of these alone. The number of serious producers in the Third World is too small to make possible any statistical analysis beyond the analysis carried out in this chapter, but even superficial observation shows that only when both capacity and motivation are present, the resulting self-production is impressive. Each of the important Third World producers—India, Israel, and South Africa—is both politically motivated and technologically capable, at least relative to other Third World countries. Moreover, when the group of motivated *and* capable nations is compared with the group of nations that are *either* capable (e.g., Argentina and Brazil) *or* motivated (e.g. Egypt and Pakistan) *but not both*, the difference in terms of actual production is considerable and consistent. As empirically shown, indicators of both capacity and motivation help in predicting self-production as well as in explaining self-production theoretically. Moreover, the validity of this argument is enhanced if we realize that *whatever* indicators of capacity and motivation are selected, the results are consistent.

The value of this kind of analysis is two-fold. Insofar as systematic understanding of foreign policy behavior is concerned, this chapter recommends a theoretical concentration on motivational and capacity factors as determinants of such behavior. The study's findings are, thus, not only of value in and of themselves; they also point the way toward a more profound understanding of other aspects of international affairs, within a general theoretical framework.

The study of military production in Third World countries has value also in the area of actual policy-making, not only its scholarly understanding. The study unraveled the conditions leading small, relatively weak nations to seek political independence in a world controlled by large, powerful, and industrialized nations. The very same conditions could lead to other routes of action on the part of Third World nations. Thus, nuclear proliferation in the 1980s would be determined by the capacity and the motivation of these nations to "go nuclear".

NOTES

1. The different alternatives are discussed by Harkavy (1975: Chs. 3-5), Leiss et al. (1970: Ch. 3), Leiss (1970: 185-226), and SIPRI (1971: 62-66). Indigenous production of arms, as a policy option, has not been extensively discussed in the literature. Exceptions are Albrecht et al. (1975: 195-212) and Oberg (1975: 222-239).

2. It is not entirely clear to what extent the Indian case is a typical one.

3. Nevertheless, Benoit (1973) has argued persuasively that, on the whole, a Third World country does not sacrifice economically even if it concentrates on military growth. For a different opinion, consult Albrecht et al. (1975).

4. Data concerning weapons production in the Third World were derived mainly from SIPRI (1971) and the SIPRI yearbooks, 1973-1978, as well as from the MIT's arms control project.

5. Though the self-production index is based on only two dimensions, these seem to be the most relevant ones from the theoretical point of view of this chapter. Furthermore, accurate and reliable data regarding other dimensions (such as number of items produced or the role of foreign scientists in the industry development) are hardly available.

6. Though Table 6.1 does not present any information regarding the production of small arms, such information would not change the general picture. For small arms, see SIPRI (1971: Table 22.1, p. 725).

7. COIN = Counter-insurgency.

8. STOL = Short take-off and landing (aircraft).

9. Oberg (1975: 231) and SIPRI Yearbook (1977: 288-289) include the relevant information. Despite developments, Brazil is still highly dependent on the supply of foreign-made military planes.

10. Oberg (1975: 232); this estimate is apparently too high.

11. Oberg (1975: 228); see also Kraar (1978: 72-76). On the Arab side a recent development is the establishment of the multinational Arab Organization for Industrialization; see Ropelewski (1978: 14-16).

12. Exact productivity levels are impossible to determine. Yet it is assessed that the levels of productivity for 1973-1974 in the aerospace industry of different countries was as follows: U.S.—$24,200, Israel—$19,000, FRG—$14,800, India—$2,732 (Oberg, 1975: 228). The Indian case is apparently quite typical for the less-developed countries. It was analyzed, inter alia, by Childs and Kidron (1973).

13. For R & D expenses, see the SIPRI yearbooks, and SIPRI (1971: 31-32, 383-386, and 398-400).

14. For lack of space, scattergrams are not presented in this chapter.

15. Oberg (1975: 239) maintains that the lack of sufficient expertise damaged significantly the Indian weaponry development. Thus, the Hindustan Aeronautics Ltd. (HAL) engine factory in Bangalore which employed 2,900 people was reported to have only two postgraduates on its staff (*Hindustan Times*, July 7, 1972).

16. Technically, the level of conflict is measured by a three-category ordinal scale, based upon the author's evaluation.

17. A review of the conditions under which the five major producers started their production efforts might help the reader to comprehend this phenomenon. South Africa, Israel, and India, all were exposed to embargoes during certain periods in the 1960s and all started developing their semiindependent arms industries during this decade. Argentina and Brazil were exposed at the same time to supply limitation; see Oberg, SIPRI, etc.

REFERENCES

ALBRECHT, U., D. ERNST, P. LOCK, and H. WULF (1975) "Militarization, arms transfer and arms production in peripheral countries." Journal of Peach Research 12, 3: 195-212.

BENOIT, E. (1973) Defence and Economic Growth in Developing Economics. Lexington, MA: Lexington Books.

CHILDS, D. and M. KIDRON (1973) "India, the USSR and the MiG project." Economic and Political Weekly 38 (September).

FARLEY, P. J., S. S. KAPLAN, and W. H. LEWIS (1973) Arms across the Sea. Washington, DC: Brookings Institution.

HARKAVY, R. E. (1975) The Arms Trade and International Systems. Cambridge, MA: Ballinger.

KRAAR, L. (1978) "Israel's own military-industrial complex." Fortune (March 13): 72-76.

LEISS, A. C. (1970) Changing Patterns of Arms Transfers. Cambridge, MA: MIT Center for International Studies, Report C/70-2.

――― with G. KEMP et al. (1970) Arms Transfers to Less Developed Countries. Cambridge, MA: MIT Center for International Studies, Report C/70-1.

OBERG, J. (1975) "Third world armament: domestic arms production in Israel, South Africa, Brazil, Argentina, and India 1950-75." Instant Research on Peace and Violence 5, 4: 222-239.

ROPELEWSKI, R. R. (1970) "Arabs seek arms sufficiency." Aviation Week and Space Technology (May 15): 14-16..

STANLEY, J. and M. PEARTON (1972) The International Trade in Arms. London: Chatto & Windus.

Stockholm International Peace Research Institute (SIPRI) (1972-1978) Yearbook of World Armaments and Disarmaments.

――― (1971) The Arms Trade with the Third World. New York: Humanities Press.

TAYLOR, C. and M. C. HUDSON (1972) World Handbook of Political and Social Indicators, Vol. 2. New Haven, CT: Yale Univ. Press.

UNESCO (1970) Statistical Yearbook.

Chapter 7

A COMPARATIVE ANALYSIS OF NUCLEAR ARMAMENT

CHARLES W. KEGLEY, Jr.
University of South Carolina

GREGORY A. RAYMOND
Boise State University

RICHARD A. SKINNER
Old Dominion University

Two sorts of uncertainty are to be distinguished. One is *risk*. We face a risk when we have knowledge of a law that operates but involves a random element. We are given a probability, but what outcome will be in the case before us remains uncertain. The other type of uncertainty may be called *statistical ignorance:* here we do not know

EDITORS' NOTE: An earlier version of this article was accepted for publication in *The Sage International Yearbook of Foreign Policy Studies* in September 1976. The version published here was received in August 1979. The authors report that the data analyzed in this paper are available to other researchers upon request to the Computer-Based Laboratory for Instruction and Analysis at Old Dominion University.

AUTHORS' NOTE: For their comments and contributions to the development of this research project, we wish to thank Philip J. Wolfson, William D. Coplin, Howard Lentner, Gerald R. Roys, Craig Neal Andrews, Roy E. Licklider, Patrick J. McGowan, and several anonymous reviewers. We are grateful to John E. Andrews for preparing the graphics presented here.

what law is operative. We are ignorant; not necessarily of all circumstances, but of the significant ones so that we cannot assign a determinate probability to possible outcomes.
—Abraham Kaplan,
The Conduct of Inquiry

The spectre of a world populated by a large number of nuclear-armed states has haunted mankind since the death of the Baruch Plan over three decades ago. Although Ailleret, Beaufre, Gallois, and other exponents of the so-called "dissuasion" school of thought contend that the spread of nuclear weapons would make interstate conflicts more dangerous and therefore less likely, most observers fear that an increase in the number of fingers placed on nuclear triggers will heighten the possibility of one of them being pulled. "We know with the certainty of a statistical truth," C. P. Snow once wrote, "that if enough of these weapons are made ... by different states ... some of them are going to blow up." It does not matter whether it is caused by accident or conscious plan, he continued. "What does matter is the nature of the statistical fact" (quoted in Schlesinger, 1967: 10). Yet, strictly speaking, the situation described here is more akin to statistical ignorance than statistical fact. We simply do not know the cumulative risk associated with the incremental addition of new members of the nuclear club. Thus, while a world of many nuclear-armed states would no doubt be fraught with uncertainty, our ignorance of the precise threshold beyond which the probability of nuclear war would increase makes each new Nth country seem even more frightening than the last.

Unlike the case of risk in which probabilities regarding the occurrence of an event are known, decision-making under statistical ignorance involves a lack of such information along a temporal and/or structural dimension. In temporal uncertainty one does not know when an event will happen, whereas in structural uncertainty one does not know if it will happen at all. The literature on the relationship between nuclear proliferation and war reflects both of these kinds of statistical ignorance: at the same time that some theorists debate ever just when the addition of another nuclear-armed state will bring the international system to "critical mass," other theorists question whether any such critical threshold would ever exist.

Needless to say, our ignorance owes much to the fact that these events have never happened. Lacking any kind of patterned historical regularity to study, it becomes impossible to generalize about the causal connection between proliferation and the onset of war. But though data-based research may be limited to the use of simulation as a tool for exploring this particular systemic relationship, it is not limited in its capacity to test rival hypotheses regarding the impact on those variables which may influence states' decisions on nuclear armament. The purpose of the present study is to address this latter question by means of a cross-national design. We shall compare forty-six potential proliferating states in order to assess the explanatory power of a set of contextual variables which are currently thought to account for the position of any given state on the nuclear armament issue.

FROM CONSTRAINT TO CHOICE IN NUCLEAR ARMAMENT DECISIONS

An inventory of the literature on nuclear armament would reveal several things to those interested in using the comparative method for the purpose outlined above. Clearly the most obvious of these is that while theorists have identified many variables which might influence a nation's posture toward nuclear armament, research on the relative potencies of these variables has been done almost exclusively by means of case studies. As a result, we possess an abundance of impressions, speculative insights, and detailed descriptions of certain national experiences, but we lack any nomic generalizations about which variables are most likely to prompt a nation to develop a nuclear weapons program. Nor is it conceivable that any such generalizations will soon be forthcoming unless analysts are able to marshal reproducible evidence in support of their conclusions. Without this kind of empirical knowledge about what the key factors are in decisions to arm, there is but slight hope that efforts to restrain proliferation can ever succeed.

Although the most obvious thing about the literature on nuclear armament may be its idiographic character, perhaps the most important attribute is that recent developments in the international market for nuclear energy have altered the way in which many theorists now think about the determinants of a nation's stance on nuclear weapons. Prior to the 1970s, nearly all of the writing on proliferation could be summarized by a model that proscribed nuclear armament for states which did not possess certain basic attributes. In essence, it was assumed that the scientific, technological, and economic investments required for the construction and operation of nuclear reactors were such that relatively few countries would be able to undertake indigenous weapons projects. Furthermore, since commercial access to both hardware and fissile material was greatly restricted, the position of most countries with regard to nuclear capability was not a matter for formulation and decision but, rather, was already set forth by a country's level of scientific expertise, technological skill, and economic wealth. Because there was no alternative to not possessing nuclear weapons for those who lacked these indigenous prerequisites, there was no real choice involved in arriving at a posture toward nuclear armament.

Several events occurred during the mid-1970s to change this state of affairs. First, owing to the four-fold increase in petroleum prices immediately following the Yom Kippur War, nuclear energy came to be viewed as an attractive alternative to oil in those countries where energy demands outstripped fossil fuel supplies. Second, the transnational rivalry which developed in the wake of the Treaty of Almelo[1] led many firms to offer uranium enrichment and reprocessing technology along with their reactors in the anticipation that this kind of package deal would attract new customers, especially among the less developed countries who had not yet been saturated by American nuclear technology. Finally, the 1974 detonation of a nuclear device by India demonstrated that, given a modicum level of technical skill, any nation could use fuel from nuclear power plants to fabricate weapons. It further showed that external assistance (in this case, from Canada in the 1960s) could help develop the skills needed for such an undertaking.

Collectively, these developments argue for new ways of thinking about nuclear armament and proliferation and for questioning the postulates of prior nonproliferation theories. They constitute the reason for suspecting that the assumptions on which the conventional wisdom rested have decidedly less relevance to a world in which nuclear technology is both increasingly attractive and available; in which the relative cost of nuclear power is being reduced as fossil fuels dwindle in supply and rise in price; in which diversion of materials from a nuclear power plant to weapons manufacture is a demonstrated fact; in short, a world in which decision-makers can make "real" choices about nuclear armament.

Given that an increased number of countries may now entertain the option of acquiring nuclear weapons despite their lack of certain indigenous scientific, technological, and economic capabilities, it is necessary for us to revise our view of who might go nuclear, when, and under what conditions. Table 7.1 contains a list of those variables which have traditionally been said to determine a nation's position and nuclear armament. Figure 7.1 shows how these variables have traditionally been organized for explanatory purposes. Simply stated, the conventional wisdom held that scientific expertise, technological skill, and economic wealth represented prerequisites for weapons development. Whether a country chose to go nuclear ultimately depended upon two sufficient conditions: the balance between its incentives and constraints, and presence of any precipitating factors that might trigger the decision to arm whenever incentives outweighed constraints.

Given the highly idiographic nature of previous research on nuclear armament, it is not surprising that a compelling theoretical statement

TABLE 7.1 Hypothesized Determinants of National Positions on Nuclear Armament

	Determinant	Level	Sources
I.	**Indigenous Prerequisites**		
	Scientific expertise	national	Barnaby (1969) Shaffer (1972)
	Technological skill	national	Barnaby (1969) Shaffer (1972)
	Economic wealth	national	Bull (1961: 152-153) Schwab (1969: 902-903)
IIA.	**Incentives**		
	Prestige	systemic	Beaton (1966: 49-61) Bull (1961: 153) Harrison (1965: 26) Inglis (1959: 161) Morgenstern (1961: 167) Rosecrance (1963: 173)
	Threat perception	systemic	Bader (1968: 98) Beaton (1966: 62-67) Bull (1961: 154) Harrison (1965: 162) Hoffmann (1968: 44) Williams (1969: 69)
	Autonomy	national/ systemic	Harrison (1965: 161) Kelly (1961: 306) Rosecrance (1972: 2)
	Role conception	systemic	Bull (1961: 153) Kissinger (1957: 222) Zoppo (1966: 581)
IIB.	**Constraints**		
	Type of regime	national	Bader (1968: 98) Kaplan (1972: 49-55) Kelly (1961: 285) Rosecrance (1963: 173)
	Domestic public opinion	national	Quester (1973: 110)
	Weapons cost	national	Bull (1961: 151-152) Hohenemser (1962) Mueller (1967: 875) Schwab (1969: 902-908)
	Reactions of other states	systemic	Harkavy (1977) Lowrance (1976: 152-153)
	International norms	systemic	SIPRI (1972)

TABLE 7.1 Hypothesized Determinants of National Positions on Nuclear Armament (Cont)

Determinant	Level	Sources
III. Precipitants		
Reduction of alliance credibility	systemic	Bowie (1965: 237-263) Hoffmann (1968: 44) Kissinger (1965: 107)
Vertical proliferation	systemic	Schwab (1969: 900-914)
Diminution of superpower guarantees	systemic	Willrich (1966: 689-690)
Adversary arming	systemic	Bull (1961: 148-149) Morgenstern (1961: 137) Wohlstetter (1965: 198)

encompassing the prerequisites argument of this conventional wisdom is not available. Nevertheless, and as Figure 7.1 suggests, perusal of that literature demonstrates common assumptions cutting across much of that argument.[2] What emerged was a perspective which viewed national wealth, scientific expertise, and technological skill as an inclusive *set* of factors a nation must possess in order to entertain the nuclear option. It was generally contended that for a nation to "go nuclear" it was necessary to possess all three attributes. Indeed, it was usually argued that possession of all three was both a precondition for and a precipitant of national decisions to join the nuclear weapons club.

In light not only of recent developments already mentioned but also in retrospect, the validity of the prerequisites model seems suspect. Previous research and emergent events have demonstrated the inability of these prerequisites to correlate with and predict to the behavior of potential proliferators. For instance, one systematic comparison (Kegley, 1979) found the relationship between both the degree of national wealth and of scientific capacity to countries' armament positions to be very weak or nonexistent (Kendall's tau_c = -.11 and .23, respectively). Other inquiries have repeatedly concluded that these conceptions are inadequate, that observed patterns "are not easily accommodated in the traditional proliferation paradigm" (Dowty, 1978: 115), and that approaches to proliferation based on past definitions are obsolete. Inasmuch as documentation of this interpretation is abundant (e.g., Greenwood et al., 1977; Feiveson and Taylor, 1977; Nuclear Energy Policy Study Group, 1977; Wohlstetter, 1976-1977; Raymond and Skinner, 1979; Epstein, 1977; Rathjens and Ruina, 1976), it is not our purpose here to test the prerequisites model of

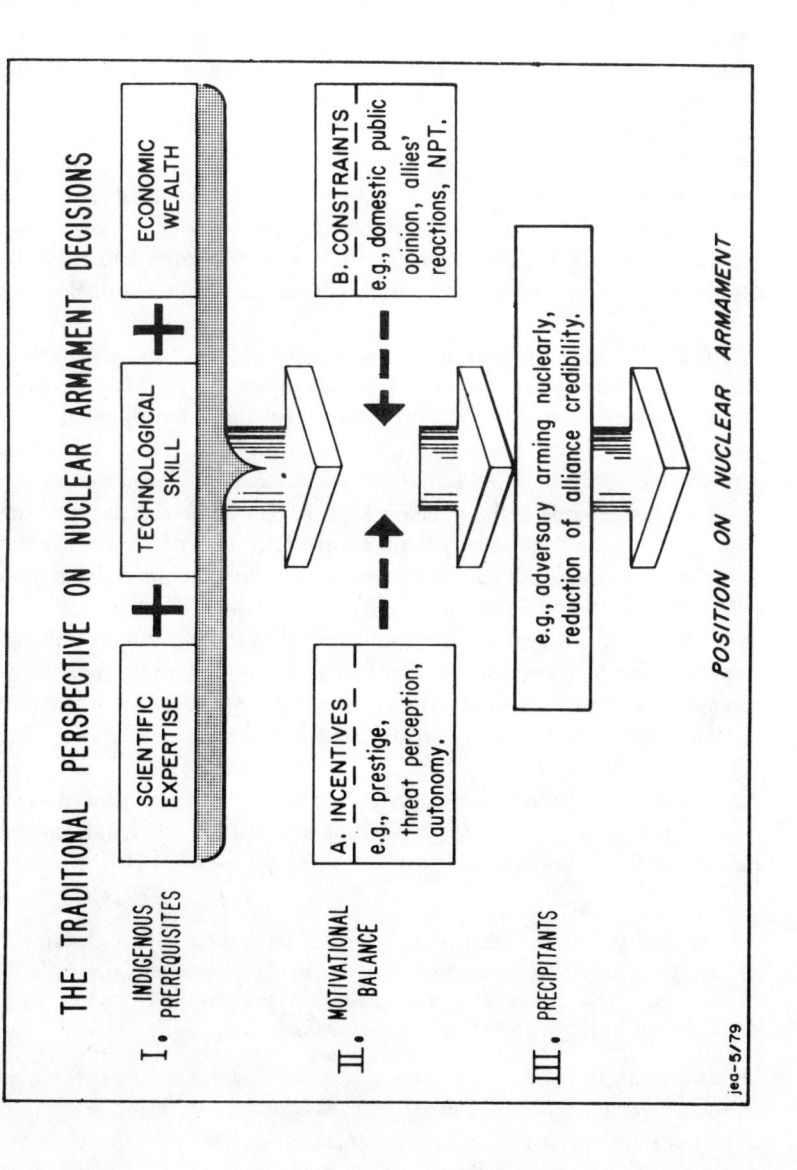

FIGURE 7.1 The Traditional Perspective on Nuclear Armament Decisions

the conventional wisdom in order to demonstrate once again what is already well known, namely, that a nation's decision to acquire nuclear weapons cannot be accounted for well by reference to these factors. Instead, we seek to develop a model which more adequately reflects current international realities by replacing the notion of "prerequisites determinism" with a revised perspective that acknowledges the synergistic link now existing (e.g., Baker, 1975) between nuclear power and nuclear weapons and that incorporates the kind of contextual variables mentioned above. That revision is absolutely necessary, in our opinion, because already "the link between civilian nuclear proliferation and the proliferation of nuclear weapons has now passed into conventional wisdom" (Falk, 1978: 19).

Figure 7.2 presents such a revised perspective on how we might profitably think about the sources of nuclear armament under present conditions. It is based on the contention that the conditions of the first twenty-five years of the nuclear age have been transformed by the cumulative effects of: (1) the economic attractiveness of nuclear energy as compared to increasingly expensive petroleum; (2) the improved availability of nuclear technology via a competitive international market; and (3) the plausibility of diverting materials and expertise from nuclear energy production to nuclear weapons fabrication. Furthermore, it also assumes that energy needs, technological availability, and diffusion pressures are the most important contextual variables to be affected by this transformation. Needless to say, a nation's energy resources were posited as important factors in early writing and it was asserted that considerable energy must be available if a country were to undertake nuclear weapons development (National Planning Association, 1972). In contrast and attendant to the rapidly increased petroleum prices since 1974, this energy-as-prerequisite has since been changed to energy-as-need. Thus we are now told:

> It is almost certain that many countries (particularly underdeveloped ones) *deficient in indigenous fossil fuel supplies* will increasingly look to nuclear power, at least as a partial solution to their energy problems [SIPRI, 1975: 34; emphasis added].

Moreover, at the same time that a new market has opened for nuclear energy, vigorous competition between exporters has made nuclear technology available to an unprecedented degree. And, as this technology spreads throughout a region, new interest is generated in obtaining its benefits. As Morgenstern (1961: 137) observed, "the spread of fission weapons is itself a kind of 'fission process': each nation that acquires weapons induces more nations to get them too." We submit that the same thing may be said today about nuclear power plants. Consequently, energy

FIGURE 7.2 A Revised Perspective on Nuclear Armament Decisions

A REVISED PERSPECTIVE ON NUCLEAR ARMAMENT DECISIONS

I. CONTEXTUAL VARIABLES

- INTERNATIONAL NUCLEAR TECHNOLOGY COMMERCE
- NEED/DEMAND FOR ENERGY
- TECHNOLOGY DIFFUSION PRESSURES

II. MOTIVATIONAL BALANCE

- A. INCENTIVES
  e.g., prestige, threat perception, autonomy.
- B. CONSTRAINTS
  e.g., domestic public opinion, allies' reactions, NPT.

III. PRECIPITANTS

e.g., adversary arming nuclearly, reduction of alliance credibility.

POSITION ON NUCLEAR ARMAMENT

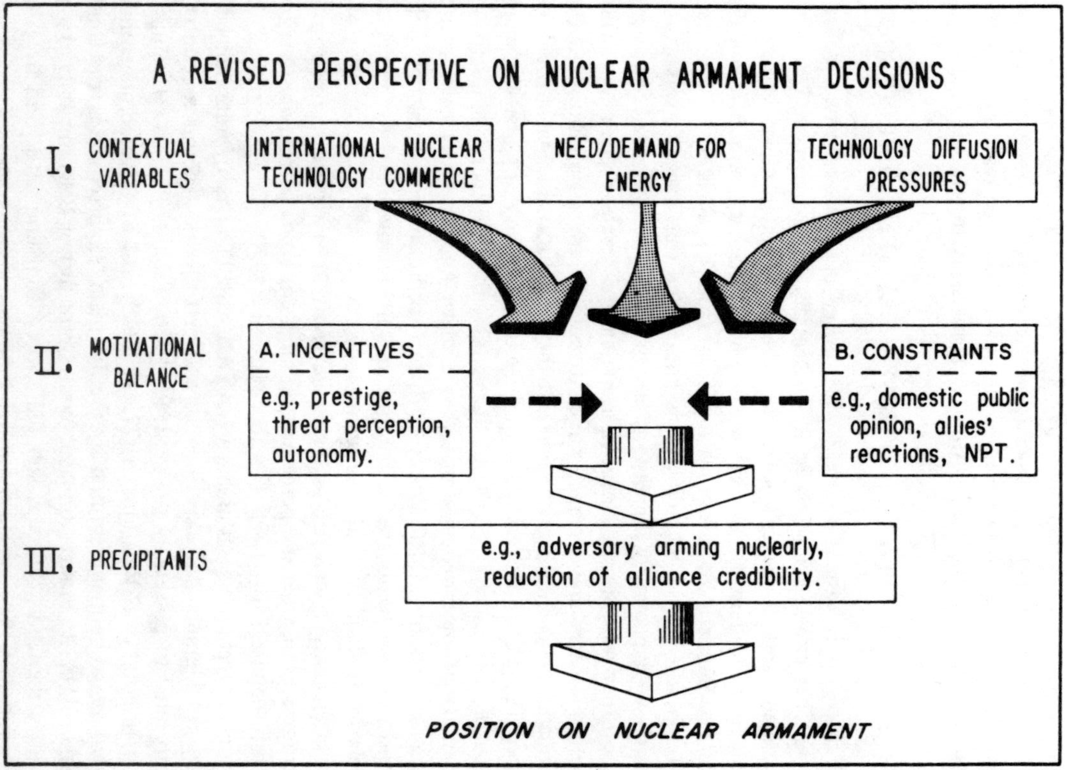

needs, technological availability, and diffusion pressures have combined to give many decision-makers the ability to make a choice—for the first time in a quarter century—on what position to take on the issue of nuclear weapons. In an international environment where the resource constraints on nuclear armament have been largely removed and where many states now have the option, we need to inquire about which factors are the most potent in influencing the position states are likely to take.

A DESIGN FOR ANALYZING NUCLEAR ARMAMENT CHOICES

In order to examine whether this revised perspective on nuclear armament has explanatory power, it is necessary to operationalize our independent and dependent variables. The three independent variables of energy need/demand, nuclear technology availability, and diffusion pressures comprise the most inviting contextual variables to be considered (Dunn and Overhold, 1976). It is anticipated that these factors will fall into two explanatory dimensions: one reflecting nations' needs for energy, the other reflecting the relative availability of nuclear technology. Diffusion pressures are expected to contribute to the composition of both dimensions inasmuch as they reflect the spatial distribution of fossil fuels (proximate countries are likely to share in the bounty or scarcity of energy sources because of geographic location) and the general trend of contiguous or proximate countries to achieve nuclear status in a complimentary fashion. On the basis of these two dimensions, countries' policy positions can be located according to both relative need for energy and relative availability of nuclear technology.

The energy need/demand variable (NEED) is measured in terms of crude oil imported as a percentage of apparent crude petroleum supply for each country for 1975 (United Nations, 1977: Table 6, pp. 62-71). Nuclear technology availability (AVAILABILITY) is operationalized as the total number of experimental and/or full-scale reactors a country is projected to possess by 1981 (SIPRI, 1976: Table 1b, 5, p. 43; Committee on International Relations, 1977: 239-248). All of the reactors enumerated are to be manufactured by the five major exporter states (the United States, USSR, France, Canada, West Germany) or Belgium, Italy, Japan, the Netherlands, Sweden, and the United Kingdom, and thus are coterminous with the growing commerce in nuclear technology.

Finally, diffusion pressures are measured in terms of the percentage of "core" and "periphery" states in a country's region (Cantori and Spiegel, 1970) that either possess or are projected to possess experimental or full-scale reactors by 1981 (SIPRI, 1976: Table 1b, p. 43). If as history suggests, Egyptian-Israeli relations imply, and the recent actions by Pakistan appear to sustain, decision-makers err on the side of cynicism in evaluating other countries' intentions and capabilities, a proximate state's attaining nuclear status is likely to encourage matching or emulative actions on the part of neighboring countries. Hence, it is expected that this measure (henceforth, labeled DIFFUSION) will contribute to nations' positions on the nuclear issue.

Having operationally defined the three independent variables in our contextual model, let us now proceed to do the same with our dependent variable. As stated earlier, our model rests on the proposition that nuclear armament is an issue on which decision-makers can exercise a choice. If foreign policy decisional behavior is conceived of as a purposeful, deliberate process directed toward the attainment of certain consciously entertained goals, and if the present tendency of states to consider military capability and national security to be related symbiotically is assumed to be universal (Boulding, 1962; Frank, 1968), then it follows that all states are compelled to take a position with respect to the desirability of acquiring nuclear weapons. According to this reasoning, nations may be classified according to the position they adopt. Moreover, these positions are relatively amenable to objective observational procedures since a country's determination to acquire nuclear weapons tends to be "an inevitably public act" (Beaton, 1966: 13).

As to the classification scheme to be used in distinguishing nations' positions on nuclear armament, the alternatives include a simple dichotomy of nuclear and nonnuclear states or an ordered scheme of categories. The case for the latter as opposed to the former is neatly summarized by Schlesinger's (1972: 360-361) phrase that "proliferation is really quite unlike pregnancy ... being a little bit proliferated may be a meaningful concept while being a little pregnant is not." The case is also captured in Quester's (1973: 102) concept of "quasi-proliferation." At the same time, however, distinguishing between being "more or less prone to arm" requires insight and/or information beyond those presently available.

This conundrum is further complicated by consideration of the fact that nations can and do entertain aspirations to arm nuclearly (or, already possess nuclear weapons) but are nevertheless opposed to further nuclear proliferation. Logical contradictions aside, the independence of states' positions on nuclear armament for themselves and their views on other nations arming calls for a more complex construct. Resisting the temptation to infer foreign policy intentions from current capabilities, nations' policy positions on the nuclear weapons issue are identified in terms of publicly observable foreign policy behavior, either overt or verbal, the latter referring to the statements of official national decision-makers.

The classification scheme employed here incorporates a given country's position on national armament and international proliferation into a single typology.[3] First, nation-states were classified into one of three categories according to their respective positions with regard to nuclear armament for themselves: (1) those states which already possess nuclear weapons; (2) those which have been observed to announce publicly at any time since 1945 that they either wish to develop a nuclear weapons program or reserve the option to do so; and (3) those states which have renounced nuclear weapons. The sample of states selected for analysis consists of those forty-six countries generally regarded as those for whom the incentives for nuclear weapons production are present and the technological impediments for that production are largely absent. Inasmuch as there exists considerable consensus as to which nations populate the so-called "potential members of the nuclear club" (compare the estimates and inventories of Walske, 1976-1977; Epstein, 1976; United States Central Intelligence Agency, 1977; Davidson et al., 1960; Coplin, 1974: 163-168; Schelling, 1976; and Rosen and Jones, 1977), it is not difficult to determine which countries are capable of going nuclear (i.e., nonmicro-states and dependencies) and which have political reasons for considering the option. As Beaton (1966) argued, "We are dealing with a definable group of countries." Hence we shall rely on that concensus to delineate our sample of forty-six countries (see Table 7.3) considered in the analysis which follows.[4]

Second, the nation-states in this sample have also been categorized according to their respective position on the Nuclear Nonproliferation Treaty (NPT): (1) those states which have both signed and ratified; (2) those which have signed but not yet ratified the NPT; and (3) those states which have neither signed nor ratified the treaty. By arraying one set of categories along a vertical axis and the other along a horizontal axis, the nine-cell typology shown in Table 7.2 is created. When the cells are collapsed in the following way (see Table 7.3), we obtain a four category nominal-level measure of our dependent variable:

(1) nuclear states (cells a and g),
(2) latent nuclear aspirants (cell b),
(3) nuclear aspirants (cells e and h), and
(4) nonnuclear states (cell c).

The statistical technique used to test the overall explanatory power of the model, as well as the relative potency of the three independent variables, is discriminant analysis. A relative of multiple regression (Kort, 1973), discriminant analysis consists of one or more linear equations of independent variables and their respective weights or coefficients (c_i) that together produce an index Z, which—depending on whether its numerical

TABLE 7.2 A Taxonomy of States' Positions on
Nuclear Weapons

		Positions on Nuclear Armament for Self		
		Possess Weapons	*Reserve Option*	*Renounced Weapons*
NPT Status	Signed/ Ratified	e.g., U.S. a	e.g., West Germany b	e.g., Austria c
	Signed	N/A d	e.g., Egypt e	N/A f
	Neither Signed nor Ratified	e.g., France g	e.g., Israel h	N/A i

N/A = Not Applicable. None of the 46 nations in sample could be assigned to cells d, f, and i.

value is above or below a certain point (K)—places each observation in one or another of the categories of the dependent variable. Whereas multiple regression provides an equation that minimizes residuals in predicting observed values of Y, discriminant analysis maximizes geometric distances between categories on the basis of groups' values on the independent variables. Like multiple regression, the standardized discriminant coefficients are estimates of the relative potencies of independent variables for predicting values of the dependent variable. Unlike multiple regression, discriminant analysis can derive more than one equation (discriminant function): each group defined by the categories of the dependent variable and measured by its centroid is treated as a point in space and each discriminant function is a unique, orthogonal dimension describing the location of that group relative to the others. The importance of any one discriminant function is assessed by its respective eigenvalue and canonical correlation. The latter measures the association between each discriminant function and the set of (g-1) dummy variables which define the group memberships.

TABLE 7.3 Classification of Nations
According to Their Policy Positions
on Nuclear Weapons (N = 46)

I.	Nuclear States	
	China	Soviet Union
	France	United Kingdom
	India	United States
II.	Latent Nuclear Aspirants	
	Australia	Netherlands
	Belgium	Phillipines
	Iraq	South Korea
	Italy	Sweden
	Libya	Venezuela
	Malaysia	West Germany
III.	Nuclear Aspirants	
		Indonesia
	Argentina	Israel[a]
	Brazil	Japan
	Chile	Pakistan
	Colombia	Spain
		Switzerland
	(Cuba)[b]	(Taiwan)[b]
	Egypt	Turkey
IV.	Nonnuclear States	
	Austria	Hungary
	Bulgaria	Mexico
	Canada	New Zealand
	Czechoslovakia	Norway
	Denmark	Peru
	East Germany	Poland
	Finland	Romania
	Greece	Yugoslavia

a. Although there has not been any public admission by the Israeli government that it possesses nuclear weapons, many reporters and intelligence analysts believe that the Dimona reactor in the Negev desert has produced sufficient plutonium stocks for approximately twenty 15-kiloton bombs. See Dowty (1978) for a review and assessment of the literature dealing with the Israeli case.
b. Eliminated from statistical treatment due to missing data.

Before turning to a presentation of analysis results, a disclaimer is in order. No attempt is made here to test the entire model depicted in Figure 7.2. As our representations of both the traditional and our revised perspectives make clear, we concur on the sequence and importance of motivational and precipitant factors in determining nation-states' positions on nuclear armament. However, we are constrained at present from undertaking a more complete empirical analysis of these factors by the Herculean requirements of measuring concepts such as "threat perception," "reduction of alliance capability," et cetera on a cross-national and longitudinal bases. Therefore our analysis is limited here to a consideration of the relative potencies of those contextual variables regarded by contemporary theorists to be most potent in predicting countries' positions on the nuclear armament option under the prevailing conditions of the present international system.

DATA ANALYSIS, RESULTS, AND INTERPRETATION

The results from our discriminant analysis are reported in Tables 7.4a-c. A preliminary inspection of the group and overall means and standard deviations (Table 7.4a) suggests that the four policy-position groups are well defined by the independent variables, although the large group standard deviations of the NEED factor and, to a lesser extent, the DIFFUSION variable indicate some overlap among the four groups. The problem of multicollinearity of the independent variables is not severe (Table 7.4b). Only the NEED-DIFFUSION relationship is of any real note, and the correlation coefficient is a moderate .47.[5]

Turning next to the multivariate model itself, we see that the results are somewhat surprising and at odds with hypothesized expectations. Recall that it was anticipated that two functions reflecting need and availability dimensions would be required to discriminate among the forty-six states classified according to their nuclear weapons positions. Instead, a single function was sufficient to discriminate. As detailed in Table 7.4c, a second discriminant function added little to the model in terms of its respective eigenvalue, canonical correlation, and statistical significance. Reversing the logic of discriminant analysis and treating the canonical correlation as comparable to the eta measure of analysis of variance, one can interpret the canonical correlation squared of the single discriminant function as indicating that 49% of the variation in the independent variables is explained by the group classification.

The model represented by the single discriminant function provides some interesting insight into the impact of international nuclear commerce. Table 7.4d reports the standardized function coefficients of the independent variables on the discriminant function. Because two functions were expected to be necessary to discriminate the four policy positions, no specific hypotheses were proferred for the case of a single function or the relative weights of each of the independent variables on that function. Nevertheless, the logic of our original argument would lead one to expect

TABLE 7.4a: Univariate Analysis

	Nuclear States	Latent Aspirants	Aspirants	Nonnuclear States	Total
n =	5	12	13	16	46
NEED(x/s.d)	58.6/41.1	68.2/46.1	52.9/42.9	76.6/31.7	65.8/39.9
DIFFUSION (x/s.d.)	53.2/44.2	45.0/29.7	49.6/25.3	76.1/19.1	58.0/29.4
AVAILABILITY (x/s.d.)	42.2/47.3	6.6/10.9	4.0/6.4	2.4/1.9	8.3/19.6

TABLE 7.4b: Intercorrelation of Independent Variables

	Diffusion	Availability
Need	0.467 (.001)	−0.046 (.337)
Diffusion		0.194 (.093)

Values enclosed by parentheses are significance probabilities.

TABLE 7.4c: Discriminant Function

Function	Eigenvalue	Relative Percentage	Canonical Correlation	Significance
1	0.95284	79.61	0.699	0.05
2	0.20531	17.15	0.413	0.21

TABLE 7.4d: Coefficients/Group Centroids

	Standardized Function Coefficients (Function 1)
Need	0.225
Diffusion	−0.685
Availability	0.948

	Group Centroids/Function 1
Nuclear states	1.709
Latent Aspirants	0.234
Aspirants	−0.083
Nonnuclear states	−0.643

TABLE 7.4e: Prediction Results

Actual Group	N	Nuclear States	Latent Aspirants	Aspirants	Nonnuclear States
Nuclear states	5	2 40.0%	3 60.0%	0 00.0%	0 00.0%
Latent aspirants	12	1 8.3%	6 50.0%	4 33.35	1 8.3%
Aspirants	13	1 7.7%	3 23.1%	4 30.8%	5 38.5%
Nonnuclear states	16	0 0.0%	0 0.0%	3 18.8%	1.3 81.3%

Percentage of cases classified correctly: 54.35%

that the NEED factor would have the greatest weight in determining a single function, followed by the AVAILABILITY and DIFFUSION measures. Moreover, it was hypothesized that the contributions of each variable would be positive as reflected in the sign attached to function coefficients.

In contrast to these expectations, AVAILABILITY is by far the most important factor (0.948), followed by the DIFFUSION variable. The NEED measure contributes but slightly to the function. Equally surprising is the negative weight attached to the DIFFUSION variable (-0.685). Given the small sample size used here, any interpretation of these results is necessarily tentative; still, it seems apparent that the burgeoning commerce in nuclear technology is more critical in determining nations' positions on the nuclear issue than are objective energy needs. Furthermore, the relative size and the sign of the DIFFUSION coefficient appears to lend some credence to the once-heretical view that the dissemination of nuclear technology may not be the destabilizing force feared. Stated differently, the onset of market processes in nuclear technology coupled with increased needs for alternatives to fossil fuels appears to have transformed the nuclear issue from one of politico-strategic concern for the consequences of nuclear diffusion to one of economic exchange. The face validity of this conclusion would seem to be enhanced by the marked ascendancy of economic terminology in the policy rhetoric governing discussion of the proliferation problem in contemporary international discourse.

The indication that there might be overlap among nations' positions is sustained by the group centroids reported in Table 7.4d. The single function derived from discriminant analysis constitutes a continuum (ranging from positive to negative values) along which nations can be located according to their respective Z values. Both nuclear and nonnuclear groups are relatively distinct of one another, 1,709 and −0.643, respectively. The closeness of the centroids for the latent aspirant and aspirant groups serves to indicate that the function does not clearly discriminate these countries. Further evidence for this is provided by the prediction results reported in Table 7.4e. The function is quite strong in distinguishing the nonnuclear states, fair in discriminating latent aspirants and nuclear states, but quite weak in predicting aspirants. This last weakness is especially vexatious inasmuch as these nations pose serious challenges to current safeguards against nuclear weapons proliferation.

CONCLUSIONS

These results are not as robust as one might wish and we have not encompassed the entire model in our analysis. The omission of motivational and precipitant factors leaves much to be done in the way of research before a full understanding of nations' positions in nuclear armament is realized. As noted, inquiry into those factors is likely to be far more laborious than the one undertaken here.

Nevertheless, we are sufficiently encouraged by these results to tender a few conclusions. The availability of nuclear technology means that the indigenous capabilities are no longer immutable restraints which prevent some nations from going nuclear; instead, low levels of scientific, technological, and economic capability have become factors which can be overcome through international commerce. If, as suggested here, market mechanisms are supplanting historical oligopolies in the transfer of nuclear technology, then increasing numbers of countries will soon be able to entertain options about acquiring this technology and, more ominously, about the ends to which it will be applied. The emergence of this development would seem to comprise a serious threat to international order.

What makes this latter issue even more frightening is that much of the technology which will become available to these countries presents the Non-Proliferation Treaty with a major dilemma. Under the terms of the NPT, all parties may use nuclear power for peaceful purposes, though nuclear weapon states are obliged to assist in the development of civil nuclear energy, and nonnuclear weapon states are required to accept safeguards over their nuclear activities as set forth in an agreement negotiated with the International Atomic Energy Agency (IAEA). One of the assumptions behind the NPT is that IAEA safeguards would detect any attempt to divert fissile materials from civilian to military programs soon enough to allow other countries to exert countervailing pressure on the potential proliferator. However, the marketing of new, short lead-time technologies for obtaining fissionable material raises serious questions about this assumption. Countries which purchase these new uranium enrichment and reprocessing technologies could be in a position to manufacture weapons components in advance and then acquire the necessary nuclear material from their reactors whenever they feel the international situation would seem to warrant full-scale production.

In 1977, a two-year study of this very problem was initiated under the auspices of the International Nuclear Fuel Cycle Evaluation (INFCE).[6] A total of fifty-three nations and four international organizations began to study ways to reconcile the development and promotion of civilian power plants with their desire to control weapons proliferation. Thus far the proceedings have been polarized. On one side stands various less developed and advanced industrial countries interested primarily in the development and commercial promotion of nuclear energy. On the other side stands the United States, which is more concerned with the question of proliferation control. At present Washington contends that the transfer of short lead-time technologies should be halted by multilateral agreement until some method is found to solve the control problem. According to the Carter Administration, this could be done by improving the efficiency of uranium utilization and shifting international nuclear commerce to diversion resistant technologies.

In other words, such a two-fold strategy contains what is hoped to be both a means of reducing the need to reprocess spent fuel and a way to decrease the opportunity to extract plutonium if reprocessing is attempted. The first part of the strategy is designed to cope with a world where the demand for enriched uranium will soon exceed the supply. Only nine countries possess major deposits of uranium ore, and even fewer sources of enriched uranium exist. Nevertheless, by the mid-1970s some 168 nuclear power plants were operating in 19 countries, and the list is expected to include anywhere from 10 to 20 more countries by the early 1980s (Atlantic Council Nuclear Fuels Policy Working Group, 1976: 7). Adding this to the fact that an ordinary 1,000 megawatt light water reactor requires 5,500 tons of uranium oxide to operate during its 30-year life (Rose and Lester, 1979: 205), it is not surprising that many countries have been attracted to fuel recycling. To lessen the need to reprocess spent fuel, several steps could be taken to improve fuel management and reactor design. For instance, slightly higher levels of uranium enrichment would increase the residence time of the fuel assemblies in the reactor, thereby allowing for a greater fraction of the U_{235} to be used while decreasing the discharge of plutonium. If one were also to institute steps like reducing the tails assay of the uranium waste stream and using thorium in the fuel cycle, it could be possible to have a uranium savings of over 40% in those power plants that come on line at the turn of the century (Hafemeister, 1979: 60). But should the desire for reprocessing still exist, the second half of the strategy would strive to limit the extraction of plutonium from the spent fuel rods. Two possibilities exist in this regard: coprocessing, and a tandem fuel cycle. The former separates uranium and plutonium from the waste in spent fuel but does not separate them from each other. Hence it would be more difficult to divert these materials because direct handling would not be safe. The latter uses spent fuel from light water reactors to power heavy water, natural uranium reactors. Therefore it likewise reduces the danger of plutonium diversion at the same time that it helps preserve existing uranium supplies.

All of these proposals notwithstanding, other technology-exporting nations nevertheless question whether INFCE is simply a forum where the United States is attempting to orchestrate world opinion toward its position on nuclear commerce. Needless to say, the international nuclear energy market is the scene of a multibillion dollar transnational rivalry. Prior to 1975, the United States earned more than $3 billion in reactor sales and $700 million for providing low-enriched uranium fuels. According to government estimates, within five years revenues could climb to over $1.2 billion annually (Energy Research and Development Agency, 1976: 10-18). Privately, France and West Germany have complained that they have lost contracts because of a tacit American threat to withhold deliveries of enriched uranium unless U.S. reactors were purchased. Thus, as they interpreted the situation, it was necessary for them to include provisions for enrichment and reprocessing with their reactor bids if they were to be competitive with Westinghouse and General Electric.

In summary, then, our skepticism toward the conventional wisdom and its emphasis upon indigenous prerequisites allegedly necessary for states to be able to exercise choice in the area of nuclear armament is increased in light of our findings regarding the impact of contextual variables on armament decisions. Furthermore, we have also seen that of the contextual variables we have analyzed, technological availability is the most potent factor in accounting for the choices exercised by states. As we approach the second review conference of the NPT, there does not seem to be much indication that the availability of nuclear technology will decrease so long as the commercial rivalry among the exporting nation continues. Our discovery that technological availability has more to do with decisions regarding nuclear armament than any other factor considered suggests that the problem of proliferation will continue to grow in the 1980s.

But despite our knowledge about the role of availability, need, and diffusion pressures as determinants of individual nations' positions on the armament issue, we still remain statistically ignorant about the systemic pattern of proliferation which will result from these individual decisions. As Schelling (1978: 3-14) has pointed out:

> There are easy cases, of course, in which the aggregate is merely an extrapolation from the individual. If we know that every driver, on his own, turns his lights on at sundown, we can guess that from our helicopter we shall see all the car lights in a local area going on at about the same time. We could even get our compass bearings by reflecting that the cascade of lights on the Massachusetts Turnpike will flow westward as dusk settles. But if most people turn their lights on when some fraction of the oncoming cars already have their lights on, we'll get a different picture from our helicopter. In the second case, drivers are responding to each other's behavior. People are responding to an environment that consists of other people responding to *their* environment, which consists of people responding to an environment of people's responses. Sometimes the dynamics are sequential: if your lights induce me to turn mine on; mine may induce somebody else but not you. Sometimes the dynamics are reciprocal; hearing your car horn, I honk mine, thus encouraging you to honk more insistently.

The lesson here is not that of highway illumination or horn blowing. Rather, Schelling's analogy points up the need for the next wave of theorizing about international proliferation to explore models that link macropatterns with microdecisions.

NOTES

1. Under the Treaty of Almelo (1970), Britain, West Germany, and the Netherlands agreed to establish a commercial centrifuge uranium enrichment consortium known as URENCO.

2. This reconstruction of the traditional interpretation of the sources of nuclear proliferation represents a synthesis of the dominant propositions articulated in the sources enumerated in Table 7.1. For recent reviews of past and present theorizing about nuclear armaments proliferation, see Schlesinger (1972), Quester (1975, 1972), and Dunn and Overhold (1976).

3. Data on the "issue-positions" (Coplin and O'Leary, 1972) of states regarding nuclear armament were derived by coding the public statements of national leaders on their respective positions vis-à-vis nuclear armament, supplemented by a content analysis of the expert opinions of scholars who have studied the policy positions of states on this issue. Sources for classifying states' positions included, among others: ACDA (1969), Bader (1968), Barnaby (1969), Beaton (1966), Bull (1961), Fischer (1971), Imai (1969), Northedge and Kumar (1968-1969), Quester (1971), Redick (1972), Rosenbaum and Cooper (1970), Russett and Cooper (1966), Sapir and Van

Hyning (1956), Schwab (1969), Young (1969), and Zoppo (1966). As further evidence on countries' issue-positions, data on the current status of various countries with respect to the Non-Proliferation Treaty were derived from coding *Treaties in Force* and from information supplied by Philip J. Wolfson of the U.S. Department of State.

4. Due to the unavailability of information on central variables from Cuba and Taiwan, these two countries usually considered to be potential proliferators had to be eliminated from the analysis. The reader should note that their absence from the sample might effect the results, but probably only moderately given the sufficient size of the sample.

5. Following Koutsoyiannis (1973: 231), additional tests for detecting multicollinearity were performed. Inasmuch as our dependent variable is a nominal measure, these tests were performed by means of a series of step-wise regressions of four dummy-coded dependent variables (representing the four categories of nation-states) on the independent variables of AVAILABILITY, DIFFUSION, and NEED, and by examining the effects of each on the regression coefficients, their standard errors, and the overall R^2. A comparison of the four sets of step-wise regressions indicated that the effect of multicollinearity was to render the NEED variable even more inconsequential to the overall model than was depicted by discriminant analysis results. We have retained the NEED variable in order to facilitate discussion.

6. The International Fuel Cycle Evaluation is composed of eight working groups which analyze specific matters pertaining to the commercial development of nuclear energy, a technical coordinating committee that ties together the activities of the working groups, and a plenary conference which assesses the reports which are produced by the groups.

REFERENCES

Atlantic Council Nuclear Fuels Working Group (1976) Nuclear Policy. Boulder, CO: Westview.
BADER, W. S. (1968) The United States and the Spread of Nuclear Weapons. New York: Western.
BAKER, S. J. (1976) "Nuclear proliferation: monopoly or cartel?" Foreign Policy 23 (Summer): 202-220.
--- (1975) "Commercial nuclear power and nuclear proliferation." Cornell University Peace Studies Program Occasional Paper 5 (May): 1-66.
BARNABY, C. F. (1969) "The development of nuclear energy programmes," pp. 16-35 in C. F. Barnaby (ed.) Preventing the Spread of Nuclear Weapons. London: Souvenir.
BEATON, L. (1966). Must the Bomb Spread? Baltimore: Penguin.
BOULDING, K. E. (1962) Conflict and Defense: A General Theory. New York: Harper & Row.
BOWIE, R. (1965) "Strategy and the Atlantic alliance," pp. 237-263 in H. A. Kissinger (ed.) Problems of National Strategy. New York: Praeger.
BULL, H. (1961) The Control of the Arms Race. New York: Praeger.
CANTORI, L. J. and S. L. SPIEGEL (1970) "The international relations of regions." Polity 2 (Summer): 397-425.
Committee on International Relations (1977) U.S. House of Representatives factbook on Nuclear Proliferation (September 23). Washington, DC: Author.

COPLIN, W. D. (1974) Introduction to International Politics. Chicago: Rand McNally.

——— and M. K. O'LEARY (1972) Everyman's Prince. Belmont, CA: Duxbury.

DAVIDSON, W., N. KALKSTEIN, and C. HOHENEMSER (1960) "Technical report," in The Nth Country Problem and Arms Control. Washington, DC: National Planning Association.

DOWTY, A. (1978) "Nuclear proliferation: the Israeli case." International Studies Quarterly 22 (March): 79-120.

DUNN, L. A. and W. H. OVERHOLD (1976) "The next phase in nuclear proliferation research." Orbis 20 (Summer): 497-524.

Energy Research and Development Agency (1976) U.S. Nuclear Power Export Activities. Washington: Author.

EPSTEIN, W. (1977) "Why states go—and don't go—nuclear." Annals of the American Academy of Political and Social Science 430 (March): 16-28.

EPTSTEIN, W. (1976) The Last Chance. New York: Free Press.

FALK, R. A. (1978) Nuclear Policy and World Order: Why Denuclearization. New York: Institute for World Order.

FEIVESON, H. A. and T. B. TAYLOR (1977) "Alternative strategies for international control of nuclear power," pp. 123-183 in T. Greenwood, H. A. Feiveson, and T. B. Taylor (eds.) Nuclear Proliferation: Motivations, Capabilities, and Strategies for Control. New York: McGraw-Hill.

FISCHER, G. (1971) The Nonproliferation of Nuclear Weapons. London: Europe.

FRANK, J. D. (1968) Sanity and Survival. New York: Random House.

GREENWOOD, T. et al., [eds.] (1977) Nuclear Proliferation: Motivations, Capabilities, and Strategies for Control. New York: McGraw-Hill.

HAFEMEISTER, D. W. (1979) "Nonproliferation and alternative nuclear technologies." Technology Review 81, 3: 58-62.

HARKAVY, R. (1977) Israel's Nuclear Weapons: Spectre of Holocaust in the Middle East. Denver: Univ. of Denver Press.

HARRISON, S. L. (1965) "Nth nation challenges: the present perspective." Orbis 9 (September): 155-170.

HOFFMANN, S. (1968) Gulliver's Troubles. New York: McGraw-Hill.

HOHENEMSER, C. (1962) "The nth country problem today," pp. 238-276 in M. Seymour (ed.) Disarmament: Its Politics and Economics. Boston: American Academy of Arts and Sciences.

IMAI, R. (1969) "The nonproliferation treaty and Japan." Bulletin of the Atomic Scientist 25 (May): 2-7.

INGLIS, D. (1959) "The fourth-country problem: let's stop at three." Bulletin of the Atomic Scientist 15 (January): 22-26.

KAPLAN, M. A. (1972) "The unit veto system reconsidered," pp. 49-55 in R. Rosecrance (ed.) The Future of the International Strategic System. San Francisco: Chandler.

KEGLEY, C. W., Jr. (1979) "International and domestic correlates of nuclear proliferation: a comparative analysis." Presented at the annual meeting of the International Studies Association, Toronto, March 20-24.

KELLY, G. A. (1961) "The political background to the French a-bomb." Orbis 4 (Fall): 284-306.

KISSINGER, H. A. (1965) The Troubled Partnership. New York: McGraw-Hill.

——— (1957) Nuclear Weapons and Foreign Policy. New York: Harper & Row.

KORT, F. (1973) "Regression analysis and discriminant analysis: an application of

R. A. Fisher's theorem to data in political science." American Political Science Review 67 (June): 555-559.

KOUTSOYIANNIS, A. (1973) Theory of Econometrics. New York: Harper & Row.

LOWRENCE, W. W. (1976) "Nuclear futures for sale: to Brazil from West German, 1975." International Security 1 (Fall): 147-166.

MORGENSTERN, O. (1961) "The n-country problem." Fortune (March): 136-137, 205-208.

MUELLER, J. E. (1967) "Incentives for restraint: Canada as a non-nuclear power." Orbis 11 (Fall): 864-896.

National Planning Association (1972) "The nth country problem and arms control," pp. 323-333 in M. L. Rakove (ed.) Arms and Foreign Policy in the Nuclear Age. New York: Oxford Univ. Press.

NORTHEDGE, F. S. and V. KUMAR (1968-1969) "The nuclear nonproliferation treaty." Political Scientist 5 (July-December; January-June): 1-114.

Nuclear Energy Policy Study Group (1977) Nuclear Power Issues and Choices. Cambridge, MA: Ballinger.

QUESTER, G. (1975) What's New on Nuclear Proliferation?" Aspen, CO: Aspen Institute for Humanistic Studies.

——— (1973) The Politics of Nuclear Proliferation. Baltimore: Johns Hopkins Univ. Press.

——— (1972) "Some conceptual problems in nuclear proliferation." American Political Science Review 66 (June): 490-497.

——— (1971) "The nuclear nonproliferation treaty," pp. 437-453 in S. L. Spiegel and K. N. Waltz (eds.) Conflict in World Politics. Cambridge, MA: Winthrop.

RATHJENS, G. and J. RUINA (1976) Nuclear Power and Weapons Proliferation. Adelphi Paper 130. London: IISS.

RAYMOND, G. A. and R. A. SKINNER (1979) "Nuclear energy exports, nonproliferation, and U.S. foreign policy," in M. O. Heisler and R. M. Lawrence (eds.) Energy Politics: Comparative and International Perspectives. Lexington, MA: D. C. Heath.

REDICK, J. R. (1972) Military Potential of Latin American Nuclear Energy Programs. Beverly Hills: Sage Publications.

ROSE, D. J. and R. K. LESTER (1979) "Nuclear power, nuclear weapons, and international stability," pp. 203-215 in Progress in Arms Control? San Francisco: W. H. Freeman.

ROSECRANCE, R. [ed.] (1972) The Future of the International Strategic System. San Francisco: Chandler.

——— (1963) "The nth country problem." Orbis 7 (September): 171-173.

ROSEN, S. J. and W. S. JONES (1977) The Logic of International Relations. Cambridge, MA: Winthrop.

ROSENBAUM, H. J. and G. M. COOPER (1970) "Brazil and the nonproliferation treaty." International Affairs 46 (January): 74-90.

RUSSETT, B. M. and C. C. COOPER (1966) Arms Control in Europe. Denver: Univ. of Denver Press.

SAPIR, M. and S. J. VAN HYNING (1956) The Outlook of Nuclear Power in Japan. Washington, DC: National Planning Association.

SCHELLING, T. C. (1978) Micromotives and Macrobeahvior. New York: W. W. Norton.

——— (1976) "Who will have the bomb?" International Security 1 (Summer): 77-91.

SCHLESINGER, J. R. (1972) "The strategic consequences of nuclear proliferation," pp. 360-369 in M. L. Rakove (ed.) Arms and Foreign Policy in the Nuclear Age. New York: Oxford Univ. Press.

——— (1967) "Nuclear spread: the setting of the problem," pp. 8-28 in S. D. Kertesz (ed.) Nuclear Nonproliferation in a World of Nuclear Powers. Notre Dame: Univ. of Notre Dame Press.
SCHWAB, G. (1969) "Switzerland's tactical nuclear weapon policy." Orbis 13 (Fall): 900-914.
SHAFFER, H. B. (1972) "Nuclear balance of terror," pp. 51-72 in W. B. Dickinson (ed.) Editorial Research Reports on the Global Community. Washington, DC: Congressional Quarterly.
Stockholm International Peace Research Institute (1976) World Armaments and Disarmament Yearbook, 1976. Cambridge, MA: MIT Press.
——— (1975 The Nuclear Age. Cambridge, MA: MIT Press.
——— (1972) The Near-Nuclear Countries and the NPT. New York: Humanities Press.
United Nations (1977) World Energy Supplies, 1971-1975. New York: Author.
U.S. Arms Control and Disarmament Agency (1969) International Negotiations on the Treaty on the Nonproliferation of Nuclear Weapons. Washington, DC: Author.
U.S. Central Intelligence Agency (1977) The International Energy Situation: Outlook to 1985. Washington, DC: Author.
U.S. Department of State (1972) Treaties in Force. Washington, DC: Author.
WALSKE, C. (1976-1977) "Nuclear electric power and the proliferation of nuclear weapon states." International Security 1 (Winter): 94-106.
WILLIAMS, S. L. (1969) The U.S., India and the Bomb. Baltimore: Johns Hopkins Univ. Press.
WILLRICH, M. (1966) "Guarantees to non-nuclear nations." Foreign Affairs 44 (July): 683-692.
WOHLSTETTER, A. (1976-1977) "Spreading the bomb without breaking the rules." Foreign Policy 25 (Winter): 88-96.
——— (1965) "Nuclear sharing: NATO and n + 1 country," pp. 186-212 in H. A. Kissinger (ed.) Problems of National Strategy. New York: Praeger.
YOUNG, E. (1969) The Control of Proliferation. Adelphi Papers 56. London: Institute for Strategic Studies.
ZOPPO, C. E. (1966) "Nuclear technology, multipolarity and international stability." World Politics 18 (July): 579-606.

PART III

MODELING ARMS RACES

Chapter 8

ACCOUNTING FOR SUPERPOWER ARMS SPENDING

MICHAEL DAVID WALLACE
*University of British Columbia,
Vancouver*

INTRODUCTION

Since Richardson began his pioneering work over a generation ago, scientific studies of arms races have become ever more numerous, and are today proliferating at what seems to be an accelerating rate.[1] Yet few would claim that we are close to answering Richardson's original question: What drives the arms race?

To a very large extent this lack of progress is attributable to the methods used to explore the problem. By far the largest number of arms race studies are little more than speculative mathematical manipulations, in which little or no attempt at empirical verification is made. But even the relatively few data-based studies have run into great difficulties when they have tried to construct a model of the dynamics of the arms race. One of two results almost invariably obtains: either the model fits the data rather

EDITORS' NOTE: This chapter was first submitted for review September 5, 1979. The version published here was received July 25, 1979. The data reported upon here are part of the Correlates of War Project, J. David Singer principal investigator. Inquiries regarding use of these data should be made to Dr. Singer at The Mental Health Research Institute, University of Michigan, Ann Arbor, Michigan.

AUTHOR'S NOTE: Revised version of paper presented to the annual meetings of the Japanese Peace Science Society, Hiroshima, 1979. This research was assisted in part by a Leave Fellowship Grant from the Social Sciences and Humanities Research Council of Canada.

poorly, or else there exist two or more models that fit the data almost equally well.

The problem of obtaining a uniquely satisfactory empirical fit has become particularly acute with regard to one of the most interesting and policy-relevant issues in the arms race literature: the debate between those who conceive the arms race to be the result of a self-feeding action-reaction sequence operating with neither important stimulus from, nor significant check, by the political process, and those who believe, on the contrary, that the arms race is primarily the result of autochthonous forces within one or both of the superpowers. After elaborate modifications and extensions of the Richardson action-reaction model, Gillespie and Zinnes were unable to obtain good fits for the superpower arms race (Gillespie et al., 1977; see also Gillispie and Zinnes, 1976; Zinnes, 1976). Nincic and Cusack (1978) had similar difficulties with a model based solely on political and economic forces within the United States. Ostrom (1977; 1978) had better luck in obtaining a good fit; but even with the aid of sophisticated econometric techniques, he was unable to discover a statistically significant difference between the predictive capacities of his "arms race," "organizational politics," and "bureaucratic politics" models, or indeed between any of these and the naive "no change" model. Luterbacher and Lamballet (forthcoming) experienced much the same problem in choosing between their "mutual stimulation" (action-reaction) model and their "self-stimulation" (autochthonous forces) model.

Now, the causes of this sort of impasse are well known from modeling efforts in other fields. If a model fails to produce a good fit, it must be somehow misspecified; either the variables or the function which links them are incorrect. Less obvious, but equally familiar to modelers, is the case in which a model fits fairly well, but one or more alternative, incompatible models fit equally well. In such instances it is a virtual certainty that one or more variables in the several models are either identical collinear, or empirically indistinguishable. Such collinearity is often harder to cure than simple misspecification, since it is often far from obvious that apparently distinct models are related in this fashion.

It shall be my contention in this chapter that both misspecification and collinearity characterize many of the models which have contributed to the "internal-external" debate. I shall contend further that these flaws are not incidental characteristics of these models, but are fundamental to their structure, which in turn implies that basic reformulation, rather than mere tinkering, will be required to remedy the situation. I shall then suggest a possible avenue along which this reformulation could take place, and shall proceed along one of these avenues to propose and execute a different sort of "critical experiment" which may help to decide the respective merits of the "action-reaction" and "autochthonous forces" hypotheses. Finally, I shall explore the possible policy consequences of my findings, particularly in the light of the current debate in the United States over the recently signed Salt II treaty.

RICHARDSON MODELS

Several studies (Gillespie and Zinnes, 1976) have shown that the classical Richardson model does not do a satisfactory job of accounting for the Cold War superpower arms race. Nor has mathematical tinkering with the basic model proven very fruitful (Gillespie and Zinnes, 1976; Busch, 1970). This author has argued previously (Wallace, 1979; Wallace and Wilson, 1978) that there are two main reasons for this poor fit. For one thing, the Richardson model consists of linear differential equations, meaning it assumes that each superpower's actions are in strict proportion to the perceived gap between itself and its rival, without threshold effects, jumps, or accelerations. Such linear, continuous models usually—and in this case certainly—produce prediction curves that are simple linear exponentials (Wallace, 1976). But much of our pretheoretical discussion of the Cold War arms race—its rapidly changing qualitative character, its multidimensionality, its mutually reinforcing links with crisis and confrontation (Singer, 1958; Gray, 1972; Luterbacher, 1978)—all suggest a process that is likely to be discontinuous and highly nonlinear (Wallace, 1979). Thus, it may well be that the reason for the poor fits of existing action-reaction models is not the absence of an action-reaction sequence, but rather the misspecifications of this sequence in the model.

A second reason for the poor fits obtained by these models is the omission of other variables which influence the action-reaction pattern. The outbreak of war (be it major or minor), confrontations and crises both between themselves and with other powers, and military actions to quell unrest in allied states or at home will all have two important effects: first, they will create direct exogenous disturbances in the level of military spending; second, they will generate an indirect effect as well by affecting the speed and intensity of the action-reaction sequence. Unless these variables are brought into the model explicitly, good fits are unlikely to be obtained. In fact, in the Richardson model and its many variants, there are no true exogenous variables, making them "implicitly autoregressive" (Ostrom, 1977). I shall return to this point later.

AUTOCHTHONOUS MODELS

Partly inspired by the poor fits obtained from Richardson-type models, and partly by the burgeoning literature on the formal modeling of organizational behavior (Davis, Dempster, and Wildavsky, 1966; Kanter, 1973), a number of studies have attempted to model superpower arms spending as the resultant of various *domestic* forces. These efforts may in turn be divided into those which view defense expenditures as the end product of a complex bureaucratic process (Ostrom 1977, 1978) and those which view it as a product of political and economic forces essentially external to the bureaucratic process (Nincic and Cusack, 1978).

Unfortunately, these efforts have not met with spectacular success either. Nincic and Cusack find that military spending is correlated with the amount of excess capacity in the economy, implying that budgetary decision-makers use arms spending as a tool of economic policy. They also find some relationship between arms spending and the proximity of presidential elections, suggesting that the president may use military expenditures as technique for vote-getting. But the amount of variance explained by these two variables is rather small, and the overall fit is not good. Nevertheless, their study represents an importance advance in two respects: (a) they have introduced genuine exogenous variables into their model, and (b) they use the rate of expenditure *increase,* rather than raw expenditures, which, as I shall explain below, has both methodological and substantive advantages.

No such statement can be made concerning the various "organizational process" models. Most of these assume a simple first-order autoregressive scheme, with the request for each succeeding year being a fixed proportion (usually > 1) of the previous year's request. Such models don't produce very good fits either, and it's not too surprising. While we might expect such bureaucratic incrementalism to play a major role in determining military expenditures, it cannot possibly be the only important factor; we would surely wish to reject, on theoretical grounds alone, any model not containing *any* explicit exogenous variables.

More generally, it is difficult to give credence—again on theoretical grounds—to any model with *no* explicit international variables. After all, defense expenditures are *for* making war, threatening enemies, or obtaining strategic advantage, and however much these goals may be shaped or modified by domestic political and economic considerations, their origins lie in the external environment.

TESTING THE RIVAL MODELS— A PROBLEM OF COLLINEARITY

Since neither the Richardson action-reaction model nor the various autochthonous models have proven satisfactory by themselves, an intuitively appealing strategy is to combine them into a single model. In principle, this approach would appear to have two advantages. On the one hand, it produces a "hybrid" model more intuitively satisfactory than either of its simpler parents; on the other hand, it would seem to allow us to test the relative potency of "domestic" and "international" influences on arms spending by the use of multivariate regression on empirical data. While the theoretical improvement in the model is indubitable, there is an important methodological obstacle to such a straightforward empirical comparison of "internal" and "external" variables.[2] Simply put, the problem is this: there will inevitably be a large degree of linear dependence or collinearity between the term representing the action-reaction component of a nation's military expenditures, and the term representing the bureaucratic-incremental component.

While this can easily be demonstrated from the equations of the general linear model, it is more appropriate here to put the matter more simply and intuitively. Reduced to its essentials, the point is this: if the arms level of nation X at time t is dependent upon the level of nation Y at t-1, and if, in turn, the level of Y at t is dependent upon the level of X at t-1, then it follows that the level of X at t must be dependent upon the level of X at t-2. (Formally, $E(Y_t) = X_{t-\tau}$ and $E(X_t) = Y_{t-\tau}$ then obviously $E(Y_t) = Y_{t-2\tau}$ and $E(X_t) = X_{t-2\tau}$.)

In other words, if the "true" process is a simple Richardson action-reaction one, the two nations' arms levels will exhibit a strong degree of autoregression. If this autoregressive component is extracted and labeled as an organizational or bureaucratic effect, the result may well be the spurious confirmation of a false hypothesis.

The converse is true as well. Suppose that the "true" process were a bureaucratic incremental one, so that the level of each nation's expenditures at t were a function of its history at t-1. Mathematically, then, we would write $E(Y_t) = Y_{t-\tau}$ and $E(X_t) = X_{t-\tau}$ so that,

$$Y_t = \beta_1 \hat{Y}_{t-\tau} + u_1$$
$$X_t = \beta_2 \hat{X}_{t-\tau} + u_2.$$

Now further assume that $\beta_1 \cong \beta_2$, in other words, that their average rates of growth are approximately the same (a state of affairs that is quite likely to occur in practice). We then can substitute and obtain $E(Y_t) = X_{t-1}$ and $E(X_t) = Y_{t-1}$. In other words, even if the "true" situation is a bureaucratic incrementalist one, it may not be possible to isolate a spurious action-reaction component.

Thus, even in principle it is likely to prove difficult to distinguish between the two models when formulated in this fasion. When the waters are further muddied by unspecified exogenous variables, poor quality data, and autocorrelated disturbance terms, our ability to do so will be virtually nonexistent.

Should we then simply abandon the "internal-external" debate on the grounds that the problem is mathematically ill-posed? It would be tempting to do so but for the fact that the debate is so crucially important in determining the optimal strategy for bringing the superpower arms race in check (Luterbacher and Lambelet, forthcoming). If the United States and the Soviet Union are truly caught up in an action-reaction competition, then clearly the preferred strategy is to proceed with bilateral agreements such as SALT. If on the other hand the arms race's driving force is to be found in the political and economic systems of one or both superpowers, the only possible remedy will be institutional reform. Because this question has lost none of its urgency—if anything, it has become even more vital a concern in the past decade—it behooves us to at least attempt to reformulate the debate so that it is more amenable to a precise empirical test. There are probably many ways of doing this, but one in particular suggests itself to this writer as especially promising.

REFORMULATING THE DEBATE—
EXOGENOUS VARIABLES AND FIRST DIFFERENCES

The strategy adopted here to avoid the collinearity problem is twofold.[3] First, the model will be wholly specified in terms of exogenous variables, thus eliminating any explicit autoregressive term. In other words, any variable which appears as a dependent variable in one equation will not appear as an independent variable (whether lagged or not) on the other side of that or any other equation.

Second, the dependent variable is not the absolute *level* of arms expenditures, but their *rate of increase*. First differencing is a standard method of eliminating the autoregressive components of time series, and makes sense in theoretical terms as well (Kmenta, 1971). If, after all, the arms race were merely a matter of incremental bureaucratic growth, then we would expect a steady rate of increase year by year. Thus, we would predict that the first differences would be constant, and that any variation in them would be entirely random. On the other hand, if the arms race were an action-reaction process, then the first differences would not be constant, would be some function of the arms growth or arms level of the other side. Thus, if we move from absolute levels of arms spending to first differences, the predictions made by our two models diverge sharply.

Having discussed the model-building strategy to be used, let us now turn to the specifics of the model itself.

Specifying the Model

Since we are attempting to account for changes in the military expenditures of *both* superpowers, we will be constructing a two-equation model. The two dependent (currently endogenous) variables are, as discussed above, the time rates of change (deltas) of the military expenditures of each superpower in constant dollars or rubles from 1950 to 1976.[4] On the other side of each equation we will have variables representing six important hypothesized influences on these rates of change: (a) the effect of the military expenditures of the other superpower, (b) the impact of the military efforts of other salient powers, (c) participation in shooting wars, (d) the presence or absence of crisis and confrontation in the international system, (e) the impact of domestic political competition, and, lastly, (f) the effect of salient economic events. Now let us specify these in detail.

To begin with, we have the impact of the other superpower's military expenditures, the action-reaction term. This term is *not,* however, simply the other superpower's rate of increase in the previous year, for both computational and theoretical reasons. For one thing, to introduce a current endogenous variable on the right-hand side of each equation would give a pair of simultaneous equations, with all of the problems of identification and estimation that follow (Johnston, 1972). Second, it is doubtful if budgetary decision-making is so narrowly sensitive to a single annual change. It is more plausible that the military, and those that control their appropriations, will react only gradually to shifts on the other side. Consequently, we use a moving average of the opposing superpower's expenditure changes for the preceeding three years; this ensures that the reaction term in the equation represents a genuine trend, and not an unrepresentative short-term fluctuation.

We must also take account of the military expenditures of other powers which can pose an important independent military threat. Since 1950 the only power in this category has been China. Since it has several times engaged in or threatened armed hostilities with both superpowers, it is reasonable to suppose that its expenditures will react to its growing military might. Therefore, the second term we include in the equation for each superpower is a three-year moving sum of changes in China's military expenditures.

Obviously, military expenditures will react sharply to a nation's participation in a full-scale war. Rather than using an elaborate index to represent this effect (Nincic and Cusack, 1978; Ostrom, 1978) we shall employ a simple dummy variable. Its value is +1 when a shooting war was in progress during the previous year, -1 for the two years after the end of the war (to take account of demobilization) and zero for all other years. Since the Soviet Union did not engage in any full-scale international wars during this period, this variable is only used for the United States, to take into account the effect of the Korean and Indochinese Wars.

International crisis and military confrontation is the fourth variable to be entered into the equation. It seems clear that, ceteris paribus, periods characterized by major crises and confrontations, either between the United States and the Soviet Union themselves, or between either superpower and China, will produce a propensity for military increases. Thus, we introduce another dummy variable whose index value is 1 when each country had a serious dispute or military confrontation in the previous year either with the other superpower or with China, and zero for other years.

Domestic political competition is accounted for by still another dummy variable, although of course its form must change to account for the differences in the two political systems. For the United States we may hypothesize that the main political pressures on the defense budget occur during presidential election years; during the quadrennial campaigning, pork-barrel pressures are the greatest, and "scare" issues such as the so-called "missile gap" are likeliest to have an impact. Thus, for the United States we use a dummy variable whose value is 1 during presidential election years, and zero otherwise.

The construction of a similar index for the Soviet Union is obviously more difficult, since so little of the Soviet political process is "visible." Nevertheless, since it is our purpose to measure the impact only of important political change, a fairly gross index will suffice. Here we use a dummy variable whose value is 1 for those years in which the general secretaryship of the CPSU changed hands, and zero for all other years.

Finally, we wish to introduce a variable to measure the effect of a superpower's economic fortunes on its changing military expenditures. Once again, the two states' differing systems force us to vary our approach in each case. Beginning with the United States, it has been persuasively argued that economic "lead times" will augment the military budget as the executive and Congress use increased military spending as the handiest and least politically contentious means of "priming the pump" (Nincic and Cusack, 1978). If this is so, then we might expect that a high unemployment rate among adult breadwinners in the first quarter of the year (right before the budget is considered) would have an upward impact on expenditures;[5] we therefore use this as our economic index for the United States.

For the Soviet Union we would be likely to propose the opposite hypothesis; operating with a far smaller pool of economic resources, suffering from a chronic labor shortage, and not subject to the vagaries of the business cycle, economic setbacks are likely to produce a *downturn* in the budget, as the pressures to divert capital and resources to other sectors intensifies. To measure this effect, our index is the rate of change in the Soviet GNP for the previous year.

Having specified the variables to be used, let us mention briefly the data sources employed.

Data Sources

Arriving at data values for superpower military expenditures is at once the most important and the most difficult part of the data-making task. A great deal of controversy—both scholarly and ideological—has surrounded various attempts to arrive at the "true" levels of expenditure for the superpowers.

Our task here is simplified by the fact that we are not required to compare directly the spending levels of the three powers. As long as our figures are in constant currency units, we can estimate the mutual impact of changing expenditures without conversion. Nevertheless, there remains the problem of "hidden" expenditures included in the budgets of civilian agencies (such as NASA and the NRC in the United States) as well as the difficulties posed by the common Soviet practice of pegging the price of military goods and services at artificially low levels. Several studies have attempted to find ways around these problems.[6] The Correlates of War Project at the University of Michigan is engaged in an ongoing effort to analyse and collate the various estimates, with a view to their eventual publication; what are used here are interim estimates.

The data on serious disputes and military confrontations were also obtained from colleagues on the Correlates of War Project; it is shortly to be published in a volume by Charles Gochman and Thomas Kselman, to which the reader should refer for a complete listing, along with data-making procedures.

While economic statistics for the United States are readily available from published sources, accurate Soviet GNP figures are much harder to come by. With considerable trepidation, we base the index on the figure published annually by the CIA; at the very least these estimates are likely to be generated in a consistent fashion over the life of the series.

Estimation Techniques

The problem of estimating the coefficients of the model is not a trivial one. As was discussed above, the use of a moving average index representing the reaction term means that the two equations of the model are not, strictly speaking, simultaneous. Nevertheless, it is almost certain that the disturbance terms (residuals) the the U.S. and Soviet equations will be correlated, perhaps highly correlated. In such cases it is possible to show that ordinary least squares (single-equation) techniques produce inefficient estimates (Malinvaud, 1966). Therefore, the Zellner procedure for iterative estimation of seemingly unrelated regression was employed; this technique is merely the limiting case of three-stage least squares, performed without any right-hand side endogenous variables (Zellner, 1972). In every case, it produced estimates superior to the OLS ones, and so only the results of the Zellner estimation are reported here.

Now, the Zellner technique is perhaps even more sensitive than OLS to autocorrelated disturbance terms; therefore, the Durbin-Watson coefficient is computed for all equations. As a double check, the exact probability of autocorrelation is computed by applying Householder transformations to the equations and then using the Pie-Jian and Niehoff methods (White, 1978).

The Results

The coefficients produced by applying Zellner iterative estimation to the complete model are displayed in Table 8.10. It is clear that for each superpower, three predictor variables are of crucial importance, while the others have little or no impact. For the United States, the Soviets' expenditures obviously play a crucial role, as do war mobilization and the international climate as represented by the presence or absence of serious

TABLE 8.1 Original Equations

Predictor Variables	USA		
	b	β	t-ratio
USSR moving average	1.17	.55	7.61
Chinese moving average	−1.28	−.12	−1.75
War	15.54	.56	7.29
Serious disputes	6.00	.42	5.85
Elections	−1.28	−.12	−1.75
Unemployment	.27	.05	.66

$R^2 = .92$ Durbin-Watson = 2.66

Predictor Variables	USSR		
	b	β	t-ratio
USA moving average	.29	.62	14.32
Chinese moving average	1.38	.27	5.68
Serious disputes	2.66	.58	7.67
Leadership changes	.59	.12	1.56
GNP growth	.05	.10	2.14

$R^2 = .96$ Durbin-Watson = 2.54

disputes. On the other hand, Chinese expenditures do not appear to produce a corresponding reaction in American spending; indeed, the coefficient is in the wrong direction, although not significantly. Moreover, neither presidential elections nor unemployment appear to have any significant impact at all.

The results for the Soviet Union show two major points of similarity with those for the United States. The first is the importance of the reaction term; the second is the emergence of serious disputes as a major factor in changing military expenditures. But unlike the U.S. case, Chinese expenditures play a significant (albeit secondary) role in accounting for Soviet arms growth. On the other hand, neither leadership changes nor fluctuations in the GNP seem to have much impact.

These results appear quite clear-cut, and the model produces a very satisfying fit. Nevertheless, the Durbin-Watson coefficients indicate the presence of significant negative autocorrelation in the residuals, a perennial bugbear when using first differences. As many statisticians have pointed out (Malinvaud, 1966), this may result in estimates that are both inefficient and biased. Now, there are a number of elaborate techniques to deal with this problem (Johnston, 1972), but before we attempt these, it usually pays to try something simpler: eliminating the superfluous variables from the regression equation. In this case, we reestimate the model after eliminating from the equations all variables not significant at the .05 level. As noted above, this leaves three variables in each equation. The results of this reestimation are shown in Table 8.2.

It is obvious that our reestimated model produces almost as good a fit

TABLE 8.2 Reduced Equations

USA

Predictor Variables	b	β	t-ratio
USSR moving average	1.12	.53	7.59
War mobilization	14.16	.51	7.42
Serious disputes	6.39	.44	6.65

$R^2 = .90$ Durbin-Watson = 2.09

USSR

Predictor Variables	b	β	t-ratio
USA moving average	.30	.64	12.26
Chinese moving average	1.44	.28	5.64
Serious disputes	3.04	.66	12.72

$R^2 = .94$ Durbin-Watson = 2.26

as the original, and that the coefficients for the remaining variables in the model have changed little. Moreover, there is one considerable improvement: the Durbin-Watson coefficients now suggest that there are no significant autocorrelation in the disturbance terms, and this is confirmed by the Pie-Jian and Niehoff tests.

Thus we have produced a model which accounts for 90% and 94% of the variance in the annual changes in the military expenditures of the United States and Soviet Union respectively. What are we to make of the findings?

Some Caveats

Before we discuss the findings themselves, it is important to enter a few cautionary notes. Although the fit is quite good—very good indeed for a model based on first differences—this study is by no means the last word. To begin with, the usual caveat must be entered concerning the data, particularly in the case of the Soviet Union. Although the estimates used here represent a considered distillation of many sources, all who have worked with them (including the author) are well aware that there is a substantial margin for error. The impact of such error, moreover, is aggravated by first differencing. Only if the findings can be replicated using *different* estimates for the Soviet Union ought we to feel truly confident in them.

Second, it is unlikely that we have yet identified *all* of the important influences which act to change arms spending, if only because there still remains a fair bit of variance to account for. Moreover, there is always the possibility (however small) that the model is *misspecified,* because one or more of the variables we have selected for the final model is in reality unimportant, which fact is masked by its spurious relationship to the dependent variable.

Third, and more likely still, we may have chosen invalid indices of some of our independent variables, especially those standing for domestic influences. If we have, then we may have falsely underestimated their importance. Again, only replication can settle the issue with certainty.

Finally, this study touches upon only one aspect of the arms race, the *fiscal* competition (Luterbacher, 1978). However, there is no reason to believe this is the most significant aspect. In fact, in the case of the superpowers, the competition to develop a secure second-strike retaliatory force, (perhaps) the off-and-on race to develop a counterforce capability, and—most important of all—the dynamic interaction *between* these two races, is probably of far greater theoretical and practical significance. We can only hope that the immense practical difficulties in constructing indices of counterforce lethality and second-strike survivability will not deter scholars from undertaking systematic studies of these phenomena as well.

These limitations should not, however, lead us to lose sight of the four major substantive points that emerge from the findings. First and most importantly, our modeling efforts lend considerable weight to those who argue that the major impetus of the arms race lies not in the domestic political and economic processes of the superpowers, but rather in the external environment which impinges upon them *qua* superpowers.

Second, within the group of external variables, it is noteworthy that the influence of the other superpower's spending is especially important; it has the largest β-weight (normalized regression coefficient) in each equation. In other words, the largest component (though by no means all) of the arms race is an "action-reaction" process.

Third, the model shows clearly as well that the occurrance of crises and confrontations in the international environment have an important impact on the arms race; for both superpowers, such crises produced a strong and significant upward pressure on military expenditures.

Finally, it is interesting to note the differential sensitivity of the two nations to Chinese military expenditures. While they exercised no significant effect on the United States, they had a significant effect on the Soviet Union. This seems to reinforce the widely held view that the Soviets must gauge their military effort to meet challenges to *both* the United States *and* China, while the Americans can more or less afford to ignore China.

POLICY IMPLICATIONS

These findings have some important implications for the debates and discussions about the arms race which are frequently held in both the Western and Socialist camps. To begin with, they offer no support whatever to those who are convinced that the arms race results from the ineluctable nature of the political or economic systems on either side. Rather, it would appear that both superpowers are reacting to *external*, rather than internal stimuli. In other words, ideological diatribes which seek to establish that the "other side" is responsible for the arms race in an attempt to justify unbalanced or inequitable concessions are neither grounded in evidence nor likely to achieve any practical arms limitations. Rather, they are likely only to provoke the other side, and prevent genuine bilateral limitations from being negotiated.

Second, the importance of the action-reaction process suggests strongly that the process of bilateral and multilateral arms limitation remains an important and fruitful avenue for controlling the arms race. Thus, rather than bewailing the limited scope of SALT II, those committed to arms control and disarmament would do well to throw their weight behind the treaty, the sooner to begin negotiations for a more comprehensive treaty. And, certainly, the argument that the arms race can only be held in check by unilateral aquisitions seeking to "balance" future gains on the other side seems to be convincingly refuted. Such a policy can only result in still greater arms growth, rendering the assertion upon which it was based a self-denying prophesy.

Furthermore, the findings seem to show clearly that the process of arms control cannot be kept entirely separate from the general climate of relations in the international system. If the superpowers engage in continual confrontations and crises with one another, it cannot but help stimulate the arms race and retard the process of arms control. Thus, the argument that each side can engage in whatever sort of behavior it wishes while continuing arms control talks. Unless some restraint is shown—at least to the extent of avoiding open military confrontations—it is difficult to see how the arms race can be held in check.

Finally, the findings demonstrate clearly that the military threat posed by China impinge quite differently on the two superpowers, a factor which must be considered in assessing their military budgets. In particular, it is important that those in the West realize that the Western alliance is only *one* of the military challenges to the Soviet Union, and that many Soviet weapons aquisitions decisions are taken with China rather than NATO or the United States in mind. If more Western analysts kept this in mind, perhaps the Soviet spectre would appear less awesome.

NOTES

1. The number of arms race studies has now proliferated to the point where they cannot be cited in toto. Excellent bibliographies of this literature are to be found in Bush (1970); Gillespie et al. (1977); and Ostrom (1978).

2. Apparently, Bruce Bueno de Mesquita and I came across this idea simultaneously.

3. Nincic and Cusack (1978) introduced exogenous variables into their equations, and used first differences; it does not appear, however, that this was done to avoid the above-mentioned problem.

4. Ostrom (1978) uses current dollars, on the grounds that spending decisions are made in actual currency and not in constant dollars. Nevertheless, unless the effect of inflation is removed, an additional source of autocorrelation is introduced into the data series, one which in fact will virtually negate the advantages of first differencing.

5. Nincic and Cusack (1978) use a complex measure of slack economic capacity, but it was felt that the index used here should reflect the *political* pressures of economic recession. The unemployment rate, more than any other index, both reflects and constitutes these pressures.

6. Complete citations are to be found in Gochman and Kselman.

REFERENCES

BUSCH, P. C. (1970) "Mathematical models of arms races", in B. M. Russett (ed.) What Price Vigilance? New Haven, CT: Yale Univ. Press.

DAVIS, O. A., M.A.H. DEMPSTER, and A. WILDAVSKY (1966) "Towards a predictive theory of government expenditures." British Journal of Political Science 4: 419-452.

GILLESPIE, J. V., D. A. ZINNES, G. S. TAHIM, P. A. SCHRODT, and M. RUBISON. (1977) "An optional control theory of arms races." American Political Science Review 71, 1 (March): 226-251.

GILLESPIE, J. V. and D. A. ZINNES (1976) Models of Mathematical Systems. New York: Praeger.

GRAY, C. (1972) "The arms race phenomenon." World Politics 24: 39-79.

JOHNSTON, J. (1972) Econometric Methods. New York: McGraw-Hill.

KANTER, A. (1973) "Congress and the defense budget, 1960-1970." American Political Science Review 66: 129-143.

KMENTA (1971) Elements of Econometrics. New York: Macmillan.

KSELMAN, T. and W. RUBIN (1978) "Military expenditures and currency conversion rates." Unpublished memo, Mental Health Research Institute, Ann Arbor, Michigan.

LUTERBACHER, U. (1978) "Towards a convergence of behavioural and strategic conceptions of the arms race." Unpublished paper.

——— and J. C. LAMBELET (forthcoming) "Dynamics of arms races: mutual stimulation vs. self-stimulation." Jerusalem Journal of International Relations.

MALINVAUD, E. (1966) Statistical Methods of Econometrics. New York: Rand McNally.

NINCIC, M. and T. CUSACK (1978) "The political economy of US military spending." Presented to the Midwestern regional meetings of the Peace Science Society (International), Ann Arbor, Michigan.

OSTROM, C. W., Jr. (1978) "A reactive linkage model of the U.S. defense expenditure policymaking process." American Political Science Review 72, 3 (September): 941-973.

——— (1977) "Evaluating alternative decision-making models: an empirical test between an arms race model and an organizational politics model." Journal of Conflict Resolution 21, 2 (June): 235-266.

RICHARDSON, L. S. (1960) Arms and Insecurity. Chicago: Quadrangle.

SINGER, J. D. (1958) "Threat-perception and the armament-tension dilemma." Journal of Conflict Resolution 2, 1 (March): 90-105.

WALLACE, M. D. (1979) "Arms races and crisis escalation." Journal of Conflict Resolution 23, 1 (March): 3-16.

——— (1976) "Arms races and the balance of power: a preliminary model." Applied Mathematical Modelling 1, 2 (September): 83-92.

——— and J. M. WILSON (1978) "Non-linear arms race models." Journal of Peace Research 15, 2: 175-192.

WHITE, K. J. (1978) "A general computer program for econometric methods—SHAZAM." Econometrika.

ZELLNER, A. (1972) "An efficient method of estimating seemingly unrelated regressions and tests for aggregation bias." Journal of the American Statistical Association 57: 348-368.

ZINNES, D. A. (1976) Contemporary Research in International Relations. New York: Praeger.

Chapter 9

SENSITIVITY ANALYSIS OF AN ARMAMENTS RACE MODEL

JOHN V. GILLESPIE
DINA A. ZINNES
Indiana University

PHILIP A. SCHRODT
Northwestern University

G. S. TAHIM
General Electric Space Center

INTRODUCTION

Of critical importance in maintaining international order and reducing added risks in the further evolution of sophisticated nuclear weapons systems are the perceptions which national foreign policy decision-makers hold toward their adversaries. Slight changes in perceptions as well as slight

EDITORS' NOTE: This chapter was originally submitted for review and accepted for publication in 1975. Changes in the editorial format of the *Yearbook* made it impossible to publish this important study before this volume. The editors deeply appreciate the patience and understanding of the authors. The version published here was received July 25, 1979. The authors report that the data sets used in this study are available from the ICPSR, Ann Arbor or from them at the Center for Inter-

alterations in the domestic assessments of needs for national security can have dramatic long-term effects on the continuing armaments races between adversaries. Although general strategies pursued by nations may seem to be consistent and stable over fairly lengthy time spans, the specific weightings associated with the perceptual factors that determine the general strategies may be altered to a degree, such that the effects, although subtle at the time, constitute long-term impacts on such outcomes as defense expenditures, procurement, and more rapid research and development into more highly destructive weapons systems.

Studying rigorously the impact of perceptual changes and changes in assessments of domestic needs on armaments races necessitates several requirements. First, a model which incorporates reasonable foreign policy objectives of nations needs to be provided. Second, estimates of the parameters in the formulated model need to be obtained. Third, an instrument for assessing perturbations or slight fluctuations in the estimated parameter values must be employed. Fourth, the impact of the perturbations on armaments behavior must be measured. Although these steps may seem laborious, to assess adequately the temporal impacts of perceptual changes requires rigorous methods. Let us begin with a reasonable model incorporating the foreign policy objectives of nations.

AN OPTIMAL CONTROL MODEL

Lewis Frye Richardson's (1960) simple differential linear equations model of armaments races has served as the basis for considerable research.[1]

$$\dot{x} = \ell y(t) - bx(t) + h \qquad [1a]$$

$$\dot{y} = kx(t) - ay(t) + g \qquad [1b]$$

In Richardson's formulation x and y are the armaments (generally measured in terms of defense expenditures) of two antagonistic nation's X and Y; $\dot{x}$ (read dx/dt) and $\dot{y}$ (read dy/dt) are the rates of change through time

---

national Policy Studies, 825 East Eight Street, Indiana University, Bloomington, Indiana 47401.

AUTHORS' NOTE: Support for this research was granted by the National Science Foundation, Research Grant GS-36806. The Center for International Policy Studies at Indiana University is supported by Grant 750-0514 from the Ford Foundation. The authors would like to express their appreciation for numerous helpful comments and suggestions to Jose B. Cruz, Jr., Dagobert L. Brito, Michael Intriligator, Irwin Sandberg, Esther Thorson, and Stuart Thorson. A previous draft of this chapter was presented at the 1974 Meetings of the Midwest Peace Science Society.

of the armaments of the two nations; and k, ℓ, a, b, g, and h are constants. Richardson reasoned that arms races could be explained by three factors: (1) threat from one's opponent (the terms ℓy(t) and kx(t)); (2) economic burden and fatigue (the terms -bx(t) and -ay(t)); and (3) grievance held against one's opponent (the terms g and h).

Richardson's model, although frequently used, has also been criticized for its failure to incorporate the goals and objectives of nations locked into an armaments race (Alker, 1968; Rapoport, 1957 and 1960). In essence,, Richardson's equations model the armaments behavior of nations involved in an arms race rather than modeling the goals of nations. If Richardson's model is to be adopted as an appropriate description of the empirical world, nations would follow the model irrespective of their goals and objectives. A nation may perceive its adversary to pursue a defense policy as modeled by Richardson; however, in selecting a strategy to "best" or "optimally" meet its adversary's defense policy behavior, the nation would derive its policy from its objectives as constrained by the defense policy of its adversary. In Richardson's terminology, the policy of nation X, if it perceives of nation Y as modeled by Richardson, may not be equation (1a), but instead some other mathematical expression derived from nation X's goals (Brito, 1972).

Let us suppose we have two nations, U and X (the notation "U" has been purposively selected so as to distinguish our approach from that of Richardson). Nation X, it will be assumed, follows the basic Richardson equation (1a). Nation U will be assigned an objective function, i.e., a set of goals with respect to its objectives concerning armaments. We will further assume that nation U operates as a "team" once its objectives are formulated, i.e., nation U has one utility function the values for which are not differentiated among its decision-makers.

One plausible assumption about the national objectives of nations is that derived from the balance-of-power literature, namely, that nations pursuing a defense policy based upon the balance of power not only desire to have sufficient arms to assure their national security, but also are concerned, at least to some degree, about the proliferation of armaments (Zinnes, 1967; Claude, 1962; Zinnes et al., 1978 a, b). There are two components to such an objective. The first component argues that a nation arms to a specified level of its adversary's armaments so as to assure national security. Let us call this goal J_1.

$$J_1 = \int_{t_o}^{T} [(u(t) - ax(t))^2] \, dt, \qquad [2]$$

where t_o is the initial time, T is the terminal time, u(t) is nation U's arms through time, x(t) is nation X's arms through time, and "a" is the proportion of nation Xs arms which nation U assesses as its need for national security. If the expression J_1 is minimized through the time horizon $[t_o; T]$ then nation U will satisfy its goal maintaining the desired "armaments balance" with nation X.

A second component of national objectives, according to balance-of-power theory is the desire to ward off unnecessary proliferation in armaments. If nation U increases its armaments, nation X is expected to increase its armaments because of the increased threat imposed by nation U's increment (1a). Likewise, if nation X increases its armaments, then nation U, to satisfy its concern for national security, would augment its arms (2). Hence, not only is it important for nation U to satisfy its goal with respect to an arms balance with nation X, but also to satisfy its goal of minimizing the total arms owned by both antagonistic nations. Let us denote this "arms minimization" goal by J_2:

$$J_2 = \int_{t_o}^{T} [c(u(t) + x(t))] \, dt, \qquad [3]$$

where "c" is the significance which nation U assigns to the arms minimization goal. If expression (3) is minimized through the time horizon $[t_o; T]$, then nation U will satisfy its goal by maintaining the desired "arms minimization" objective with nation X.

Expressions (2) and (3) can be combined into the single objective function:

$$J = \int_{t_o}^{T} [(u(t) - ax(t))^2 + c(u(t) + x(t))] \, dt \qquad [4]$$

Accordingly, nation U's task is to select an optimal armaments policy, call this policy $u^*(t)$, such that its objective (4) is satisfied (minimized). The two component parts of equation (4) are not mutually compatible. A policy which satisfies one part may not satisfy the other. Given this incompatibility, nation U needs to select a strategy which best compromises among the two components of its objective.

Since nation U, however, is in an arms race with nation X, nation U must also take into account the behavior of nation X. The behavior of nation X, we will assume, is, as modeled by Richardson (1a), which represents how nation U *perceives* its adversary, nation X, to behave. Equation (4) represents the objective of nation U with respect to nation X.

Given equations (1a) and (4), there are two kinds of parameters of interest: (a) parameters involving assessment of domestic objectives in foreign policy (we will call these "assessment parameters"), and (b) parameters involving perceptions of one's adversary (we will call these "perceptual parameters"). Table 9.1 summarizes the parameters and their meanings. No restrictions have been placed on the specific parameter values (Zinnes and Gillespie, 1976). These values of the assessment and perceptual parameters are obviously the product of nation U's defense policy decision-makers. Of interest here are the consequences of changes or perturbations in the values of these parameters on the optimal defense policy of nation U, and the consequences for the anticipated response of nation X. By answering the question posed we will not only be able to state which perceptions or assessment when altered have the greatest effect on nation U's defense policy and nation X's anticipated response, but also chart the course of this effect through time.

Using equations (4) and (1a), the optimal defense policy for nation U can be derived. Since the derivation has been presented elsewhere (Gillespie et al., 1977), there is no need to repeat it here. Equation (5) provides the results:

$$u^*(t) = ax(t) - [\xi/2] \cdot [(ca + c) / (\ell a - b)] \cdot [1 - e^{(b-\ell a)(t-T)}] \qquad [5]$$

TABLE 9.1 Parameters in the Optimal Control Model

Parameters	Interpretation
	Assessment Parameters
a	Nation U's arms balance proportion with nation X to assure U's national security
c	Nation U's significance attached to arms proliferation between itself and nation X.
	Perceptual Parameters
ℓ	Nation U's perception of its threat imposed on nation X by nation U's armaments
b	Nation U's perception of nation X's economic fatigue and expense from nation X's armaments
h	Nation U's perception of nation X's grievance toward nation U.

Equation (5) yields the optimal defense policy for nation U. Given that nation U pursues policy u*(t), we also desire to know the anticipated response of nation X. Substituting u*(t) into equation (1a) and solving for x(t), we obtain:

$$x^*(t) = [(\ell c - 2h)/(2(\ell a - b)) - (\ell^2 c)(a+1)/(2(\ell a - b)^2)] + [x(t_o) + ((\ell^2 c)(a+1))/(2(\ell a - b)^2 + (2h - \ell c)/(2(\ell a - b))] \cdot [e^{(\ell a - b)t}] - [(\ell^2 c)(a+1)/(4(\ell a - b)^2)] \cdot [e^{(\ell a - b)(T+t)}] + [(\ell^2 c)(a+1)/(4(\ell a - b)^2)] \cdot [e^{(\ell a - b)(T+t)}] + [(\ell^2 c)(a+1)/(4(\ell a - b)^2)] \cdot [e^{(\ell a - b)(T-t)}], \quad [6]$$

where x*(t) is the anticipated response of nation X given nation U's optimal policy u*(t). Whereas equation (5) presents the policy of nation U through time, equation (6) provides the policy nation U expects nation X to take given nation U's policy selection. Given estimates of the perceptual and assessment parameters, we can attempt to measure the consequences of perturbations in these parameters on u*(t) and x*(t).

ESTIMATING THE PARAMETERS

We are interested in estimating the parameters in equations (5) and (6) for a set of nations involved in armaments races over a fairly lengthy time horizon. We have chosen three nations and three alliances or groups of nations for the purpose of this analysis. The three nations are the United States, the Soviet Union, and Israel and the three alliances or groups of nations are the Arab states (Egypt, Syria, and Jordan), the North Atlantic Treaty Organization, and the Warsaw Treaty Organization. For each of these three sets of nations we will assume that the alliance or set of nations operates as a "team" in pursuing its foreign policy objective. Each nation or group of nations will be analyzed as nation U with its adversary nation or group of nations as nation X.[2]

Following the standard operationalization of arms races models, we have defined the variables u(t) and x(t) to be defense expenditures. The data collected on the defense expenditures of the six nations or groups of nations for the post-World War II era (1948-1975) have several important characteristics. First, the data all have been converted into American dollars. Second, the domestic inflationary monetary effects have been removed from the data. As a result the defense expenditures are in terms of noninflationary dollars across the time period. Third because the Soviet Union experienced a major accounting change in 1960, the data for the Soviet Union were adjusted to compensate for the accounting alteration. These procedures are summarized elsewhere in greater detail (Gillespie et al., 1977).

Given these data it is possible to estimate the parameters in equation (5). Setting T, the terminal time equal to the number of years in the data series, the values of the parameters in equation (5) can be estimated for each country or group of countries. The procedure, using functional minimization with pseudo-parameters for estimating these parameters, is complex and is detailed in Gillespie et al. (1977); Schrodt et al. (1978) and Gillespie et al. (1979). Table 9.2 presents the results from the analyses for each of the six cases.

Much can be said about the particular parameter values displayed in Table 9.2 (see Gillespie et al., 1977, for a full discussion of these results). However, our interest here is not in these particular sets of values, but in the consequences for defense policy when they are perturbed. It should be noted, nonetheless, that our model seems to hold exceptionally well for three of the six cases (WTO, Israel, and the Arab states). In these cases, even when adjusting for autocorrelation effects, we are able to estimate 88% of the variance or better. For NATO the fit of the data to our model is less successful (58% variance explained), and for the United States and the Soviet Union the model does not perform admirably.

Knowing the parameter values for a, c, ℓ and b in equation (5), we now know all the parameters in equation (6) save for h. The parameter h in

TABLE 9.2 Values of Parameters in Equation (5) Based on Generalized Least Squares Analysis

Parameter	Cases					
	USA	USSR	NATO	WTO	Israel	Arabs
a	.94	.18	1.21	.16	.15	.83
c	−383.83	−323.18	−189.58	−134.16	−3270.77	−902.62
ℓ	0.00	0.00	.15	−.18	−.22	0.00
b	−1.07	−.25	.80	.30	.22	−.13
GLS[a]R^2	.32	.42	.58	.88	.99	.97
No. of Transformations[b]	2	1	3	0	0	1
h	1.67	.68	2.39	.97	6.22	5.80

a. GLS refers to generalized least squares.
b. The number of transformation is the number of times the control for autocorrelation needs to be exercised so that it can be reduced to the criterion level. It can also be interpreted as the order of the autocorrelation.

equation (1a) and Table 9.1 refers to nation U's perception of nation X's grievance toward nation U. A reasonable estimate of h is the mean change in defense expenditures of nation X to determine the value of the grievance parameter. This estimate is especially meaningful with respect to equation (1a). If equation (1a) is viewed in terms of a linear regression model, the parameter h will be the intercept. The intercept in a regression model is the point at which the path of means intersects the Y-axis. Assuming that all the assumptions of the linear regression model are satisfied—this assumption is made any time regression analyses are performed—the value of h for a time series analysis on our problem would be the mean change in the expenditures of nation X. The values for h, computed in billions of American dollars, are recorded in Table 9.2.

Given these parameter values we now know the value of the perceptions and assessments for each of the six cases. Our objective is to analyze the consequence when these perceptions and assessments are perturbed. In so doing a rigorous method must be developed for analyzing the effects of these perturbations.

SENSITIVITY COEFFICIENTS

In asking questions about the consequences of perturbation in perceptions of adversaries and assessments of domestic foreign policy objectives, we want to know how sensitive defense policies are to perceptual and assessment changes. Perceptual and assessment changes are important in understanding defense policies because they may be the basis for an arms race moving toward more rapid escalation, the beginnings of arms reduction agreements, or be the basis for increased hostility and threat between nations. Perceptual and assessment changes can take place under many circumstances. Most obviously they can occur when the foreign policy decision-makers of one or both nations locked in an armaments race are replaced by other decision-makers. Perturbations in perceptions and assessments may take place as a result of exogenous forces such as conflict elsewhere in the world, international "power plays" such as embargoes or blockades, shifts of domestic public opinion, etc. Indeed, foreign policy decision-makers commonly reevaluate situations and although not altering the structure of their objectives or their perceptions of their adversaries' defense behavior, change their minds about the specific weights associated with factors involved in domestic foreign policy assessments and perceptions of an adversary's behavior. Most importantly, if citizens are to have some perspective on the consequences of electing one of a set of contesting candidates for a public office exercising influence over defense policy, it is important that some analyses be performed to understand how changing the office holder, and hence perhaps changing the perception of an adversary's behavior and domestic foreign policy assessment, affects defense policy. Sensitivity analysis offers a rigorous method for measuring the consequences of these important perceptual and assessment changes.

To perform a sensitivity analysis, a set of sensitivity coefficients need to be derived from the model (Perkins and Cruz, 1969; Ogata, 1970; Tomovic, 1963; Tomovic and Vukobratovic, 1972; Cruz, 1973). The sensitivity coefficients can be obtained by analyzing an expression of the partial derivative of the variable trajectory with respect to a parameter in a perturbed state. The logic of the use of the partial derivative is straightforward. Simply put, the partial derivative provides an expression of the amount or degree of the variable trajectory that is "explained" by the parameter. Even though the parameters, strictly speaking, are assumed to be constant for the time horizon of the model, slight perturbations are introduced treating the parameters as "almost perfect constants." These perturbations are of the small unit value ϵ and can be thought of as very slight forces affecting the parameter values. For larger forces affecting the parameter values, multiples of ϵ can be taken.

As noted in Table 9.1, our model contains two assessment parameters (a and c) and three perceptual parameters (ℓ b, and h). Our model also contains two variables: $u^*(t)$, the optimal defense policy of nation U and $x^*(t)$, the anticipated response of nation X given nation U's optimal defense policy. We desire to know the impact of perturbations in all five parameters on both $u^*(t)$ and $x^*(t)$. Although in the original statement of our model (equations (1a) and (4)) only the parameter a and c affect u(t) and only the parameters ℓ, b, and h affect x(t), since our model incorporates interactions between the parties in the armaments race through feedback, changes in any one of the parameters, or in some combination, can affect both nation U's defense policy and nation X's anticipated behavioral response. Given five parameters and two variable trajectories, there are ten sensitivity coefficients to derive. For the sake of brevity, we will not present the derivations here.

In general, each sensitivity coefficient will be a function of other parameters and time. From equation (5) we can derive sensitivity coefficients with respect to the optimal defense policy, $u^*(t)$. The derivations involve considerable manipulation and the resulting expressions are complex. Table 9.3 records the sensitivity coefficients for the assessment parameters and Table 9.4 records then for the perceptual parameters.

TABLE 9.3 Sensitivity Coefficients for Assessments Parameters[a]

Parameter	Trajectory	Expression
a	u*	$x + a(\delta x^*/\delta a) + [k_3/(2k_1)] \cdot [e^{-k_1(T-t)}] + [k_2\ell^2 c)/(2k_1^2)] \cdot [e^{-k_1(T-t)}] \cdot [x\ell(T-t) - [k_3/(2k_1)] + [\ell^2 ck_2)/(2k_1^2)]$
a	x*	$[(-\ell^3 ck_2)/(k_1^3)] + [h\ell - \ell^2 c)/(k_1^2)] + [e^{-k_1 t}] \cdot [(\ell^2 c - h\ell)/(k_1^2) + (\ell^3 ck_2)/(k_1^3) + \ell t \cdot x_0 - (\ell^2 ck_2)/(2k_1^2) + (\ell c - 2h)/(2k_1)] + [e^{-k_1(T+t)}] \cdot [(\ell^2 c)/(4k_1^2)] \cdot [(a\ell + 2\ell + b)/(-k_1) - \ell k_2(T+t)] + [e^{-k_1(T-t)}] \cdot [(\ell^2 c)/4k_1^2)] \cdot [(a\ell + 2\ell + b)/k_1 + \ell k_2 (T\ell t)]$
c	u*	$a(\delta x^*/\delta c) + [(\ell k_2)/(2k_1)] \cdot [e^{-k_1(T-t)}] - [(\ell k_2)/(2k_1)] - 1/2$
c	x*	$[\ell/(-2k_1)] - [(k_2\ell^2)/(2k_1^2)] - [1-(\ell k_2)/(k_1)] \cdot [\ell/(-2k_1)] \cdot [e^{-k_1 t}] - [(\ell^2 k_2)/(4k_1^2)] \cdot [(e^{-k_1(T+t)}) + (e^{-k_1(T-t)})]$

a. Notations for time have been suppressed. Expressions of the partials of x* can be obtained from other entries. $k_1 \equiv b - \ell a$; $k_2 \equiv a+1$; $k_3 \equiv \ell c$.

SENSITIVITY ANALYSIS–OPTIMAL DEFENSE POLICY

In sensitivity analysis we are interested in the effects of perturbations in the assessment and perceptual parameters in the model on the optimal defense policy of a nation and the anticipated response from the nation's primary antagonist. There are three important attributes of the sensitivity values which allow for the assessment of the impact of parameters. First, the *magnitude* of the sensitivity values allows for comparison of the degree which unit changes of ϵ in the parameters have impact on the trajectories. Second, the *direction* of the sensitivity values allows for assessment of whether the impact of positive perturbations increases the value of $x^*(t)$ and $u^*(t)$ or decreases those values. Third, the *shape* of the sensitivity values taken through time provides an analysis of comparison across time of perturbations in the various parameters. Since the variables $u^*(t)$ and $x^*(t)$ have both been measured in identical units (billions of American dollars), we can not only compare across parameters, but also across time and across cases.

TABLE 9.4 Sensitivity Coefficients for Perceptual Parameters[a]

Parameter	Trajectory	Expression
ℓ	u^*	$a(\delta x^*/\delta \ell) + [(ck_2 e^{-k_1(T-t)})/(2k_1)] \cdot [1 + (\ell/k_1) + \ell x_0 a(T-t)] - [(ck_2)/(2k_1)] \cdot [1 + (\ell a)/(k_1)]$
ℓ	x^*	$[c/(-2k_1)] + [(2ah - 2k_3 - 3ak_3)/(2k_1^2)] + [\ell^2 cak_2)/(-k_1^3)] + [e^{-k_1 t}] \cdot [\ (2k_3 - 2ah - 3ak_3)/(2k_1^2)\ -\ (\ell^2 cak_2)/(-k_1^3)\ -\ c/(-2k_1)\ +\ at \cdot x_0 + (\ell^2 ck_2)/(2k_1^2) + (2h-k_3)/(-2k_1)\ ] + [e^{-k_1(T-t)} \cdot [(k_2 k_3)/(2k_1^2) \cdot [1 + (\ell/k_1) + (\ell a(T+t))/2] + [e^{-k_1(T-t)}] \cdot [(k_2 k_3)/(2k_1^2)] \cdot [1 + (\ell/k_1) + (\ell a(T-t))/2]$
b	u^*	$a(\delta x^*/\delta b) - [(k_2 k_3)/(2k_1)] \cdot [(-1/k_1) + e^{-k_1(T-t)} \cdot (1/k_1) + x(T-t)\ ]$
b	x^*	$[(1/k_1^2)] \cdot [\ (k_3 - 2h)/2\ +\ (k_2 \ell^2 c)/(-k_1)\ ] + [e^{-k_1 t}] \cdot [\ (\ell^2 k_2)/(-k_1^3) + (2h-k_3)/2k_1^2\ -\ t\ x_0 + (\ell^2 ck_2)/(2k_1) + (k_3-2h)/(2k_1)\ ] + [e^{-k_1(T+t)}] \cdot [(\ell^2 ck_2)/(2k_1^2)] \cdot [\ (T+t)/2\ -\ 1/-k_1\ ] + [e^{-k_1(T-t)}] \cdot [(\ell^2 ck_2)/(2k_1^2)] \cdot [\ 1/-k_1\ -\ (T-t)/2\ ]$
h	u^*	$a(\delta x^*/\delta h)$
h	x^*	$[1 - e^{-k_1 t}] \cdot [1/k_1]$

a. Notations for time have been suppressed. Expressions of the partials of x^* can be obtained from other entries. $k_1 \equiv b - \ell a$; $k_2 \equiv a+1$; $k_3 \equiv \ell c$.

Taking the assessment parameters first and measuring the effects of perturbations on the optimal policy, $u^*(t)$, for each of the six cases, Table 9.5 provides a display from which we can begin to arrive at several conclusions about the sensitivity of the parameters. Table 9.5 and all subsequent tables are presented in scientific notation. The reader is reminded that in scientific notation the values are to be read as the number of significant digits. Table 9.5 only reports the sensitivity values in scientific notation of the first and last time periods and the points at which a change in the scientific notation takes place. For a given entry the sensitivity value for all previous times is the same in terms of scientific notation unless otherwise noted. As a companion to Table 9.5, Figure 9.1 presents miniturized graphic displays of the shape of the sensitivity values

TABLE 9.5 Sensitivity Values for Assessment Parameter and the Optimal Defense Policy[a]

	Parameter a					Time		Parameter c			
USA	USSR	NATO	WTO	I[b]	A[c]		USA	USSR	NATO	WTO	I[b]	A[c]
+E+12	+E+04	+E+02	+E+02	+E+03	+E+04	1	−E+10	−E+02	−E+00	−E+00	−E−01	−E+01
+E+13				+E+02	+E+05	2	−E+09	−E+01				
						3						
+E+14						4	−E+10					
						5						
+E+15						6	−E+11					
				+E+01		7						
+E+16				−E+01		8	−E+12					
				−E+02		9						
					+E+06	10	−E+13					
+E+17						11						
						12						
+E+18						13	−E+14					
						14						
+E+19						15	−E+15					
				−E+03		16	−E+16				−E+00	
+E+20	+E+05					17	−E+17					
						18						
+E+21						19						
						20						
+E+22						21	−E+18	−E+02				
						22						
+E+23						23	−E+19					
+E+23	+E+05	+E+02	+E+02	−E+02	+E+06	24	−E+19	−E+02	−E+00	−E+00	−E+00	−E+01

a. All values are recorded in scientific notation. Only values for the initial and terminal time, and time points when there is a change from preceding values (in terms of scientific notation) are reported.
b. Israel.
c. Arab states.

through time. In Figure 9.1 the scales are not comparable. The sensitivity values for each sensitivity coefficient have been scaled using the minimum and maximum values for a given sensitivity coefficient. In cases where the sensitivity values for a given coefficient change sign in the time horizon, the location of the horizontal axis indicates the zero point. A horizontal axis appearing at the top of a given miniturized display indicates that the values are always negative. If the horizontal axis appears at the bottom of a given display, the values are always positive. If the horizontal axis appears at some point between the top and bottom, the axis appears at the zero scale value and the sensitivity values change sign through time. The vertical axis measures magnitude (not in scientific notation).

FIGURE 9.1 Graphic Displays of Sensitivity Values Through Time

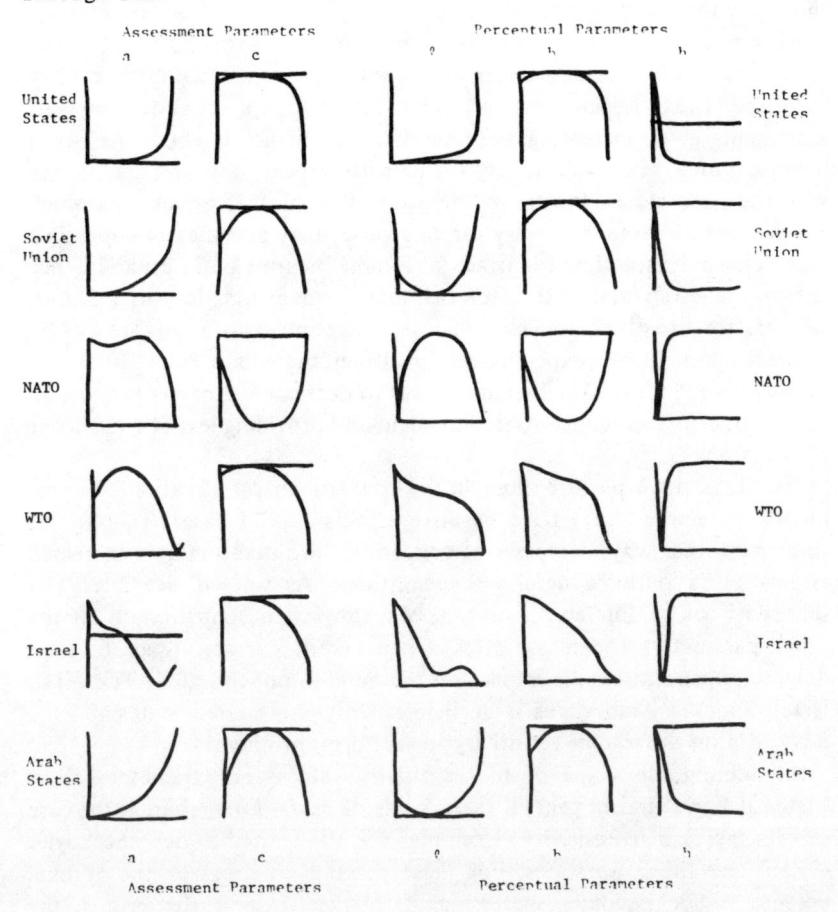

In examining Table 9.5 several conclusions can be reached. First, for all cases and for all moments in time the parameter "a" (the need for arms) is more sensitive than the parameter "c" (the concern for proliferation). This implies that positive (or negative) perturbations in a nation's assessment of its needed arms balance proportion with its adversary will have greater impact on its own defense optimal policy than will positive (or negative) perturbations in a nation's assessment of the significance of arms proliferation. Simply put, assessments of national security needs are more sensitive than are assessments of the need to restrain proliferation. Second, with one exception (Israel) slight increments in the assessment of needed arms balance proportions leads to increases in a nation's defense outlays, i.e., the sensitivity values of the optimal defense policy with respect to the parameter "a" are positive. The case of Israel is, interestingly, deviant. At time 8 in the horizon, perturbations of the parameter "a" for Israel begin to have negative consequences. In other words, as the proportion of Arab armaments which Israel assesses as necessary for Israeli national security increases, Israel begins—after a while—to "give up" and decreases its armaments given increasing assessment needs for armaments. The Israeli defense policy, as a result, is very fragile with respect to its armaments race with the Arab states. Increasing the proportion of Arab armaments which are deemed by Israel necessary for its own security becomes an impossible task. The only solution for Israel is to limit its arms build up and hence entice the Arab states to decrease their armaments. In other words, whereas for the other five cases, increased assessments of needs are met by increased armaments expenditure, for Israel there is a point at which increased need for national security leads to decreased armaments expenditure in an effort to reduce Arab armaments by providing less of a challenge to the Arabs.

Third, positive perturbations in the concern for proliferation of armaments (parameter "c") have negative effects for all cases. To put this finding another way, decreases of concern for proliferation have increased effects on a nation's defense expenditures. As we will see later, the sensitivity of parameter "c" is generally low when compared to all the other parameters for all six cases. When taken as a percentage of total defense expenditures, the impact on the defense policies of NATO, WTO, Israel, and the Arab states is negligible. Only the United States and the Soviet Union show some sensitivity toward arms proliferation.

Examining the shape of the sensitivity values for parameter "a" in Figure 9.1, we find in general three kinds of cases. First, there is the case of ever-increasing sensitivity. Examples are the United States, the Soviet Union, and the Arab states. For these cases, as time passes, the optimal defense policy becomes increasingly sensitive to perturbations in the assessment of the needed proportional arms balance. This is especially pronounced in the case of the United States. Somewhat interestingly, the Arab states show greater sensitivity toward national security needs than the Soviet Union. For all times perturbations in the parameter "a" have greater effects on the Arab defense policy than on the Soviet optimal policy. The second kind of shape of the sensitivity values for parameter "a" is the case of increasing then decreasing sensitivity. This case is typified by NATO and WTO. Actually, for NATO there is a slight decreasing sensitivity followed by an increase followed by a decrease. Also for WTO toward the end of the time horizon there is a slight increase of sensitivity. For WTO and NATO the sensitivity is greatest midway through the time horizon. The third kind of shape is Israel where there is a decreasing sensitivity to a negative impact with a slight increase, although still negative, toward the end of the time horizon.

For the parameter "c" there are essentially two kinds of shapes in Figure 9.1. Five cases exhibit increasingly negative impacts of increased concern for arms proliferation. For four of these five cases (USA, USSR, WTO, and the Arab states), at the beginning of the time horizon there is a decreasing negative impact of positive perturbations in the parameter "c" followed by rapid increasing negative impact. The case of NATO is deviant in that the NATO countries, taken as a group, exhibit increasing negative impact of perturbations in the concern for proliferation followed decreasing negative impact. For all of the cases save NATO, the concern for arms proliferation is its greatest toward the end of the time horizon. The second greatest impact for these five cases is the beginning of the time horizon. For NATO the greatest impact is midway through the time horizon.

Table 9.6 compares the six cases by magnitude and direction on the sensitivity of the assessment parameters. Even though the NATO and WTO countries have the largest defense expenditures, it is not the case that these alliances are the most sensitive to parameter fluctuations. The comparison in Table 9.6 is especially meaningful in that the units of measurement are comparable across the six cases. As Table 9.6 indicates there is a relationship between the two assessment parameters. Nations or groups of nations that exhibit the greatest positive sensitivity toward perturbations in their assessment of need are also those that exhibit the greatest negative sensitivity toward the assessment of proliferation. The generally low and consistent pattern of sensitivity shown by NATO and WTO implies that the defense policies of these two alliances are the least vulnerable. The United States, the Soviet Union, and the Arab states are the most vulnerable to slight changes in the assessment parameters. As noted earlier, the behavior of Israel is sensitive in a rather fragile way to the need assessment parameter.

TABLE 9.6 Rank Ordering of Cases for Sensitivity Values of All Parameters and the Optimal Defense Policy

		Rank of Cases					
		Least Negative Impact			*Greatest Negative Impact*		
		Greatest Positive Impact			*Least Positive Impact*		
Parameter	Time	1	2	3	4	5	6
a	1	USA	Arabs	USSR	Israel	NATO	WTO
	2	USA	Arabs	USSR	Israel	NATO	WTO
	3-5	USA	Arabs	USSR	NATO	Israel	WTO
	6-24	USA	Arabs	USSR	NATO	WTO	Israel
c	all time	Israel	WTO	NATO	Arabs	USSR	USA
ℓ	1-5	USA	USSR	Arabs	Israel	NATO	WTO
	6-13	USA	Arabs	USSR	Israel	NATO	WTO
	14-24	USA	USSR	Arabs	Israel	NATO	WTO
b	1-8	Israel	WTO	NATO	USSR	Arabs	USA
	9-11	Israel	WTO	NATO	Arabs	USSR	USA
	12-24	Israel	WTO	NATO	USSR	Arabs	USA

Perturbations in the perceptual parameters can also have effects on the optimal defense policy of a nation. The perceptual parameters are of three sorts: the parameter "ℓ" which refers to the perceived threat a nation's armaments present for the nation's opponent, the parameter "b" which is the perceived economic fatigue and expense from armaments for a nation's opponent, and the parameter "h" or the perceived grievance of a nation's adversary. Because the expression, $u^*(t)$ (equation (5)) contains both "ℓ" and "b," these perceptual parameters are a part of nation U's calculation. Also, since equation (5) contains $x(t)$ and $x(t)$ (equation (1a)) contains the parameter "h," there is an impact of the grievance perception parameter on nation U. Table 9.7 provides the sensitivity values in scientific notation for the six cases.

There are several important findings in Table 9.7. First, the threat perception parameter "ℓ" is always positive across the six cases. This implies that if there is a perception of increased threat imposed on the adversary (nation X), the impact is an increase in defense spending by nation U. In fact, when examining all three of the perceptual parameters, we find that the threat parameter has the greatest impact on the optimal defense policy of nation U. For the six cases the defense policy of the United States is the most sensitive to threat perception followed by the Soviet Union for time periods 1-5 and 14-24 and the Arab states for time

TABLE 9.7 Sensitivity Values for the Perceptual Parameters and the Optimal Defense Policy[a]

Parameter ℓ					Time	Parameter b					Time	Parameter h				
USA	USSR	NATO	WTO	I[b]	A[c]		USA	USSR	NATO	WTO	I[b]	A[c]		USA	USSR	NATO	WTO	I[b]	A[c]
+E+14	+E+06	+E+03	+E+03	+E+04	+E+06	1	−E+14	−E+05	−E+03	+E+03	+E+04	−E+05	1	+E−01	−E−00	+E+01	+E+00	+E+00	−E+01
						2	−E+13						2	−E+00					
						3							3						
+E+15						4	−E+14						4						
						5							5						
+E+16						6	−E+15						6						
	+E+05				+E+05	7							7						
						8	−E+16						8						
+E+17						9		−E+04					9						
						10	−E+17						10						
						11							11						
+E+18						12	−E+18	−E+05					12						
						13							13						
+E+19					+E+06	14	−E+19						14						
						15							15						
+E+20						16	−E+20			+E+02			16						
						17							17						
+E+21						18							18						
						19	−E+21						19						
+E+22						20					+E+03		20						
						21	−E+22	−E+06					21						
+E+23						22							22						
+E+24	+E+07					23	−E+23						23						
+E+24	+E+07	+E+03	+E+03	+E+04	+E+06	24	−E+23	−E+06	−E+02	+E+01	+E+02	−E+05	24	−E+00	−E+00	+E+01	+E+00	+E+00	−E+01

a. All values are recorded in scientific notation. Only values for the initial and terminal time, and time points where there is a change of value from preceding values (in terms of scientific notation) are reported.
b. Israel.
c. Arab states.

periods 6-13. The remaining three cases show the least vulnerability to perturbations in threat perception imposed on their adversaries. In order of magnitude they are: Israel, NATO, and WTO. As with the analysis of the assessment parameters above, NATO and WTO again show the least vulnerability to changing perceptions while the United States, the Soviet Union, and the Arab states continue to be the most vulnerable.

Figure 9.1 contains the miniturized graphic displays of the sensitivity values through time for the threat perception parameter for the six cases. Three patterns are evident: the generally increasing pattern (the United States, the Soviet Union, and the Arab states); the generally decreasing pattern (WTO and Israel); and the first increasing and then decreasing pattern (NATO). For the generally increasing pattern it is the case that as the time horizon passes, the response to increased threat perception is met with ever-increasing arms expenditure. Although in the cases of the Soviet Union and the Arab states at the beginning of the time horizon, positive perturbations in the threat perception parameter "ℓ" are met with decreasing degrees of armaments expenditure, after the passage of a few time periods, positive perturbations are met with rapidly increasing armaments expenditures.

Concerning the sensitivity values of the fatigue and economic burden parameter "b" (Table 9.7), four of the six cases respond to positive perturbations in their perception of their adversaries' fatigue and economic burden by decreases in arms expenditures. The optimal defense policies for the United States, the Soviet Union, NATO, and the Arab states are all affected negatively by positive perturbations in the adversaries' economic burden. For WTO and Israel, positive perturbations in their opponents' economic burden lead to increases in armaments and higher levels of expenditure. Although these sensitivity values are small when compared to the sensitivity of the "ℓ" parameter, it is nevertheless the case the increased values of the parameter "b" lead to increased values of $u^*(t)$. This result is meaningful, however, in light of the earlier findings concerning the need assessment parameter "a." For Israel, increased needs for national security were met in the later part of the time horizon by decrements in armaments (in constant dollars). Since we infer that Israel does not desire to impose additional threats on the Arab states by increasing its armaments, Israel does take advantage of its perception of the economic burden encountered by the Arabs. In other words, although Israel is "giving in" to the Arab states by not meeting its assessed needs for national security, it is at the same time "taking advantage" of the economic burden it perceives the Arabs are encountering.

The WTO countries also exhibit a deviant on the "b" perceptual parameter. As with Israel, the WTO nations take advantage of the NATO nations when it is perceived that there are positive perturbations in NATO's economic burden. Although the positive push on WTO's armaments policy is generally small in comparison to the perceived threat parameter, it is nevertheless somewhat counter to normal intuition. In the WTO case the effect is a compensation for two factors. The responses of WTO to assessed needs, although positive, is small and exhibits fluctuation across the time horizon. In other words, by avoiding large responses to assessed needs, the WTO nations are attempting to reduce increased threats to the NATO countries, and by avoiding large responses to increased perceived threat to NATO, the WTO nations are attempting to reduce increased need assessments. As a result, the point at which WTO feels free to increase its arms expenditures is when it perceives increments in economic burden in the NATO alliance. As we will see later, perturbations in the perceptual parameter "b" have a sizable effect on WTO expenditures throughout the vast proportion of the time horizon.

Figure 9.1 clearly demonstrates that both Israel and WTO exhibit positive patterns in the sensitivity values of the "b" parameter. As observed with the previous analyses of other parameters, the United States, the Soviet Union, and the Arab nations all have similar patterns. For these cases the impact of perturbations in "b" is always negative. The curves rise slightly at the beginning of the time horizon and fall dramatically to comparatively large negative values near the end of the time horizon. The display for NATO in Figure 9.1 is a near mirror image to the curves for the United States, the Soviet Union, and the Arab states. Although always negative in impact, the least negative impact is found at the beginning and conclusion of the time horizon. For NATO the sensitivities of the assessment parameters and the "ℓ" and "b" perceptual parameter all achieve their maximum absolute value midway through the time horizon. At the conclusion of the time horizon there is the least impact of perturbations on NATO's optimal defense policy. In other words, the policy pursued by the NATO alliance is highly insensitive to fluctuations, and there is solid evidence that the defense behavior of the NATO countries is resistant to change. The magnitudes of the sensitivity values further reinforce this finding. Whereas perturbations move the defense policies of the United States, the Soviet Union, and the Arab states into dramatic shifts, NATO exhibits a stability unfound in the other cases. For Israel there is a fragile "balancing" of factors, and for the WTO there is some stability but yet disturbances introduced by the effects of the "c" and "b" parameters.

The last of the perceptual parameters is the grievance parameter "h." As can be seen in Table 9.7, the sensitivity values of "h" with respect to the optimal policy trajectory exhibit little variability. For all six cases, after a brief change at the beginning of the time horizon, "h" achieves a near constant value for the remaining time periods (see Figure 9.1). In fact, the sensitivity values of the "h" parameter are so small that for most of the cases, the differences between positive and negative values have almost no impact on the optimal defense policy, i.e., the perceived grievance parameter is for most cases very insensitive. Only the Arab states and the NATO countries exhibit moderate sensitivity to the grievance parameter. As with the "c" parameter, in general, perturbations in perceived grievance have negligible impact.

The sensitivity values of the "h" parameter show there are three negative impact cases and three positive impact cases. The division of the two groups of cases is consistent with the previous findings. The cases showing negative impact are the United States, the Soviet Union, and the Arab nations. The cases exhibiting positive impact are NATO, WTO, and Israel. For the negative impact cases, perceived perturbations in the adversaries' grievance are met by slight decreases in armaments. The negative impact cases respond to momentary grievances of their opponents by decreasing their defense expenditures. Such a policy strategy is aimed at containing the grievance rather than permitting the perturbation to have a lasting effect on the arms race. Contrary to the United States, the Soviet Union, and the Arab states, the NATO, WTO, and Israel respond to increased grievance by increasing their armaments (see Figure 9.1 and Table 9.7). Perception of increased grievance is met in these cases by escalation rather than by containment of the grievance. However, since increased armaments because of increased perceived grievance may lead to increased perceived threat, there is a moderating influence in that for these three cases, increments in perceived threat, although responded to positively, are met with decreasing amounts of increments in expenditure.

Because the sensitivity values for the "h" parameter rapidly achieve a near constant value, the "h" parameter is less interesting than the other parameters. In the aggregate its impact is plus or minus a small constant. Because the sensitivities of the other parameters exhibit variability in their values through time, these parameters can have differential impacts. The "h" parameter in the main has little differential impact.

Table 9.6 ranks the cases according to sign and magnitude. As can be noted in the table, the cases cluster consistently into two groups. The first group is composed of the United States, the Soviet Union, and the Arab countries. For this group, the United States is always at the extremes, and hence exhibits the greatest sensitivity (positively or negatively) to parameter fluctuations. The second group is composed of NATO, WTO, and Israel.

Table 9.8 reports the ranking of the magnitude of sensitivity of the optimal defense policy with respect to perturbations in all five parameters.

For all cases, save the second part of the time horizon for the Arab states, perceived threat is the most significant parameter. Perturbations in the perception which a nation or alliance has of its threat to its opponent has the greatest effects on defense policy. With the exception of the Arab states, economic burden is the second most sensitive parameter for the bulk of the time horizon. The Arab states are more sensitive to their own assessment of needs than to their perception of Israeli economic burden. In fact, sensitivity to need assessment becomes most significant for the Arabs in the later part of the time horizon. For five of the cases, again the Arab states being the exception, assessment of needs is the third most significant parameter for the bulk of the time horizon. The perception of Israeli economic burden is the primary third-ranking component for the Arab states. For all cases the lowest sensitivity is exhibited toward perceived grievance and assessment of the importance of arms proliferation. It is important to note, however, that for the two superpowers, the sensitivity of arms proliferation is greater than that of perceived grievance. For the other six cases, there is little sensitivity to arms proliferation.

Table 9.8 allows us to take a different perspective when comparing the six cases. If we ignore the "h" and "c" parameters which have limited effects, five of the six cases are more responsive in their defense policies to changes in perceptions of their opponents than to their own assessment of needs. Such a defense policy is less related to domestic security and more related to "what the other fellow is doing." In this sense the defense policies are more a response to the defense calculation of the opponent

TABLE 9.8 Ranking of the Magnitude of Sensitivity Values of All Parameters on the Optimal Defense Policy

Case	Time	1	2	3	4	5
USA	all time	ℓ	b	a	c	h
USSR	all time	ℓ	b	a	c	h
NATO	all time	ℓ	b	a	h	c
WTO	1-22	ℓ	b	a	h	c
	22-24	ℓ	a	b	h	c
Israel	1-23	ℓ	b	a	h	c
	24	ℓ	a	b	h	c
Arabs	1-2	ℓ	b	a	h	c
	3-8	ℓ	a	b	h	c
	9-24	a	ℓ	b	h	c

than a response to domestic assessments of national needs. Only the Arab states show sensitivity to assessments of national needs. Whereas the optimal defense policies of the United States, the Soviet Union, NATO, WTO, and Israel are more "other-directed," the defense policies of the Arab states are more "inner-directed."

SENSITIVITY VALUES—ANTICIPATED RESPONSE POLICY

Not only is it important to understand how perturbations in the assessment and perceptual parameters affect the optimal defense policy of a nation or alliance, it is also important to understand the consequences of perturbations on the anticipated defense policy of a nation's adversary. The model we have formulated posits an objective function (equation (4)) for nation U subject to the model of the response calculation of nation X. Nation U is trying to satisfy its objective. However, U must take into account the anticipated behavior of nation X in formulating its policy to satisfy its objective. Nation U's goal is to find the "best" or optimal policy to satisfy its objective given nation X's response. In essence, nation U is attempting to find that policy which best satisfies its objectives by "controlling" the response of nation X. If nation U is to pursue its optimal policy and if there are slight changes in either nation U's assessment or perceptual parameters, it is important to understand the consequences of these perturbations on the response nation U anticipates from nation X.

Earlier we derived the expression for the response policy of nation X. Equation (6) provides the description of the $x^*(t)$ trajectory. We also presented the sensitivity coefficients for the assessment and perceptual parameters with respect to the $x^*(t)$ trajectory (Tables 9.3 and 9.4). Using these sensitivity coefficients and the parameter estimates in Table 9.2, we can calculate the sensitivity values for each moment in the time horizon.

Table 9.9 provides in scientific notation the adversary's anticipated response for each of the six cases given perturbations in the assessment parameters. The results tell us the effects on nation X's defense policy anticipated by nation U when nation U shifts its assessments of its needs and concern for arms proliferation in a positive direction.

The nation labels in Table 9.9 refer to nation U, the perceiving nation, not nation X, the nation being perceived. The numerical entries refer to the amount and direction of change that nation U anticipates in nation X's defense expenditure when nation U's assessment parameters are perturbed.

Several conclusions can be drawn from Table 9.9. First, the sensitivity values for the need assessment parameter "a" are positive for all six cases. All cases anticipate that their adversary will increase its armaments expenditure in light of increased need assessment. If nation U, where nation

TABLE 9.9 Sensitivity Values for Assessment Parameters and the Anticipated Response Policy[a]

	Parameter a					Time	Parameter c				
USA	USSR	NATO	WTO	I[b]	A[c]		USA	USSR	NATO	WTO	I[b]	A[c]
+E+11	+E+02	+E+02	+E+02	+E+03	+E+02	1	−E+08	−E+00	−E−01	−E+00	−E+00	−E−01
+E+12	+E+03					2	−E+09					−E+00
+E+13						3	−E+10					
+E+13						4						
+E+14					+E+03	5						
+E+14						6	−E+11	−E+01				
						7						
+E+15						8	−E+12					
						9						
+E+16	+E+04			+E+02		10	−E+13		−E+00			
						11						
						12						
						13						
+E+17						14	−E+14					
						15	−E+15	−E+02				
E+18						16	−E+16					
+E+19				+E+03		17	−E+17					−E+01
						18						
+E+20	+E+05				+E+04	19	−E+18					
						20						
+E+21						21						
						22	−E+19					
+E+22	+E+05	+E+02	+E+02	+E+03	+E+04	23	−E+19	−E+03	−E−01	−E−01	−E+00	−E+01
						24						

a. All values are recorded in scientific notation. Only values for the initial and terminal time, and time points when there is a change from preceding values (in terms of scientific notation) are reported.
b. Israel.
c. Arab states.

298   THREATS, WEAPONS, AND FOREIGN POLICY

U is any one of the six cases, increases its assessment of need, nation U anticipates an increased armaments expenditure from nation X. Second, the sensitivity values for the proliferation parameter "c" are all negative. All cases expect opponents to decrease their armaments effort in light of increased concern for arms proliferation. If nation U increases its concern for arms proliferation, nation U expects a decrease in armaments expenditure on the part of nation X. Third, for all cases the magnitude of the absolute sensitivity values is greater for the need assessment parameter than for the proliferation parameter. As a result, the impact of perturbations in need assessment is greater than the impact of perturbations in proliferation. Nation U can have a greater effect on nation X's defense expenditures by alterations in need assessment than by alterations in concern for arms proliferation.

FIGURE 9.2   Graphic Displays of Sensitivity Values Through Time: Anticipated Response Policy

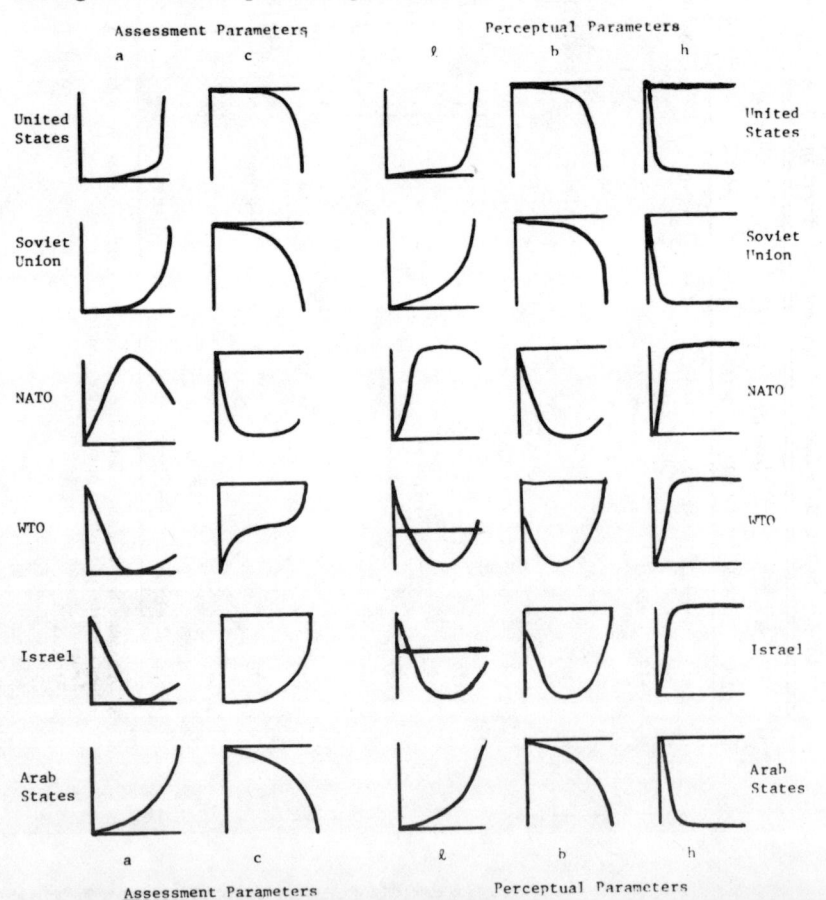

If we examine the miniturized graphic displays in Figure 9.2, the varying effects of perturbations in the assessment parameters across time can be analyzed. Whereas the United States, the Soviet Union, and the Arab states all perceive their opponents to react with ever increasing expenditures to positive perturbations in the need assessment parameter, Israel and the WTO countries anticipate declining sensitivity in the first part of the time horizon followed by increasing sensitivity in the later part of the time horizon. Whereas the United States, the Soviet Union, and the Arab states view their adversaries as "strict escalators" of armaments, the views of NATO, WTO, and Israel are far more subtle. NATO views the WTO nations as responding first by increasing escalation and later by decreasing escalation. The differences in views of the various cases as we shall see later, are closely linked to the anticipated consequences on the other parameters.

Figure 9.2 also displays the anticipated responses on the proliferation parameter. Again, the United States, the Soviet Union, and the Arab states all show the same pattern. For these three cases, as they increase their concern for arms proliferation, they expect their opponents to decrease their arms expenditure at ever-increasing rates. Israel and WTO expect their opponents to indeed decrease their expenditures but at decreasing rates throughout the time horizon. Increased concern for proliferation on the part of Israel and WTO is viewed as having less effect on the Arab states and NATO toward the end of the time horizon than at the beginning. For NATO the expectation is that the WTO nations will decrease their armaments in light of NATO's concern for arms proliferation, but that WTO's reaction will level off midway through the time horizon and in fact be less toward the conclusion of the total time period.

Comparing the six cases on the assessment parameters Table 9.9 clearly demonstrates that the United States expects its opponent to have the greatest shift in policy when the United States slightly alters its policy. At the initial part of the time horizon the Israelis expect the Arabs to show the second greatest impact, but shortly into the time horizon, the Soviet Union's expectations toward the United States become larger than those of Israel toward the Arabs. For the bulk of the time horizon the NATO and WTO alliances expect the least amount of change in their opponent's defense policy. Both NATO and WTO view each other as being comparatively insensitive to the policy shifts of each other. It would take very major shifts of policy for NATO and WTO to have impact on each other equal to the impacts of very minor shifts in the defense policies of the United States and the Soviet Union. The NATO and WTO alliances would have to greatly shift the weighting of their objectives to even come near the consequences of very small shifts of the weighting of goals for the

United States and the Soviet Union. Table 9.10 ranks the six cases on the assessment parameters. It summarizes, by comparison, the expectations of impacts on adversaries.

Alterations in perceptual parameters can also have impact on the anticipated responses of nation X. When nation U alters its perception of its threat to nation X or nation X's economic burden and fatigue or nation X's grievance, nation U desires to adjust its defense policy to the perceived changes in nation X's calculus. The sensitivity coefficients of the $x^*(t)$ trajectory (nation X's anticipated policy) when evaluated provide numerical assessments of the anticipated consequences for nation X's defense policy when there is a positive shift equal to ϵ in the value of nation X's parameters as perceived by nation U. These values are displayed, using scientific notation, in Table 9.11, where the labels in the table refer to nation U.

Table 9.11 demonstrates that four of the six cases (the United States, the Soviet Union, NATO, and the Arab states) anticipate that their adversaries always respond with increased arms expenditure when faced with increased threat. Both Israel and the WTO nations anticipate that

TABLE 9.10 Rank Ordering of Sensitivity Values of All Parameters and the Anticipated Response Policy

Parameter	Time	Least Negative Impact / Greatest Positive Impact 1	2	3	Greatest Negative Impact / Least Positive Impact 4	5	6
a	1	USA	Israel	USSR	WTO	Arabs	NATO
	2-4	USA	Israel	USSR	Arabs	WTO	NATO
	5-7	USA	USSR	Israel	Arabs	NATO	WTO
	8-23	USA	USSR	Arabs	Israel	NATO	WTO
	24	USA	USSR	Arabs	Israel	WTO	NATO
c	1	NATO	Arabs	USSR	WTO	Israel	USA
	2	NATO	Arabs	WTO	USSR	Israel	USA
	3-4	NATO	Arabs	WTO	Israel	USSR	USA
	5-16	NATO	WTO	Arabs	Israel	USSR	USA
	17-22	NATO	WTO	Israel	Arabs	USSR	USA
	23-24	WTO	NATO	Israel	Arabs	USSR	USA
ℓ	1	USA	USSR	Israel	Arabs	NATO	WTO
	2	USA	USSR	Arabs	Israel	NATO	WTO
	3-24	USA	USSR	Arabs	NATO	WTO	Israel
b	1	NATO	WTO	Arabs	Israel	USSR	USA
	2-3	WTO	NATO	Arabs	Israel	USSR	USA
	4-24	WTO	NATO	Israel	Arabs	USSR	USA

TABLE 9.11 Sensitivity Values for Perceptual Parameters and the Anticipated Response Policy[a]

Parameter ℓ

USA	USSR	NATO	WTO	I[b]	A[c]	Time
+E+13	+E+04	+E+03	+E+03	+E+04	+E+03	1
+E+14	+E+05	+E+02	+E+02	+E+03	+E+04	2
				-E+02		3
+E+15			-E+01	-E+03	+E+05	4
			-E+02			5
+E+16				E+04		6
						7
+E+17	+E+06					8
						9
						10
+E+18						11
						12
+E+19						13
						14
+E+20						15
+E+21	+E+07				+E+06	16
						17
+E+22						18
						19
+E+23						20
			-E+01			21
+E+24			+E+02	-E+03		22
+E+24	+E+07	+E+03	+E+02	-E+03	+E+06	24

Parameter b

USA	USSR	NATO	WTO	I[b]	A[c]	Time
-E+12	-E+03	-E+02	-E+02	-E+03	-E+03	1
-E+13	-E+04					2
				-E+04	-E+04	3
-E+14						4
						5
-E+15						6
	-E+05					7
-E+16						8
						9
-E+17						10
						11
-E+18						12
					-E+05	13
-E+19						14
	-E+06					15
-E+20						16
						17
						18
-E+21						19
						20
-E+22				-E+03		21
						22
-E+23	-E+07		-E+01			23
-E+23	-E+07	-E+02	+E+01	-E+03	-E+05	24

Parameter h

Time	USA	USSR	NATO	WTO	I[b]	A[c]
1	+E+01	-E+01	+E+01	+E+01	+E+01	-E+01
2	-E+00					
3						
4						
5						
6						
7						
8						
9						
10						
11						
12						
13						
14						
15						
16						
17						
18						
19						
20						
21						
22						
23						
24	-E+00	-E+01	+E+01	+E+01	+E+01	-E+01

a. All values are recorded in scientific notation. Only values for the initial and terminal time, and time points where there is a change of value from preceding values (in terms of scientific notation) are reported.
b. Israel.
c. Arab states.

their opponents will respond at times by decrements in armaments when threat increases. Whereas Israel perceives the Arab states to counter increased threat after the beginning of the time horizon by reductions in armaments, and the WTO group of nations perceive the NATO states to counter increased threat in the middle of the time horizon by decreases in armaments, the United States, the Soviet Union, and the Arab states all perceive their opponents to counter increased threat by escalation in armaments. The perceptions of Israel and WTO are in pursuit of a different strategy than the other four cases. By decreasing armaments expenditure an adversary is actually reducing or "controlling" for the total threat (total threat is the parameter "ℓ" multiplied by arms expenditure of nation U (equation (1a)). Given the values of the need assessment parameter, by reducing total arms expenditures, adversaries are encouraging reduced rates of arming. As we observed earlier (see Table 9.9) for both WTO and Israel, when the need assessment parameter is perturbed in a positive direction, the NATO countries and Arab states are not expected to respond by ever-increasing arms expenditures. As the time horizon passes, the anticipation is that there are decreasing rates of increase in armaments expenditure, except toward the conclusion of the time horizon when the rate of expenditures increases slightly. Hence as WTO and Israel view their arms races with NATO and the Arab states, there is a balancing between perceived threat and need assessment. In some senses both WTO and Israel anticipate that their opponents will "yield" under increased threat. However, this yielding is done in the context that Israel and WTO will not dramatically increase their armaments given the sensitivity of the need assessment parameter. Both Israel and WTO perceive their opponents as avoiding arms build-up in light of increased threat and hence controlling, at least to some degree, the outright confrontation or risk of confrontation in war. The sensitivity results for the parameter "ℓ" are especially meaningful when it is realized that the arms expenditures of NATO and the Arab states are considerably greater than those of WTO and Israel. Decreased arms expenditure for NATO or the Arab states, in the light of increased threat, is only a small proportion of total arms expenditure. Such decrements in order to avoid increased need assessment by the opponent do not alter the arms advantage which both NATO and the Arab states hold. The decrements only allow for the satisfaction of the opposition's objectives and are a small price to pay for reducing the risk of a run-away armaments race. Figure 9.2 presents the graphic displays of the sensitivity values for the perceptual parameter "ℓ" through time.

The sensitivity values for the parameter "b" are negative for all cases except for the final time period of WTO (see Table 9.11). All six cases perceive their opponents to reduce armaments expenditures in light of increased economic burden and fatigue. Examining the displays in Figure 9.2 it can be seen that the United States, the Soviet Union, and the Arab states all perceive the impact of increased economic burden on their adversaries to be an exponentially increasing function across time. The sensitivity to economic burden is especially pronounced in the United States' perception of the Soviets. As has been observed in the previous findings, Israel and WTO tend to exhibit the same pattern in Figure 9.2. For both cases the least sensitivity to economic burden anticipated in the defense policies of the opponents of WTO and Israel occurs at the conclusion of the time horizon. The greatest sensitivity is midway through the time period. NATO also exhibits a differing pattern in Figure 9.2. NATO anticipates that the WTO nations will respond with decreases in armaments expenditure when faced with increases in economic burden, but the anticipated response occurs at a declining rate until the end of the time horizon when the rate of change in response actually increases. Consistently throughout the time horizon both NATO and WTO perceive each other as comparatively insensitive to shifts in economic burden (see Table 9.11). As was observed with respect to the threat parameter "ℓ," it is also these same two cases which consistently expect each other to be the most insensitive to parameter fluctuations. Also it is consistently the case that both the United States and Soviet Union perceive each other as comparatively the most sensitive to parameter fluctuations of the threat and economic burden parameters. These findings are consistent with the earlier findings. Whereas the United States and Soviet Union are both highly sensitive responders to slight changes in perception and assessment *and* perceive each other to be highly sensitive to such fluctuations, NATO and WTO are comparatively highly insensitive responders to parameter fluctuations *and* perceive each other in this light. The optimal defense policies and anticipated defense policies of opponents for both the Arab states and Israel are generally less sensitive than those of the United States and the Soviet Union, but more sensitive than those of NATO and WTO.

Table 9.11 also records the sensitivity values for the grievance parameter "h." As noted in the earlier discussion of the $u^*(t)$ trajectory (optimal defense policy trajectory), the grievance parameter becomes a constant shortly into the time horizon. This finding is also revealed in Table 9.11 and Figure 9.2. All cases perceive fluctuations in grievance to have constant impact shortly into the time horizon. Three cases (the United States, the Soviet Union, and the Arab states) anticipate that their opponents will respond negatively to increases in grievances, while three cases (NATO, WTO, and Israel) anticipate increases in armaments when their opponents increase their grievance. The Soviet Union, the United States, and the Arab states all anticipate "restraint" by their opponents and a desire to keep the armaments race from further frustration. For NATO, WTO, and Israel the expectation is that increases in grievance will be met by increases in armaments. Figure 9.2 displays the curves for the sensitivity of the "h" parameter.

The sensitivity results for the "h" parameter are not especially interesting because the values quickly become a constant and are relatively small. Perturbations in grievance, as a result, have little changing impact on the optimal and changing defense policies.

Table 9.12 presents the ranking of the parameters in terms of absolute magnitude of impact on the anticipated defense policies of adversaries. The labels in Table 9.12 refer to nation U, the perceiving nation. For four of the six cases, threat perception is viewed as having the greatest impact on the adversary's defense policy (the United States, the Soviet Union, NATO, and the Arab states). For these same four cases need assessment and economic burden have less impact. For all cases grievance and concern for arms proliferation have the least impact. The cases of WTO and Israel deviate from the other four cases. For the bulk of the time horizon economic burden, when perturbed, has the greatest impact on the defense

TABLE 9.12 Ranking of the Magnitude of Sensitivity Values of All Parameters on the Anticipated Response Policy

Case	Time	1	2	3	4	5
USA	all time	ℓ	a	b	c	h
USSR	all time	ℓ	b	a	h	c
NATO	1	ℓ	b	a	h	c
	2-4	ℓ	b	a	c	h
	5-23	ℓ	b	a	h	c
	24	ℓ	b	a	c	h
WTO	1	ℓ	a	b	h	c
	2-3	ℓ	b	a	h	c
	4	b	a	ℓ	h	c
	5	b	a	h	ℓ	c
	6-21	b	ℓ	a	h	c
	22-23	a	b	ℓ	h	c
	24	ℓ	a	b	h	c
Israel	1	ℓ	b	a	h	c
	2-3	b	a	ℓ	h	c
	4-11	b	ℓ	a	h	c
	12-24	ℓ	b	a	h	c
Arabs	all time	ℓ	b	a	h	c

policy that WTO anticipates from NATO. For the first half of the time horizon Israel views the Arab states as being most responsive to fluctuations in economic burden, but in the last part of the time horizon threat perception becomes more significant. For all cases, except the United States, economic burden is generally viewed as having a greater impact on the opponent's defense policy than need assessment. Whereas the United States views the Soviet Union as more responsive to the American assessment of needs for national security than to Soviet economic defense burdens, the Soviet Union views the United States as more responsive to American economic burden than to Soviet assessments of its own need for armaments. It is also interesting to note that the Soviet Union views the United States as more responsive to grievances than to Soviet concern for arms proliferation, whereas the United States anticipates that the Soviet Union is more responsive to American concern for arms proliferation than to Soviet grievances.

In comparing NATO and WTO, several interesting conclusions arise. Whereas NATO views the WTO states as reacting to threat, economic burden, and NATO's assessment of needs in that order, the WTO states view NATO as having various different responses depending heavily on the particular moment in time. Certainly for the major portion of the time horizon WTO views NATO as reacting most strongly to changes in economic burden followed by threat and then WTO's need assessment. For the largest portion of the time horizon, for both alliances, the impact of changes in concern for arms proliferation is less important than the opponent's grievances.

The Israeli-Arab arms race also exhibits differing responses depending on the moment in time. The Israelis view the Arab states as most sensitive to economic burden during the first half of the time horizon and most responsive to threat in the second half of the time horizon. The Arabs view the Israelis as most responsive to threat for the entire time horizon. Economic burden is perceived by the Arabs to be of secondary importance in Israeli defense policy, whereas the Israelis view threat for the larger proportion of the first part of the time period to be second in importance to the Arabs and economic burden to be second in importance in the later half of the time horizon. Except for small time slices when the Israelis deviate from the Arab ranking, for both adversaries need assessment ranks third followed by grievance and concern for arms proliferation.

CONCLUSIONS

We have now analyzed several sensitivities of nations' or alliances' defense policy and the defense policy they expect from adversaries. Two primary questions remain.

The first question is whether a nation or alliance by parameter shifts encounters greater consequences for itself than for its opponent. In other words if nation U changes its parameter values, are the consequences greater for nation U or are they greater for nation X? Second, and perhaps the most intuitively interesting, our results have shown that the sensitivity of the USA-USSR arms race is considerably different than the sensitivity of the NATO-WTO arms race. The consistency of this finding deserves further comment. Let us explore each of these inquiries in order.

For each case we have analyzed two trajectories: the optimal defense policy trajectory ($u^*(t)$) and the anticipated defense response policy trajectory ($x^*(t)$). The sensitivity of the $u^*(t)$ trajectory measures the impact on nation U under pertrubations in the assessment and perceptual parameters. The sensitivity of the $x^*(t)$ trajectory measures the impact nation U expects in nation X's defense policy given perturbations in the assessment and perceptual parameters. We can ask if a given parameter perturbation from the view of nation U has greater impact on nation U's or nation X's policy. This is accomplished by comparing the results of the sensitivity analyses of the $u^*(t)$ and $x^*(t)$ trajectories with respect to absolute magnitude. Table 9.13 summarizes these results.

For four of the six cases there are parameter changes which can have greater impacts on the adversary than on the nation or group of nations itself. For example, from the viewpoint of the United States greater impact on Soviet defense policy can be attained by increasing concern for arms proliferation shortly after the beginning of the time horizon. Likewise for the Soviet Union, greater impact is achieved when there is a perceived increase in American economic burden. For the United States, the Soviet Union, Israel, and the Arab states, greater impacts on the adversaries by perturbation in some of the assessment and perceptional parameters are possible; the costs of policy changes can be imposed upon the adversary without enduring the same amount of cost. For these four cases there are policy options open for compelling the adversary into costly responses. As a result there is greater policy flexibility, but also as a consequence of this flexibility, there is greater instability. Action-reaction cycles can be initiated by slight perturbations in the assessment and perceptual parameters. Such cycles may lead to a level of instability which may force direct confrontations in armaments and may prove highly problematical for international security.

However for the cases of NATO and WTO such political flexibility is lacking. With the exception of a very brief period of the "a" parameter, for both NATO and WTO, the consequences of perturbations are always viewed as greater for the alliance itself than for the opposing alliance. Hence shifts in the assessment and perceptual parameters simply imply

TABLE 9.13 Absolute Magnitude of Impact on Defense Policies

Nation U	Parameter	Time	Greatest Impact
USA	a	all time	USA
	c	1-3	USA
		4-24	USSR
	ℓ	1-3	USA
		4-24	USSR
	b	all time	USA
	h	all time	USSR
USSR	a	all time	USSR
	c	1-7	USSR
		8-24	USA
	ℓ	1-6	USSR
		7-24	USA
	b	1-7	USSR
		8-24	USA
	h	all time	USSR
NATO	a	all time	NATO
	c	all time	NATO
	ℓ	all time	NATO
	b	all time	NATO
	h	all time	NATO
WTO	a	1-2	NATO
		3-24	WTO
	c	all time	WTO
	ℓ	all time	WTO
	b	all time	WTO
	h	all time	WTO
Israel	a	1-14	Arabs
		15-20	Israel
		21-24	Arabs
	c	1-22	Israel
		23-24	Arabs
	ℓ	all time	Israel
	b	1-11	Israel
		12-24	Arabs
	h	all time	Arabs
Arabs	a	all time	Arabs
	c	all time	Arabs
	ℓ	1-14	Arabs
		15-24	Israel
	b	1-13	Arabs
		14-24	Israel
	h	all time	Israel

greater "domestic" consequences. Our findings demonstrate that it is impossible to impose greater consequences on the opposition by a parameter change than those imposed upon the alliance itself. Such stability means that the alliances themselves are not particularly eager to initiate changes in policy objectives or perceptions because the costs of such changes are greater at home than they are abroad. There is no way either alliance can gain on the opposition. The USA-USSR and the Israeli-Arab armaments races do permit strategies to be employed for domestic advantage and punishment abroad. The NATO-WTO armaments race contains no such options.

Since the United States is a member of NATO and the Soviet Union is a member of WTO, it is interesting to note that whereas in the context of NATO and WTO there are constraints on the defense policies of the USA and USSR, outside of that context such constraints break down. Consistently throughout all the sensitivity analyses, we have shown that both the Soviet Union and the United States are far more sensitive to slight perturbations in parameter fluctuations than the NATO and WTO alliances. Several speculations can be offered for these findings. However, it does seem obvious that the other nations involved in the NATO and WTO alliances serve as a major modifying influence on the United States and Soviet Union. Even though the United States and Soviet Union are predominant in their respective alliances, the collective influence of the other "smaller" nations is such as to counter the American-Soviet penchant for sensitivity and instability.

The policy lesson is obvious. If radical changes in defense policies are to be avoided, it behooves both major powers to formulate policies in consort with their alliance partners rather than unilaterally. Especially in this age of massive capabilities for destruction by simple errors in judgment or even in mechanical engineering, the alliances become especially important to modify and control the American and Soviet penchant for hypersensitivity and instability.

Sensitivity analysis offers a perspective on armaments policy not commonly recognized in the arms race literature. Certainly, to correct what might be assessed as an undesirable situation, some sensitivity is required. An automobile's performance at less than maximum fuel efficiency can hopefully be rectified by a set of small adjustments. An explosive arms race might be contained by shifts in some parameters. However, sensitivity is a two-edged sword. The automobile in unskilled hands can be converted into the worst of "gas guzzlers." Arms races which are seemingly orderly and hence allow decision-makers to anticipate reactions from an adversary, if highly sensitive, may become disorderly when subject to slight changes in perception and assessment. The adversary perhaps somewhat unaware of or uncertain about the slight perturbations, views the alterations in the opposition's armaments behavior and might respond by new levels of arms expenditures. The US-Soviet arms race is of this sort, and it is on the precarious edge of extraordinary change given slight alterations of parameters. A new weapons system, new decision-makers with different perceptions than those presently in power, new surges of fear in public opinion, however slight, can alter the course, not only for the one of the participants, but for both adversaries.

As a form of policy analysis, sensitivity analysis allows us to answer the "what if" question. What if the next president of the United States takes a tougher stand on arms balancing with the Soviet Union? Our analysis clearly shows that U.S. and Soviet arms expenditures would rapidly escalate. What if the U.S. concern for arms proliferation increases? Our results clearly show that, much to the dismay of those concerned about arms proliferation, the impact would be slight. A slight positive increase in the need for armaments is only offset by a massive increase in the concern for proliferation. If our model is in any way an adequate reflection of the empirical world, then the optimal strategy for those seeking to contain seemingly ever increasing armaments is to reduce the perceived need for arms than to preach against proliferation.

Similar strategies for others can be deduced from our analysis. For the American defense industries, with defense policy decision-makers assessing greater need for arms, increased expenditures result. These increases cannot be easily offset by simultaneous perturbations in any parameters. Small changes in need, at least for the United States, require large changes in other assessments and perceptions to offset the expenditure increments.

Our analyses can be easily extended to consider combinations of sensitivities in parameters. We could combine perturbations in one parameter with perturbations in another asking how much change in one parameter is required to offset or match changes in another. Furthermore, we might examine various alternative policy postures (parameter values) to determine their effects on a nation's defense expenditures and those of its adversary.

As our analysis has shown, the sensitivity of need assessment and threat perception are dominant in almost all instances. Although this general finding may not surprise defense analysts, it does clearly point to a fundamental characteristic of arms races, namely, they are difficult to control, but easily frustrated.

NOTES

1. There are several surveys of the arms race literature available. See: Gillespie and Zinnes (1975), Luterbacher (1975).

2. Several other arms races could be selected. The analyses presented here have been run on thirty contemporary and historical arms races. However, to report the findings from all thirty races would yield excessive numbers of tables. We have chosen the six nations or groups of nations to be consistent with our previously reported research (Gillespie et al., 1977; Gillespie et al., 1979).

REFERENCES

ALKER, H. R., Jr. (1968) "The structure of social action in an arms race." Presented at the North American Peace Research Society (International), Cambridge, MA.
BRITO, D. L. (1972) "A dynamic model of an armaments race." International Economic Review 13: 359-375.
CLAUDE, I. L. Jr. (1962) Power and International Relations New York: Random House.
CRUZ, J. B., Jr. (1973) System Sensitivity Analysis Portland, OR: ISBS.
GILLESPIE, J. V. and D. A. ZINNES (1975) "Progressions in mathematical models of international conflict." Synthese 31: 289-321.
——, P. A. SCHRODT, G. S. TAHIM, and R. M. RUBISON (1977) "An optimal control model of arms races." American Political Science Review 71: 226-244.
GILLESPIE, J. V., D. A. ZINNES, G. S. TAHIM, M. W. SAMPSON III, P. A. SCHRODT, and R. M. RUBISON (1979) Deterrence and Arms Races: An Optimal Control Systems Model." Behavioral Science (forthcoming).
LUTERBACHER, U. (1975) "Arms race models: where do we stand?" European Journal of Political Research 3: 199-217.
OGATA, K. (1970) Modern Control Engineering. Englewood Cliffs, NJ: Prentice-Hall.
PERKINS, W. R. and J. B. CRUZ, Jr. (1969) Engineering of Dynamic Systems. New York: John Wiley.
RAPOPORT, A. A. (1975) "Lewis Frye Richardson's mathematical theory of war." Journal of Conflict Resolution 1: 249-299.
——— (1960) Fights, Games and Debates. Ann Arbor: Univ. of Michigan Press.
RICHARDSON, L. F. (1960) Arms and Insecurity. Pittsburgh: Boxwood.
SCHRODT, P. A., J. V. GILLESPIE, and D. A. ZINNES (1978) "Parameter estimation by numerical minimization methods." International Interactions 4: 279-301.
TOMOVIC, R. (1963) Sensitivity Analysis of Dynamic Systems. New York: McGraw-Hill.
——— and M. VUKOBRATOVIC (1972) General Sensitivity Theory. New York: American Elsevier.
ZINNES, D. A. (1967) "An analytical study of balance of power theories." Journal of Peace Research 4: 270-288.
———, J. V. GILLESPIE and R. M. RUBISON (1976) "A reinterpretation of the Richardson arms-race model," pp. 189-217 in D. A. Zinnes and J. V. Gillespie (eds.) Mathematical Models in International Relations. New York: Praeger.
ZINNES, D. A., J. V. GILLESPIE, and G. S. TAHIM (1978a) "Modeling a chimera: the balance of power revisited." Journal of Peace Science 3: 31-44.
——— (1978b) "A formal analysis of some issues in balance of power theories." International Studies Quarterly 22: 323-356.

PART IV

BIBLIOGRAPHY

Chapter 10

BIBLIOGRAPHY OF RECENT COMPARATIVE FOREIGN POLICY STUDIES, 1975-1979

CONSTANCE J. LYNCH
University of Southern California

This bibliography is the fifth in the series that has appeared in the *Yearbook* surveying the field of comparative foreign policy studies. While the preponderance of works listed in this year's edition have been published since 1976, there are some listed which have not been noted in the four previous bibliographies.

The criteria for inclusion in the bibliography cover several aspects. First, the work must be comparative in its approach to studying either: (1) two or more actors on the national or subnational levels; or (2) the international behavior of one national actor in two or more cases. Second, the work must systematically approach the description, explanation or prediction of foreign policy behavior as a dependent or independent variable. Third, the work must approach foreign policy behavior empirically through an attempt to operationalize that behavior. Qualitative as well as quantitative research fits this criterion, as the works listed include comparative case studies, time-series analyses, all manner of quantitative studies and other types of research designs.

The increased number of works cited in this year's bibliography, as compared with those of past years, suggests that comparative foreign policy analysis has continued in the trend of expansion of the field.

EDITORS' NOTE: This chapter was first received June 27, 1979. The version published here was received September 15, 1979.

Interesting to note is the burgeoning number of titles which discuss international interactions of a political-economic nature, particularly taking a dependency or Marxist approach. This trend may be seen as a reflection of changing directions in the field of international relations as a whole.

As the editors have expressed the intention to continue with the inclusion of the bibliography in future editions of the *Yearbook,* any corrections and addenda to this listing are most welcome, and should be forwarded to the editors.

ABOLFATHI, F., J. J. HAYES, and R. E. HAYES (1979) "Trends in United States response to international crises: policy implications for the 1980s," pp. 57-81 in C. W. Kegley, Jr. and P. J. McGowan (eds.) Challenges to America: United States Foreign Policy in the 1980s. Sage International Yearbook of Foreign Policy Studies, Vol. 4. Beverly Hills: Sage Publications.

AVERY, W. P. (1978) "Domestic influences on Latin American importation of U.S. armaments." International Studies Quarterly 22 (March): 121-142.

AXELROD, R. (1977) "Argumentation in foreign policy settings: Britain in 1918, Munich in 1938, and Japan in 1970." Journal of Conflict Resolution 21 (December): 727-744.

BLANNER, C. (1976) The Hovering Giant: U.S. Response to Revolutionary Change in Latin America. Pittsburgh: Univ. of Pittsburgh Press.

BRADY, L. P. (1978) "The situation and foreign policy," pp. 173-190 in M. A. East, S. A. Salmore, and C. F. Hermann (eds.) Why Nations Act: Theoretical Perspectives for Comparative Foreign Policy Studies. Beverly Hills: Sage Publications.

BRUCE, J. B. and R. W. CLAWSON (1977) "A zonal analysis model for comparative politics: a partial Soviet application." World Politics 29 (January): 177-215.

BUNCE, V. (1976) "Elite succession, petrification, and policy innovation in Communist systems: an empirical assessment." Comparative Political Studies 9 (April): 3-42.

BUSCH, P. and D. PUCHALA (1976) "Interests, influence and integration: political structure in the European communities." Comparative Political Studies 9 (July): 235-254.

BUTTERWORTH, R. L. (1978) "Do conflict managers matter? an empirical assessment of interstate security disputes and resolution efforts, 1945-1974." International Studies Quarterly 22 (June): 195-214.

CAPORASO, J. A. (1978) "Dependence, dependency, and power in the global system: a structural and behavioral analysis." International Organization 32 (Winter): 13-43.

––– and M. D. WARD (1979) "The United States in an interdependent world: the emergence of economic power," pp. 139-169 in C. W. Kegley, Jr. and P. J. McGowan (eds.) Challenges to America: United States Foreign Policy in the 1980s. Sage International Yearbook of Foreign Policy Studies, Vol. 4. Beverly Hills: Sage Publications.

CHASE-DUNN, C. (1978) "Core-periphery relations: the effects of core competition," pp. 156-176 in B. W. Kaplan (ed.) Social Change in the Capitalist World Economy. Political Economy of the World-System Annuals, Vol. 1. Beverly Hills: Sage Publications.

CLARK, C. and R. L. FARLOW (1976) Comparative Policy and Trade: The Communist Balkans in International Politics. Bloomington, IN: International Development Research Center, Studies in East European and Soviet Planning, Development and Trade No. 23.

CLAUDE, R. P. [ed.] (1976) Comparative Human Rights. Baltimore: Johns Hopkins Univ. Press.

COBB, R., J.-K. ROSS, and M. H. ROSS (1976) "Agenda building as a comparative political process." American Political Science Review 70: 126-138.

CZUDNOWSKI, M. M. (1976) Comparing Political Behavior. Beverly Hills: Sage Publications.

DORIAN, C. F. (1979) "Resource politics and U.S. foreign policy," pp. 117-138 in C. W. Kegley, Jr. and P. J. McGowan (eds.) Challenges to American: United States Foreign Policy in the 1980s. Sage International Yearbook of Foreign Policy Studies, Vol. 4. Beverly Hills: Sage Publications.

DRUCKMAN, D. (1976) "The person, role and situation in international negotiations," in M. G. Hermann (ed.) A Psychological Examination of Political Leaders. New York: Free Press.

DRIVER, M. J. (1976) "Individual differences in ideological content and conceptual structure as determinants of aggression in the Inter-Nation Simulation," in M. G. Hermann (ed.) A Psychological Examination of Political Leaders. New York: Free Press.

EAST, M. A. (1978) "National attributes and foreign policy," pp. 123-142 in M. A. East, S. A. Salmore, and C. F. Hermann (eds.) Why Nations Act: Theoretical Perspectives for Comparative Foreign Policy Studies. Beverly Hills: Sage Publications.

——— (1978) "The international system perspective and foreign policy," pp. 143-160 in M. A. East, S. A. Salmore, and C. F. Hermann (eds.) Why Nations Act: Theoretical Perspectives for Comparative Foreign Policy Studies. Beverly Hills: Sage Publications.

———, S. A. SALMORE and C. F. HERMANN [eds.] (1978) Why Nations Act: Theoretical Perspectives for Comparative Foreign Policy Studies. Beverly Hills: Sage Publications.

FALKOWSKI, L. [ed.] (1979) Psychological Models in International Politics. Boulder, CO: Westview.

FELD, W. J. (1979) "Global allies or competitors: U.S. policy toward an ascendant European community and Japan," pp. 171-200 in C. W. Kegley, Jr. and P. J. McGowan (eds.) Challenges to America: United States Foreign Policy in the 1980s. Sage International Yearbook of Foreign Policy Studies, Vol. 4. Beverly Hills: Sage Publications.

FERRIS, E. G. (1979) "National political support for regional integration: the Andean pact." International Organization 33 (Winter): 83-104.

FREY, B. S. and W. W. POMMEREHNE (1978) "Toward a more theoretical foundation for empirical policy analysis." Comparative Political Studies 11 (October): 311-336.

HARKANY, R. E. (1975) The Arms Trade and International Systems. Cambridge, MA: Ballinger.

HERMANN, C. F. (1979) "Why new foreign policy challenges might not be met: constraints on detecting problems and setting agendas," pp. 269-290 in C. W. Kegley, Jr. and P. J. McGowan (eds.) Challenges to America: United States Foreign Policy in the 1980s. Sage International Yearbook of Foreign Policy Studies, Vol. 4. Beverly Hills: Sage Publications.

——— (1978) "Decision structure and process influences on foreign policy," pp. 69-102 in M. A. East, S. A. Salmore, and C. F. Hermann (eds.) Why Nations Act: Theoretical Perspectives for Comparative Foreign Policy Studies. Beverly Hills: Sage Publications.

——— (1978) "Foreign policy behavior: that which is to be explained," pp. 25-48 in M. A. East, S. A. Salmore, and C. F. Hermann (eds.) Why Nations Act: Theoretical Perspectives for Comparative Foreign Policy Studies. Beverly Hills: Sage Publications.

HERMANN, M. G. (1978) "Effects of personal characteristics of political leaders on foreign policy," pp. 49-68 in M. A. East et al. (eds.) Why Nations Act: Theoretical Perspectives for Comparative Foreign Policy Studies. Beverly Hills: Sage Publications.

——— [ed.] (1977) A Psychological Examination of Political Leaders. New York: Free Press.

HOLLIST, W. L. (1977) "Alternative explanations of competitive arms processes: tests on four pairs of nations." American Journal of Political Science 21 (May): 313-340.

HOLSTI, O. R. (1976) "Foreign policy formation viewed cognitively," pp. 18-54 in R. Axelrod (ed.) Structure of Decision. Princeton, NJ: Princeton Univ. Press.

——— and J. R. ROSENAU (1979) "America's foreign policy agenda: the post-Vietnam beliefs of American leaders," pp. 231-268 in C. W. Kegley, Jr. and P. J. McGowan (eds.) Challenges to America: United States Foreign Policy in the 1980s. Sage International Yearbook of Foreign Policy Studies, Vol. 4. Beverly Hills: Sage Publications.

HOPMANN, P. T. (1978) "Asymmetrical bargaining in the conference on security and cooperation in Europe." International Organization 32 (Winter): 141-177.

——— and T. C. SMITH (1977) "An application of a Richardson process model: Soviet-American interactions in the test ban negotiations 1962-1963." Journal of Conflict Resolution 21 (December): 701-726.

HOPPLE, G. W. (1979) "Elite values and foreign policy analysis: preliminary findings," in L. S. Falkowski (ed.) Psychological Models in International Politics. Boulder, CO: Westview.

———, J. WILKENFELD, P. J. ROSSA, and R. N. McCAULEY (1977) "Societies and interstate determinants of foreign conflict." Jerusalem Journal of International Relations 2 (Summer): 30-66.

KATZENSTEIN, P. J. [ed.] (1978) Between Power and Plenty: Foreign Economic Policies of Advanced Industrial States. Madison: Univ. of Wisconsin Press.

——— (1978) "Domestic and international forces and strategies of foreign economic policy," pp. 3-32 in P. J. Katzenstein (ed.) Between Power and Plenty: Foreign Economic Policies of Advanced Industrial States. Madison: Univ. of Wisconsin Press.

——— (1978) "Domestic structures and strategies of foreign economic policy," pp. 295-336 in P. J. Katzenstein (ed.) Between Power and Plenty: Foreign Economic Policies of Advanced Industrial States. Madison: Univ. of Wisconsin Press.

KEGLEY, C. W., Jr. and P. J. McGOWAN [eds.] (1979) Challenges to America: United States Foreign Policy in the 1980s. Sage International Yearbook of Foreign Policy Studies, Vol. 4 Beverly Hills: Sage Publications.

——— and P. J. McGOWAN (1979) "Environmental change and the future of American foreign policy in an introduction," pp. 13-33 in C. W. Kegley, Jr. and P. J. McGowan (eds.) Challenges to America: United States Foreign Policy in the 1980s. Sage International Yearbook of Foreign Policy Studies, Vol. 4. Beverly Hills: Sage Publications.

---, N. R. RICHARDSON, and G. RICHTER (1978) "Conflict at home and abroad: an empirical extension." Journal of Politics 40 (August): 742-751.

KINDER, D. R. and J. A. WEISS (1978) "In lieu of rationality: psychological perspectives on foreign policy decision making." Journal of Conflict Resolution 22 (December): 707-735.

KLINGBERG, F. L. (1979) "Cyclical trends in American foreign policy moods and their policy implications," pp. 37-56 in C. W. Kegley, Jr. and P. J. McGowan (eds.) Challenges to America: United States Foreign Policy in the 1980s. Sage International Yearbook of Foreign Policy Studies, Vol. 4. Beverly Hills: Sage Publications.

LOEHR, W. and T. SANDLER [eds.] (1978) Public Goods and Public Policy. Comparative Political Economy and Public Policy Series, Vol. 3. Beverly Hills: Sage Publications.

LUCIER, C. E. (1979) "Changes in the values of arms race parameters." Journal of Conflict Resolution 23 (March): 17-39.

McCALL, L. A. (1976) Regional Integration: A Comparison of European and Central American Dynamics. Sage Papers in Comparative Studies. Beverly Hills: Sage Publications.

McCLELLAND, C. W. (1977) "The anticipation of international crises: prospects for theory and research." International Studies Quarterly 21 (March): 15-38.

McGOWAN, P. J. with T. H. JOHNSON (1979) "The AFRICA Project and the comparative study of African foreign policy," pp. 190-241 in M. W. Delaney (ed.) Aspects of International Relations in Africa. Bloomington, IN: African Studies Program, Indiana University.

--- (1976) "Economic dependence and economic performance in black Africa." Journal of Modern African Studies 14 (March): 25-40.

McGOWAN, P. J. and D. L. SMITH (1978) "Economic dependency in black Africa: an analysis of competing theories." International Organization 32 (Winter): 179-235.

McKINLAY, R. N. and R. LITTLE (1977) "A foreign policy model of U.S. bilateral aid allocation." World Politics 30 (October): 58-86.

NAU, H. R. (1974) National Politics and International Technology: Nuclear Reactor Development in Western Europe. Baltimore: Johns Hopkins Univ. Press.

NUECHTERLEIN, D. E. (1976) "National interests and foreign policy: a conceptual framework for analysis and decision-making." British Journal of International Studies 2 (October): 246-266.

ORGANSKI, A.F.K. and J. KUGLER (1978) "Davids and Goliaths: predicting the outcomes of international wars." Comparative Political Studies 11 (July): 141-180.

PETERS, B. G., J. C. DOUGHTIE, and M. K. McCULLOCH (1977) "Types of democratic systems and types of public policy: an empirical examination." Comparative Politics 9 (April): 327-355.

PHILLIPS, W. R. (1978) "Prior behavior as an explanation of foreign policy," pp. 161-172 in M. A. East, S. A. Salmore, and C. F. Hermann (eds.) Why Nations Act: Theoretical Perspectives for Comparative Foreign Policy Studies. Beverly Hills: Sage Publications.

RAICHUR, S. and C. LISKE [eds.] (1976) The Politics of Aid, Trade, and Investment. Comparative Political Economy and Public Policy Series, Vol. 2. New York: John Wiley.

RICHARDSON, N. R. (1976) "Political compliance and U.S. trade dominance." American Political Science Review 70: 1098-1109.

RICHMAN, A. (1979) "The U.S. image under stress: trends and structure of foreign attitudes toward the United States," pp. 201-228 in C. W. Kegley, Jr. and P. J. McGowan (eds.) Challenges to America: United States Foreign Policy in the 1980s. Sage International Yearbook of Foreign Policy Studies, Vol. 4. Beverly Hills: Sage Publications.

ROSSA, P. J., G. W. HOPPLE, and J. WILKENFELD (1979) "Crisis indicators and models." International Interactions (forthcoming).

RUMMEL, R. J. (1978) National Attributes and Behavior: Data, Dimensions, Linkages and Groups, 1950-1965. Dimensions of Nations Series, Vol. 3. Beverly Hills: Sage Publications.

RUSSETT, B. (1978) "The marginal utility of income transfers to the Third World." International Organization 32 (Autumn): 913-928.

SALMORE, B. G. and S. A. SALMORE (1978) "Political regimes and foreign policy," pp. 103-122 in M. A. East, S. A. Salmore, and C. F. Hermann (eds.) Why Nations Act: Theoretical Perspectives for Foreign Policy Studies. Beverly Hills: Sage Publications.

SALMORE, S. A., M. G. HERMANN, C. F. HERMANN, and B. G. SALMORE (1978) "Toward integrating the perspectives," pp. 191-210 in M. A. East, S. A. Salmore, and C. F. Hermann (eds.) Why Nations Act: Theoretical Perspectives for Comparative Foreign Policy Studies. Beverly Hills: Sage Publications.

SIEGEL, R. L. and L. B. WEINBERG (1977) Comparing Public Policies: United States, Soviet Union and Europe. Homewood, IL: Dorsey.

SIGELMAN, L. and M. SIMPSON (1977) "A cross-national test of the linkage between economic inequality and political violence." Journal of Conflict Resolution 21 (March): 105-128.

SMALL, M. and J. D. SINGER (1979) "Conflict in the international system, 1816-1977: historical trends and policy futures," pp. 89-115 in C. W. Kegley, Jr. and P. J. McGowan (eds.) Challenges to America: United States Foreign Policy in the 1980s. Sage International Yearbook of Foreign Policy Studies, Vol. 4. Beverly Hills: Sage Publications.

SNYDER, G. H. and P. DIESING (1977) Conflict Among Nations: Bargaining, Decision Making, and System Structure in International Crises. Princeton, N.J.: Princeton Univ. Press.

STARR, H. and B. A. MOST (1978) "A return journey: Richardson, 'Frontiers,' and wars in the 1946-1965 era." Journal of Conflict Resolution 22 (September): 441-467.

--- and B. A. MOST (1976) "The substance and study of borders in international relations research." International Studies Quarterly 20 (December): 581-620.

SULLIVAN, M. P. (1978) "International organizations and world order: a reappraisal." Journal of Conflict Resolution 22 (March): 105-120.

TANTER, R. (1978) "International crisis behavior: an appraisal of the literature." Jerusalem Journal of International Relations 3 (Winter-Spring): 340-374.

THOMPSON, W. R. and G. MODELSKI (1977) "Global conflict intensity and great power summitry behavior." Journal of Conflict Resolution 21 (June): 339-376.

TOMLIN, B. W. and M. A. BUHLMAN (1977) "Relative status and foreign policy: status partitioning and the analysis of relations in black Africa." Journal of Conflict Resolution 21 (June): 187-216.

WALLACE, M. A. (1979) "Arms race and escalation: some new evidence." Journal of Conflict Resolution 23 (March): 3-16.

WALLERI, R. D. (1978) "The political economy literature on North-South relations: alternative approaches and empirical evidence." International Studies Quarterly 22 (December): 587-624.

——— (1978) "Trade dependence and underdevelopment: a causal-chain analysis." Comparative Political Studies 11 (April): 94-127.
WILDGEN, J. K. and W. J. FELD (1976) "Evaluative and cognitive factors in the prediction of European unification." Comparative Political Studies 9 (October): 309-334.
WILKENFELD, J., G. R. HOPPLE, S. J. ANDRIOLE, and R. N. McCAULEY (1978) "Profiling states for foreign policy analysis." Comparative Political Studies (April): 4-35.
——— and P. J. ROSSA (1979) "Indicators of conflict and cooperation in the interstate system, 1966-1970," in J. D. Singer and M. D. Wallace (eds.) To Augur Well: Early Warning Indicators in Interstate Conflict. Beverly Hills: Sage Publications.
YOUGH, S. N. and L. SIGELMAN (1976) "Mobilization, institutionalization, development and instability: a note of reappraisal." Comparative Political Studies 9 (July): 223-232.

ABOUT THE AUTHORS

FARID ABOLFATHI is Senior Research Associate at the Policy Sciences Division, CACI, Inc.-Federal, Arlington, Virginia. He was born in Iran and received his education in Iran, Britain, and the United States. He has published in the field of international relations, comparative politics, and economics. His most recent publications include *The OPEC Market to 1985* (1977), "Defense Expenditures in the Persian Gulf" (1978), and "Trends in United States Response to International Crises" (1979). His research has been sponsored by the Department of State, the Defense Advanced Research Projects Agency, and the Department of Commerce. His latest research involves evaluating Soviet international crisis performance in terms of Soviet goals.

RICHARD P. CLAYBERG received his M.A. in Soviet Studies from Columbia University in 1966. Mr. Clayberg was a career Soviet area studies specialist in the United States Army, from which he retired as a Lieutenant Colonel prior to joining CACI, Inc.—Federal as a Senior Associate in 1977. He is a frequent guest lecturer at the School for International Studies, U.S. Army Institute for Military Assistance, Fort Bragg, North Carolina. Since joining CACI, Mr. Clayberg has been involved in research on Soviet and Chinese crisis behavior.

JOHN V. GILLESPIE was Professor of Political Science and Director of the Center for International Policy Studies at Indiana University. He held fellowships from the National Science Foundation, and his research was supported by grants from the National Science and Ford Foundations and the Advanced Research Projects Agency. He was a member of the NSF Panel in Political Science and Associate Editor of *Behavioral Science*. In 1978 he was the recipient of an Amoco Foundation Award for distinguished instruction. He authored four books and over twenty-five articles. His most recent publications included articles in *International Studies Quarterly, Journal of Conflict Resolution, International Interactions, Comparative Political Studies,* and *Systems, Man and Cybernetics.*

NORMAN A. GRAHAM (Ph.D. Columbia University, 1978) is a Research Associate at the Columbia University Institute on Western Europe and is Visiting Assistant Professor of International Relations at James Madison College, Michigan State University. He has served as a Research Associate and consultant with the United Nations Institute for Training and Research.

GERALD W. HOPPLE is Senior Research Analyst at the International Public Policy Research Corporation (IPPRC), a private research firm in McLean, Virginia. Dr. Hopple formerly taught at the University of Maryland, where he received his Ph.D. in Political Science in 1975. He is the author of a forthcoming book from Westview Press on political psychology and international politics (*The Psychological and

Biopolitical Foundations of Elite Foreign Policy Behavior) as well as the editor of and contributor to *Expert-Generated Data: Applications in International Affairs,* a forthcoming volume on the use of expert data in international politics. A specialist in crisis analysis, political psychology, and comparative foreign policy, he is also the author or coauthor of a number of articles and book chapters.

CHARLES W. KEGLEY, Jr. received his undergraduate education at the School of International Service, the American University, and his doctoral degree from the International Relations Program at Syracuse University. Currently Professor of International Relations at the University of South Carolina, he has taught previously at Georgetown University and the University of Texas. His publications include coauthorship of *American Foreign Policy: Pattern and Process* (1979) and coeditorship of *Analyzing International Relations* (1975), *Challenges to America* (1979), and *After Vietnam* (1971). He has contributed articles to a number of edited books and journals, including *International Studies Quarterly, International Organization, Armed Forces and Society, Simulation and Games, International Interactions,* and *Journal of Politics.*

EDWARD A. KOLODZIEJ is Professor of Political Science and former Head of the Department of Political Science at the University of Illinois. He is the author of the *Uncommon Defense and Congress: 1945-1963* and *French International Policy under De Gaulle and Pompidou: The Politics of Grandeur* (1974). A specialist in American and European foreign and security policy and policy-making, he is a frequent contributor to professional journals in areas of his interest.

DAVID J. LOUSCHER (Ph.D. University of Wisconsin, 1972) is an Associate Professor of Political Science, University of Akron, Ohio. He has served as a consultant to the House of Representatives and to the Department of Defense. His principal research interests and publications are in the area of arms transfers.

CONSTANCE J. LYNCH received her B.A. in political science from the University of California, Los Angeles, and her M.A. in international relations from the University of Southern California, where she is currently a Ph.D. candidate. Her fields of study include international political economy, international relations theory, and foreign policy analysis. She has also served as a member of the research team for the Current World Stress Studies project under the direction of Charles A. McClelland.

ROBERT B. MAHONEY, Jr. received his Ph.D. in political science from Northwestern University in 1974. Since October 1977 he has been manager of the Projections and Plans Department of CACI, Inc.-Federal. Previously, he was on the professional staff of the Center for Naval Analyses. His current research interests include Soviet, U.S., and Chinese crisis behaviors and the role played by European leaders' perceptions and public opinion in European national security affairs.

PAT McGOWAN received his Ph.D. from Northwestern in 1970 and is now Professor and Chairman, Department of Political Science, Arizona State University. He has taught at Syracuse University and the University of Southern California. He has edited the *Yearbook* since 1973. His most recent publications are articles in *International Organization* (Winter 1978) and *Teaching Political Science* (October 1979) and a monograph in the Denver University series on *Culture and Foreign Policy Behavior* (1979). His current research focuses on imperialism in the nineteenth and twentieth centuries.

About the Authors

ILAN PELEG (Ph.D. Northwestern) is currently the chairman of the International Affairs Program at Lafayette College. He is the author of articles published in *Journal of Modern African Studies, Ethnicity, International Problems* (Tel-Aviv), and *International Development Review*. His areas of interest are arms transfer, nuclear proliferation, international terrorism, and the Middle East.

GREGORY A. RAYMOND is Assistant Professor of Political Science at Boise State University. He received his Ph.D. from the University of South Carolina in 1975. Dr. Raymond has authored *The Other Western Europe: A Comparative Analysis of the Smaller Democracies* (1980) and coedited *International Events and the Comparative Analysis of Foreign Policy* (1975) and *Military Policy Evaluation: Quantitative Applications* (1979). He has also published articles on foreign policy behavior in such journals as *International Interactions, German Studies Review*, and *Modeling and Simulation*.

PAUL J. ROSSA is a Research Analyst at IPPRC and doctoral student at the University of Maryland. He specializes in international relations and quantitative methodology, has served in senior research positions on several projects in comparative and international political analysis, and is the coauthor of chapters in books and articles in *International Interactions* and *Jerusalem Journal of International Relations*.

PHILIP A. SCHRODT is Assistant Professor of Political Science at Northwestern University. In 1979 he received a NATO Postdoctoral Fellowship to pursue study of the Arabian Sea region. His other research interests include models of coalition formation and international environmental law. He is the author of several articles published in such journals as *Peace Science, American Journal of Political Science, American Political Science Review*, and *International Interactions*.

RICHARD A. SKINNER is Assistant Professor of Political Science and Director of the Computer-based Laboratory for Instruction and Analysis (CLIA), Old Dominion University. In addition to articles in *International Interactions* and *Journal of Political Science*, he has coedited *International Events and the Comparative Analysis of Foreign Policy* (1975) and *Evaluating Military Policy: Quantitative Applications* (1979). His current research includes a critical assessment of contemporary public program analysis and evaluation.

G. S. TAHIM is a Control Systems Engineer with the General Electric Space Center at Valley Forge, Pennsylvania. He had held various academic appointments with Indiana University and the University of Illinois. His research has been reported in numerous articles including *Transactions on Automatic Control, Systems, Man and Cybernetics, Peace Science, Behavioral Science*, and *International Studies Quarterly*.

MICHAEL DAVID WALLACE was born in Montreal and educated at McGill University and the University of Michigan and is presently an Associate Professor at the University of British Columbia in Vancouver. He is the author or coauthor of numerous publications on the causes of war and the dynamics of the arms race. With J. David Singer he coedited *To Augur Well* (Sage Publications, 1979).

JONATHAN WILKENFELD is Associate Professor of Government and Politics at the University of Maryland. He is a former editor of *International Studies Quarterly* and has served as the coprincipal investigator of several government-supported research projects. His publications include work on the comparative analysis of foreign policy and conflict research. Professor Wilkenfeld is the editor of and a contributor to *Conflict Behavior and Linkage Politics*.

DINA A. ZINNES is Professor of Political Science at Indiana University. She has held fellowships from the Ford Foundation, the American Association for University Women, and the NATO Postdoctoral Fellowship Program. Her research has been supported by the Ford and National Science Foundations and the Advanced Research Projects Agency. She has held offices in many professional societies and is President-Elect of the International Studies Association. She is a member of the editorial boards of seven journals. She is the author of five books and over forty articles. Among her recent publications are *Contemporary Research in International Relations* (Free Press) and articles in *International Studies Quarterly, World Politics, Journal of Conflict Resolution,* and *Peace Science.*